what makes juries listen

what makes juries listen

Sonya Hamlin

a communications expert looks at the trial

Law & Business, Inc.
Harcourt Brace Jovanovich, Publishers
(New York   Washington, D.C.)

Requests for permission to make copies of any part of the work
should be mailed to:

Permissions, Law & Business, Inc.
855 Valley Road, Clifton, N.J. 07013

Printed in the United States of America

Library of Congress Cataloging in Publication Data

Hamlin, Sonya.
    What makes juries listen.

    Includes index.
    1. Jury--United States.   2. Trial practice--United
States.   3. Psychology, Forensic.   4. Persuasion
(Psychology)   I. Title.
KF8972.H28   1984   347.73'752   84-25057
ISBN 0-15-004292-2   347.307752

for Mama, Papa and Esther;

for Bruce;

for Ross, Mark and David

who taught me the frailty and strength
of being human. I'm still learning . . .

CONTENTS

ACKNOWLEDGMENTS

When it's over, the seemingly endless task of writing a book telescopes itself in time. Looking back, all those painful months become a blended memory and, just as in childbirth, you find yourself forgetting the pain in the joy of the tangible product. Fearing this, I took notes along the way about all those who helped my anxious, faltering steps in writing this book and developing this material so that I could properly and publicly thank them.

First let me thank Robert F. Hanley for his enduring support of my work from my earliest teaching. His willingness to read and critique my manuscript as each chapter came through the meat grinder, his helpful suggestions and enthusiasm were invaluable and deeply appreciated. Ed Stein, Marshall Simonds, James Brosnahan, Tom Singer, Keith Roberts, Desmond Fennell, Q. C., Tom McNamara, Barbara Caulfield, Fred Bartlitt, Judge Rya Zobel, Judge Hiller Zobel and the Honorable William J. Bauer also took time to read individual chapters and offer incisive comments and suggestions and I thank them all.

Let me also thank all those lawyers who answered my questions and sent me their transcripts for reproduction in this book. Their willingness to share their insights and creativity are appreciated not only by me but, I'm sure, by all the readers who will benefit from them.

To the judges who answered my questionnaire so fully, with

such candor, I extend my heartfelt gratitude and belief that their advice will indeed make a difference.

Let me thank Judge Robert Keeton, who, as a Harvard Law School professor, gave me the opportunity to first begin to explore this field, to create my first lectures and critique sessions and essentially to launch my career in his Trial Advocacy Workshops at Harvard.

My thanks to the National Institute for Trial Advocacy on whose faculty I have taught all these years, where the bulk of my material has been developed. To all of you dedicated lawyers and judges with whom I have taught, who give of your time and share your expertise so that the profession will grow and deepen in its skills, you have been an inspiration and have taught me well. Thanks also to the U.S. Department of Justice Attorney General's Advocacy Institute where I serve on the faculty, to the American Bar Association's Litigation Section, to ALI-ABA and the many Bar Associations and lawyers' groups I have addressed. You challenged me to continue to grow and find new ways to explain the jury's point of view.

To the endless lawyers whose fate it has been to come under my scrutiny, I hope I have been as helpful to you as you have been instructive to me. I thank you all for the chance to keep learning through you.

I thank Professor Donis A. Dondis and the M.I.T. Press for permission to reproduce or to adapt excerpts and figures from pages 22, 23, 25, 27–30, 32–35, 44, 46 and 51 from *A Primer of Visual Literacy*. Thanks also to Veda R. Charrow et al. for permission to reproduce lists from the American Institute for Research on the Behavioral Sciences workbook on "Teaching Legal Writing" and the Document Design Centers' "Guidelines for Document Designers." Thanks to William C. Brown Co., publishers of Lyle V. Mayer's *Fundamentals of Voice and Diction* for permission to reproduce some exercises. A special thanks to Elinor Bunin for her expertise in graphics and illustration.

My thanks to my editor Steve Seemer, to Kathleen Kelly, Tom Saettel and Dan Mangan for their help and to Steve and Lynn Glasser for their faith and support. A deep genuflection in the direction of Louise Chastain whose ability to decode my handwritten manuscript and turn it into readable typed pages was nothing short of miraculous.

Finally, my deep gratitude to Alexis Parks who was there at my faltering start with support and encouragement and who gave me the spirit to go on and to write.

Sonya Hamlin

1

HOW WE COMMUNICATE: A NEW VIEW OF THE TRIAL AND THE JURY

Let me put you in a movie. It begins with the following scene.

You're walking down the street and see a friend coming toward you:

You: (*touching his arm, smiling*) "Hi, Jack—haven't seen you for a while. How are you?"

Jack: (*hastily, avoiding eye contact*) "Fine, fine."

You: "What's up? Are you O.K.?"

Jack: (*dropping his paper, scrambling for it, getting up very quickly and looking past you as he shifts from one foot to the other*) "Yeah, sure, I'm fine. Everything's just fine."

You: "Gee, you seem a little distracted."

Jack: (*stepping back, finally looking at you*) "No, no—believe me, I'm O.K. (*heaving a sigh*) Everything's—just—uh—dandy . . . (*looking off*) Yeah, dandy . . ."

Now, finish this scene. Do you believe Jack? Would you accept what he says about everything being fine? What do you think is really going on? How do you know? What clues give you the answers?

Go back and read the scene again without the directions in parenthesis. The words alone don't tell you what you need to know, do they? Actually, the information about how Jack is really feeling becomes much clearer and more poignant because of the contrast between what he's saying and what he's doing. And if you turned the sound off in this scene and just watched it, you'd get a much clearer message more directly, wouldn't you?

Well, let's say goodbye to Hollywood and get back to reality. *But this scene is reality.* It shows what we all do, every day, from our beginnings on to the end of our days. We have a primary human need to evaluate what is communicated to us, and not just to accept it. We filter incoming messages through such questions as, "What does this really mean? Can I trust him? Why is she saying or doing this?" This need to fully understand requires us to look for as much information as we can.

To see how we do this, go back to the scene with Jack. Look at all the information you would automatically gather as you watched or lived it:

• *Body language*: Jack shifts his feet; he twitches, gestures, nervously drops papers, scrambles hastily.

• *Eye contact*: Jack can't look at you; he looks off, thinking.

• *Space relationship*: You get closer, even touch him; he backs away.

• *Speech rhythm*: Jack speaks hastily. There are long pauses between his words and he sighs as he speaks. His last words are delivered slowly and thoughtfully.

• *Words*: He says "Fine," "Dandy," "No, no, believe me."

See how each image calls forth your judgment; how you know what each gesture means, how hollow the words seem. He is neither fine nor dandy, is he? And you know it from all the instinctive judgments you have made.

Now, this is all very interesting but what is it doing in a book about trial advocacy skills? Simply this.

Our innate ability to evaluate behavior and to judge instinctively is why the jury system works.

Consider. The jury system is actually bizarre. Where else in our society would you invite disparate laymen, novices with absolutely no experience or previous information in a given field, to be the ultimate judges about issues in that field, with almost no restrictions on their qualifications except direct, personal bias, willingly admitted? Bizarre, yes? They've never been to court, know nothing about trial procedure or the law. They hear the case just once—orally. They may have little schooling and little information about most aspects of our society, let alone expertise in the subject in question. They may be innately bright or slow, interested or disinterested, privately prejudiced or not. They're recruited and pressed into service, not even willing volunteers. And then, this motley crew, this questionable "board," is given ultimate authority to judge crime and punishment, life and death, right or wrong. Why? What did our tribal elders, our societal sages have in mind when they designed this system?

Just this. We can all judge human behavior because we have all shared the human experience. In order for us to judge anything, we depend on our backlog of experiences. We ask ourselves is that true, is it possible, is it practical, what would someone normally do and what would the consequences be? When jurors sit in court and listen to you or to witnesses' testimony they're thinking, "C'mon, people don't act like that," or "Look at him, he's lying," or "That was cruel," or "Ha! That's just greed." They know about living and being human. Their process of evaluating and judging is in the gut; it's automatic and unthinking but very reliable. That's why it doesn't matter that jurors don't know about the law or the case. That's your job. You'll tell them that. What they know about, what you rely on, is that they've lived within our society's format of acceptable behavior. That's how they'll judge who's overstepped the bounds and who should be blamed and punished. Jurors know what's fair; they know what would happen if we let some breach of the code continue. They know what's expected of each of us if we are to have a workable system of living together. That's what laws are all about. We all know instinctively what's permitted or not based on what the consequences would be to other people we share our space with, what will preserve the system, and what will shatter it. And *that's* what most of us care about—the old self-preservation syndrome. And *that's* where you finally win your case.

So jurors decide by evaluating against their standards. They evaluate the facts. They evaluate the witnesses. They evaluate you, the teacher, the interpreter of the facts. They think through and interpret the facts against their standards. But the final energies are sympathy, empathy, and self-preservation; and the final judge is instinct.

We can all internalize the truths and concerns of others because we share the common thread of being people, living now, in the same town, state, country, planet and we are affected by similar outside forces. But our most compelling common denominator is that we all share similar inner drives, needs, fears, and common human secrets. Therefore, the jury already knows almost all it needs to know to judge the human conflict in a trial. All it still needs is an explanation of context, precedent, and consequence.

How to get the jurors involved so they bring their best judgment and attention to your case and how to get them to take your ideas and information to shape their opinion is what the rest of this book is about. But let's start out knowing that juries are extremely competent and wise in the oldest wisdom we have—common survival sense. You have an extremely knowledgeable, critical audience to play to and to persuade. And those visceral intuitive skills, the ones *you* used to analyze your mythical friend Jack's real meaning a few pages ago, *the jury* uses to judge with as well, to color and weigh the logic of your arguments. This intuition, combined with good common sense, is the jury's greatest strength.

Now let's see how these attributes interact with what you bring to the courtroom.

THE ADVOCATE'S JOB; THE
ADVOCATE'S CHALLENGE

An interesting thing about work: when we first learn how to do something, it always seems so complex. We're filled with anxiety when we realize how much there is to learn and master and how hard it all seems. Details, techniques, and what we don't know all loom so large they almost blot out the view of the job itself. So we start, with a narrowly focused intensity, to master the parts. By the time we've got them all working and synchronized, we're inside the job, performing, and rarely seem to take a further step back after we've learned it to gain perspective and see an overview of the job itself. We flow between the parts and the whole of our work but rarely see its broader outlines, or how it fits into the patterns of our society. Most of all, the longer we do it and the more skillful and comfortable we get, the less we realize how our job looks to others or how it affects them. We tend to stay with our peers, talking shorthand, enjoying membership in our private mutual "club," refining and polishing the fine points of our work. We move further and further away from the early days when we stood on the threshold as an outsider, looking in at the formidable, strange new world, still closely linked to the rest of society and its view of our chosen work.

Remember your first year in law school? The incredible maze that faced you and your fear that you'd never get it all in? Remember how much of your recognizable self you felt you lost as you went underground to master at least the rudiments of the law? The more you learned, the more you practiced your role as advocate, the farther away you got from that original self and from all the rest of us who didn't become trial lawyers. Yet it is that very "rest of us" whom you confront in the jury box every time you try to persuade and explain.

In order to gain some new insights about the jury and to add other perspectives to what you already know about your job as a trial lawyer, step back to that outsider's threshold again with me. Let's look at what your work requires you to do and how the system of the trial, the conditioning of our current society and the role of the advocate interacting with lay people creates a series of intrinsic dichotomies and problems in your job before you even begin a trial.

Emotion vs Order

What is a trial? It's the retelling of a human event, the re-enactment of a human drama, the evaluation of human conflict.

In each of these there is some aberration, some trauma, something unusual that happened outside the norm of acceptable social behavior. Human behavior went awry. If not, it would never reach the courtroom.

Take the dramas. What are the origins of most of these events? They're emotional, spontaneous and unpredictable.

They're visceral, not logical. The moment of trauma is explosive, uneven, disorderly, fitting no pattern. This the jury can readily grasp and understand. They know the volatile nature of life. They can respond to emotion and drama. After all, their skills are geared to understanding the emotional areas; their judgments are based on "gut instinct," not the head.

Now you come as a lawyer and say, "I must lay over this volatile, irregular, amoeba-shaped happening the cool, linear order of the law. I must take a uniquely shaped, original human drama and fit it into a pre-existing structure." Instead of responding to the events as a person normally would, you must represent objectivity and precedent. You must make logic of illogic; bring a learned, analytical response to a basically intuitive, unpredictable act. You must speak, coolly, of the law. And present all of this to a lay jury that has previous knowledge only of human events, not the law; of spontaneous emotion, not order and precedent. Look what that does to you and your image.

Remembering that the only skills the jury brings into the courtroom are those visceral responses, those intuitive judgments they need to rely on, you confront them with needing to take another, cooler view, an unfamiliar approach. In the seemingly cerebral and unemotional process that you work in, can you come through as a feeling and fallible human being too, with first-hand knowledge of how human events happen? Can you be recognizable to the jury as one of them, as you participate in this logical, controlled, orderly process? Look at the distance automatically created between you and the jury.

How about the supposedly cool civil actions that deal with dehumanized business structures looking for interpretations of the law? Again there is a conflict between your job and what the jury sees and feels. Here your job is to present the rigid, geometric, right-angled shapes of a company, to discuss facts and figures and statutes. Think of the dry, distanced, dehumanized image this presents. All thought, no heart. No recognizable human dimensions showing. Here your problem is relating, making abstract issues and concepts rounder and more human. You must put the jury in touch with the facts but somehow make them care and be concerned. Unless you connect the cerebral contents with what people did and why, and with the effect it has on all of us, you are again isolated from the jury. All they can see in such a trial are the steel and glass facades, the stereotypical two-dimensional cardboard cutouts of "The Corporation," a cold, unfeeling, powerful monolith. And they see you as an extension of them. To bridge the intrinsic space between you, you must show them the human-scale motivations and processes in three-D living color. You must show them you know about all of life, as they do, not just an isolated, powerful, unfamiliar corner.

So the first dichotomy in your job is the contrast between squares and wavy lines; the law and the spirit; the cerebral and the emotional; the left and right brain; and how you must bridge the gap between them for a jury mainly oriented and experienced in only one direction. You must make the jury think, not only feel, yet you must recognize what your essentially cool role and the rigid trial format does to the jury's perception and image of you.

Oral Presentation

The basic form of communication used in the courtroom is oral presentation and that presents another problem. Just picture this image:

> Speaker (preacher, teacher) walking towards lectern, large sheaf of papers in hand, clearing throat, ready to begin his speech (sermon, lecture).

How do you respond to this image? What does it make you anticipate? What are the first words that come to your mind to describe how you feel? "Interesting?" "Exciting?" "Can't wait to hear this?" Or do your eyes glaze over and some large capital letters float to the surface that spell out B O R I N G   L O N G D U L L   W O R D Y   P O M P O U S   O B S C U R E.   Here, then, is dichotomy number two.

Our preconditioned responses to verbal communication have reached an alltime low in this half of the twentieth century. Now, if you were practicing law in earlier times you'd be golden. That was the time of the Chatauqua circuit, when entertainment meant speeches, not vaudeville. The traveling stars were speakers, not dancers. People paid money to sit for two or three hours and hear

famous orators of the day hold forth, weaving a magic web to capture the audience with their superior forensic skill. We know
William Jennings Bryan as the "Silver-Tongued Orator" even now.
People walked away savoring the creative use of words by someone
admired purely for his ability to talk. There was a love of language.
There was pleasure in the sound of the human voice. Elocution
teachers abounded. Debating societies were everywhere. People
used to recite poetry or read aloud for an evening's entertainment
at home. They considered the amount of time that it took for an
idea to be presented orally a time of pleasure. The pace of life was
such that everybody could wait until an idea was developed verbally, slowly, eloquently, formally, carefully, and a point finally
made. The phrasing, the timing of describing and telling was
lengthy and leisurely. People responded to that not only by wanting to go and hear someone deliver oral arguments, but also by being willing to read books in order to get information. They were
accustomed to coming to the process of communication prepared
to take an active role.

That was yesterday. Television, film, and computers have
changed all that forever. You now practice law in a society that has
permanently altered the way it gets and gives its information. Yet
your form of giving information is still based on the old mode. It
presupposes those attentive audiences that could sit still and hang
on a well-turned phrase; that would thrill to a booming voice, or
relish a thought, carefully developed.

Oral presentation in a trial depends on a jury listening, understanding, and being persuaded by seamless streams of words and
eagerly following them with a level of concentration high enough to
register and remember facts and explanations heard just once.
What is the reality? We just don't do that anymore. You're stuck
using an outmoded tool to get your message across to a twentieth
century audience that wants its information quickly and expects
the old speechmaking form to be *boring, long, dull, wordy, pompous, and obscure*.

You Can't Tell It All Yourself

Not only must you present the case in oral argument, *you* personally cannot even tell most of it! Even if you're a brilliantly skilled
communicator, a great deal of what happens in the trial is not in

your hands. You have to depend on others to tell it. All you can do is elicit and extract the information from them—from lay people and experts in specific fields. You may only hope your witnesses will remember and tell again a story they've told you in a certain way, a way you depend on as you plan your case. This system presents several problems.

Most people are amateurs, not skilled raconteurs. Their instincts do not naturally bring them to presenting information with logic and order. Yet the jury needs to hear chronology and order, not only to help them understand but to help them remember; not only to get the information but to know what's important and how one point relates to another. The stress and unfamiliarity of a trial setting, as well as people's natural anxiety about performing or being unique and visible before an audience, combined with the pressure of being judged by their peers, causes this retelling system to break down—often.

Therefore, you are cast in a pejorative role and involved in a visible aggressive act—pulling out information by manipulating people. Not only do you need to go in and get the testimony from your witnesses, you must actively scrutinize, dissect, and question the testimony of your opposition's witnesses as well. Not only because the format of a trial requires it, but also because the performances of the witnesses usually demand intervention and clarification.

Now here's the dichotomy. The jury judges *you* based on how you examine the witnesses. They're there to judge and judge they do—everything and everybody, including you. They watch how you get other people to talk, how you extract information, how aggressive or manipulative you are, how disinterested or supportive you seem, how respectfully you behave to lay people like themselves.

Not only that. They will accept or reject the testimony they hear based very much on how you get it. Is the witness mouthing pre-rehearsed lines, cued by his lawyer? Is the opposition's witness being cowed and confused by a predictably hostile lawyer to the point where he is unduly forced into retracting or admitting something? The jury's judgment of why something is said colors not only what they hear but how they feel about the inquisitor.

So you're in a bind. You can't tell it all. You're required to go get the information from others. Yet, that very act is open to interpretation. If the jury sees you doing your job with too much force or hostility, or too little sensitivity, they will not only question your work product, the testimony, but your character and qualifications as well. All of which affects their decision and judgment in the case.

The Attention-Span Syndrome

Your work as an advocate in a trial is to persuade, to teach, to explain, and to analyze. You work with difficult, strange, often abstract or technical information the jury has never seen or heard before. Much of it they will never need to know or care about again. You need their total and continuous attention. When you refer to what was said in court yesterday, you depend on their having heard it and remembered it. You build toward your final argument by delivering blocks of information throughout the trial, and you need the jury to follow you with each step.

But it takes only 15 percent of the human mind to understand English, if that is your native language. That leaves 85 percent of that mind free to wander in any direction—daydreaming, contemplating personal thoughts, worrying over personal problems, criticizing or arguing with a speaker, experiencing irritation or boredom. You have sat in countless audiences and classrooms and you know exactly what I mean. Just sitting in a chair, looking like you're listening, guarantees nothing. The odds (15 percent versus 85 percent) say you're not.

So you're dealing with gauze, with holes and gaps, with information that falls through the webbing, with illusion. You don't know what is getting in and what will last. What you should know is that really listening and paying attention is extremely hard for all of us and mustn't be taken for granted. Since the nature of simply understanding your words is accomplished by such a small percentage of the brain, people are not compelled to pay close attention.

But that's not all. None of us likes to feel that we're stupid. We avoid being put in a position of feeling incompetent and inadequate, like we're failing. To many people, learning is a threat, not a challenge. Since a large majority of people have not had exciting, successful school careers, the idea of learning and being exposed to unfamiliar material which they must work to absorb feels like a test—and a threat. A test because they will have to discover if they grasped it and understood, if they rose to the occasion, or not. A threat because it will call up again and possibly demonstrate those feelings of inadequacy, incompetence and failure from their time at school or other learning experiences.

What effect does this conditioning have on attention span? Are most people very motivated to dig their heels in, to stick to it and listen when confronted with new, strange, complex, or abstract material requiring feats of understanding and memory, like your material in a trial? Or does that self-protective mechanism alive in all of us do a quick cut-off? Does it circumvent or avoid this personal confrontation by diverting attention from the seeming threat at hand and retreating to the safer and sunnier climes of daydreaming and not paying attention?

All of this adds up to bad news for people like you who need to command attention and to sustain interest. Capturing a juror's mind and building your case in it is uphill work. The odds are against your developing a smooth progression of information which the jurors absorb and retain as you give it. That's dichotomy number four. You need total attention and they are neither physiologically compelled to give it nor conditioned to try very hard.

How People Learn Today

At the heart of your work is giving information. Throughout the trial, you must teach people things they didn't know before—whether it's technical data or legal statutes, helping the jury understand the issues or explaining the facts. But today our information-gathering has been redesigned, primarily as a result of our exposure to television. The contemporary televison-trained audience versus the way lawyers present a case in court—this is the fifth dichotomy. Here's the reality of how people learn now and the problems it causes you in the courtroom.

The Effect of Television

Television has permanently altered how we learn and listen; how we gather new information. Other formats have affected us as well, but television's pervasive, all-encompassing presence, free for the looking, with the convenience of easy accessibility in everyone's home has been the greatest force.

First—you need do nothing to gain information. It's all done for you and delivered in the most painless, least challenging, most pureed form—with built-in, ultra-sophisticated techniques to keep you staying tuned.

Next—it has taught us to listen with barely half an ear. In the past, to hear or learn you went to a totally focused environment where that was the only activity; school, college, lecture hall, auditorium, forum, library. Now consider the environment in which television plays. Kitchen, den, living or bedroom. Phones ring, kids play, moms and dads cook, talk, or read. The business of life— shouting, eating, arguing, disciplining, attending to daily details— all vie for equal time with the tube. Television becomes an obligato, a hum, a drone in the background and only occasionally rises up to command total attention from the disparate group pursuing their activities in the vicinity. What does that teach us? Even more inattention and lack of concentration than we already naturally suffer from as an audience.

Television also teaches us lack of continuity. We get comfortable about coming in to the middle of a subject, having others fill us in with an even more edited version than the television show itself presents or bumbling along till it begins to come clear what's going on.

Commercials condition us to expect breaks in concentration and continuity. Information—hard or soft—is delivered in bite-sized pieces and we've learned to expect to get off the hook every 9-11 minutes, and much more often during the news.

We've also learned to switch subjects as soon as the first inklings of boredom hits us. Snapping the dial, hunting for something that tickles the palate and pleases us more creates competition for getting and holding an audience. The gimmicks become more vital than the content.

Television has added other information to our culture. We now automatically know what to consider unpalatable and boring, worthy of little attention. We are told what information appeals to only a very select, very small section of the audience as "fact shows"—news and public affairs, documentaries, and the "serious" interview shows—are all relegated to no-man's land hours of nonviewing time, or public (read "egg-head") television. Our television culture tells us what's key, what's prime (it's even called prime time). That's when we get mindless sit-coms, "adult" soap operas and generally anything that says "Entertainment and Escape." This conditions us to expect to be bored by heavy water and serious subjects (like those often found in a trial) and that to be entertained is the best of all possible pursuits.

Assaulted by all these messages and programmed by what is now the greatest communications device ever created, we have come to expect our information to be delivered in such a way that a single presenter, armed with only words and ideas, would have a hard time competing. But that's not all.

What Most Adults Learn

Most people stop learning when they leave school. A very small percentage of us continue to pursue new information and new ideas or try to understand something we didn't know before. Most people don't continue to go to the library, read new books or sign up for courses on their own. Generally, once people's jobs are in place, they don't learn how to do them better or differently. Even when people at work are challenged to learn, like converting to using computers or other complex machinery, many resist or some even quit because they fear they cannot learn. Adults generally tend to stay with what they know and divert themselves from ever really looking at deep basic questions like: "What else is there to know," "Is this what I'm all about. What do I hunger for and how can I get it?"

This, then, is the common-denominator level, the mental set of how your potential jury feels about what you want them to do: take in, digest and remember the new information you'll teach them. But there is one area in their lives in which they are continually challenged to learn and in which techniques have become highly developed to make people learn, understand and pay attention.

The only new information everyone gets and must continue to process almost daily is the news. It's the only new thing most people have to learn, absorb and, using internal reference points, to understand. Local, national, and international news requires some thought and assimilation, critical appraisal, agreement or disagreement, judgment and decision. Since statistics show that 77 percent of all the people in the country get 90 percent of their news from television and 41 percent get *all* their news from television, discovering how television tells the news can be a gold mine of information about what techniques make people learn now. As you read about these new forms of giving information, think about how they compare with what you normally do in the courtroom and how these new, but now familiar, techniques affect the demands of your potential audience.

The New Techniques of Telling

• *Television news stories are short.* Basically headlines, one-and-a-half minutes long, they're designed for short explanations, not in-depth analysis.

• *They use magic to suspend time.* The unquestioned illogic of going from the studio (CUT), to a live scene on location, (CUT), to a suspended head talking, (CUT), to graphics appearing on the screen, without ever seeing how any of it got there has made us believe in, and expect, magic. Most of all, it has telescoped time and therefore raised our impatience level.

• *They reinforce.* Using graphics and descriptive written words to identify and clarify is actually an excellent teaching technique. But this can also encourage inattention, passivity and lack of concentration. "If you don't catch on, we'll help you." "You don't have to listen hard, we'll tell you again." Even when they show pictures, a voice-over explains them again. Although these are good teaching techniques, capturing attention and reinforcing, they also lull the viewers into not working too hard to figure anything out on their own.

• *Visuals are the message.* Words are no longer the primary message-givers. Now it's pictures that tell. Human tellers corroborate and embellish but are no longer the major source of information. Television has taught the viewer to demand visual proof—flawed as it may be.

• *What looks true is not true.* Since pictures are edited by the reporter, and their content and angle of presentation are chosen by reporter, cameraman and/or director, what the beholder gets is not pure truth, exactly as it happened. Time and reality are distorted by the use of quick, unconnected shots of a scene, closeups impossible to do with the naked eye and dispassionate scanning views of a real human drama—and only the juiciest parts are selected.

• *Conditioned responses to oral presentation.* A "talking head" (a closeup of a person just talking) is considered so boring that it's generally given only about 30 seconds on the air. Not only that, television producers know that people are basically garrulous and verbally disorganized. Therefore, most "talking head" statements are given as a "bite" from a speech or edited by taking part of this sentence, the middle of that and a startling or memorable line to finish, creating one cogent (albeit manufactured) thought, a pithy "made-by-TV" statement. As a result, television viewers are accustomed to hearing and wanting only essences—the bottom line— from people. No strolling through the language. "Just the facts, Ma'am." And short.

• *Seamless flow of words.* Consider the anchorperson with his/her seamless delivery. They don't make mistakes or cast about for a word very often, do they? They don't look at notes. They just look at you—directly, keenly, sincerely, seductively—and talk. Of course, they're reading from a teleprompter, designed with mirrors to roll their whole script right up before the lens so their eyes don't move and give it all away. What does that teach the audience? People don't stumble, falter, think or try again. They don't rephrase or rework an idea. Just deliver the lumpless chocolate pudding by the spoonful, Mr. Speaker, and don't bother me with trying to follow you or watching you work.

• *We're becoming inured to privacy and sensitivity.* The camera zooms in where you and I would fear to tread. The lens and microphone intrude on a weeping person, wracked by tragedy. Heartless, banal "how-does-it-feel" questions are opened to the scrutiny of the audience who watch while munching a sandwich. Result? Non-involvement and passivity. We remove violence and conflict to an abstraction and a commonplace, becoming voyeurs whose natural caring and sense of concern about setting things right is dulled and dismissed by the easy reproduction of such scenes in the safety of our homes. This alters our view of connected, responsible citizenship—a bulwark the jury system depends on.

So your job as teacher, as clarifier and explainer is made even harder because the popular system for learning and gathering information has little to do with how you will deliver your message. The juror's conditioned reflexes brought to the courtroom can defeat your need for attention and continuity. Your audience now expects to be cajoled, tantalized, shocked, titillated and entertained to keep them from reaching for the dial or the OFF button. And they have developed a finely tuned aversion to "commercials"—thereby turning a deaf ear on being sold any point of view.

*   *   *

Now what can all these startling perspectives teach you?

• That there are built-in dichotomies between your intentions in the trial and what the jury thinks and can absorb.
• That the system of the trial puts you in a difficult role in the eyes of jurors.
• That the communications systems you use are not geared for greatest effectiveness.
• That listening, learning and information-gathering in the old ways are gone. Audiences expect an edited, telescoped version of anything new and unfamiliar, amply laced with visual reinforcement.

Therefore you can no longer do business in the old way and be unaware of what audiences—your jury—now expect and respond to. To be effective you need a much deeper understanding of the psychology and dynamics of being in a jury. To reach them and keep them with you, it's necessary to rethink the communications systems you use.

THE PROCESS OF COMMUNICATION

What a way to begin a book—presenting you with a rather bleak picture of the difficulties built into your chosen career! It could prompt you to not only close the book, but to take up playing the recorder or vegetable farming. But I tell you all this to give you some additional perspective on your work; to put you in touch with all the issues surrounding the trial that have an impact on the litigator's role. My goal is to focus and stimulate you; to show you the obstacles, the barriers, so you'll want to find solutions to them. And the solutions are the purpose of this book.

They all fall under one broad heading—communication. Knowledgeable, sensitive, effective communication to the jury is at the heart of the jury's ability to judge fairly. In the succeeding chapters, we shall explore each phase of the trial to give you some surprising new insights into what you've always seen as familiar territory. We'll explore many kinds of techniques to tell your story well. And we'll discover what makes juries listen.

Let's begin by looking at the communication process itself—at the most basic principles of how we all reach and affect each other anywhere. Let's discover how we normally learn and absorb information and what makes us pay attention in order to adapt these principles to the trial.

Why People Listen

Most of us think of "communicating" as a one-way street. We get very involved and invested in what *we're* saying, why we want it said, how we're saying it, what choices we should make to communicate it better. But, in our zeal to achieve our goal of getting a message across to others, we lose sight of the fact that at the other end of our message is someone with his own goals, his own zeal, and his own concerns which do not often coincide with ours at the outset.

That is perhaps the greatest single stumbling block to real communication. Communication cannot be a monologue in which only the sender is at work. To be effective, both parties, the teller and the receiver (be it one or many), must be actively involved. It profits you nothing to send your words into the air addressed "To Whom It May Concern." Unless your communique has specific addressees who will become involved in reading or hearing, absorbing, and accepting your message, it's a space shot with no destination.

Therefore, good communication means a dialogue between you and your receiver; a dialogue made up of telling *and* listening.

It must involve two people actively engaged in the same pursuit—one giving, the other getting. The big question then is—how do we get people to listen to us?

The answer lies in motivation. What makes us do anything? What motivates our lives? What is at the heart of why we do whatever we do? Think about it. Do you agree that the answer is. . .

Self-Interest

Confronting this issue creates some small conflict. Although we're all born with a crucial self-preservation instinct that motivates all our behavior, our parents spend years trying to curb and civilize it. Their attempts to teach us acceptable, socialized behavior while this "selfish" instinct ran its blatant, unbridled course through our childhood stay with us and continue to play in our ears. Our parents identified "self-interest" with unseemly, "bad" behavior. Remember "give that back, it's not yours," "don't hit that little boy," and "stop screaming or go to your room."

Although we seem to learn that lesson and manage to curb and mask our appetites externally by the time we grow up, our powerful prime motivating force internally continues to be—self-interest. We do what we do because it's good for us, fun for us, exciting, useful, valuable, fulfilling, aggrandizing, alluring, or problem-solving for us.

Therefore, the way to make people listen is to identify your message in some way as being connected to their self-interest.

Test yourselves. What makes you listen or pay attention? What do you read in the paper and why? What gets you past the headlines? When do you stop and read the whole article? Because at some point you thought: "I want to know that. I need to know that. I'm curious about that. I've never heard of that." It all has to do with "I".

What do you do on the weekend? Even if you may not want to go somewhere, if it's in your self-interest to keep peace in the family, you acquiesce and do it. Whom do you call or call back and whom do you not answer? See how that little flame directs and motivates whatever we do?

Therefore, if you can tap into anyone's self-interest you could create an attentive, willing, thoughtful audience. But to do so, you must know your audience so well that at every step of the way, you can capture them by pointing out and fulfilling what they need and want from you. The number one way to make people listen is to discover and show what's in it for them.

Who's Telling

Another factor that makes people listen is how they perceive the teller. Look back on your own experience. Whom do you like to listen to and whom do you resist? Are there some basic characteristics that always attract you? What adjectives come to mind? "Warm," "friendly," "interesting," "exciting," "knowledgeable"?

What words symbolize the quick turn-off speakers? "Pompous," "dull," "removed," "formal," "stuffy," "complex," "vague," "irrelevant"?

Members of any audience share some basic problems. They feel anonymous, passive, without power, often defensive or resistant as they are being told what to do or think. Therefore, the audience's perception and personal measurement of the speaker and whether he or she is a likely, palatable leader or information-giver can make them listen or not. People have different ideas about what makes some speakers more appealing than others, but some universal truths cut across the differences and seem to be basic qualities that all audiences respond to.

• The speaker needs to be compelling and able to capture the audience by force of personality and/or subject.

• He or she needs to be identifiable as a total, recognizable human being who transcends his or her moment on the stage and feels related to, and knowledgeable about life as the audience members know it.

• The speaker needs to be either an eminent, recognized figure or one who shows specific, useful knowledge in an area of the audience's self-interest.

• He or she must show awareness of the audience's needs with a clear perception of what they want to know and the commitment to fulfill their desires.

These are characteristics audiences quickly perceive as they seek signals about the speaker through his or her techniques.

How They Tell

The next issue in what makes people listen is technique: the content, structure and style of telling. Here, too, there are some basic components.

• Strong opening
• Identifying and stating audience's needs and interests
• Structure—telling where they're going and what the content will be
• Organization of material
• Recognizable language
• Analogies and/or apt, familiar examples
• Rhythm, pace, drama
• Visualization and/or using visual aids
• Audience involvement and participation
• Warmth
• Humor
• Energy level and commitment
• Succinctness
• Recapitulation and repetition
• Memorable close

These techniques, when well used, can add up to presentations with enough variety, relatedness and order to keep an audience following and being willing to absorb information.

The Spoken Word and Non-Verbal Language

Since we use words as the basic form of communication currency, we should look at them for a moment to see what people think of words, what words can and cannot do and what other forms of personal communication are equally, if not sometimes more, eloquent.

• Words are symbols—they're cerebral. They require us to translate those symbols into meaning.

• Non-verbal body language is visceral. We absorb its meaning viscerally, instinctively, through the gut, not the head. We feel—we don't think—about what it means.

• Words are self-edited. They're controlled. We pick what we say; we filter our choices through the constraints of our super-ego and verbalize only what seems fitting, non-damaging or not too self-revealing. Audiences know that because we all do it.

• Body language is not edited. It's unconscious and involuntary. It's spontaneous and we all know that, too. That's why we use it as our best measure, our barometer and truth-teller about what's really happening and what any communicated message really means. Remember the scene on the first page? The non-verbal message in that scene with Jack was so potent that you could play the scene with no words and instantly get the answer to what you wanted to know—"Jack, how are you?" If you heard the words after you'd seen the scene, you wouldn't believe them. You'd ignore them and go with your gut response to what you saw.

• Words are exact. As symbols they mean specific things and call forth the same images for all of us. "Three o'clock" says only 🕒 to everyone at once. Words can explain concrete ideas and facts.

• Movement, posture, gesture, and space relationships are inexact. They demand interpretation. They deal with nuance, with feelings. They modify facts. They can't say exactly 🕒 but they can say how you feel about the fact of 🕒 . Think of and actually try to do the gestures that say: "Oh, I'm, late!"; "What, already?"; or "Finally!" They come to you at once, don't they? See how recognizable and universal they are?

• Words can eventually describe and tell but gestures *show* feelings much more directly, succinctly and eloquently.

• Words and movement can exist together making a dual dialogue. If they match and are consistent with each other, they strengthen and underscore meaning. If they are inconsistent, saying two different things, the viewer disregards the words and believes the body language.

The significance to you of all the above is this: Oral presentation depends on the spoken word. You use it to reach the jury and present your case. You polish your words, think about them, write them out, re-do and worry over them. But, they're often erasable; forgettable; ignorable. They are superceded and can get canceled by unconscious gesture—not the direct route you thought they were to people's consciousness.

Knowing that audiences watch as well as listen and that they put more credence in and can be more affected by what they see you do rather than say, it's important to analyze all your forms of communicaton to understand what's most effective and why.

*   *   *

All the above-listed explanations of how people listen are useful to know but the basic underlying motivation for audience attention is still self-interest. To capture them with that net you must have a much deeper knowledge of your audience—who they are, how they feel, what they anticipate and what they need, especially from you. How do you learn this? Ladies and gentlemen, meet— the jury.

KNOWING THE JURY

Communicating is gift-giving. But it's useless and totally ineffective if the receiver says, "Ugh, I don't want your gift." To work it must be wrapped in the communicator's commitment to give and the receiver's willingness to receive. How do you insure that your gift will be accepted? By knowing your audience. And by remembering that each member's basic question is, "Why should I listen?"

Remembering that the prime motivator is self interest, you must know, understand, feel for, and actually become your audience. You must be able to internalize:

- What are the jurors' anxieties?
- What are their preformed images of the trial?
- How do they see themselves?
- What are their goals?

Knowing these answers will help you decide on the most compelling form, tone and text for your message. You will answer their question "Why should I listen?" by obviously and instinctively fulfilling their needs, assuaging their fears, and meeting their goals.

How They Feel; What They Need

Environment

Can you remember the first time you walked into a courtroom? Close your eyes for a moment and imagine the scene—the colors, shapes, symbols, the overall ambience. What do you see?

• *Colors?* Brown. Wood. Dark.

• *Shapes?* Boxes. Rectangles. Enclosures. Specifically defined areas.

• *Symbols?* The flag of the United States, a state seal or state flag, too. These symbols that say, "The Government and the People are represented here. They made this happen."

• *What dominates the room?* The bench, a great high, imposing, dominant shape. Does it feel or look like any other form you've seen? An altar, perhaps? (It even has a judge—robed, like a high priest, raised and exalted behind his inaccessible barrier, treated with special respect and ceremony.)

• *What adjectives come to mind* to describe the quality of the scene? Serious. Stately. Intimidating. Formal. Powerful.

Think about this environment for a moment. Think of its message—a ritual, religious atmosphere, with a sense that whatever happens here must be done in certain ceremonial ways—learned, correct, required ways. Like a church that says "Sssh. Behave yourself. Don't break the rules." Only, strangers don't know the rules.

Now become a juror who walks into this stage set. What does he see? How does she feel? And who are they to begin with? Mostly the disenfranchised, since the enfranchised ones often get off, don't they? Generally, they're people whose lives haven't turned out to be a giant success; who are not accustomed to wielding power, cutting a swath, making a dent in society. They walk into this chamber (it's hardly a room) where nothing is self-evident. No recognizable human activity can be imagined here. You can't eat here, play here, dance or study here. The layout says "unique," "strange."

Unlike walking into a foreign restaurant or a new ball park, nothing here says, "You're competent, you'll figure out how to behave here, this is like something you've seen and done before."

So the jury begins its work, before you ever begin yours, feeling intimidated, alien and incompetent. This feeling is created by the stylized ritual environment of the courtroom—their first introduction to their role in the trial.

Competence

Consider the jury's job. What are they asked to do? To make a decision. Now how many people find that on top of their list of favorite things to do? We all hate making decisions. Why? Because we could be wrong. When you go shopping around for the best, cheapest, most dependable, practical, beautiful shoes, car or idea you're trying to hedge your bets against being wrong. You know if you passed the first book of wallpaper samples or the third couch you see, you will begin to lose your mind. Why? Because we keep looking for the "most"—The "10"—The "A". Our reluctance to decide comes from the anxiety of being wrong, visibly, and of the consequences of regret and self-berating we will suffer.

Take this perfectly human universal trait and lay it over the juror's work—to decide fairly about an issue of right or wrongness. Not only what's right or wrong but to feel so sure about it that they can mete out punishment as well. To feel so secure about their decision, to stand on such solid ground, with such a suitcase full of good reasons and precedents for making their decision that they can also say, "You may win, you must lose; you shall live and you shall die; you shall pay and you go free." At every level of trial, what's right, what's fair and what the consequences are is the basic process, the questions that need to be answered, the decisions the jury must make.

Now picture this process with the typical jury cast of characters: people unaccustomed to making consequential decisions, especially those affecting other people's lives. Here they are, involved in a trial; a process which they don't understand and have never experienced and in which they have no skills. Their lives have taught them the fear of being wrong—whether it's in the classroom, answering a parent, or at their job. They all have the usual human complement of insecurities about themselves, their wisdom and their ability to grasp and understand. Now add the intimidation of the courtroom itself and the sense of incompetence it creates. And balance all this against each juror's high-minded resolve to be eminently just and fair. What a way to begin!

Absorb this inner turmoil. Really feel it in your gut. What do jurors need, therefore? To get so clear about the information of the trial that they can dare to say "I know. I'm sure." To see fathomable, logical reasons for punishment and blame, reasons that will make them comfortable with their decisions. And to feel someone clapping them on the back, saying, "C'mon—you can do it."

That's a picture of some internal needs. Now let's take a look at the external demands of the trial on the juror.

Passivity

The jury is passive. They are not able to move, actively affect or really participate in any part of the trial. This is a terribly important point for several reasons.

• *They are cast in the role of dependents.* They can't interrupt and say, "Listen, lawyer, ask him about this" or "I can't hear, what did he say" or "Never mind that legal stuff, tell me so I can understand." So they can be frustrated and feel out of control of their own work.

• *Adults don't generally like seeing their own dependency.* It can create resentment about the person in power, especially if that person doesn't anticipate their needs and give them what they want, since they can't get it themselves.

• *Passivity creates a loss of impulse to keep listening.* Since the jury's activity is delayed till the end of the trial, their lack of ongoing participation can be translated into encouraging total passivity and total lack of participation, namely tuning out entirely.

• *Their physical passivity has bad physiological consequences*. Concentration and thinking operates through electrical impulses in your brain. The waste products of such activity are discharged into your blood stream, which needs to purify itself. One of the best ways is physical activity, improving circulation. Sitting still all day just listening, with no refreshing input, no change of pace or ability to move around makes the physical act of concentrating twice as difficult as it normally is. Just watch what you do when you've been sitting for a while. Doesn't your body push you to stretch or to get up and do something?

• *Even where they sit affects them*. The enclosed jury box by itself is confining and pen-like in nature. It has a specific visual focus and exposure and certain designated sight lines. The background is always the same: the angle for viewing the witness, the judge, the side view, the audience—all are static.

• *There is an open-ended, no-limit time frame of servitude over which they have no control and which is unpredictable*. Although for some jurors the trial is a welcome relief from a dreary life, not knowing when they'll be done and having no hand in deciding how long the trial will continue also adds to their sense of helplessness and anonymity.

The physical passivity of the jury therefore has great consequences in their need, desire or ability to concentrate and listen.

Identification

Now, given this alien environment with the personal problems it creates ask yourself: What's familiar to the juror? With what or with whom could he or she identify?

With the judge—that exalted, parental figure of righteousness? Hardly.

With the lawyers—those efficient, business-like attache-case packing practitioners, who talk a language only *they* think is English, who seem so comfortable at home in this strange world? Not likely.

Who, then?

With the witnesses, those lay people who but for the grace of God could be the jurors themselves.

Think about the edge that gives the witnesses in the eyes of the jury.

This dynamic must be factored into everything you do in examination. Since it's in there, the jurors do not only see the facts unfold, but are quite involved in how you get them and what you're doing to a fellow stranger on your turf.

Which leads me to the last facet of this juror-montage. What do you think they think of you?

Images Of Lawyers

Jurors bring a set of stereotypes about you to the courtroom, just as you bring some of them. You both start out working from conditioned images, not really perceiving human beings at all. After all, lawyers are abroad in the land. Jurors have seen "Witness for the Prosecution," "Inherit the Wind," and "The Verdict," not to mention that ever-present, ever-ready, ever-successful practitioner, Perry Mason.

What do you think their images of lawyers are? Manipulative, not to be trusted, shifty, crafty, sly, a hired gun, insincere, dry, stuffy, rich? Jurors imagine your lives as being glamorous, trouble-free, martini-quaffing, party-going, golf-filled, with weekends at some expensive retreat and a Porsche purring at the curb.

Is it all true? Yet, what in the trial can let you tell them that it's not? What can you do to cut down the distance their stereotypes can create between you and them? And how does their canned image of who and what you are qualify you to fulfill the juror's needs we've just discovered, or even to understand them?

*   *   *

Now what have we learned?

The truth is that the prognosis is a difficult one. There they are, jurors entering into a ritualized performance, frightened and insecure about their role in it, feeling unable to function in a normal, familiar way. They feel unprepared, with little or no knowledge. They must watch and wait, seeing only mysterious strangers—lawyers whom they can suspect—and empathizing with the recognizable ones, the witnesses. And they come armed only with intuitive people-skills that don't seem the right outfit for the game.

On the other side is what you wish to be: their teacher, their guide, their leader and explainer. You want their trust; belief; attention; concentration; understanding; agreement. You want to persuade them. But that would require that the jury see someone with whom they can identify, someone with a set of standards and ethics like theirs, whose version of truth and justice, good behavior and honesty is like their own.

What's the answer?

It's to look again at the trial, at the accepted, correct legal ways of conducting a trial, and to add something to make your own performance more human.

It's to find how to engage and excite, involve and capture this audience, this anxious, motivated jury, this group of people in a foreign land.

It's to approach the subject, the techniques, the processes with full knowledge of how the jury would react and what would make them listen.

Most of all, it's to show yourself as a fellow-member of their tribe, fallible, courageous, sincere, hard-working, knowledgeable and deeply committed to helping them understand.

For in the final analysis, what you do boils down to a simple, human scene.

It's made up of just you, one person, reaching out to your audience—your jury—and of their choosing to listen and be persuaded, or not.

It comes back to basics, to the essence of why people listen to each other and what finally gets us. It comes back to how well, how fully you must know your audience. That you must discover their needs and self-interest and feel them so keenly and fulfill them so clearly that this twentieth-century talkproof audience will absorb your complex concepts and your simple truths and be persuaded.

2

VOIR DIRE

Voir dire is a curious process. It's a system of diometric opposites. It represents, at the same time, the best and the worst of ourselves.

The best—because it shows our gifts. By using our shared human experiences and our remarkable instincts, we can intuitively sense, recognize and read basic characteristics or responses in each other. What a wonder. We really can do it. That's the best part.

The worst—because we use these instincts to reinforce decisions based on preconditioned, uninformed, automatically accepted stereotypes. Voir dire plays on, relies on prejudice. It admits that we are all prone to believe the unproven, to accept the myth, to follow the group. Since it's a human failing, it also affects you as lawyers.

Demonstration:

You will smoke out and choose conservative, authoritarian or puritanical men if you're against a woman defendant who's single, pregnant and has been a go-go girl in Las Vegas.

You will choose dependent, disenfranchised women with children if your widowed client is suing a large corporation for damages in her husband's wrongful death.

In each instance, you assume that their previous experiences will prejudice those jurors toward or against one aspect of the case.

You do not select as much as you "de-select" people whose prejudices you feel are so ingrained that they can't hear your side or decide fairly. In both how they think and how you select, prejudice is
the key ingredient. Prejudice, not so much in the pejorative sense,
but as simplistic, primary-colored assumptions and commonly held
beliefs, without shadings or hues. Prejudice as popular, recognizable stereotypes which route our thinking into easy slots. They're
recognizable because we all use them, without looking for much
new input.

That's how people are and how we operate most of the time;
flawed, biased, unable to shake old beliefs, unwilling to accept new
ideas, yet trying to live up to expectations, wanting to be good and
judge fairly—in a word, mortal and fallible, somewhat predictable,
and apparently able to be put into categories.

Except when they surprise you.

In a medical malpractice case in California involving a question of infant brain damage at the time of delivery, the plaintiff's
lawyer chose a jury made up entirely of mothers, counting on their
natural empathy for the mother to deliver a verdict for his client.
But the jury awarded no damages at all because, as they stated in
an interview later, they could tell, when the plaintiff was on the
stand, that "that mother did not love or feel for her child; she was
only interested in the money."

Lesson? The plaintiff's lawyer needed more information beyond the most basic "prejudice" of "a mother is for a mother." He
needed to know about his jurors' commitment to and feelings about
motherhood so he'd know how quickly they would recognize that
in others. He needed to see beyond the "mother" title of his client
to her real feelings and how perceptible those would be to people
attuned to looking for them. That lawyer needed to understand
that one must look deeper: at the jurors' value systems, beliefs,
morality; at the quality of their lives; at their level of disappointment or satisfaction with the hand life has dealt them; at how impotent or empowered they feel to make changes and get what they
want. These issues are reflected in how jurors handle their momentary power. This is where decisions and human responses
really lie. This is where those instinctive human skills of sensing
and recognizing must take you if you wish to find out what you *re-*

ally need to know in voir dire. You need to reject the simplistic categories in a search for the "but" and the "however."

Unfortunately, this is very hard to do. There are a number of volatile yet unseen factors that affect voir dire:

- Potential jurors are multi-layered with only the tip of the iceberg showing and available to you.
- Your system of gathering information gives jurors great choices and editing capability.
- There is a hidden sub-text in the voir dire process, with the jurors having agendas other than what seems to be happening.
- The questioning process itself has built-in flaws that lead to problems.
- The information you get needs interpretation and thought to be useful, while voir dire is a fairly instantaneous process.

Therefore, with these givens, a successful and effective voir dire requires much more from you.

- You need to deepen your knowledge of who people are and how they behave, to see and understand more.
- You must sharpen your instincts and all your senses in order to gather information from the jurors' unguarded sources rather than from their careful answers alone.
- You need to take a hard look at your questioning techniques to see if and how they work, as well as what effect you have on the jurors.
- You need to analyze the kinds of questions you ask to see what you really get from their answers and how revealing or helpful they are.
- You need to look into some new areas of questioning that will net more incisive and telling information.

These processes are what this chapter is all about. In order to build a foundation, let's begin by taking a moment to orient ourselves to where voir dire is right now, what the basic process is and isn't, and what it can and cannot do.

ISSUES AND INSIGHTS

Where Voir Dire Is Now

Voir dire is in a strange state right now. Some say voir dire is a dinosaur, losing its tenure as a system in the trial. Lawyers and the judiciary are not in agreement about what it's for and who should do it, if it even serves a purpose or if it is perhaps an unjust practice. The future of voir dire is open to question and its present is confusing. For example:

• Most lawyers would like to conduct their own voir dire in their jury trials. However, they may not.

• Most judges feel that the system of voir dire is abused by lawyers, mishandled, overlong and that only judges should conduct it. Judges conduct voir dire in the federal courts and in some courts they may permit submission of attorneys' questions, but they may or may not use them.

• Some say the state court system of voir dire is better. However, attorneys do voir dire in 44 percent of the state courts, judges in 30 percent, and both attorneys and judges in the remaining 26 percent.

• Even when attorneys conduct voir dire, the judge can decide the duration and the kinds of questions he or she will allow. At any level, the practice varies according to the judge.

• Voir dire is conducted sitting, standing behind a lectern or moving about. The manner of questioning is open to individual judicial decision.

What Voir Dire Is and Isn't

Voir dire is not a science.

• It is not exact.
• It is unpredictable, almost unteachable.
• There are no hard and fast rules that can create guaranteed success.

• The same question in the hands of two different lawyers can bring totally different answers.

• It presupposses honesty and forthrightness from jurors, which is inaccurate and naive.

• It is ultimately based on hunches, feelings and other intangibles.

The essence of voir dire is to find those jurors most favorable or fair to one side of a case, or at least not too heavily influenced against one side by previous experiences. It is based on a sketchy personal profile drawn in court from answers to a lawyer's or judge's questions.

• You extrapolate from this profile who a juror is, how he or she thinks and how he or she will probably judge this case.

• You base your decisions on commonly held beliefs and clichés about how certain kinds of people usually feel about certain issues.

• You don't know and you can't find out whether it's true. You have no authentic way of judging which stereotype really fits.

Can It Be Learned?

The above list makes it sound impossible to transmit any relevant, objective information about voir dire. Yet, by becoming aware of what is real versus what voir dire hopes for, by discovering how jurors see the process and what their inner motivation is, by learning how and where to look for information, there is a vast area of personal skills that can be learned.

Wouldn't it be valuable to discover whether all those stereotypes, and assumptions *are* true? How often they are true? What are the mitigating factors that make them untrue? What else do you need to know about human behavior to understand the clues you are gathering? Are there other kinds of clues you should be aware of and notice? What of your personal skills—can you ask your questions differently or ask different kinds of questions to get better, truer results?

How Social Sciences Can Help

There have been some innovative new developments in the jury selection process, using social science services such as market research, demographic studies, public opinion surveys and community interviewing, as well as calling on communications experts, psychologists and social scientists as consultants. Their insights into human behavior, economic and ethnic strata, and regional beliefs can be very helpful in deepening your understanding of your venire and helping to predict your jurors' leanings. The objective and factual information you can gather to orient yourself to what potential jurors feel, do and care about in any specific area can not only help you select with more understanding, but can actually help you design your whole trial to be more pertinent, affecting and clear to your specific jury.

All these adjunct materials are very useful in preparing for your voir dire. Yet the action which ultimately determines the outcome is in the courtroom, and this will be our focus. Let's look at the courtroom, where you would think everyone is engaged in the same process. Actually, there are very different scripts being played simultaneously by you and the jury.

WHAT ELSE IS HAPPENING IN THE COURTROOM

It's understandable that your main focus as you enter the voir dire process is what techniques you will use, what the answers will tell you and what will help you decide.

But these factors deal only with you. What about the potential jurors? What are *they* doing while you're busy evaluating them? The fact is that every event has at least two points of view—that of the mover, the initiator, and that of the perceiver, the recipient of the action. Nor do the interaction and the response rise full-blown at the moment of impact in court. Both parties bring a long history and a series of previously conditioned responses to any new event in which they participate. So what happens in the courtroom has hidden layers that affect and often mask the visible action. Let's focus on the potential jurors to discover what you don't see and may not know: What do the jurors bring with them to the courtroom?

Since you gain your voir dire information through questioning, we should look first at that process. Is it foolproof? Is it enough? What issues does it raise? What problems underlie the fact of your extracting personal information from strangers? How do people feel about being questioned and how do they usually answer?

The Act of Questioning

Of all the acts that man perpetrates on his fellow man, the most aggressive act, short of touching someone, is questioning them. Questioning is a classic system—recognizable in every culture, done for myriad reasons. Just picture any questioning circumstance: your parents at home, your teacher at school, a policeman at your car window, a personnel director's interview, a banker, rental agent, admitting nurse, IRS auditor . . . the list is endless. And we've all experienced it: A questioner asks the questions, in the way he wishes, at the pace he wishes, in the order he wishes, on the subjects he wishes and then expects an immediate and total response.

The most amazing part of this aggressive act is that our society has trained us to accept the questions, imbue the questioner with special permission to use this power, and then automatically, without resistance, to answer.

When you were a kid would it occur to you to say, "I won't answer" or "None of your business" to your parents or your teacher? You answered. You did what you were told. And we all still do, most of the time.

I've done a number of experiments on the act of questioning in the seminars I teach. In an audience filled with very canny, prestigious lawyers, I walk into the audience, select one lawyer at random and, standing over him or her, begin to ask a string of questions that range from "Who are you? Where do you live? What do you do?" "How many children do you have? Why? Do you mean to have any more? When?" or "Are you married? Why not?" And I find these wise, tough lawyers answer every question automatically, in front of a large room of people, never questioning why

I ask it, what I will do with the information or even saying, "Get lost." Why? Why do they acquiesce and answer? Why aren't they more resentful of my rudeness?

It has to do with power. We're trained to give in to the person in charge and in every situation we automatically sense who that is. Anyone who asks questions in a formal setting seems to have the endowed right to do that and we all have learned to submit to their aggression. But what effect does this have on the person being questioned and on their answers?

Think back on your years in school. Imagine yourself in arith-metic class, or whatever was your least favorite subject. The teacher calls on you, asking for an answer. The spotlight is on you while everybody cringes in his seat and thinks, "Thank God it isn't me." Not only did you have to answer, but the moment you did, you were exposed to the challenge: Was the answer right or wrong? If it was wrong, would someone then top you with the right answer? What was everyone thinking about you? Were others making judgments about you? As you read this, can't you immedi-ately conjure up those images—can't you see yourself in class and remember those feelings and what you were worried about? These feelings stay ingrained in our subconscious for good, even though we're all grown up and supposedly in charge now.

How People Answer Questions

When we're questioned, especially in a group setting, we automat-ically strain our spontaneous answers through a whole series of filters—blocks built from childhood.

• Our major concern is always the issue of right versus wrong and the possible attendant humiliation. Our culture likes winners.

• Not only that but there's built-in competition in a group—"I hope no one else knows it either."

• Since we all want acceptance, there is an attempt to anticipate what kind of an answer will please the questioner or what kind of answer is expected.

• There is caution and self-censorship around areas of privacy and what answering may cause us to reveal about them.

• There is fear around the consequences of an answer—what the fallout may be if we tell. This puts the brakes on candor as we sift and choose a reply.

• Visibility, the focus of a spotlight on ourselves in a group while others watch and listen creates anxiety which greatly interferes with how we answer.

• The need to fit into a group also invites comparison with others, what they said, what's acceptable, what's the norm.

All of these concerns have set up grooved pathways we travel whenever we are questioned—in any situation.

Jurors' Responses to Voir Dire

The significance to you of the ways we filter our answers to questions is that jurors bring a suitcase full of those conditioned responses into the courtroom and your right to voir dire examination.

They are preprogrammed to resist, to censor, to alter, to give half-answers because they have experienced the questioning process endlessly in their own lives. Therefore, their answers to many of your questions are somewhat predictable because that is how they would answer all questions.

Additionally, there are unique factors present in voir dire that further affect how jurors will answer you. To fully understand what you're getting when a venireman answers, let's put you in his or her place, and ask you to experience the voir dire process from his or her point of view.

Concerns of Potential Jurors

Let's assume that for most jurors this is their first time in a courtroom. Focus in on them as they file into the jury box (or into the courtroom itself) to be questioned in voir dire. There is an inner soliloquy as they quickly try to orient themselves and assess the situation.

People are already here. What have they been doing? What will they want of me? How will I handle this?

We're all filing into an enclosure like a corral. Boxed. No one can get out or leave until they tell you. I am sitting with strangers. The judge talks to us. This is serious.

They start out feeling passive and defenseless, vulnerable, disoriented and, typical of us all, wary and resistant to an unknown process.

Lawyers are going to ask me a lot of questions. Assault. Strangers. Who are they to get to my insides, maybe even to my secrets . . . .

Yet underneath this polyphonic anxiety-chorus hums one constant, basic chord: the desire to win, to be chosen, not to be rejected.

What's Behind the Jurors' Answers

"I Want To Win, To Be Chosen"

Picture this. If someone walks into a room and says, "I need three people—let's see, you, you, and you," and leaves you out, that means he didn't pick you. Human nature creates a momentary flash of disappointment—"Why not me? Something's happening and I'm going to miss it."

Although some people may not want to serve and give the time, no one voluntarily wants or likes to be rejected or to be dismissed. Panel members are engaged in a process that has a win, a prize in it. The lawyers will say, "You shall live and you shall die. You can play and you can leave." Who wants to lose in the USA?

"What Kinds of Answers Are Acceptable to the Lawyers?"

It's the old right versus wrong answers again. "What are these lawyers really looking for? What does it mean if I answer this way or that? What should I hold back? What makes me acceptable? What would you like in order to pick me?" Their agenda is, "What do you want? What's the right thing to say?" rather than, "What do I really think about this?"

"What Will Other Jurors Think of Me?"

Who's ready to hang their life-story on the wall and say, "Read it"? "How do I know who's sitting next to me and how terrific their life is going to sound? How do I rate in my society? If I get chosen, some of these other jurors will be on the case with me. They will know forever that I dropped out of high school, that I recently lost my job, that my wife divorced me, that my son ran away." Answers can expose areas of his or her life that are not the norm or that he or she is not proud of. There's a consequence to live with as the venireman answers, knowing he or she could become part of a group that's heard his or her personal story.

"What Does the Judge Think?"

The symbol of authority, the parent, is a source of great concern to jurors. He or she symbolizes what should be the best in us, the purest, the fairest, the most correct. "What would he think is right, good, just? How would she like me to answer? Is that the same sort of thing I want to tell the lawyers?"

"Who Wants To Volunteer or To Go First?"

Jurors have a great concern about the consequences of volunteering; not only are they concerned about what you meant but also how the group perceives and deals with the question. "I'd better watch and see what kind of answers they want and what other people say before I raise my hand. I'm better off to stay hidden. Why should I expose myself?"

"Who Ever Even Asks My Opinion?"

Most people in our society are not asked their opinions and beliefs about anything publicly. Rarely, if ever, does someone call you up to be part of the Nielsen ratings or stop you in the street and ask you to become a part of a poll. (Did *you* ever get phoned?

Have *you* ever been polled?) It is not common in our society for the average lay person to be put in a position of authority or judgment. We don't even get asked our opinion too much at home—by spouses or children. It is, therefore, anxiety-producing to have your opinion asked in public about anything.

"My Ideas Are Being Evaluated"

"The lawyers and the other jurors will be hearing how I think, my approaches to everything from the death penalty to how I feel about insurance companies. I know that the lawyers will then be judging me and my ideas. The other jurors will, too. Better not tell too much—or better yet, keep quiet."

"I'm Worried about How I Will Say It"

"Am I eloquent enough? I never could use words too well and I never made a speech. Will I talk all right? How will it sound for *me* to speak out on abstract subjects or serious issues like this in front of other people, in a courtroom with the flag waving. Will I make a fool of myself?"

"How 'm I Doing?"

We all need to feel acceptable. "How'm I doing on the Richter scale? Where do I fit in this group? What's the norm?" This is especially true if they heard other people answer the same questions quite differently. Being compared with others, the possibility of being found wanting or inferior in some way, makes jurors avoid forthrightness.

"These Questions Are Pretty Personal"

"Most of my *friends* don't even ask such questions. That's not the sort of thing that I would volunteer any information about, to a stranger." We are all naturally reticent and private. A conflict develops between feeling invaded and answering because it's required. The jurors' unease can sometimes be translated into bellig-erence and resistance. People don't like anyone asking "nosy" questions but especially dislike strangers, lawyers, in this public evaluation process.

"It Feels Like I'm Under Attack"

It's human to feel defensive when being grilled and scruti-nized. Potential jurors can react as if under personal attack by the lawyer. The feeling of being "aggressed upon" builds up as the questions accumulate and the process wears on.

What Else Jurors Are Thinking

Jurors not only filter the questions, but have other thoughts as well:

"Why Did They Dismiss Her?"

Watching you excuse jurors makes them wonder why. Not only do they wonder what you are evaluating and what are dismiss-ible answers but also what you are thinking about them. The choices look arbitrary to them and since there seems to be no rhyme nor reason, it feels almost like a popularity contest.

"He's Really Being Rough on That Nice Lady in the Front"

Veniremen and women spend quite some time together, just waiting. They share a common bond by the time you see them and they are quite protective about each other. They're a "we," a bonded group, and they see you as a "they," an outsider and the possible enemy. Because they feel connected to each other, pro-spective jurors are especially sensitive to how you treat the other panel members, assuming you could do that to them, too. It makes them judgmental of you and your character before they've even gotten to know you.

"Who Is This Who's Asking All These Personal Questions?"

There is a feeling of inequality as jurors are "grilled" and lawyers stay private, cool and manipulative. This can build not only resentment but a hostile and distorted view of the "nosy," aggressive lawyer who will later need to win over the jurors to his side of the case.

"How Long Is This Crazy Process Going To Take?"

If you've ever interviewed potential jurors after voir dire you discover that the "Number 1" complaint is waiting. And waiting. And waiting some more. That means their attention span is very short by the time you get them and they're impatient to get on with it and to participate. Not a good environment for a long-winded or dull voir dire or one in which they are not asked very much.

*   *   *

All of this adds up to a series of cautions about how much direct, straighforward information you can expect from a venire going into voir dire. Obviously, there is a need for more skills to circumvent these roadblocks, different kinds of information-getting techniques beyond just plain old questioning in order to get what you need for the kinds of judgments you wish to make.

How the Jury Sees You

The lawyer's role in voir dire is two-fold: to judge and be judged.

You are making decisions, almost instantaneous decisions, based on gut feelings and preconceptions and perhaps adding some previous information you have gathered. You're tightly focused and concentrated. It's hard work. While trying to stay open to all the stimuli and clues you get from the jurors, you're also, literally, narrowing and squeezing your thoughts into the boxes and labels on the chart before you. You're tense, trying to maximize each moment.

But there is another activity going on. This is the first time the potential jury sees you. At the same time that you are busy doing your evaluation, they have begun to evaluate you, a major process they carry on through the whole trial. While you're looking at their human qualities, they're looking at yours. What kind of person are you? What is your relationship to them and to other strangers? What can they learn about you as you question them? The way you dismiss jurors, for example, or how sensitive you are when you ask personal questions tells them a great deal about you. Just like you, they're drawing a personal profile based on the style and substance of your questions, your questioning techniques, your non-verbal signals—in a word, how they react and respond to you.

The most important part of this process is that it will affect how they answer your questions. Liking you or not liking you predisposes them to be honest and relaxed or guarded and suspicious.

Potential jurors, like all of us when we first meet, work from their previously accepted stereotypes. Your role, as you meet them, blinds them at first:

- They see you as being all powerful.
- They see you as being intrusive.
- They see you as carrying out their old stereotypes of lawyers: aggressive questioners, manipulators, finger pointers, penetrating, getting to the heart of the matter, no matter what.
- They watch uneasily as you ask seemingly rude questions quickly and make all sorts of mysterious decisions.
- They see you as a source of personal criticism. You may whisper (rudely, they think) to your associate; you make notes about them, you write things down as they answer.
- They see you as a person who has some power over their lives at this moment. You can say, "You may become a juror, an active anointed citizen, or you may go back to being just what you've always been: John Doe, USA, without any additional power or the opportunity for this rare plum. I can give you a chance for an experience of novelty, excitement and some power, a chance to exercise a very unique right or I can take it away."
- They see you as a sly manipulator; as a person who knows why he's asking these questions, and who's going to get this information

out of them. They won't know if you've done it or how you've done
it or how to stop it once it happens.

*   *   *

How you ask your questions will dispel or reconfirm the decisions potential jury members are already making about you. They
bring to the courtroom nothing but their own past experience and
how *they* have made decisions all their lives about other human beings. They bring their prejudices. They evaluate based on images
their mothers and fathers gave them about acceptable behavior.
They bring the canned unreality the media presents about lawyers.
They bring their own angers, frustrations and fantasies they would
like to act out. They react negatively to people who remind them of
some of these angers and frustrations, who point up the disappointments in their lives and the secret places they don't tell anybody
about. They bring their own universal, deep-seated insecurity,
common to us all: "Will they like me? Am I acceptable?"

This total human package is all they have when they sit in the
jury box and choose what they choose and believe what they believe. It begins at the very moment they take a look at you. What
they see, what they feel they can judge (and care very much to
judge), is what kind of a human being you are. The best way to
measure that is by how you treat and manipulate them. They'll
watch that throughout the entire trial but especially at the beginning, and the amount of trust you develop in them right at the start
will be reflected at the end of the trial in the jury room. Therefore,
it's time to look at the communication processes you use and what
the jury sees you do.

**PREPARING FOR VOIR DIRE
EXAMINATION**

How To Begin

As I mentioned earlier, the social science services, such as
analyzing the jury lists for occupations and addresses, doing surveys and polls that gather additional data and insights are very
helpful in giving you a base to begin planning your voir dire. But
with or without them, the next few steps can help you focus on the

basic thrust of your jury selection and prepare you for the courtoom.

Design an Optimum Jury

Analyze the issues in your case and list the major ones. Now try to figure out what kinds of people, with what kinds of vital statistics and life experience or basic personality characteristics, would be good or bad for your case. List them. Then create an optimum jury by category. Although I have made a case about getting too committed to stereotypes, stereotypes are a good way to begin, provided you stay alert and open-minded.

Decide what kinds of people would relate well to your client, your key witness and the issues involved in your case. Someone of a certain age group, ethnic background or profession; someone who is older and retired, young but female, or has a certain breadth of experience. Be clear about why certain kinds of people would be useful to you and what kinds of experiences could make people feel or think one way or the other.

Then, make a chart or a grid with your optimum jury listed by category based on the above questions. As you begin interviewing your jurors, you can fit them into those slots; you can then quickly look down your list and see, "I've got one of those and one of those, but I still need the male, retired, 55 year old and I need the young unattached professional woman." It helps you to make decisions more readily when you categorize in advance rather than casting about on the spot and and wondering, "If I take this truck driver and I like that widow, how would it affect me if I had the teacher, too?" It also helps channel your thinking and focus your attention on certain key areas to search out, while retaining the basic mix you want. You might make your categories Column A, Column B and so on, listing the basic qualities and experiences you're looking for under each one. Then, develop a shorthand, "He's an A, she's a G," so that you have a very clear picture of what you're looking for. But—a word of caution here: Don't get so committed to your stereotypical images that you don't hear the deviations and the variables as they come up. As you hear them, think about what effect they might have on your neat theories and classifications. Don't forget that the exception proves the rule. Be aware. Don't be complacent. Look for the extra clues that can tell you that although this man is a member of an ethnic minority, who never finished high school, his hobby is building and fixing mechanical toys (and you're the defendant in a faulty toy suit).

Since what happens in the courtroom requires such a high level of concentration, the more prepared and organized you are in advance and the more highly focused you are on the issues and pitfalls, the more room you'll have to take in *all* the clues given you during voir dire.

Remember Group Dynamics

The jury will be a group. They will function as any group of people does. There are leaders, followers, opposers and bystanders. Note: Once you've gotten your jury, be sure you look at them again to see the group dynamics and what mix you actually have. But during voir dire, think about whom you see as a leader, or an opposer and who are the weak ones. Who looks like a swing juror? Group members each have a major function and will play roles against or for each other that can affect the outcome of the trial. Therefore, along with the personal data you seek, keep in mind the personality types you're putting together. Is the obvious leader type on your side? Are there too many followers or bystanders waiting to be led? Keep a lookout for the non-conformist. Who is the opposer? How strong will that opposer be? Is the group strong enough to overturn him or her? You might use some abbreviated signs to indicate the personality types of the potential jurors you're questioning and add them to your decision-making list. (Later in this chapter you'll discover ways to discern these types.)

Handling Your Notes, Lists, Charts

How do you normally write notes? Do you use yellow pads? A clipboard? Horizontal charts made of small poster board? Are you more comfortable sitting at the counsel table and writing or writing at the lectern? How portable is your form of writing notes?

The most important issue is how much your notes confine you to a certain space. The goal is to be as free and as flexible as possible. Try to be economical and efficient by deciding on initials, abbreviations and symbols in advance that define the various things you're looking for. For example, "A" could stand for prior accident; "LS" for prior law suit; "M" for medically informed; "U" for unemployed and so on. It makes for less writing and less distraction and helps the flow of your questions. Don't be afraid to carry your note pad with you as you get closer. Don't write down everything said to you. It looks too condemnatory, like a police dossier. It also makes you look at your paper instead of looking at the jurors, giving them confidence and showing interest. Whatever your system, handle the writing of notes as a comfortable but unobtrusive part of your questioning. Take the time to learn to do it in a relaxed way.

THE QUESTIONING PROCESS

The essence of voir dire is getting familiar, "getting to know you." If you removed this process from its purpose in the courtroom, you'd find you do this all the time, with everyone you meet. We all do. The process of getting acquainted is natural. That's important because, since we all do it, we all bring a vision and a prototype of how to do that into the courtroom. We've all gotten acquainted with strangers—lawyer and juror alike. Consequently, we have an instinctive measurement of what's seemly and what isn't, what's permitted and what isn't, and a variety of acceptable, recognizable ways we get to know someone.

Therefore, the premium in voir dire is to look and act natural, to put the potential juror at ease and to make the process look familiar. This can do more to disarm and encourage forthrightness than any fancy ploy or clever, devious trick. Developing an atmosphere of "I'm interested. I'd like to get to know you a little better. I'm a pretty nice person, too," is the essence of successful communication in voir dire.

But there the analogy must end, for there are other issues at work here. The potential juror finds him or herself in a strange milieu where he or she is not on equal ground. Unlike you, he or she questions. Unlike you, he or she can be dismissed as you get to know him or her better. And unlike you, he or she has no idea what you're after as you ask your questions, but he or she surely knows you're after something specific.

So the focus is to overcome these suspicions that distance you and come as close to the "getting to know you" feeling as you can.

Openings

The courtroom is a theatre. You enter as a trial lawyer but you are visible as an actor throughout the trial. Everything you do—how you talk to your associate, whether you tap your pencil or jiggle your knee, the color and pattern of your tie or dress, how you move—becomes a clue that tells the juror about how pleasant, friendly, uptight or aloof you are. It helps the juror imagine, "Would I like him? Would I have a beer with him? Does he drink beer? Can I imagine him or her relaxed, in jeans, at play?" The same system of perception and judgment they rely on when they bring in a verdict is what they use to evaluate you, too, the system of extrapolating from what they see that's familiar, to what else they can imagine you would be and do. Actually, it's the same system you're using on them.

They start out assuming you're different from them. Wouldn't it help if, in the beginning of this performance, in which they will see you in a very powerful role for a rather long time, you could let them know, "I also wear old clothes, I love football and good music and my kids absolutely baffle me half the time"? How can you help them see a three-dimensional person right from the beginning?

Let the Jury See You in a Human, Not a Lawyerly Role

The jury will observe you closely to see the unguarded you. From the beginning, and when you're not actively involved in voir dire, show many facets of relaxed behavior with colleagues and the courtroom staff. If you are in the halls, call the clerk, the elevator man, the bailiff, and other people that work in the courtroom by their first names, greet them, do a little bantering with them. The

potential jury notices this and sees you as having an additional dimension, not just all business. They see someone who takes the
trouble to discover who else works there, even at menial tasks, and
gives them some recognition. They see your warmth, your sense of
humor, your humanity. They see themselves.

Let Them See You on the Move

Let the jury see you laugh and move. They will rarely see
your physical, human dimensions, your relaxed, natural, everyday
behavior again in the trial. Let them hear you talk and greet
friends. Let them get a chance to see what you'd be like on Satur-
day and Sunday outside the courtroom.

How do you relate to your colleagues? How do you handle
your materials? How do you open your briefcase? Are you neat and
orderly? Do you move with confidence, competence, comfort? Are
you a very active person? Do you fiddle with things?

Move about freely. It's one of the few chances they'll have to
see you do that. Be visible, be at ease—they are watching you.
Help them fill in or deviate from their own lawyer stereotypes.
Make them see who else you are, and what to expect from you as
you move into their world. These suggestions are true for all the
days of the trial, but most important as people get their first
impressions.

Introduce Yourself

If you have a difficult or unusual name, spell it. Use some humor about how tough it was in grade school or something that
makes it sound human, like a real introduction and outreach, not
just a perfunctory announcement. Even if your name is Smith, you
might find something distinctive to say about it to make the moment memorable: "not hard to spell" or "but my first name is *really*
unusual—John." Use the first moment to make contact.

Introduce the Case

The judge usually permits a brief preliminary statement. Use
your opportunity well, but don't harangue or proselytize.
Continuing to explain the case in small succinct bites as you go

along is much more effective than making one long speech. Don't argue. Be factual, but let the potential jurors get your theory of the case. It may be better to introduce different aspects of the case as you introduce different categories of questioning, to explain why you are asking, but your orientation to the jury up front should draw the basic parameters and issues.

Make It Conversational

If the intention is to make this experience feel like getting acquainted, then talk to them and don't lecture. Use an easy, conversational tone. Your goal is to explain and reassure, even to charm, not just to tell. Give them your warmth, not your smarts.

Tell Them What You're Going to Do and Why

A very important aspect of anticipating a new experience is to feel informed and competent. Do not rely on a few perfunctory sentences to explain voir dire. Your introduction to what you're going to do colors their approach to it and their state of mind.

Tell Them First About Your Goal

Explain that the purpose of jury selection is "to find a jury that will be most comfortable with the material and issues of the trial and, therefore, most open about the subject matter." They need to know what this process is actually going to do.

Professor James Seckinger of the Notre Dame Law School and director of the National Institute for Trial Advocacy, explains it this way to a jury panel: "What we are doing here is selecting a jury to hear and decide this case. In the interests of justice, we'd like to have the best possible jury to listen and decide. We're looking for people who do not have special knowledge about or a relationship to this case or a similar case. For example, I would not be a good juror, since I have a lot of information about one side of this case."

Never Say, "We're Looking for People Who Can Be Fair."

It automatically says "some of you are not fair." We all pride ourselves on trying and wanting to be fair when making decisions, especially in this competitive, sports-oriented country. We depend on referees to make impartial judgments based on rules, and trust their fairness (although sometimes we question their ability to see).

Potential jurors want to bring the best of themselves to do this important job correctly. The venire are already filled with pride and nobility about how they will judge. I heard one juror, when asked if he could be fair, say, "Isn't that what we're supposed to do?"

Say things like, "This is a case about XYZ and for some it may be difficult to handle or to hear." Or, "It may involve things that affected your own life which would interfere with your desire to be impartial." Or, "Some of you might not want to be involved in such decision making." Or, "We know you all want to be fair. Sometimes it's not possible." Or, "We're looking to put together a jury that could listen to this case with the least interference from their personal concerns."

Tell Them About the Process

They need to understand and be prepared for what's going to happen.

• Tell them you'll go about selecting a jury in the classic way—by asking questions.

• Show them you have a chart with their names listed in proper seating order to keep them all straight in your mind. This takes the mystery out of your note-taking.

• Explain that you will be writing notes next to their names with their "vital statistics," the basic information they give you, as you talk together. This will help deal with the seeming secrecy of note-taking and relieve the anxiety and curiosity they will feel about what you're writing about them.

Your Time Together Is Limited

Explain that you'll include all the venire, as much as possible, in your questioning but you know you won't get to know them all as well as you'd like to, since "I'm only allowed a limited time," or, "I only need to get some general ideas about you" (or whatever else is true and comfortable for you). "I hope you'll forgive me and understand if I can't ask everything of each one of you." This takes care of those you'll find less interesting or worrisome, and won't spend as much time with.

Prepare Them for Intrusive, Personal Questions

Tell potential jurors that some of the material in this trial is of a delicate, personal, controversial or rather gruesome nature and it's important that you and they talk about these matters in voir dire, although normally that's not your common conversation, either. Tell them you're aware of their sensibilities and will be as sensitive and discreet as you can be and that although you're a lawyer and supposedly used to these things, it's a little uncomfortable for you, too. Based on the jurors' need for privacy and how they feel about intrusive questions, this can allay some negative responses to your prying later. It also shows your sensitivity and your understanding of their needs.

Explain How You Will Dismiss Some of Them and Why

Prepare them in advance with face-saving devices for the fact that some will be excused. It helps the veniremen and women you reject to exit more gracefully. It also brings out into the open what your purpose is—to *select* a jury and not to automatically accept everyone. Tell them you know they would all like to serve, that they'd all like a chance to practice their privilege and responsibility as citizens in this unique way. However, one of the best advantages of the jury system is to pick the most balanced jury you can and, therefore, you and the other lawyer will need to excuse some of them to accomplish this.

Where You Question Them

It's imporant to think about where and how you will sit or stand as you question. The spatial relationship you set up between yourself and the potential jurors can color how they will feel about answering your questions. Based on social science research, there are four kinds of spaces or distances that make people comfortable, depending on the quality of the encounter:

- Intimate—0 to 1½ feet
- Personal—1½ to 4 feet
- Social—4 to 12 feet
- Public—12 feet or more

Of course this all depends on your personality and style. You need to discover your feelings about how close you instinctively like to be. Then, you need to analyze the situation to see what is seemly and what is called for.

Some basic truths:

- Standing, while the venire sits, sets up a power relationship, with you automatically in the role of special authority, distinctively different and superior.

- Standing behind the lectern is the most powerful, removed, authoritarian place you can be—especially if it's fairly far from the jury box.

- Sitting at a table has a softer look, but there's still a barrier between you and them. Yet it looks more relaxed and is easier to write at.

- Getting too close too soon is overwhelming. People have strong gut feelings about this, especially if they don't know what you're going to do. It's uncomfortable and intrudes on their space.

Studies show that the optimum distance for one-on-one interviews is 3 to 6 feet between the two people involved. "Public" distance is greater. For the kinds of personal contact and intimate disclosure you're looking for, you could use this as a gauge, moving in and out, while recognizing at all times that closeness must suit your individual personality and your physical size as well as the circumstances and activity you're pursuing.

Suggestions:

• If you are required to use the lectern, step to the side and in front of it. Keep your notes on the lectern but walk around to the front and come back to look or write. This makes you look more intimate.

• Even if you can move around, you might like to leave your notes and chart on the lectern. It's easy to see and to write there. Feel free to go back, look and write before you move away again to talk.

• Relax your posture. Stand with more weight on one foot (looks easy, relaxed and vulnerable). Lean on the lectern with one arm. Put one hand in your pocket (if it feels right). These are all off-balance gestures that disarm a wary audience and make you look less formidable and aggressive.

• Don't take an aggressive stance. Standing with your weight evenly balanced, legs apart, arms crossed over your chest or behind your back are all signals of authority and challenge. They will get the jury uptight and resistant before you begin.

• If you can move about freely in your jurisdiction, find a comfortable distance from the jury. Your instincts will tell you what's right—listen to them. Look at the makeup of the group—who's in it? How do you feel towards them? Most of all, how big and physically powerful or threatening are you? How close should you be?

• If you're an informal, easygoing type, you can allow yourself to get closer.

• Women and older men can get closer.

• Tall men should stay much further back. Men do not like looking up to another man (too challenging). Older men can resent a young, very tall, physical looking man and younger men can feel competitive.

• If you're more formal by nature, stay back a little. Getting closer than you normally would in real life situations will make you tense and you'll look uncomfortable.

• Find ways to get closer and change your position when you change the subject or are about to get into some delicate or controversial issues. Make a visual and physical separation between categories of questions to give the jury panel a chance to change gears.

• Sitting at a table looks more relaxed and makes writing easier. You're down at their level, too, which is good. But it gives you a much narrower range of movement and less ability to change gears from subject to subject or to warm things up. It also creates a physical barrier between you and the jurors. Use the table to go back to but allow yourself to stand and walk around as well. Stand when they come in, as a form of greeting and respect; they'll like that. Don't get stuck behind the table (it's paralyzing and uninteresting) unless of course that's your jurisdiction's requirement.

• If you must sit, you should lean forward, keep your voice and energy up and *never* lose eye contact. That's one of the biggest things you've got going for you—it's evidence of your interest and a warm, friendly voice and manner.

• You might consider sitting down on a chair near them (as I've seen some lawyers do) to lower the height/power differential and look friendlier, more informal and less threatening.

• Don't come up and lean on the bar. It's much too soon in your "getting-acquainted" process for such intimacy.

The most important thing to remember is that the jury responds to the messages you give off non-verbally, and these messages can markedly color the opinion the jurors are forming of you.

Humanize Your Client

Defendants, especially criminal defendants, need to be presented to the jury early with human regard and respect. The jury judges from the beginning.

Standing near your client shows the panel that you, an upstanding citizen who has worked with and knows this defendant, are not afraid. Touching his or her shoulder as you introduce him or her is another sign of warmth. Some lawyers even suggest letting the defendant say. "I accept this juror." It makes a subliminal connection between the juror and the defendant.

In a civil action, find a way to characterize your client; if the client is a big corporation, it's "the people at XYZ Company." Explain why no one is there from the company to represent them except you. Or, if someone is there, explain that person by his or her title in simple job-like terms. Show your relationship and respect. The future jury will remember this and be affected by it.

Questioning Techniques

The goal is to get the potential jurors to answer openly with as little
evasiveness, suspicion or hostility as possible. Good questioning
techniques, therefore, must take into account how they already
feel about the questioning process and about your ultimate goal.
You must be aware of what else they'll notice and respond to and
how you can disarm their defensiveness.

Start with Their Names

Everyone has strong feelings about his or her name and
getting it pronounced correctly. If you have a difficult name you
know exactly what a pain it is to constantly correct people. You anticipate it and probably have developed some clever ways to get
people to remember how to say it. Tap into this common experience with your veniremen and women.

Ask them how to say their names. Repeat them. Make a small
comment: "That's an interesting spelling. Where does it come from
originally?" Or, "Sounds like your grandparents came from
Sweden, like mine." Or, "I'll bet you've had people mispronounce
that before." Let them answer you. That small exchange not only
warms them up, it gives them power and recognition from you in
their first moments. It will also help you remember them. It'll give
you an excuse when and if you mess it up again (use humor and
self-blame: "There I go again," or, "I was never very good at lan-
guages. Please help me with it."). Most of all, you're saying, "I see
you. I'm interested in you." By the way, if you go from "Ignatz
Papashvili" to "Joe Jones" don't just ignore Jones. You can use humor again: "No excuse to mess that one up, Mr. Jones," or, "Joe—
that's my son's name."

Ask Them What They Do or
How They Spend Their Time

Don't ask about their "job," since some people are unemployed or go to school, and some women will say "just a housewife"
and feel put down. This is the next logical get-acquainted question.
People want to establish themselves, to be grounded in your mind.
Their name and what they do in society are their most manifest in-

dividualizers. You can comment on their work or ask another question or two as follow-up just to get the picture clear and make them feel important. (What they're really telling you and how to use those clues will be explained in the next section on "Kinds of Questions.")

You can also use the question of their work to identify them with your client. For example: "In your job at the ABC Company, do you work in the home office or out in the field? In the field? Well, then you're a salesman, just like my client Bill here."

Get Everybody to Answer at First

Go right down the line. Everyone wants to participate and be heard. This is the time to give equal weight to each person. They all want recognition. At the beginning, do not stay with one person and use them as a guinea pig or a device for asking, "Does anyone else do that?" Say to everybody, "I'm going to ask all of you, one after the other." It's necessary for you to get everybody to feel that he or she is participating and that each one of them is equally important to you. It creates anxiety to watch one person get "grilled," knowing he or she will be next. It creates impatience—"When will he get to me?" It also gives jurors a great deal of time to formulate carefully screened answers as they try to analyze what your questions are for and how to answer them. If you wish to follow up, go back to a particular juror after everyone has answered and say, "I was interested in your answer. Would you tell me a little more about it?" Be sure that you do not intimidate a juror when you follow up. That juror may become wary and wonder why you've come back to him or her. Rather, phrase your questions so that he or she will know you're interested in clarifying, in getting a little more information. But at the beginning, give everyone something to do, a chance to participate and be heard.

Show Them What You Want to Hear

An excellent device for getting jurors to tell their basic dossier (name, address, job, family, etc.) used by Professor Seckinger is to demonstrate what you want by doing it yourself. He starts by saying "I'd like to get to know you. Will you give us a statement about yourself? Something like this: 'My name is Jim Seckinger. I'm forty-two years old. I'm a lawyer and a teacher here at Notre Dame Law School and have been working here in South Bend for ten years. I'm married and have four boys, aged 5 to 15, who all go to school here in town. My wife started working outside the home three years ago as an administrator. We live at 309 Elm, right across from the university. My hobbies are reading, jogging and doing things with our family.' "

Such a demonstration:

• Allows each juror to tell you his or her resume spontaneously without your repeated questioning—a much more benign and active beginning.

• Allows you to give the jurors a mini-introduction to you and some dimensions they might not get otherwise.

• Gives you an extra source of information as you notice what they deem important and choose to tell you, in what order and with what kinds of descriptive phrases.

• Starts individualizing the jurors in some key areas like hobbies, predilections and personal style.

Be sure your judge will allow this technique, however, before you sally forth, although a number of judges actually use it themselves when they conduct voir dire. The only problem may arise with describing yourself. If that's not permitted, create a character, but the use of the demonstration is invaluable in encouraging important information to be offered.

Don't Ask for Volunteers

The old classic Army line, "Never volunteer," is grounded in reality. People automatically think, "Why should I stick my neck out? Who knows what could happen?" Also, people by nature are more willing to blend in and follow the group than to stick out as different and individual. Volunteering information at the beginning is too dangerous a move for most people. It's too exposing, too frightening. Nobody really knows what you're asking or why and that makes them afraid to volunteer. They'll keep their hands down and you'll get no information at all. They also may feel that you're asking too much of them in the beginning. Not only are you asking them to answer your questions, but also to be more aggressive than people normally want to be in a group of strangers. In time they will feel safe enough to begin to volunteer but be sure you get to everyone in the first and second round. Then you can ask collective questions, "How many of you do . . . ?" They'll feel a little more at home that way. This technique can also be a way to find the leaders or more aggressive jurors, as you see who volunteers and speaks up.

Indicating which Juror Should Speak

• Don't point at them with your finger. It's too demanding and harsh, and is reminiscent of inquisitional tactics.

• Don't point with your pen. It looks lethal (with a point and ink), and seems too anonymous. It's also an object removed from you personally and symbolizes that you're "grading" them.

• Don't gesture with your clipboard. That's also impersonal and demeaning, a power symbol.

• Use your whole hand, palm up, to indicate which person should speak or which one you're talking to. This is an entreaty, an open, unhostile, unthreatening gesture.

• Use eye contact and a nod of the head or an inquisitive uptilting of the chin and/or eyebrows.

• Best of all—use the jurors' names as often as you can. This is the greatest recognition you can give of your personal interest and contact. Having made something of their names at the beginning of your questioning, try to develop the skill of remembering them, or look quickly down at your notes. If you use a name and mispronounce it, don't get serious or embarrassed when you're corrected. Rather, use some humor, "That's a great way to make friends," or, "I'm sorry—I'm sure you're tired of people mispronouncing your name," or whatever comes to mind. Lighten up and use it as a sharing moment to show your human fallibility.

• Don't say "Juror Number 4." It fulfills their sense of being just a cipher or a pawn to you. Never use first names! It's demeaning, disrespectful and patronizing. You haven't earned the right for such intimacy nor have they invited you.

Give Before You Get

Earlier in the chapter I discussed how people felt about being questioned. Internalize this now. Feel the anxiety those pointed fingers and accusing questions used to create in you. Be aware. You need to do something to soften that inquisitor's image when you have all the marbles, so that you don't seem as all-powerful and aggressive as the act causes you to be.

You need to give something back.

Since you now know that people worry about their answers and your perceptions of them, give them a safe environment in which to answer. Reassure them in advance as you ask something of them by making them feel part of the norm. Let them first see and hear you tell how you might answer. Show them how much you have in common. Be willing to invest yourself in your question before you get an answer or admission from a potential juror, to add a piece about yourself before you ask it of someone else. Example: "I know when I come home at night I'm so tired I find it hard to relax. What do *you* normally do?" Adding yourself in a common framework is reassuring and much less anxiety-producing than saying, "What television programs do you watch?" That question can make them worry too much about the consequences. They wonder, "What's the wrong answer? What does he really want to find out? Should I say PBS to show I'm smart?"

Preface your questions with a comparison to something that you do or that many people do, or something you've heard or read. They will not only be willing to talk on the subject, they'll amplify on what you're really looking for since they won't feel so guarded, exposed or alone when they answer. You're also letting out some personal information about yourself, which scores general human "Brownie points."

Be Sensitive and Show You
Share Their Feelings

When you get into more personal or delicate areas, warn them that that's what you're going to do. Let your voice reflect a change of focus and feeling. Tell them it may seem intrusive or too inquisitive or perhaps even rude. "This may sound like prying but . . . ." Tell them you know how they feel and that you'd probably feel uncomfortable, too. Then explain why it's necessary, what you're looking for, that you are trying to find out how they feel about the delicate or gruesome issues of the trial, or whatever the reason is. Don't just go from ordinary, factual talk to this area without making an obvious and sensitive transition. It's shocking and will make them think you have no feelings.

Show Them You Really Listen

Stay interested in their answers and maintain eye contact for the entire time they are answering you. Nod your head, lean in to show you're listening. Murmur a few comments—"really," or "that's interesting." One of the greatest pitfalls in asking a question is that you get busy thinking about your next question and seem inattentive to their answer. Forget your next question. You will have time to think of it after the answer is over and besides, their answer may take you in another direction. Write notes *after* they talk. Jurors give you permission to think. They know you're working. All the other potential jurors are watching to see how you listen and what you will do with these answers. They wonder, "Do you really want to know? Are you really paying attention? Am I being used? Are we just an anonymous group?"

Show Approval

Give them a feeling that you accept and understand their answers to encourage further conversation by saying, "Uh-huh" "Mm-hm" or some small positive comment, and/or nodding your head.

Remember to Smile

Look pleasant. Make a conscious effort to relax your features. People usually smile and look interested when they first meet and ask opening questions.

Listen Hard for Clues

How they say what they say, and what they leave out and don't say, is as important as their answer. Ask yourself, "What else

are they saying besides the words that they use?" Answering with
"I guess so" or "probably" shows a tentative or very careful, or par-
tial answer. Ask yourself, why? Notice clues and think of what they
mean, how they affect or alter what's being said. What inflections
do the jurors use? What kinds of adjectives? Where do they pause?
What do they emphasize and why? "Well, when I park my
Mercedes . . " "Of *course* I do!" "I have *five* lovely children."
What do they fumble with? When do they try to rephrase your
question? Notice what they avoid in your question. Also notice
who's very definite and absolute, answering "Certainly" or "I always do," who answers very quickly or stops to think. These additional unconscious statements should form a framework for you to
evaluate the answers. They are a vital source of additional authentic information about jurors and what they really think. They add
dimension and color for your consideration—over and above the
words.

Follow Up When You Notice
Hesitancy

Focus on what was not answered. Go in again for it. "But
could you be a little more specific?" "Could you give me an example?" "Do you mean thus and so?" Then, depending on the response, you will sense that either this is not in his or her experience or that it's a topic he or she wants to avoid. Don't press too
hard. Notice and go on. You can come back to that person if his or
her reason for avoiding the question seems to fall into an important
category you're concerned about.

Don't Pursue or Seem to Harass
One Juror

Remember the group has already spent time together and
done some bonding as a "family." A friend of mine was a venire
person and tells an interesting and cautionary tale about this.
Having waited for several days in very cramped quarters, the
panel members made friends. Joking and complaining about their
common plight and about the waiting, they developed some concern and loyalty for each other and eventually saw themselves as a

unit, or several units, defending themselves against the formidable system that treated them so cavalierly.

When they were finally called in and were being questioned, one of the lawyers had great concern about my friend, who is a very bright school teacher. He kept coming back to her, rather aggressively pressing her for more information about how she really felt about a specific issue in the case. After he grilled her for the third time, a fellow panel member attacked the lawyer, saying, "Hey, what do you want from her? She's telling you the truth. Why don't you lay off?"

As you read this you're probably thinking, "But that lawyer was a fool. I'd never do anything like that." Yet, your zeal in uncovering what you want to know and your natural bent towards intensive examination to get at "the facts" can make you seem like you're attacking one of their "family members." Be careful and be subtle.

Use Open-Ended Questions

Compare the answers you would get to the following questions:

"Did you read about the issues of the trial?"

"What do you remember reading about the issues of the trial?"

Yes or no answers are good for a census or poll taker. All you get from them is quantity and percentage. You're not learning anything you can use. Qualitative answers—feelings, reasons, other experiences—can only come when the question is open-ended, not closed, and when the answer must be a paragraph, not a word.

The classic open-ended questions always begin with a why, what, how, when, where or who. If your goal is to get past basic statistics to find out how this person thinks and feels, and therefore how he or she would think and feel about your case, you must elicit responses that reveal: "How do you feel about . . ?" "What do you think about . . ?" Even if you wish to smoke out who's been involved in a trial or an action against an insurance company, once you've got the hands raised, go for the story: "Tell me about it." Or "What happened?" This encourages people to let go and in doing so, lets you find the meaningful dimensions you want to know about.

When to Ask Everyone to Join in

When you've asked a good question and gotten a pretty full answer, you should ask the others what they think about that subject, too. Seeing someone answer openly makes the rest of the group feel confident and willing to answer, too. Just turn to the next person, or random people, and say, "How do you feel about that?" or "What do you think?"

Cutting Off a Garrulous Juror

"I'm so glad you feel comfortable telling me this. But I need to hear from your neighbor Mr. X, too." Or, "That's interesting. Let me come back to that a little later." Or, "I'm afraid I got caught up in your story—but time forces me to move on." Anything that gracefully stops someone shows your awareness of his or her feelings and saves face for both of you, since the implication of cutting someone off is that you're disinterested or he or she is irrelevant. It's important not to look judgmental when you cut someone off. Looking or sounding bored, impatient or irritated can cut off the general flow of information you're trying to establish from all the jurors.

If You Get Negative, Hostile, or Controversial Answers

Many lawyers fear negative answers because they think it will influence the jury in advance. If those thoughts are there, that juror can influence others throughout the trial and surely in the jury room. It's best to get it out early to know where your problems may lie.

In order to encourage honesty and self-revelation, be prepared for undesirable answers. The most important thing for you to do is to encourage disagreement with you in order to discover it. Therefore, you can't be punitive or judgmental. Show how big you are: "I'm glad you were so honest, Mrs. Jones. That's just what I was hoping for." Or, "I admire people with the courage of their convictions—who dare to speak out or disagree." Or, "I thank you for being so straight with me." These are signals that will encourage similar forthrightness from the other potential jurors. It also makes the dissenting answerer feel comfortable and remain a part of the group if you decide to keep him or her. Doing this gracefully can potentially get him or her on your side.

Make Your Questioning
Upredictable and Interesting

Don't be repetitive or boring. Don't use rigid formulae—good for all occasions and all venire men and women. Remember how long they've been waiting before they get into the courtroom. Their patience is at a low ebb and their interest span—which starts out, like most people's, classically short—is getting even shorter as the boredom and predictability set in. If you want real, alert and complete answers, put on an interesting show. Get people to participate. Make them look forward to the next question. After the first group of simple data—be conversational and involved. Get them involved. Make them think. Find new ways to phrase the same question. Ask new ones. You have to fight hard to keep their attention.

*   *   *

A final word: Techniques are important. I heard a noted judge in New Mexico tell members of the bar, "For every one voir dire that's too short because of time restrictions, ten are too long. We'd give voir dire back to the lawyers if they could prepare it and do it well."

CREATING A PERSONAL PORTRAIT
OF A JUROR

Voir dire is an extraordinarily fallible way for you to find out what you want to know. Instead of the in-depth one-on-one interview sessions with endless time to think, investigate and follow up that might provide some accuracy, you're going for a one-shot, stop-action resume, on the fly, hoping all your senses will gather enough information in that timed exposure for you to end up with a profile you can use and understand.

You then ask yourself to extrapolate from that short-form information, saying, "This is the kind of person who, in a situation relating to violence or embezzlement or cruelty, would feel like this." What you're actually doing is not so much looking for general information but clues, taking pieces from someone's personal profile and matching them against a stereotypical image:

> A person who has this many children, was married twice, has this kind of a physical, tough job, lived in this sort of a neighborhood, played a lot of football when he was a kid, and loves hunting, is probably the kind of person who wouldn't get too upset about a violent assault. He has experienced violence and might not think that beating somebody up would be as disastrous as would someone who served in the Peace Corps, lives in a solar home and is into jogging, health foods and raising animals.

But those profiles and assumptions are not enough. Have you found out how he or she *really* feels about violence? Have you looked at the clothing to see how narcissistic he is about his inviolate body? Have you looked at the body language as she talks about brutal physical contact to see how much more that is telling you? Did you find out if she was ever badly hurt and, if so, how?

How quickly do you feel you've gotten enough answers to decide on your potential jurors? What more could you do to make this process more efficient and informative? What kind of information do you really need? What subjects should you explore? What techniques can you use? The next sections are designed to answer these questions.

Non-Verbal Clues

From the first moment, one of our best sources of truth is tuning into non-verbal behavior. It can help you understand much more about who the jurors are, how they really feel, and what their personalities are like. These subconscious gestures and visual statements can tell you more than most of a juror's self-edited words. They help to round out the picture, to make a truer composite. See where the contrasts are—what people say versus what they're doing. The clues serve as signals to help stimulate your searching out more information and can also show you who is being receptive to you.

Obviously, the quest for non-verbal information requires great attention. Although you must train yourself to see clues on your own, I strongly urge you to bring someone with you if you can—an associate, a paralegal, a professional observer, even a sensitive friend whom you've trained in what to look for. Let them watch for clues and take notes for you. Create an efficient symbol system for note-taking that you both understand at a glance. Introduce your associate as a colleague when you introduce yourself. The panel will readily accept this person, if explained, rather than seeing a surreptitious "spy" whose function they don't understand.

Various kinds of clues should trigger your thinking about what personal trends they signify. Knowing the kinds of jurors you will need, that are capable of certain ways of thinking and understanding, these signals should alert you to possible difficulties a juror may have with your case. A sloppy-looking man sprawled on his chair, with a button open on his belly and day-old stubble on his face might not get too upset about a case with sloppy records and many human errors. An obviously uptight, correct-looking woman with hair exactly in place, color-coordinated clothes and ribbon bow-tie, sitting primly on the edge of her seat, might not have sympathy for a "crime of passion." Non-verbal clues also alert you to the level of forthrightness in the answers you're getting or can hope to get.

The most important thing to remember is that your "gut feelings" are a gold-mine of information, if you make yourself alert to non-verbal behavior. You have a great capacity for understanding it and extrapolating what it means if you look and notice. Here are some areas to be especially aware of and some possible meanings to think about.

Watch Them as They Wait

This is the place to see them move and interact. Notice this and think how you can extrapolate from that behavior how they would respond to your client and the issues in the case.

- Who is gregarious and who is a loner?
- Who chooses to make friends (likes people, trusting)?
- Who starts up a conversation (aggressive, more secure)?
- Who chooses aloneness and doesn't automatically give of him or herself? He or she isn't easily reached and may not like feeling empathy or understanding for people.
- Who chats around and likes to be liked? He or she may be a crowd pleaser who turns chameleon in order to be accepted. Or is this a natural leader with a politician's gift for getting people to like and follow him or her? He or she may be your foreman. How do other people respond to the person who seems to be the natural leader? Notice any competition?
- Who jokes and kids around?
- Who seems to relax and take life lightly? Note his or her behavior and find out more during questioning. He or she may be more forgiving and less judgmental.
- Who carries books versus newspapers? Who sits down and cutting others out, tries to read? He or she may be more interested in and have more patience with gathering information. Also, he or she may not respond so well to purely verbal communication.
- Who carries something to read yet reaches out to others to socialize?
- Who carries handiwork, needing to do something with his or her hands all the time? He or she is organized, efficient, needing to make every moment count, product-oriented and physically charged.
- Who's very disciplined and inner-directed, taking care of some chore while waiting, like doing paperwork?
- Who paces? A pacer is a hard person to make sit in a jury box for two or three weeks. Discover who has that kind of energy. An energetic person needs to be wooed and channeled into listening to you, but he or she also has a lot of energy and commitment to give.
- Who sits quietly? A person who can sit still is a person who may be thoughtful and analytical, who likes to think things through, an observer.
- Who goes running to the phone, preoccupied, with other things on his or her mind? He or she may not be delighted to be

part of your jury. Find out more about the nature of his or her work.

• Who smokes? How much? How itchy will a smoker get sitting through a long trial? Does the fact that he or she smokes tell you of his or her approach to life and death or health, addiction or reality? If there are many smokers, will you be aware of how far apart recesses are and how to time your most important examinations or final argument? Will you remember to ask for a recess for the smokers? That makes friends.

Notice Their Posture

Posture is formed in childhood. It represents how that person felt about him or herself. Posture is also copied from the family. Did he or she see themselves or their role models as winners or losers? Look at shoulders, chest and back.

• Round shoulders and caved-in chest—apologetic, unsure, defeated.

• Thrust-out chest, arched back—overcompensating, belligerent, feisty.

• Easy, relaxed back and squared shoulders—confident, comfortable.

• Shifting weight (standing)—insecure, doesn't feel that he or she belongs, looking for a stance or position that will please or feel comfortable.

• Shifting position (sitting)—highly charged, impatient, perhaps uncomfortable with his or her role in the court.

• Weight on one foot—more relaxed and confident.

• Two feet apart—military: "I'm ready for anything. I expect to be confronted."

Notice How They File in and Sit Down

• Who looks about anxiously to be sure he or she has the right seat? Such a person is insecure, needs to be correct and is willing to follow authority.

• Who checks out the room and looks around curiously? He or she is more comfortable with him or herself, wants and needs more information, likes to get oriented to each situation and think independently.

• Who sits tentatively on the edge of his or her seat (a follower) and who sits back and takes his or her space (more secure)?

• Who crosses legs and arms? He or she is closed and challenging: "You can't get in and I won't give out. I'll protect myself."

• Who fidgets and doesn't sit still? He or she doesn't have much patience for a long, technical trial.

• Who grips the arms of the chair? He or she is nervous and in need of support.

• Who clasps hands on his or her lap? The sign of a "goody," someone who likes to behave and depend on tradition and self-control.

• Who looks cocky and bored (resistant) or extremely attentive (wants to please)?

• Who leans way back or slumps ("I couldn't care less")? Check on his or her hostility.

• Who crosses legs, and how (man's macho foot-on-the-knee vs. softer knee-crossed over-knee)?

• Who kicks a leg or jiggles (not much patience, physically tense or physically expressive person)?

• Does anyone drum his or her fingers on the arm of the chair (quickly irritated)?

• Who primps and fusses with clothes or hair? He or she is fussy, a perfectionist, a narcissist and cares about orderliness and discipline.

Notice What They Carry in

• A book: This person doesn't like to waste time, is happy to spend time alone, can make independent decisions and learns visually.

• A tote bag or briefcase: What does it look like—expensive or ordinary? What seems to be in it?

• A newspaper or a magazine: (*Sports Illustrated, Times, Wall Street Journal, tabloid?*) This can tell about special interests, point of view and style of information people want and are exposed to.

• Umbrella when it's only cloudy: This person is highly organized, cautious, likes to be prepared for all events and is not so able to adapt to or allow for variable or flawed solutions or answers.

Notice Any Unusual Physical Characteristics

We all adapt to our own givens, but many aspects of our personal development can get bent as we do. Noticing what unique physical characteristics someone has had to deal with in their lives can trigger your thinking toward how he or she could have responded to this circumstance and what kind of residue it has left.

• Is anyone handicapped? He or she could be angry, fiercely independent, prejudiced about physical disability, supersensitive, strong willed, feel disenfranchised by society or wary of other people.

• Is anyone very overweight? He or she could be depressed, or feel out of control, defiant and used to masking or denying feelings.

• Is someone extremely unattractive? How will he or she feel toward your young, pretty client—jealous, punitive?

• Is someone very tall or very short? How has the world related to him or her and what patterns have been developed to deal with it? How does he like himself? How powerful does she feel? What did adolescence teach him or her about aggression, acceptance, self-consciousness and other people?

Notice Their Clothing

Noticing clothes is not only informative on its own, but it also alerts you to a line of questions you should enter.

Not only does choice of clothing tell about a person's inner predilections and sense of self, but at a jury selection, it also speaks of his or her attitude toward the court which is, after all, the establishment. People's clothing can tell you what status they feel they have or what class they think they belong in. It also speaks of where they'd like to fit in or even *if* they'd like to fit in. Observing clothing is a great way to collect information on who's casual or an indulger, who's a perfectionist, a narcissist, a conformist, a combatant or an individualist. Here are some manifestations:

• *Everything matches*—fussiness, attention to detail, a perfectionist who might be unforgiving if your client goofed up specifications or broke the law. These people try hard to live "by the book."

• *Running shoes, sports-oriented clothes*—could be a body and health lover, disciplined, inner-directed. Notice them. Ask if he or she runs and why. (If you run, too, you can say you recognize their shoes—they're like yours.) This conversation can uncover some of their characteristics as well as identify you as a health and exercise aficionado, too.

• *A showy, flashy, opulent display*—means "notice me." This ego needs attention and is self-involved. That person may not be much of a listener or an empathizer. He or she may also be intolerant or bored with ordinary, lower-class people or issues.

• *Very casual dress*—indicates someone who is not so fussy or formal. This person is not so concerned with proprieties and the correct way to behave, but is looser, more able to live and let live. But—notice and compare the age of the wearer to the clothes. What is this older heavy-set man saying with his jeans, sneakers and "Rolling Stones" T-shirt? Is he emulating youth? Unable to accept his age? Dealing with unfinished business about growing up?

• *Anti-social clothing* (punk hair, mini-skirt, black leather jacket)—indicates hostility to existing institutions. This obviously inappropriate clothing in the courtroom speaks of his or her feelings about trials and courts, as well as other establishment symbols. What else is going on? What heat fuels this person? How will this affect your case?

• *Women*—How do they feel about themselves as women? What statement are they making?

   • Who wears frilly feminine things? That speaks of the traditional views of women—dependent, soft, nurturing, pampered, non-violent.

   • Who wears classic suits? That's the new image of successful, independent women making it in a man's world. She is often more knowledgeable and worldly, more able to stand alone, more factually and practically oriented, with more work and systems-oriented experience.

• If the clothes are expensive, think of the self-interest of that economic bracket and how it affects your case.

• Modish clothes indicate a concern with current fashion and how one *must* be in order to fit in and be accepted. Think of that goal in the jury room.

• If the outfit is striking and flamboyant, she has a need to get ahead of everyone and be noticed, with an independent flair and some personal courage.

• Understated dress indicates a need for self-control and containment of feelings and is a reaction against individuality and public visibility.

Noticing clothes is informative on its own; it also alerts you to a line of questions you should enter.

Notice Women's Purses and how They Hold Them

Does she carry a shoulder bag? This is more efficient, leaves hands free and speaks of a more physical person. Is it large or dainty, soft and pouchy or hard-edged and boxy? What response do you have to these shapes and who do you think chooses which kind? Watching women handle their purses can tell you how they feel about money. Who puts her purse on the floor and who holds it in her lap? Does she let it swing in a relaxed fashion or clutch it under her arm (habits born of suspicion, nervousness, unsafe neighborhoods, feeling old and vunerable)? Can you imagine her assumptions about your rough-looking teenaged client or your embezzling accountant?

What Shoes are People Wearing?

New, old, resoled? Work shoes? Low heeled and comfortable or high heeled, dressup and sexy? Extrapolate what shoes can tell you about a person's life and status in society and how that will bear on his or her decision.

Colors

Colors show people's attitudes toward themselves, toward life and toward jury duty.

Pastels are soft and romantic; gray colors are subtle and understated; clear, primary colors are strong and positive; patterns talk of regularity, of small repetitions or free-form flamboyance.

Reds, yellows, oranges, greens show positive feelings, outgoing people, youthful, vigorous approaches to life.

Green shows growth and expansion, while blue indicates a cool, trustworthy, more cerebral personality. A blue suit on a man means that it is his best dress-up outfit and he takes the trial seriously.

Brown, black and muted colors indicate serious, somber, careful, more private approaches.

Beige and gray for a woman show a neutral, more self-contained personality. Such people are understated and sophisticated; they use a background color for themselves rather than a strong statement.

Pink, pale blue, green or lilac are dreamy and show a fantasy-oriented, softer approach to life.

Notice How They Listen to Other People's Answers

• Do they notice and pay attention—alert and curious about the whole procedure? If they do, they're good listeners and will probably pay attention to you and the trial.

• Do they keep their heads cocked and frown—thinking, listening, perhaps analyzing, as someone answers? They ruminate and judge carefully.

• Are they checking out the answers nervously, then looking away trying to formulate their own and get it right and play it safe?

• Are they being judgmental, rolling their eyes as someone fumbles or doesn't understand or expresses an opinion they disagree with? That opinionated, impatient person might be tough in the jury room.

• Are they nosy—looking to see who's talking? Group status matters to them.

• Do they smile with approval or look concerned—with empathy?

Notice all this to help discover which people fit your pre-arranged categories.

Notice How They Answer

Listen to their voices and speech patterns.

• Who speaks up, loud and clear, with some assurance?

• Who hesitates, looking for the exact word, showing some screening and critical self-evaluation? Who shows a need for excellence and for getting something just right before he or she can give it their approval or get yours? That person is a perfectionist, a sifter and an evaluator.

• Who has a full vocabulary and who seems uncomfortable expressing him or herself verbally? This matters when, in designing your opening statement and final argument, you need to choose the level of language you'll use.

• Who answers in short, cryptic monosyllables? Is he or she resistant and holding back or just very self-conscious?

• Who giggles or smiles nervously—betraying insecurity and a need to be accepted?

Watch Their Eyes

• Who makes and keeps eye contact when answering? That indicates a forthright answer.

• Who keeps watching you as you ask questions of others? That's a sign of concentration and an attentive listener.

• Looking off to an upper corner is a sign of thinking, searching the brain for a deeper truth. You'll get a genuine answer about feelings when you see that. It also shows if he or she is using the right (creative, subjective) or left (factual, didactic) side of the brain. (You look in the opposite corner from the side of the brain you're using.)

• Looking straight up indicates a more thought-out, cerebral answer that could be self-edited.

• Looking at you expectantly when they finish answering means they are checking out your response and how you liked it.

Notice Who Seems Responsive to You

Who nods his or her head when you ask the group if they understand? Who leans forward? Some lawyers try little ploys like saying, "Now everyone sit back and relax" when they first introduce themselves to see who automatically complies and therefore is more responsive and compatible with them. Trust your gut feelings on this one. Whom do you feel drawn to? Who gives you rapt attention and a kind of energy feedback as you talk? That's palpable. You can really feel it, if you look for it.

*   *   *

I cannot emphasize enough how totally revealing unconscious and unplanned non-verbal behavior is and therefore how vital it is as a primary source of information. Use these clues as a counterbalance on your measuring scale. Don't just hear what the jurors answer—watch to see *how* they answer. What else is going on? What character traits can you see and uncover without asking? What signals concern you, alert you to go on and find out more? Work out a method in advance with your assistant so that as you need to make your decisions, you can discuss and/or look at his or her notes, too, for input and confirmation.

KINDS OF QUESTIONS TO ASK

In all my work on voir dire one amazing fact stands out: Lawyers are sometimes naive.

In every voir dire examination I've seen, at least one lawyer will ask each juror individually (or all of them collectively, which is even more bizarre) to promise him they will be fair. And they always say yes. The lawyer walks away, satisfied that he has gotten their promise, that they've given him their word, that therefore, they will be fair. Not really *fair*, just fair to his or her client and his or her side of the case.

I have also seen another remarkable charade played out. A lawyer walks up to a potential juror, looks him or her in the eye and says, "Does the fact that my client is black have any effect on you?" What does the juror say? "No." Satisfied with that result and the juror's reassurance, the lawyer lays that subject to rest.

Every time I see it, I can't believe it!

Think about this for a minute. How many of you will volunteer, to a stranger, that you're prejudiced and unfair? Does it mean you're not? Or does it mean it's shameful, unfashionable and not reflective of your best Sunday school lessons or your college degrees? That's how people act and how we really are. We have an image of how we're supposed to behave and we try, especially in public or at work, to live up to our images of acceptable behavior. But that doesn't have much to do with our inner selves—what we really think and feel deep down and what affects our decision-making.

But that's not all.

You're in a court of law. There sits the berobed and elevated judge, the ultimate parent, looking down on you. There sit the flags and seal of the state—symbolizing justice and the law of the land. The law of this land says it's illegal to discriminate. And you're applying for a job as a juror. Do you, in your wildest dreams, think anyone will say, "Yes, I'm prejudiced. I hate blacks and they're taking over my neighborhood"? Can you imagine that anyone in this country, which prides itself on fair play, will say, "No, I can't be fair. And I'm not going to be in this case, either. I hate corporations and nothing you say will convince me that they have a heart." Can you imagine that? Is that reasonable? Is that human nature? Would you do it?

Let's face facts. We're all prejudiced. It's the shorthand of life, a system for making decisions fast. Prejudice is not just a negative feeling. We're prejudiced about small things (clothes, colors, tastes) and big things (whom we'd like to make love to or marry). Our prejudices cut down exhaustive shopping surveys and discussions. This form of automatic thinking, however, is also harmful and restrictive. It cuts down our options and the chance for clear, untrammeled judgments. It cuts down the windows of our minds and doesn't let new information in. But it's how most of us operate much of the time; we're either not conscious of many of our prejudices or ashamed of the ones we know we have. One thing is sure: we're not about to admit to the big ones, especially in public.

As far as extracting a promise is concerned, it's a bit like your promise as a teenager to your father that you'd never drive over 45 or smoke a cigarette. We all know how that promise fared. A juror's peers in the jury room (like your teenage friends) are going to influence him or her more than you, the lawyer, will, playing a temporary parent-figure with a very tenuous hold on the juror.

Consider this. Who are you to this stranger? What is the nature of your relationship with him or her? He or she wants to be picked and accepted by you and you want him or her to like you and vote for your side of the case. Don't you think you both know that? Promises to be kept are given to people who are part of our ongoing lives, who matter to us, who can see us keep them or not, whose trust and approval is an ongoing need of ours. Why should a juror promise you anything and feel beholden to keep it? You can't see him in the jury room; you can't get inside her mind, watching her filter the information and absorb the trial. What is that promise actually worth? The lip service it's given. That promise is predictable, but not binding. It's given to get the job; to be self-protective and not to expose oneself to the disapproval of other jurors or the judgment of the judge.

So much for what not to do. . .

What *can* you do to find out how these people really think and feel? What do you need to know to predict how they might respond to your client and your case? Given how people normally respond to being questioned, especially in the unique circumstances and purposes of voir dire, what kinds of questions can help you get some insights?

To be effective, questions must be indirect; they must draw a pithy, three-dimensional picture of a person, of his or her life and attitudes. They cannot be frontal or direct, dealing flatly and obviously with self-explanatory issues of the trial, and causing the juror to be guarded and secretive in his or her answers, as described earlier.

I suggest you look to an area I call "quality of life" questions. Focus on the places where people make choices in their lives. Just collecting data about the facts of their lives leaves too much to chance and misinterpretation. If you can discover and understand their *choices* and then consider what those choices mean, what they reflect about a person's general thinking and how they describe this person's approach and exposure to life, you're in the right area for making value judgments. Then, when you measure that information against the issues of the trial and the decisions that need to be made in the jury room, you can begin to predict who will think what, who will care about what, and how the jury will make choices and decide in your case.

The Basic Approach

Many things happen to us in our lives over which we have no control. People don't choose to be poor or unemployed. An uneducated person may be so because of environment, lack of opportunity or immature judgments, not real choice. But the places where people choose—where they select what they do, wear, eat, read, like and believe—these are the places for you to explore. Furthermore, these are areas of relative safety for the juror to expose to you. Not only is everyone an expert on his or her own likes and dislikes, but people don't feel too concerned about the consequences of telling you about them. Those subjects seem benign. The ultimate use you will make of this information is not visible. Answering doesn't feel strange or dangerous, yet the answers will give you the deeper, more meaningful information you need to draw your personal profiles of each potential juror. They will get you to the places you need to go—to the gut feelings people live by and to the protected private selves you seek to discover.

The major goal of asking such questions is to discover these key facts about jurors:

- How do they feel about themselves and about life?
- What do they believe in?

- With whom and with what do they identify?
- What do they know and how do they feel about our systems and our society?
- Where is their anger?
- Whom do they want to punish?

These are the hidden factors that influence decisions. This is why, no matter how clear and just your case sometimes seems, the jury can still decide against you. Of course, what happens in the trial influences them, but to choose your jury you need to find what they already bring to your case.

The following list of questions is representative, not exhaustive. It is designed to trigger your imagination as you adapt the questions to your case. They represent a point of view about how to gather personal information. They can give you a general picture of lifestyle, of cultural and educational background, of possible prejudices, of what people believe in, of how they think, learn or analyze and of how they feel about themselves and their lives.

Read the following categories, questions and insights in several ways:

- First, re-think critically what you *have* been asking in voir dire and why. Do your questions give you what you want? Can you make judgments from your questions?

- Second, use these questions verbatim when appropriate. Pick and choose which parts of which category you need to know about. Be selective and know why you picked them and what you're after. You needn't use all of everything. I'm just giving you many choices.

- Third, be stimulated by this new point of view to create your own insightful questions that deal specifically with the issues of your case.

This approach and many of these kinds of questions may be new to you and you may think judges would not allow them. As a matter of fact, I've spoken to many, many judges who say they are quite in order since they deal with uncovering prejudice. I'm sure

I don't have to teach you how to get something in if you want to. My concern is that you change your thinking from the closed question, yes-or-no frontal approach to this much freer, subtler and more effective way of getting the full, substantive, and useful answers you want and need.

Questions on the Basics of Life

These questions are rather straightforward. It is important, however, to know what else to listen for and discover as they are answered, as well as to realize what potential these seemingly simple questions have to give valuable data.

"What Do You Do?"

Where people are in their lives is a vital source of insight and information for you to evaluate. It is logical to ask people their name and what they do when getting acquainted, but there are many other things to listen for when people describe how they work or spend their time.

• Are they proud or embarrassed, apologetic or hesitant? Knowing how people feel about their work will tell you something about their self-esteem and sense of fulfillment. This affects how they will evaluate your client and the case.

• Listen for their tell-tale phrases: "I'm just a . . . ." "I guess you'd call me . . . ." "I've been the general manager of X Company for twenty years." "I'm a certified . . . ." "I own my own business." Such phrases tell you if they think they've made a mark in society, especially if they've reached what they considered *their* mark. A 55-year-old retired postal worker will not only not have much rapport with or understanding for your stockbroker-entrepreneur client indicted for fraud, he or she might want to punish your client for having the courage or temerity to reach for the moon instead of walking the usual route.

• Find out how they feel about their work. Ask if they like it, how they got into it, did they always want to be one—"Must be hard work, isn't it?" Ask people to describe their actual work to hear if they like how they spend their time.

• Think about how much money they earn and how independent or dependent they are.

• Listen for and think about their experiences with authority and decision-making in their work, how they're affected by it or how often they exercise these rights.

• Listen for anger and frustration.

• Listen for the scope and range of their understanding of the way the world works, especially as it relates to aspects of your case.

• Understand that certain kinds of work develop or attract certain personality types with certain predilections and develop not only certain types of expertise, but also affect and reflect one's basic approach to life.

• Precision workers (engineers, computer or lab technicians, accountants, bankers, craftsmen) need and like to understand precision and judge exactness, correctness, and following the rules.

• People who choose to take risks, who face danger or become accustomed to pain (medical workers, bank loan officers, physical laborers, military personnel, motorcycle riders) are not as sympathetic to personal injury suits.

• Weight lifters, runners, models, and athletes are accustomed to body awareness, even narcissism, and care about damage to the human body.

• Housewives and retired people are realistic about money, dealing with budgets, actual costs and struggling to manage. They would resent a "free ride" and wouldn't be so quick to give money away for nothing.

• Service people (salesmen, flight attendants, hotel personnel) are better judges of human nature and are more understanding than "thing-oriented" workers.

• Age and work experience also affect how people feel about life and death, and what they expect from the future.

The deeper meanings you can think about as you listen to a question being answered will start you on this new method of observation and learning by indirection.

"Do You Own Your Home?"

This can uncover anything from the deeply-vested political and emotional interests one can have in not changing the status quo to a person's racial attitudes.

• It can pinpoint economic status. Find out how long they've owned it. Have they made repairs and additions? A big investment and financial security are involved. These jurors care about property, taxes, quality of products and good workmanship. Chances are they've all had some tough expenses and disappointments from depending on someone else to make things work correctly, as promised.

• Homeowners' lives are more regulated and their responsibilities are keenly felt. They would tend to look less kindly on change—on a "rolling stone," a person who only takes from society's coffers or performs an irresponsible act. Their imagery is their town, their street, their children and a fairly predictable way of life. "Do not disturb" is their motto.

• Know your neighborhoods in advance. What is the quality of life there? Is it ethnic? Which groups? How religious? New immigrants? Old, entrenched families and systems? What are the prevailing problems? Crime? Decay? Inflated prices? New real estate developments? Knowing this, you have a base for further questioning.

• Attitudes toward racial or ethnic groups can be uncovered by asking, "Tell me about your neighborhood. Has it changed? Are people moving out? Why? Are you planning to sell? Why?" Listen for anger and resentment.

• Find out who the juror's neighbors are, how long they've been there. Are they friendly? Do they visit back and forth? This gives you insights into his or her sense of belonging or deprivation. Is there blame or desire to punish a representative of the new intruders?

• Homeowners could be selling because the kids are gone, the house is too expensive to keep up or he or she is retiring. Find out why. This is important. These people are in a state of flux. The several jobs in their lives are ending and with them go status, security, regularity, growth. The future might look bleak to these people. They may feel uprooted and cast aside. They might resent someone in the prime of life with plenty of financial security. Were they retired after long years with one company? Ask how they feel about that. Then think about their attitudes toward companies.

This should demonstrate that a simple question can lead you to uncover those attitudes you're really looking for, if you go past just taking the census and probe for feelings and implications.

"Tell Me about Your Children"

One of our greatest sources of pride and fulfillment, or frustration and feelings of failure, is how our chidren turn out. Using an open-ended, non-leading question, watch what they choose to tell you first about their grown-up children.

• Do they tell first of their children's jobs or careers? That they're married and have children? This tells us something about their sense of values. Notice what matters to them, what they think is impressive and important. Notice how they describe it. Others are listening and they're reaching for approval as they describe their kids.

• Do they sound angry? Disappointed? Apologetic? Proud? How do they describe their children's work? Proud of the daughter who's a computer analyst? Proud or embarrassed by the construction worker son? How receptive are they to modern live-in life styles? How have they adapted to the changes in our society? The new ideas of childlessness? The individuality? What do they say when you ask about grandchildren? This can demonstrate how flexible they would be with the givens in a case that involves, say, adultery or an entrepreneurial career-woman's decisions.

• Are there many children? Are there grandchildren? How does the fact of a life filled with people and daily problems and the knowledge, patience, caring and commitment one develops as a parent affect the issues of your case?

• Listen for their children's occupations for another reason. The parents learn a great deal about those fields, too. Could any of them be knowledgeable about something in your case because of that kind of exposure?

• Do they see their kids often? Are they lonely? Notice the women's answers. Empty nest syndrome? Superfluous in society? What do they do now? With warmth and shared understanding you can get people to tell you a great deal about themselves as they describe their children.

• Are they parents of little kids? Think of their goals and how hard it is to make it today. Find out their biggest worries or hardships in relation to being a parent today. It's easier to talk about that than about yourself directly. Extrapolate how those concerns might intrude on the trial.

Ask about Women's Lives

• Notice how a woman describes her husband's work. In the traditional model of the old marital sweepstakes, a woman threw her lot in with a man, guessing what kind of breadwinner he'd be. Some were lucky and their husbands made it, many didn't. Those women who live the more passive life of "only a housewife" could be bitter or frustrated by their economic hardships and envious of someone who flaunts or doesn't appreciate affluence or an easy life. Notice how a woman feels about her husband and her economic position as she describes her husband's work. Is she knowledgeable about what he does? Proud of it?

• Asking her about her work gives you an idea of her own feelings of worth and personal accomplishment, as well as her level of defensiveness. How does she describe herself: 'Well, I guess you'd call me a housewife." Or, "I don't work, I'm just a . . ." Or does she say "I'm a homemaker."? Or, "I stay home to bring up our children." Or, "I'm a "domestic engineer and proud of it!" See how she looks—hair, make-up, clothes, to see how she feels about herself as a woman and what kind of woman she imagines herself to be.

• What does she do daily? Drive the kids? She knows about cars and accidents. Volunteers at the hospital or teaches remedial reading in the ghetto? Think of the added information she has picked up. Jogs? Does aerobics? Note her body awareness and health consciousness.

• Ask her if she was ever known by any other name to discover widows or divorcees. This is a tremendous area for anger and feelings of disenfranchisement or, conversely, understanding. Follow up if you sense it. Ask how long ago. Does her new name mean she's married again? Things are therefore better now and some of the anger may be gone.

• Most of all, notice how she feels about her life. Listen hard. Her level of disappointment, her retrospective view of an arduous life whose validity is now questioned by the younger generation can be expressed in her moment of power when as a juror delivering her verdict, she can get even.

Quality of Life Questions

These are questions relating to taste and lifestyle that give great insight into people's general tastes, predilections, knowledge and experience.

"How Do You Get Your News?"

I think this is one of the most valuable areas of questioning. By the time most Americans reach adulthood, they have given up on their quest for new information and they are unlikely to go in for much original thinking. After high school and learning how to do their job, the only new information most people come across is learning new job skills or getting the news. The latter is most likely to be the only new information that comes into their homes automatically each day. This is meaningful to you because you will be presenting new information daily—hoping the jury will listen and understand. You need to know how they will respond and how they are conditioned to absorb information.

Therefore, how people get their news is a vital clue as to how they learn and how they assimilate data, and from what point of view. It is also a clue to the processes by which they learn best or most frequently. For example, if someone says he or she gets his or her news only from television, you have already learned a great deal about that person. This is an individual who is probably inclined to accept authority, not question and investigate too much, because basically what the usual television news gives him or her is a headline and some visuals to put that bit of news into context. There's not much depth in the nightly news but plenty of variety—it's one story after another, short and sweet.

The television news viewer is likely to want his or her news information pre-digested and spoonfed. Dan Rather tells him or her what's new, and he or she would prefer leave it at that. As a lawyer, you have to deal with this person's acquired system of learning. You are going to have to prod him or her into staying with the legal process—to sit through a thorough understanding of one idea, a statement and a deeper analysis and multiple corroborations of that statement, and be sure the juror is not checking his or her watch for commercial time and a recess from these complicated legal proceedings. It's not an easy task because television viewers have been programmed and quickly become bored with a lot of talk. And here you are, locked in oral combat, while they expect simplification and visual reinforcement. You could lose them to an early death of the attention-span.

Getting the news from a newspaper is a different matter. Regular newspaper readers are much more active participants in the absorption of the news. They have had to pay for the paper; television is free. Moreover, there is effort involved in their getting information. The newspaper reader has to go through the active process of picking up the paper; silently reading it, alone, and looking for the page where the story is continued. This can mean he or she is not only more interested in learning on his or her own, but may be more likely to want to follow up on an idea, to get all the facts. Newspaper readers are more individualistic and self-determining. They not only select the kind of paper, but also select which parts to read, as opposed to letting television hand them the blue-plate special of the day, with no choices or substitutions, please.

"Which Paper Do You Read?"

Find out what paper the juror reads. *The New York Times, The Washington Post,* the local tabloid—each tells you something about how he or she thinks, about possible prejudices, and what points of view are most often absorbed. *The Wall Street Journal* reader may be more understanding of the employer in a case about unsafe working conditions, while the reader of the *National Enquirer* might have a more tolerant view of a little cocaine possession ("They're all doing that these days").

Think about what your case is about and what you want the juror to know and care about. With what point of view? What paper gives what point of view and what additional information would he or she be likely to get?

It is useful to ask how one gets the paper. Does he or she go and buy it (on purpose and means to read it) or is it delivered to the door (automatically)?

"What Is the First Thing You Read in the Paper?"

The sports page, Dear Abby, the television listings, the ads, the obituaries? What does that tell you? What's his or her favorite columnist, if any? Answers to these questions will give you some insights into interests and attitudes. Be aware that there can be some sensitivity to a possible value judgment perceived here. To get at the truth share one of your secrets, something like, "When I pick up the paper, the first thing I turn to is Doonesbury (or the baseball scores or the horoscope). "What do you read first?" Such an approach is likely to make the juror feel more comfortable about confiding that he or she doesn't always start with the editorials either.

"What Magazines Do You Read?"

Magazines cost much more money than newspapers . They reflect total voluntary choice, not necessity. Magazines are a vertical, in-depth, very specialized form of reading that indicates a hobby or a passion.

Field & Stream, Fortune, Golf Digest, Health, Psychology Today, and *The National Geographic* all tell you something of past experiences, possible life styles and special interests, as well as the

kinds of exposure to and understanding of certain issues like shooting, competition, money, the body, how we think and the world
around us.

Time, Newsweek, Sports Illustrated, Playboy or *The New
Yorker* are all a quick way to get a profile of the kinds of tastes and
basic interests people have. Think about your own subscriptions or
those of friends. Don't those choices sum them up to quite a
degree?

You can even pursue the information further, asking questions like, "How long have you been reading it? Why, are you a
hunter?""Do you play golf, too? So do I. What's your usual score?"

A *Fortune* or *Forbes* follow-up question could be, "Are you
interested in investments or just general business trends? How
come?" You're much more likely to get information about who is
really knowledgeable and cares about government, taxes, business
and finance that way than by asking, "Does anybody have
investments?"

"What Books Have You Read Recently?" (Or, "What Was a Favorite Book?")

You can learn a great deal about anyone by examining his or
her bookshelf. In the courtroom, ask what's on the juror's
bookshelf to find out the kinds of interests and previous information people have been exposed to.

• Reading books means "alone" time—individual, not consensus thinking—and curiosity about ideas. It says, "I can listen and
decide." It says, "I question and judge, too." It says, "I take the
time to learn something."

• Find out if the books are paperback or hard cover. Hard cover
means money, but I think paperbacks are also bought by book
lovers—people who haven't got a great deal of money, but who really would like to read, and who perhaps often wait for books in
paperback. Someone with a book in his or her pocket, reading on
the run, is likely to be more attentive and analytical.

• What do they read? Gothic novels? Their life must need an escape valve. What's the subject? Romance? Spy thrillers? Sci-fi? Violence? Sex? How do these subjects tell you about their interests or hidden desires and how do they intersect with your case?

"What Organizations Do You Belong to?"

This, too, places people. Friends of the Earth, The Republican Club, the ASPCA, Juvenile Diabetes Foundation, A.C.L.U., League of Women Voters, American Legion, National Association of Retired Persons, National Rifle Association, and American Cancer Society not only indicate preferences, but can describe principles one lives by or problems in someone's life. These could also describe with whom the person would socialize and what view of the world he or she gets from that.

• Find out what role the juror plays in the organization. How active is he or she? Has he or she held office? If so, that person likes being in charge and has confidence; such people are leaders, not passive followers.

• Is anyone involved in fund raising? A missionary spirit—someone who dares to expose him or herself to personal rejection for an ideal. Going out to solicit money shows someone willing to be responsible—a realist, no illusions about how things get done and how hard it is, someone who knows how people are about giving or about money, someone with a practical bent. This is a doer, a worker, willing to be on the front lines. Proselytizers can be very persuasive in the jury room—be sure such a person is on your side.

• Find out why the juror belongs to a given club—"What draws you to that organization?" The country club, for example, means social conformity, with not many new ideas allowed. The P.T.A. shows interest in children and the well-being of the family. It could mean an understanding of bureaucracy. Special interests like the Historical Society, for instance, give a little perspective and a broader scope to life and to lasting values, but they may also mean rigidity about change and nostalgia for the good old days. Cancer Society or Retarded Children's Association membership could mean a major tragedy in the juror's life. How would this affect what he or she might want to act out in your case?

"What Are Your Favorite Sports?"

The answer to this question speaks eloquently in American society where sports are used both directly and vicariously to act out so many different aspects of our lives, especially for men.

From childhood, team sports are where boys learn about competition, team play, male bonding, leadership, "the thrill of victory, the agony of defeat." In effect, American business has become a game, a team sport. We continue to evaluate how we are allowed to behave based on this learned behavior. Fake a little, bend the rules if you can get away with it, placate the coach to get in the lineup, don't lose. (Of course, this is also true for girls who grew up playing team sports.)

Contact sports with their violence, team sports with their interdependence, being a spectator and only watching others express one's pent-up rage—all these considerations should be meaningful in your selection.

• It is important to find out what sports people like to watch, as opposed to those they like to play or do. That will tell you who is a passive observer, who gets his or her thrills vicariously and who is a doer willing to risk his or her body and safety. Such traits will play an important role in anyone's attitude toward a defendant who has taken a risk, is a plunger, an entrepreneur. A football player is more likely to be sympathetic toward a person who has been a success, faced bankruptcy and got up again. People who watch tend to be more cerebral and judgmental. They're not so willing or able to empathize or understand how fallible we are in the heat of battle.

• A boxing fan may delight in a good fight in the courtroom, while someone more caught up in the elegance and grace of figure skating might appreciate a dapper, aloof lawyer rather than a street fighter. If the defendant has been charged with a violent crime—assault and battery, perhaps—a hockey fan might be more sympathetic to someone who got pushed to his or her limit and struck back. (After all, what would a hockey game be without a good punch-up?)

• Compare the differences between team sports, contact sports and individual sports and what that means in terms of personality traits and preferences. These days, many men and women are runners or long-distance swimmers and these are revealing pastimes. Running, especially marathon running, takes considerable physical and mental discipline and inner direction. It calls for isolation, independence, self-reliance and a unique personal vision. The runner or swimmer as juror may be a stern and demanding sort, quite unsympathetic to a defendant who did not seem to have the discipline to say "no" to something that is basically wrong or the "starch" to stay with a difficult situation. If you are representing an alleged drug dealer, or even a gouging landlord, your ideal juror is not likely to be a purist marathon runner.

• Women's attitudes toward sports have changed radically in the past decade, so it will be important to question the women jurors about sports; don't limit your questions to the males. Ask what they like about the sports they play or watch. Women who actually like baseball or football and watch them on television or go to games because they are fans and not only to please their husbands or kids, could very well be the sort of people who are not afraid of being different, unpopular, or unconventional. They are not as afraid of physical contact and violence. That kind of information is important in selecting a jury.

• Find out about women who run. Look at their age level and see whether it's a typical 23-year-old concept, "You should be fit and healthy," or whether it's a woman of 47 or 55 who does something daring, who is self-actualizing, listening to her own drummer. She could be more inclined to understand individualism. She could be very tolerant of changing one's mind or the rules in mid-stream.

• Ask what women think about certain sports—boxing, wrestling, football, hockey. Listen to the tolerance they have for people who fight or become violent, since such women are telling you how they respond to that issue in real life, too. Notice if they feel irritated or disenfranchised by television sports taking over their weekends as they describe what their husbands watch. Ask yourself, how's their home life and, therefore, their attitude toward men?

• Find out which men were athletic stars in high school or college and which ones were really bad at sports. That issue leaves lifelong scars and a hunger for a time when belonging and being accepted were so important. Find out what the football hero is doing now. If it's all been downhill from early stardom watch out for a secret desire for vengeance in one form or another. Conversely, how will that "94-pound weakling" juror (who never made the teams) respond to your Muscle Beach hero who seriously injured a woman in a car accident?

"What Are Your Favorite Television Shows and/or Movies?"

This is an area of questioning that can reveal attitudes toward all sorts of things like crime, violence, politics, sex. Who's interested in cops and robbers shows? Anyone with Walter Mittyish fantasies about being Kojak, and "cleaning up the town" is the kind of juror the prosecutor is after, but surely not the defense.

• Everyone watches situation comedies, but some are more mindless than others, so find out the specific shows. Then think about what they deal with. The basic story line that interests someone can tell you what phases of life that person cares about or needs to laugh about. Also keep in mind that watching sitcoms and more serious programs like *60 Minutes* or *20/20* are not necessarily mutually exclusive; therefore, it's important to probe a bit deeper here and find out what it is about say, *60 Minutes*, that so enthralls him or her—the undercover investigative reports or Mike Wallace's tough style? Do you want a keenly analytical juror who enjoys probing? Maybe he or she feels one ought to watch the show because everyone claims it is so good and uplifting (a conformist, aiming to please). Does he or she like *Hill Street Blues* with its human, fallible situations or *The A Team* with its do-it-yourself macho justice? Extrapolate from this how that would affect your case.

• Asking who are their favorite stars can give you information about their attitudes toward sexuality, authority, power. Anyone who is a fan of J.R. Ewing, the *Dallas* millionaire con-artist, is bound to be more sympathetic to a client with a bit of larceny at heart. Fans of the dumb-but-sexy blonde bombshell may not work with your female scientist-expert.

• Ask women who their favorite stars are to hear their attitudes toward men, money, justice, and femininity. Then try these on the givens—your case and your client.

"What Do You Do on Vacation?"

Vacations represent fantasies. What's everybody's dream? What feels like relaxation to them? Vacations also tell what a person believes to be important.

• Choices reveal how people feel about parenting and being married. Are they trapped? Do they want to get away? Do they do things with their spouses and children? Men who take their wives and kids on backpacking vacations, who teach their children how to cope in the woods, are likely to be responsible types who feel they have certain obligations to others and like self-reliance. They are at peace with their family life and comfortable as nurturers and parents.

• Choices tell you about how they spend their money and why. What level of glamour do they look for? What level of euphoria? Do they go to Europe or the Caribbean or are they satisfied with a week at Disneyland? Do they go sailing for two weeks (one person against the elements) or do they prefer to leave the kids with the grandparents and head for Las Vegas for some serious blackjack? Gamblers want instant gratification, to circumvent the system, to do things the easy way. Think of how exposure to one form of society or another can affect the issues of the trial.

"What Do You Do on Weekends?"

Example: "I stay in the city, read and ride my bicycle fanatically—maybe 30–40 miles, rain or shine."

Q.   "Why do you stay in the city?"

A. "I don't know anyone with a country house and I'm saving for my vacation."

What do you hear? Health fiend, loner, disciplined—lives on a budget, understands working hard, saves money, delays gratification, is self-reliant, understands lower income lifestyles. But remember the reading! What kind? A thinker? Knowledgeable?

• On a weekly basis, what do people look forward to all week long? What does their weekend reflect about their lives? How many people feel so beset by responsibilities, by the fact that they're never going to get out from under them, that they spend their weekends working, fixing up, taking care of chores? Would such people feel resentful about being overburdened, about the lack of freedom? Would they therefore dislike somebody who didn't accept responsibility, who just went along with an irresponsible get-rich-quick scheme? Would they perhaps forgive someone who had the courage to try something and break the mold?

• Who's a model airplane builder or basement wood worker? These people are exacting perfectionists. They have patience and care about the correct way to do things, to handle details. They may not be sympathetic to a tax evader or a faulty product manufacturer.

• Who's escaping? How many people go off and play golf on the weekend? "I'm going to feed and take care of myself and it's going to take me six hours to do it and I want to hang around with the boys." Who watches ball games on television? Find out where they watch it. In the living room? That means they usurp the whole family's time and free space; maybe they're looking for the old hierarchical structure—"Everybody please Dad. I work hard, I earned it." How flexible would they be? How much room would they have to understand other life styles?

• Who goes to museums? These people feel connected to the seeming order and style of the past, and have respect for artifacts and property. If your case involves arson, burglary or property damage, think of their response. Because of their love of beautiful, handcrafted, one-of-a-kind works of art, their indignance at such waste and wanton disrespect would bode ill for your client.

• How do single people spend their free time? Are they lonely? Are their lives empty? Listen for clues of disappointment with life. These people have something to be angry or envious about.

• Look for the basic personality. Competitive and physical (racquet ball, touch football)? Health and ecology-oriented (cross country skiing, bird-watching)? Do they work on the house and yard (home loving)? Are they sedentary, wanting passive amusements like movies or television?

• It is very important to ask women what they do on the weekend, particularly women who work inside the home. Where is her fulfillment? What variety is there in her life? Do you her her say, "Oh well—on the weekends my husband and the boys all watch television and I don't know—I'm just busy cooking or shopping, catching up on the laundry." Or "We always have lots of company." (Ask her if she likes that.) If she is a married woman who works outside the home, does she ever get any respite from work? Is she feeling resentful? How would she feel about damages for a woman who hasn't been working? There are many other areas to explore, such as hobbies or taking courses, that can give you the dimensions mentioned above. Create your own to suit your case.

Questions about Attitudes

These next questions are designed to smoke out people's attitudes toward some of the basic issues found in most trials.

Authority

Try a multiple-choice test, listing various kinds of authority figures. Tailor these to suit the client or witnesses in your case who will need to be believed or whom you want a juror to be skeptical about. His or her answers are based on old prejudices and how this juror looks at life.

Example: "If I gave you this list, on a scale of one (lowest) to ten (highest) whom would you believe the most or least?" (Develop your list to suit your case and your witnesses.)

Minister	Television
Government official	Doctor
Policeman	Newspaper
Business executive	Scientist
Professor	

Let me show you what this does.

Aside from being a game and fun, it's a change of pace from the question and answer rhythm, it isn't blatantly obvious and it's disarming, since they don't understand quite what you're after.

When you get a "nine" for newspapers, television and the policeman, and your case has been all over the media and the police officer is a key witness against you, you're in trouble. But, if you got a "one" for TV, a "two" for newspapers and a "four" for the policeman and government officials, you're hearing a skeptic who's more sophisticated and wants to make up his or her own mind.

I suggest using a scale of one to ten since you see more shading than one to five.

Power

How do the jurors feel about power? Do they lead lives of domination or subordination? Do they feel powerless in their lives? Do they resent power or are they intimidated by it? If your client is a giant corporation or the owner of a big chain or factory this matters.

Ask the juror to describe his or her job:

• To whom do you report?
• Who reports to you?
• Describe your boss.
• Would you rather be in business for yourself or work for someone else?
• Why?
• What's good about working for yourself?
• What's good about working for someone else?

Some people are basically more passive and dependent. They're glad that someone else is in charge, taking the risks. They're all for that kind of order and are willing to step back and let others lead or be strong. They're believers and willing followers. However, a frustrated leader or resentful assistant can have a secret vote against your powerful client all stored up as the answer to his or her own sense of impotence.

Law and Order

This is a crucial issue in many trials.

Ask the jurors to give you word associations that come to mind about these words. You can also simply ask how they feel about:

Discipline	Jails
Law and order	Death penalty
Police protection	Sheriff
Law enforcement	Juvenile delinquents
Police brutality	Posse
Crime in the streets	Guns

These buzz words can give you a three-dimensional tapestry of what's at work inside when the jurors consider these issues or need to make decisions about them.

Racial Attitudes

Indirection and subtlety are the keys. Together with the questions I mentioned earlier about owning a house and how changing neighborhoods can smoke out prejudice, you want to know if they have encountered or worked with other races or ethnic minorities as a matter of course in their lives. Do they feel natural and comfortable with them?

If you can gather some information about how much exposure to people of another race or ethnic origin a venire man or woman had and the quality of that experience, then you get some feeling for the knowledge and understanding of other races and how he or she probably feels about them.

For example, in your own community you know your neighborhoods pretty well and you know which ones have been changing. Find out where people grew up and where they went to school. If those are swing neighborhoods, ask when or if they left. Ask them why.

Did they grow up in an urban, suburban, or rural environment?

• *In rural areas*, the opportunity to naturally grow up with people with great differences would be very rare. You might find less information but perhaps not less tolerance about different kinds of people since they're not seen as a threat. But rural people may have less ability to imagine other kinds of lives or allow for different cultural backgrounds. They may not necessarily see minorities as adversaries or the enemy, but surely as strange.

• *In urban areas*, of course, there's been a great deal of elbow rubbing, not all of it benign. Sometimes you find the deepest prejudices in urban environments, where people feel threatened by other groups that live too close to them or who feel that their security and economic balance are threatened.

• *Suburban areas* are notoriously segregated and the lack of opportunity to meet different people outside of one's own homogeneous society makes it difficult to relate to other groups. However, suburbanites go to and work in cities so their view can be almost more prejudiced. They compare their clean, quiet streets with the messes in the city and become very judgmental as they compare and blame, while they run for home and safety.

• The suburbs are also fairly homogeneous communities where conformity and the blatant norm are clear, obvious, and basically required and desired. However, many suburban school systems have a program that buses ghetto children out of the city to suburban schools. Ask about this and find out what they think of it, and if they were ever involved.

• What about extra-curricular or sports activities while they were growning up? Did they go to community centers, belong to church clubs, YMHAs? Who else went there? What did they play? Did they play against other schools? If you followed high school or college sports in your town, name some of the great black or Hispanic athletes. Did they know them? Ever play with or against them?

• Do they now have new immigrants entering their workforce? Racial or ethnic minorities? How do they feel about that? Ask about their unions. Some are known for discriminating against minorities. Find out if their daily work life has exposed them to different groups naturally.

• Ask how they feel and what they think about inter-racial dating, busing, school integration, or equal employment opportunities.

• Knowing that you mustn't ask people if they can be fair or are prejudiced, you might try this: Tell them that we're all prejudiced about many things, for a number of reasons, and that's just a fact. Then ask, "Would you want a person with *your* frame of mind on this or that subject to sit on a jury that would judge you?"

Attitudes toward Women

Trying to find out attitudes toward women and where one thinks women should fit in society would tell you about a venireman's tolerance for your female client or any of your female witnesses.

It could tell you how much credibility they would have or how much resentment or threat they would generate. It can also tell you their level of tolerance for changing social norms of any kind.

• Ask, "What does your wife do?" The answers are symbolic and telling. "Nothing; she's at home," which says "as opposed to the hard-working man." "She's just a housewife," which means her work or her ideas don't count for much, in his opinion. He may have heard a number of complaints about housework but he probably doesn't think it's a very big deal—it's not "real" work. That can also tell you something about his feelings and his understanding of where women fit in society or what other capabilities they might possibly have. How difficult it would be then for him to jump to believing your hot-shot, ambitious, young career woman client who's been married and is also making it in the big world.

• Suppose he answers, "She works." Ask what she works at. Hear how he describes her job. Does he describe it with some pride? Does it sound like a real job or just a nine-to-five thing that brings in some money? Does he dismiss it? Does he speak of it perhaps with some embarrassment? Many men still have left-over feelings of "I'm supposed to be earning the money. This shows that I'm probably not earning enough and she's helping out. Now you all know."

• When you hear him talk with some pride about her job, ask if he would call it a career, a job or a profession. Listen for the qualitative nouns that tell something about his attitude toward her work, his pride in it and how seriously he takes it.

• The next question to ask in this regard is who takes care of the home. Then you begin to hear about the social structure in the home. "Oh, my wife does that." Or "She has a cleaning woman." Or "The maid." Or perhaps, "We both do it. We share the work, and the kids pitch in." Now you're hearing a variety of liberal or conservative attitudes toward social change. You can use this information to connect to what is going on in your case and whom they're going to be hearing. Think about how much flexibility and respect they have for other kinds of lifestyles or other ways to relate to society. This is a good source of information about what their politics might be, as well.

• Ask if he works or has ever worked with women. What did they do? How well did they do it? How did he feel about working with them?

• Ask every juror, or those you're most suspicious of, how they feel about the E.R.A. or the women's movement, or about women as firefighters or airline pilots. If your case revolves around a determinist woman who dares to be visible or who wishes to sue or fight the system or the establishment in some way, you need to smoke out commitment to the old system and negative feelings toward women's new roles.

Money

• Who controls the money in your family?
• Do you read the financial pages? Regularly?
• How often do you go out for dinner?

- How do you feel about tipping? Do you sometimes worry about the right amount?
- Do you live by a budget? Who designs it? Can you really stay inside of it?
- Do you tip the paper boy? About how much?
- What do you think of the new style of dating, where women pay for themselves?
- How do you feel about welfare?
- Do you gamble? What do you consider a big bet?

These will all give clues to their ability to part with a buck and the kinds of amounts they think in.

Political Attitudes

- What worries you most about the U.S. today?
- Do you think we have enough or too much government regulation?
- How do you feel about welfare? Taxes?
- Which of our previous presidents do you admire?
- What do you think could help us now?

Sympathy/Empathy

- Who raises pets or owns them? Ask to hear about them. Why do they keep them in the city?
- Were they brought up with animals?
- What is their opinion of the ASPCA? The movements to preserve wildlife?
- Does anyone run a day care center or do child care at home?
- Does anyone know how to do C.P.R. (cardio-pulmonary resuscitation) or the Heimlich maneuver for choking? (Think of that sense of personal commitment to help.)
- Does anyone give blood? (These last two questions also orient you to who is not too afraid of physical problems and is more straightforward about blood and gory details.)

One More Idea

It's very valuable to stay updated about community events, about local issues and about various factions active in political questions in the community. Asking how they feel about the bond being floated for building the new park, or plans for revamping the traffic pattern, or taking a playground by eminent domain to build a shopping center, can teach you a great deal about potential jurors' personal prejudices, preferences, and concerns.

If you come from another community to try a case, be aware of what's happening in the locale of the trial. Not only can you use that to discover personal leanings, but it has another great benefit. It makes everybody in the community see you as being more caring and more connected to the community than just a hired gun from Chicago. We all like to see people make an effort to learn something about our town.

* * *

To conclude: The one underlying theme that can make you grow and develop an effective voir dire is to go back to the beginning, before you were a lawyer and remember how that person would have viewed this process.

You still know how it feels to be nervous, disenfranchised, embarrassed, and critically examined—which is what's happening to your panel members. So say to yourself—how would I like someone to talk to and question me?

You need to have empathy for their position. Be respectful of the fact that they are going to give something to a process all of you spend your lives doing—a process you could hardly do without them. They too have ownership in the courtroom, yet it's not often seen or felt.

Be sensitive and subtle. Dip into your own humanity and find all the ways you have to charm people, to get them to talk, to give them what they need. Extend yourself and *listen,* because they have as many complex dimensions as you.

3

OPENING STATEMENT

Remember the first time you went into a doctor's office knowing you were in for a new procedure? Picture yourself there. The palms of your hands got damp and you felt that knot in your stomach grow and rise to your throat as you imagined what would happen, how it would feel, how long it would last. There you were, a competent lawyer, suddenly feeling incompetent and fearful because this activity and environment were not your milieu. You had no information. You felt displaced and strangely incompetent as you discovered yourself dependent on others, with no control. You worried about how you'd handle it or if you could do it as well as you'd like to. Suddenly, your knowledge of the law, your forensic skills and that familiar advocate's stance were useless.

But then—remember how that fear eased when the doctor arrived and you could ask questions? You needed him to explain and reassure you, to guide you through each step of the upcoming process so that you could imagine it, so that you could feel yourself on safer, more predictable territory, able to marshal your own forces and feel more prepared to handle each step when it came. Now let's do a little comparison.

A juror's fears and concerns as he or she starts his or her job in the courtroom are very similar to yours in the doctor's office, and are based on the same set of human principles.

For most jurors it's the first time they're going through this process. Someone outside their own lives has asked them to make a momentous and consequential decision: a binding judgment that will affect someone else's life, a judgment of who's right and wrong and how to mete out punishment. Picture their anxiety. Housed in an unfamiliar setting, they are being asked to perform, to deal with and to handle a major procedure for the first time without knowing what's to come or if they can do it as well as they'd like to. What could help them relax and get to work, to quell those anxious inner voices and focus on you and the trial?

Enter—the opening statement.

To ease the juror's fears and confusion, you, for whom the trial is a familiar experience, become their orientation. Like your doctor, you are their expert. You can take your information and share it with the jurors, to predict and describe, to explain and re-assure. But there the analogy ends. For, unlike you in the doctor's office, they can only be totally passive listeners. They can't ask you to focus your explanation to suit each of them and their individual concerns. They cannot share with you how they feel or ask you to relate to them. They can only *hope* you'll cover everything, that you will be sensitive and understanding enough to give them the information, the support and the confidence they need to go on.

Therefore, the opening statement is crucial to jurors as an in-troduction to the "procedure" they're about to undergo: to help them focus on their job rather than on their anxieties or lack of un-derstanding. But opening statement is even more crucial to you. What the jurors hear at the beginning can:

• help them follow the whole trial from *your* point of view;

• make them hear and absorb the evidence *you* want them to remember;

• make them adopt *your* attitudes toward your client, the is-sues, what's fair and what probably happened;

• make you, most importantly, emerge in the role of helpful, thoughtful "doctor" who notices and gives them what they need.

But here's the rub: All of these benefits come your way through some very curious processes. While you're bent on simply telling and explaining the facts in the case, the jury is using other measurements, looking at several others facets and judging you and your case through filters other than just your considered legal opinions. What else is going on during opening statement, what the jury's looking for, how you can fulfill those needs and what new information and techniques you can use in your presentation are the subjects of this chapter.

WHAT THE JURY NEEDS

Before you can design your opening statement, you need a deeper look at your audience to insure that your message is truly made for them and that they will accept and use it.

Remembering that the prime motivation for listening is self-interest, let's analyze what the jury needs and is looking for and what else they're doing during opening statement.

What Else Is Going On

Let me start with a story.

In each of the seminars I teach, I ask one of the lawyers to do a demonstration of a two to three minute mini-opening statement, using all the other lawyers in the seminar as the jury. When he or she is through, having just explained a totally unfamiliar case, the first thing I do is to turn to this " jury" and ask them to tell me:

- What kind of car do you think this lawyer drives?
- What color is it?
- Does she drink wine or beer?
- Does he live in a house, on a farm or in an apartment?
- How is it furnished—formal? Modern? Early American antiques?
- What colors do you think he used?
- Is she married?
- Does he have children?
- Does she ever wear jeans?
- What vacations does he take—backpacking or Club Med?
- What kinds of movies, television shows, magazines does he or she like?

Now here's the most surprising part.

No matter what the question, the audience answers vehemently, with absolute and definite opinions.

"Oh, definitely beer!"

"Wine! And really fine wine, too."

"Oh no! He'd never work in a yard."

"Sure, she lives in a high rise. Drives a red Porsche."

"Club Med? (with a laugh) Never! Not the type."

"Nah. He drives an old VW bus. Blue. And it's messy in the back."

If you challenge them, the audience gets more definite and more convinced in their opinions. No one has "no opinion." Now stop and think about this a moment.

The opening statement given was only two or three minutes long. It was all about the facts of a case. When did the "jury" do this? When did they have time to think up all of these answers, to make these judgments and to feel it all so keenly that they'll argue about their opinions and can't be swayed? Where did they get this information? Why? Weren't they listening? After all, the lawyer was only making an opening statement; he was busy telling them information about a case. Or was he?

The hidden truth that this exercise points out is what else is going on, what else the jury is doing while they're listening for their introduction to the case. Here we come to a basic truth.

Why Juries Judge You

Like all jurors, that group of lawyers, that mock jury, had a sub-text; they were deciding about the person who was telling them the case at the same time that they listened to the story. Like all of us when we first meet a stranger, they were making an instant profile, using a series of convenient, accepted image-models.

It's a familiar and automatic process we all go through unconsciously, whenever we first meet anyone or judge anything—from picking clothes to picking a mate. The judgments are made by instinct—viscerally, not cerebrally. They're based on feelings, not facts. We use our internal library of past experiences, of early conditioning and more recent information, as a reference. We use short cuts—stereotypes and prejudices—to categorize and hasten the process. In each instance we run through "What do I need?" "How will this fit my needs?" "How do I feel about it?"

Example: picture yourself at a cocktail party, with a group of strangers. Based on your own agenda of why you're there, you select and "de-select" whom you'll spend time with.

Are you there hopefully to find a partner?

• Your ever-present filter system attracts you to what pleases you visually.

• You use your opening remarks together to measure voice, language, energy level, subject matter to see if he or she fits your "taste" (that gut instinct I'm telling you about).

• If your "target" measures up, you go on to evaluate intellect, interests and position as you continue to talk and test to see if that person fits enough of your requirements for you to stay.

How do you judge and how long does it take? In only a few minutes you go down an automatic unthinking checklist of what's acceptable and unacceptable to you and either stay for the second round or move on.

Suppose you're there for business or political reasons. Then your needs would make you seek out who's important or useful, not sexy. Your checklist would move the priorities around. "Title and position" would come long before "attractive," and you'd go about seeking those facts first. But you'd still be making your snap judgments about who appeals to you and what kind of people they are. That's just basic to us.

How can you do it so quickly and get so much information based on so little real knowledge? By using categories and stereotypes, primary-colored slots that you automatically fit people into based on very few signals. They work for you because you're only interested in the most general sorting at that time. You'll fill in more later, if there is a "later," but the initial automatic process at which we're all experienced has served its purpose. And it goes on at the same time we're carrying on a conversation and supposedly listening.

Therefore, what that mock jury of lawyers was doing was a natural process, true for us all. By extrapolating from what they saw, heard and unconsciously felt as the lawyer delivered his opening statement, they could answer my personal questions based on the slots they put that lawyer in and how they imagined that kind of "character" would behave in other situations.

Like all juries, they were using the inner agenda of why they were there and what they wanted from him to make intuitive decisions about the lawyer they had just met. The initial facts of the case being presented were vying for attention with the business of "type-casting" the lawyer.

The most important message here is that this judging process is the sub-text for all juries as you begin your trial. Being aware of it will help you design your opening statement to fulfill the jury's need, and guaranteed fact, of judging you.

What the Jurors Look For

In a sense, the opening statement is an introduction for jurors into a very intense personal relationship, which is what you will have over the next few days or weeks. It's a very dependent and needy relationship for them, which sets up cautions in their minds. There's much they need to know in order to trust you. "How much am I going to like him? What can I predict? Is he always going to be like that?

As I said, when meeting someone new, we all start with a few standard questions like, "What kind of person is this?" and "Do I like him?" However, since you're applying for the job of someone the jury has to listen to and learn from, the next thing the jury will want to know about is how you communicate. Therefore, the jury automatically begins to be aware of and judge your style. They'll notice if you're formal and stand-offish or if you're relaxed and easy to know. They'll notice what your metabolism and your energy levels are; whether you talk fast or slow, whether you're intense or low-key. They'll discover how you move, how you take your space in the courtroom, what your voice sounds like and what regional accent you have. In their effort to become comfortable with you, they'll begin designing a persona for you, to understand that this is the way you communicate, to predict that this is the way you'll behave and this is what they can expect of you, almost like families do. "Oh yes, that's Charlie, always hot under the collar and always talking fast." Or, "Aunt Margaret is always kind of laid back."

They'll decide if you're feeling secure or nervous, if you're prepared and solid or still changing your mind. They'll notice your body and your clothes and do the stereotyping I talked about, deciding about your lifestyle and family. In general, they'll start to get to know you from the outside in.

But the jury has an important job to do, so there's much more information about you that they need to gather. They have extra-sensitive antennae to pick up clues and discover who's asking them to follow him as they pursue their job. They have to judge who'll be able to fulfill their special needs. Here is what they're looking for during opening statement.

Who Is Telling Me

Remembering how the jury feels about the unfamiliarity of their role and their fear about their incompetence, they need something very special from you.

From the beginning the jurors need:

- a leader;
- a teacher;
- a helper;
- a guide.

They need someone who'll tell them what to pack for the trip, since he's been there already. Someone who'll say "Trust me. I'll tell you how deep the water is. I'll take you across to the other side and I'll never let go of your hand."

They also need:

- someone recognizable with whom they can identify;
- someone with similar goals, ethics, and standards who will help them judge according to their own version of right and wrong.
- someone who believes in them;

Therefore, the most important issues a jury must decide right at the beginning are:

- Who is the teller?
- Who's bringing the message?
- What does he or she know?
- Is it enough?
- In which of these two guides will I place more confidence?
- Who sounds like he thinks like I do? Whom can I believe in and trust?
- Who is telling me "This is wrong and this is right"?

How can they answer all these questions? By using their quick-impression "Geiger counter," they will listen and look hard for clues that show them if you are the better leader, teacher and guide. They become very aware, unconsciously, of all the choices you make in communicating with them: your choice of language, metaphor, analogy, reference points and assumptions as well as your clothes and your manner, to help them identify you.

The jury also looks for humanity and sincerity in a lawyer, since one of the major questions the jury has at the beginning is whether this lawyer is a "hired gun." It doesn't matter who you are or what case you're trying, they know that someone is paying you money, so they ask, internally, "Does he really care?" How deeply they will listen and trust and believe you is in direct proportion to their perception of your level of caring. Much of that comes through as they watch you work.

But, most of all, the jury looks to see how you feel about *them*. Do you respect them? Do you believe they can understand? They'll watch not only how well you explain but how you choose to explain to them. Are you patronizing, explaining things too simply because you think they're not intelligent or experienced enough? Are you really trying to make them understand? Do you show them you know how much they want to do their job well and bring in a fair verdict?

What Is the Case about?

Jurors need to be given the "coming attractions" in the opening statement. What is the trial about? What will they hear? What's about to take place? Jurors want to know all about the story, to become oriented to the plot.

- What's the argument about?
- Who are the players?
- What went wrong?
- What do I need to decide?
- What should I watch for?
- What should I remember?
- Will it be interesting?
- Can I understand it?

Since they are concerned and disoriented, the one thing they want to know most of all is what's going to happen. And they want it in broad strokes—a clear, simple outline.

What they don't want at this point is elaboration and detail. Just the plot, not the play. They don't yet know what facet will interest them, what they will want to understand much more deeply. They need to have an overview and then to wait for the plot to unfold, rather than listen to everything the lawyer already knows up front.

The opening statement is the only time the jurors have to sort out the facts and the players, to make a blueprint for themselves so they can follow the story. Remember, from then on, they get the story in disjointed pieces. First, the interruptive form of telling through questions and answers that is the direct examination. Then going back over the same ground in cross-examination before they can go in to hear more. Then another witness with another style shines the light on another part of the story. Then back over it with a cross before they hear still another point of view. And then they go over everything again from the defendant's point of view. The jury needs a unified, clear version of the story first, so they can begin to listen and understand its parts.

Why Should They Listen

There's another need the jury has as the trial begins. They need motivation to listen. As you start your opening statement, you're asking them to sit still and listen to you throughout a speech of uncertain length; to give you their total attention; to rise to the occasion and try to understand complex, unfamiliar material. Why should they?

When you stand up, you must tell them why. Remember, everyone's preconception is that speeches are boring. Remember, too, that it takes only 15 percent of the brain to understand your native language—leaving 85 percent free to not pay attention. Therefore, jurors need reasons to listen to what you're saying and to look forward to the story that will unfold. They need to know that you'll tell them in what context to hear the story, what the events mean and why those witnesses will be called. They need to know that they should listen because you'll clarify the story for them now, in a succinct way, and you're going to give them guidelines to help them follow the trial. Most of all, they need to know that you will help them understand their job and what they have to decide.

Telling the jury you're about to answer their needs and concerns; that you know the questions in their minds; that you will now explain what the conflict is about, what's at issue, and what the two sides of the story are; will make them tune in and listen carefully, since this is what they need and want most of all.

How Will the Trial Work

One other area the jury needs to know about is what a trial is like. Therefore, you need to explain the format of the trial itself and to orient them to some of the procedures they will see and how the trial will take place. They don't know that the plaintiff's whole case goes first; they don't know about a direct and cross and re-direct examination for each witness; they don't know that you'll be back to wrap it up in final argument; and they don't understand a number of unique procedures they'll see which can be misunderstood and might eventually hurt you. They do not understand objections and what they mean, or side bar conferences which they will hate since they look like secrets. They don't know about depositions or what evidence is or many other aspects of trial procedure you might want to explain, if the judge hasn't done so already. Most of all, since they're not at all clear about what they're supposed to decide, you need to show them how the techniques of the trial will help them do that.

*   *   *

To sum it up: From the jury's point of view, the opening statement is:

- an introduction to you;
- a road map to the content of the case: topic headlines, cast of characters, key issues, basic conflict the points of the law involved;
- your point of view in the case;
- priority information to listen for;
- "coming attractions"—a motivation to listen and stay interested.

The University of Chicago jury studies have found that 80-85 percent of jurors make up their minds about the verdict and the lawyer during or just after the opening statement and hardly ever change them during the entire trial. That's a sobering thought.

Therefore, how you tell your story and how you answer the jury's questions about who, what, why and how in your opening can be the major fulcrum on which much of your case can hinge in the jury's mind. Now that you understand what the jury needs, let's go on to discover what techniques will help you fulfill their expectations and give the most effective opening statement.

DESIGNING THE OPENING STATEMENT

As you prepare for trial, choosing what facts you will tell and what you want the jury to know seems quite apparent to you. Often, your knowledge of trial procedure and your familiarity with the facts of a case prevent you from stripping it all down to the basics that the jury needs in order to better understand and follow you. Since we now see that the opening statement must be planned to fulfill a number of requirements, let's look at how you can begin to organize your material, make choices and also include the needs of the jury.

Selecting the Material and Approach

As you sit down to design your opening statement you are awash in the sea of information you have collected about your case; details, witnesses, evidence, arguments and conflicts, points of view are all rolling around in your mind, looking to you for order and priority. It is very difficult to make categories and designate which are major headings, which are small explanatory lists and which are footnotes. Yet this process is crucial if you are to backtrack to the level of the jurors who know nothing about your case or even about trials themselves. The process of distilling the case down to the essence is of prime importance in developing your material for jury presentation. The best way to do this is to get your material out of your mind and onto paper.

Begin by asking yourself some questions to really highlight the issues in your case. Think through and then list the three or four most basic points. Keep reducing all the details in the trial down to the most essential central themes that cover what the trial is really all about. Making yourself do this, forcing yourself to edit and be critical, is a good way to focus and organize, to uncover the basics and to start making a succinct list to follow as the central core of your material. Then, in order to decide the approach to your material and the order in which it should be given, answer the following key questions:

What Are Your Goals?

List what you want the opening statement to accomplish. Remember, you must not only tell a story and give the jury your point of view, but also give them a structure in which to listen to the trial as well as introduce yourself to the jury as someone who will relate to them, who will be a welcome sight whenever he or she stands up during the trial.

What Results Do You Want to Achieve?

What do you hope the jury will walk away with? If you could test them and ask them questions at the end of the opening statement, what would you want them to be able to answer, and with what answers? List those questions. When you list them, it becomes possible for you to be sure that you have included every one of these ideas and their answers in your opening statement.

What Does the Jury Need?

Think through where they are in the trial, what they need next and how they are feeling. This will help you custom-design each segment of the trial for this unique jury in these particular circumstances. It will help you truly meet their needs. Platitudes and generalizations about trial procedure are only good as a foundation. You build a solid structure by being aware of the actual people in an immediate situation.

What Does the Jury Expect?

What do they expect from the beginning of a trial? What do they expect from you? What questions are in their minds? How helpful do they think you are going to be? Think through the ways in which you can surprise them, support them and cause them to be reinforced, reassured and better informed—all against the background of what you know they are thinking.

Think about the stereotypical images they may have about a trial and a lawyer. What can you do to lead them into new territory and new ideas? What first impressions can you change and how?

What Are Your Basic Problems in the Case?

What are the built-in difficulties you need to surmount? How will you handle the jury's possible preconditioned responses to the touching issues of your case? List what they are. This removes these issues from a sense of general unease to the clear light of day. If you see them spelled out, you can factor them into your planning and find a way to include handling them as part of your opening statement and every other part of the trial.

What Methods Should You Use?

Form follows function, as the architects say. Design your opening statement in response to the previous questions. What do you want to say? When you see your task clearly then you'll see what methods you need to do it.

Only after studying your answers to the previous five questions should you focus on what methods you'll use to achieve their solution. Is it choice of language you need to concentrate on? Making the material visual? Softening your approach to a basically unsympathetic cause? Backing up your claims with hard-nosed facts? How will you best accomplish the first impression you wish to leave with the jury?

For example: If you are a defense lawyer, and you've thought through what the jury assumes about you to begin with, perhaps your method, your approach might be to humanize you and your client. Your choices should lead them away from the stereotype of the three-piece, blue-suited, rich, grey-templed company lawyer to discover what else you are and how else they can see your client and the case.

If it's a criminal case, what will you do to establish your relationship with your client? What non-verbal messages can you send?

If you are the plaintiff's lawyer, will your approach be to depict yourself as an extension of your client? Just another good human being doing a noble job, as they would if someone asked for their help? How can you show that best? What system should you design for the extra concerns in your case?

All the above-listed categories of questions are the catalysts for how to make your choices. Now let's discover techniques for answering those questions and designing the opening statement.

Creating the Content

Making choices always creates anxiety. What's the best, most memorable or most interesting way to say it? What should the organization be? How do you add flavor, quality and drama? These are issues that always pose a dilemma. This section will suggest some approaches to handling your material, some persuasive, attention-getting techniques for developing and presenting your information and some key areas you should include in the content of your opening statement.

Tell a Story

Your case is the retelling of something that actually happened to real people. It has a beginning, a middle and an end. It always has a crisis, some problem, some drama; that's the reason it has become a trial. It has real and imaginable surroundings, often very familiar to a jury.

There is much in any trial that is instantly identifiable, images that can be brought to everyone's mind. Yet unfortunately, lawyers often lose sight of the fact that a case is a narrative, that stories have appealed to all peoples from the beginning of time. In wanting to get out the facts and a listing of the issues, you can forget that people don't like listening to dry data to which they don't relate and which reminds them of those abstract math problems at school.

A story has built-in charisma. Little children say, "Tell me a story." Someone who calls you on the phone saying, "Have I got a story to tell you," makes you eagerly lean forward and listen. You listen because you anticipate elements of pleasure or surprise, the ability to use your own fantasy and imagination to enter into it, and a chance to remove yourself from your own life and live someone else's for a little while.

Why are soap operas so incredibly successful in this country? It's because people feel, "There's enough in it that looks like my life. Yet other things happen that never happened to me. I'd love to extend myself into someone else's experiences for a while, with no risk." That's a basic, compelling drive that is always and forever interesting to any audience, that will make them listen.

Begin with a tease, a glimpse into where you're going and a little excitement about what's going to happen next. Use the story in your trial to begin your narrative. Instead of saying, "Ladies and gentlemen, this case deals with certain issues of compensation which the law provides...," begin with "The story begins on a Sunday morning;" or "Imagine looking out the window and watching the rain." Or "On a day just like this, snowing and blustery, Marion Snodgrass got in her car and was driving down Maple Street right here in town."

Use the kinds of openings that will instantly get people into the story. Include local references: "You know where Fourteenth crosses Broad Street, that place where everybody always goes to meet under the clock? Let me take you right to that spot, ladies and gentlemen, and we'll begin our story"; or, "What does it mean to a young family when the mother dies in an accident? What happens to the lives of her husband, her children, her parents?"

Can't you imagine how everyone would get involved because you have included them in something familiar rather than in something strange, abstract and cold, difficult or alien, which causes them to become concerned about "Will I understand this"? or, "Do I care?" They *will* relate to a story, however, because you've made it sound simple, so close, so—almost everyday.

Dramatize

The best way to help people remember a concept is dramatization—accent, color, emphasis, pulse-quickening. It not only moves an alien idea into a place where people can understand and will remember it, it also keeps the interest level high as you tell it. Then, as the jury hears it again in the testimony, they pay special attention.

For example, in describing the story of an accident, if you build suspense as the car inexorably approaches the victim, the jury will develop its own sense of anxiety and identification with the victim. They will anticipate and wait expectantly, horrified, for the moment that you say, "And then, at that moment, as if from nowhere, the car loomed up and hit her." They can recall that moment again and again as the trial progresses because they were there, with you. If it's done well, they will feel as you have made them feel towards both victim and driver. This is an excellent technique, but a word of caution here: The jury doesn't know you yet or even trust you very much, and they aren't ready for too much emotional appeal at the beginning. Too much drama feels maudlin and obvious, like an assault, when it's overdone.

Therefore, subtlety is the key. You have to be really careful to engage, to interest and to entice without robbing the juror of his work. Don't tell him, in advance, *how* to feel—just weave a dramatic thread that you can pluck again and again as the trial continues. Its lingering resonance can then be played as full chords in your final argument.

Humanize

Still another way to get the jury involved is to humanize the opening statement, to put the jury into the story. Remembering the "golden rule" that you can't tell them to put themselves into your client's shoes directly, you can still use phrases that help connect them to your client in common human experience: "You know how it is—when someone is driving along," or, "Can you imagine how Mr. Jones felt."

Take opportunities to move away from the theoretical to the human. Make your allusions simple and tangible. This will encourage them to feel more comfortable as you go through the unfamiliar material of the trial. But most of all, it humanizes and identifies you with them.

You can humanize by making references to a common place in town. This lets everybody know you also come from this town or know it well. Use colloquialisms or descriptions of general or local events, if they're comfortable for you. Making a reference to the local winning baseball team helps people see you in a multi-dimensional form, rather than as a cutout of a stuffy lawyer.

Using humanizing references within your description of the case in the opening statement does two things: It makes the jury relate and begin to care for your side, but it also makes them care for you. This is often very difficult if your client is the defendant and a giant corporation. The images conjured up in the jury's mind of an unthinking, unfeeling monolith with no morality or motivation except to make money and squash people has been alive and well since its eloquent start in the movies of the 1930s. References to corporate leadership and decision-makers can conjure up stereotypical images to people who've never met one. They see someone like Edward Arnold playing a cigar-smoking tycoon, waistcoat bulging, big gold watch chain hanging, ordering people around and living a life none of them can imagine.

One way of humanizing a corporation was demonstrated by a very talented attorney, Tom McNamara of Grand Rapids, Michigan, at an advanced seminar of the National Institute for Trial

Advocacy in Gainesville, Florida. He was acting as defense counsel
for a power company in a mythical case created for the program.
Here's an excerpt from the transcript:

> Ladies and gentlemen of the jury, good morning. My name is Tom
> McNamara. I'm a trial lawyer. I'm not from here. I'm from Grand
> Rapids, Michigan. I know Grand Rapids is kind of a small city—you
> can probably look at me and tell I don't live here. But I'll tell you a
> little secret. Any time I try a lawsuit in a new courthouse, the first
> thing I do . . . sneak into the courthouse when there's nobody
> there. And I sit in the chairs where the jury sits. And you know
> what I discovered about your chairs? I've probably tried lawsuits
> in—oh, 15, 20 different courthouses, and these are the hardest
> chairs I ever sat in. Because they're hard, I'm not going to try your
> patience, I'm just going to take a few minutes of your time, right at
> the beginning of this case, to tell you a little bit about what the case
> concerns. Let me tell you why I'm up here, taking your time while
> you sit in those hard chairs.
>
> Did you ever go into a book store, pick up a hard cover book, and it
> says $8.95 on the cover? Didn't know if you wanted to buy that book
> or not. Not real sure that was exactly what you had in mind. What'd
> you do? Flip that book over and you read on the back, didn't you?
> On the back of that book is something the publishers calls a blurb.
> Probably 200 words at maximum, and it tells you, in very short fash-
> ion, what that book's about. Now that's what I'm going to give you as
> to a lawsuit that's probably going to take two weeks to try—a blurb.
> I'm going to miss some of the facts, you know I am because I'm not
> going to talk to you very long. I'm going to say a few things that may
> not come out exactly that way in trial, because I don't know exactly
> what the witnesses are going to say in this case, but I promise you
> two things. One, I'll be done in six minutes, and two, I'll do my
> absolute best not to overstate the case. This case doesn't start in
> 1977 as far as my client's concerned. My client is N.I.T.A. Power
> Company, right out south of town, you see the plant. It's the only
> plant we got—four big smokestacks. Some of your friends probably
> work there.
>
> My defense in this case is real easy and I can give it to you in one
> sentence. N.I.T.A. Power Company isn't liable, because we didn't
> do anything wrong. But somebody is liable. And that somebody is
> Northern Electric Company, the folks from whom we bought that
> power plant. Let me tell you why I say that.
>
> This case actually starts way back in 1959. At that point, Northern
> Electric was building engines for nuclear submarines, power plants.
> And they were good at it. About 1960, they decided that they'd get

into the electric generating business. Why? Because the little power plant that went in the submarine was a lot like the great big power plant that could be used to generate electricity, light your lights, project my voice, and warm your houses,—the electricity that we sell.

They did something kind of funny back in 1960, this Northern Electric Company. They apparently had the strange view, as best I can tell, that if a little mousetrap is real good to catch a little mouse, then a great big mousetrap can probably catch an elephant because that's what they did. They took the exact design they had for that little nuclear reactor in the submarine and they blew it up 20 times. Didn't change the design. Didn't change the materials that were in it. Just built a great, big mousetrap to catch the elephant.

Now you don't have to spend too much time in engineering school to know that if you take a little copper wire on a mousetrap, and you blow it up that big around to catch an elephant, it might bend, might not work too well with the elephant. That's . . . (and so on)

The points to notice here are his introduction—humanizing himself by understanding the jurors' feelings (the chairs, how we buy a book) and asking to be welcomed by the city folk after he describes his small town. He used this to get closer to the jury before he got down to business.

Then notice how he made the analogy about what an opening statement is for. He let the jury in on the process easily and sensibly—a practical process to help them. He even told them it won't take too long.

Now notice how he humanized his client, company "right south of town." "Friends probably work there." "Only plant we've got." He continued by saying, "We didn't do anything wrong." A simple, strong concept. Notice how he described the value his power plant has to the jury—what we all do with the electricity they sell us.

As for emphasis—notice how he used the concept of the mousetrap, how he repeated that the power plant "didn't change the design—didn't change the materials." Just built a big one instead of a small one. Notice the rhythm that he creates and how he could come back to it again and again. See how memorable that can become.

Contrast this approach with one in which the concepts of the law, a detailed description of the materials used, the chronology of events or a description of the jury's responsibilities were the key points. Not to say that he won't get that in, too, but which would you rather hear first and which lawyer would you like better if you were a juror?

Organize Your Material

Since you know what the key issues of the case are, you also know how they will evolve and what will be important to remember in the decision-making process. However, the jury doesn't know this. The case is a jumble of facts to them. Therefore, a major goal in your opening statement should be to organize the case in such a way that you alert the jury to know what's coming and which stops along the way are the ones for them to notice and remember.

One of the most compelling ways to keep the jury with you is to have your material so organized that the logic, the chronology, the development of your ideas and the topics you're covering come through clearly and in order for them. When you lay it out, test whether or not each succeeding point you raise follows naturally, as an outgrowth of the one before. Remembering that the jury hears it only once, test your outline for organization, for logic and chronology.

You need not always start at the beginning. You might want to make three bold statements first to startle or to pinpoint your theme. But then be sure you do your flashbacks right after that, filling in why you said what you did and where it comes from.

Make Priorities

Only you know what's important as you begin your trial. In order to insure that the jury will keep listening for the major points you feel are central to your case, you need to tell them what's important, what to listen for and what to remember. Decide in advance what those issues are. When you get to those places, you should not only tell the jury to pay particular attention to these points as they develop in witness examination, you should also tell them why they're important. How will knowing or remembering this point help them decide at the end of the trial? When you make this kind of request for special attention seem useful to them, you assure that jurors will have a personal reason for listening and will surely want to do that.

Give Them a Scorecard

They really can't tell the players without some identifying markers or reminders. Just as you want to know names and some facts about each batter in a ballgame, the jury wants to get names and titles clear. But don't overload. Just be sure you get the key players' names and relationships clear.

"Who else could know that but Mr. Smith, the owner of the store? When you hear Mr. Smith testify . . . ."

The exact name of every witness is not significant. Just let the jury know what other witnesses can tell and what the jury will hear from them. Link witnesses to their area of expertise or their connection to the case, rather than merely mentioning their names. Select which names to emphasize and which players should be designated by category and subject. Detail overload can blow the fuse on concentration.

Don't Tell Too Much

Remember preparing for tests and writing "crib notes"? The purpose was to hit the most salient points of the course, to select and reduce the major facts, theories and principles you'd learned and expected to be asked about into a few themes. Well, that's the kind of information you should give the jury in opening statement. But no more! The jury's test is at the *end* of the trial. You have to ask yourself:

• What do they need as preparation to go into their "listening mode"?

• What do *you* need to do to prepare them to hear?

• What do you want them to hear first-hand from witnesses, to affect them as it happens rather than your having told them in advance?

There is a problem with over-informing the jury; with telling all the key issues plus many details and descriptions of things better left for testimony. Self-editing is crucial in your preparation and delivery. If you tell too much you not only confuse the jury but you rob them of the anticipation of what they'll hear. You dampen their ardor for listening. If you tell the plot plus all the dialogue, why should they stay tuned? Follow this motto:

"Tell them what *they* need to know, *not* all you know."

HOW TO WRITE IT

After making the decisions about what you wish to cover and designing how you'll do it, the next challenge is to create a system that will take your words, thoughts and organization of the materials and put them in a form you can use in the courtroom to support your presentation.

Oral communication at its best and most effective is a dialogue between the teller and the audience. It happens only when one speaks and the other listens and understands. This dialogue is created by the use of many techniques that insure this two-way activity, techniques we will discover in the rest of this chapter. But let's begin by analyzing a major issue: the written materials from which you speak.

Written Versus Spoken Word

Presentations to a group are traditionally written in advance, then read as they are delivered to an audience, after much rehearsal. Some people can plan and organize their material in note or outline form and then deliver their message extemporaneously. There are some major differences between these two forms, the written word versus the spoken word, that deeply affect how the message is received. These differences, which affect all of you as you plan and deliver your opening statement, need to be scrutinized and understood.

The written word is designed for delay: delay between when the message is given and received and delay in how the receiver takes the message in. When words are read, the eye has the leisure to go back over the things it didn't understand, to reread and reassimilate. When reading, people take in their information at their own pace, not the writer's. The writer of the words relies on how the reader absorbs and interprets his message since, as the writer reviews his material, he himself is reading it, following the same process. It is the reader who decides the "sound" of the author's voice.

The spoken word, however, is immediate. It depends totally on its delivery at the moment. The pace is only the deliverer's, as is the choice of when and how to pause, underline and explain. He sends the message once, at the moment it is given. He must guess how much and how fast the audience can absorb. They must keep up with him or miss it. Since a speech is usually delivered to a group, the pace chosen must of necessity reach for a common denominator. Therefore, it can leave people with slower metabolism, or with a mind that races ahead, on the sidelines, losing interest.

The form of the written word, as opposed to the spoken word, is also quite different. In written communication, the word is the total message, while in oral presentation words are only part of the whole performance.

Knowing that written words must be sent forth to stand alone as representatives of the author's ideas, this allows—actually motivates—the author to re-read and edit, to ruminate and select just the right word or image as he imagines his audience.

The spoken word, however, is improvisational. The speaker can alter, add or subtract immediately, based on his audience's reaction which he sees and feels at once. The sentences are much shorter. The meaning of a word can change dramatically just by inflection. It can be emphasized or underlined by the place on the stage (or in the courtroom) from which it is delivered or by the gestures a speaker makes. So there are vast differences in intention, preparation and delivery between written and spoken words, and that is an important aspect of how you deliver your statement.

The Effect in the Courtroom

One of the mistakes often made by many lawyers is that they try to write out the perfect opening statement. They want to ponder over, choose and select every word and polish it carefully, thinking *that* will make it the "ultimate" opening statement. But they forget the delivery system. The fact is that there is no perfect opening statement on paper alone. There is no "10" given for the words. Not only does each attorney have his or her own style, but a written statement can be more or less effective depending on the variety of techniques used in its delivery. The most crucial test is to analyze how the jury sees and hears it in the courtroom.

Lawyers can actually be trapped by writing out the entire opening statement, rehearsing it and then standing up and reading it to a jury. They feel absolutely marvelous because they think they have now got it right, after thinking it through many times, editing, rewriting, even memorizing it. But they don't understand the effect this written message has on a jury.

A written statement is made to be read and should therefore be sent so the jury can read it. A written message is not intended for live delivery; reading a written speech is acting—re-creating, not communicating. It's essentially a rote exercise, not spontaneous or seemingly genuine. It's trying to flesh out lines you know and have already rehearsed, trying to breathe new life into them as you say them to the jury. A written speech has the following effects on the jury:

• It reminds them of all the boring, professiorial or sermonizing orations everyone has ever heard.

• It is a more formal presentation than just talking. Your style is altered into a more removed and stilted one simply because you're reading.

• The rhythm of your written words is not that of your natural speech. Your supposedly seamless delivery is not how most people talk.

• The jury finds it very difficult to make eye contact with you.

• Since you are not watching them you don't know whether they're understanding you or not, whether you're going too fast, whether this is a moment for you to pause or whether they're really getting the point.

• You do not include them because your energy comes from your paper, not your audience. The best of your energy really was spent in your office when you wrote it. That's when you were engaging in the communication process. That's where the jury was alive for you.

• You are speaking from yourself, by yourself—not obviously to others. You hope the jury gets it—they may or they may not. It seems not to be your first priority.

• The jury wants you to be competent. They want to feel your comfort and security in the courtroom and with your job. Watching you read doesn't show them your freedom to speak from what you know.

The Effect on You

"But I like writing it out. I feel much more secure that way." As far as anxiety and feeling that you're much less nervous if you've written it out is concerned, the fact is that reading actually creates a bigger worry. Your greatest danger when you read is losing your place. Since your mind is turned off because reading is almost rote, you have no way to recover, to ad lib and flow back into the canned words, trying to find your place or a logical transition. You really look flustered and lost. If you do ad lib successfully, returning to the written text looks even worse, since the jury's seen the contrast between your reading and just talking.

However, if you present your opening statement improvisationally, from an outline that is organized to tell you where you're going, you actually make your job easier. By keeping eye contact with the jury, by looking directly at them, you allow them to become your catalyst, your energizer, the reason you're doing it. It gives you a tremendous push forward to present your material at a much higher energy level, at a more intense and committed level.

It's also much more secure to improvise from notes because you're alive right then, thinking of what you're saying. You can backtrack, re-route, change your mind, explain in a new way—inspired by what's actually happening with the jury, not the imagined scene you planned for in your den or office when you wrote it. You're also using the right format for what you're doing—a live presentation.

*   *   *

So, what's the upshot? If you have become a master at using the paper and reading, can lift your eyes enough to make contact, and you feel that the crutch is absolutely crucial, far be it for me to say put it down and fall flat on your face. I would say, however, it would be worth a try for you to experiment, in a very informal setting, with trying to deliver a statement from notes, to free yourself; to let the same head that put all those words on paper manufacture them right in the courtroom. Those words are yours; you *do* know what you're talking about and the words *will* be there when you need them stimulated by actual performance.

Making Usable Notes and Outlines

Of course you know how to write notes and outlines. It's the word "usable" I'd like us to concentrate on now. Spontaneous oral presentation has certain unique requirements from the written materials you use to speak from. For you to stay free, able to think and talk, notes must be:

- immediately understandable;
- be written in such a way that the order of where you're going is made visually simple and clear to you;
- able to feed you information in short, catalytic bursts that make their translation to speech self-evident;
- able to signal their various levels of importance in advance;
- able to tell you in what quality, form and style they should be delivered.

Now, here's the problem. The notes we're accustomed to writing and the outline forms we learned to use came from years in school; listening to lectures or reading books and writing notes or outlines based on our need to study or to read them again *later*. The implication is time; time to read and decipher what the notes and outlines meant, time to flesh out in your mind what else they referred to, time for you, on your own, to dip into your thoughts and make sense of them and only then, to imbue them with relative values and importance.

This time lag is the problem of using your old-style notes as a springboard for your improvisational, live presentations. Look at the five points I listed above as requirements for useful speaking notes. They all require immediacy, the ability of your notes to speak to you so succinctly that you can see and process them on the spot and use them as a catapult to launch the next idea directly toward the jury.

Therefore, let's look at a series of systems I've devised to expand the traditional forms of notes and outlines into self-explanatory catalysts for your presentation.

The Basic Process

You can write an outline in different forms to become a catalyst for different deliveries. An outline should be like dehydrating what you wanted to say and reducing it to its essence, one or two-word "bullets" or action-words. As you start talking, you "pour water" on them and the outline expands into many whole sentences again. Just seeing words like "diner," "ledger," "contract," "red light" triggers a response in you because you know just what they mean and what you want to say about them. Have faith that you can. If you can write these ideas as sentences, all those words will come to you to make sentences when you speak. Your mind goes through the same process, but you are more stimulated to edit *as* you speak. You can add more as you hear yourself, but you start out more focused as you see the trigger or action word.

Use Whole Pages

I do not recommend using little index cards. You can only write a few lines on an index card, and everybody watches you shuffling the cards and dealing out the joker. It doesn't make any sense since you can't really hide them in your hand, you know. They also give you no sense of continuity or overview.

You can write much more on a page. It gives you a better sense of where you're going and what's coming up. The jury gives you permission to bring visible notes. You're supposed to be prepared, you're supposed to have thought about this. They actually want to see your preparation and your sense of purpose and direction. Those traditional yellow-pad sheets are part of your recognizable equipment.

Short Words

The hardest thing to do is reduce the phrases and ideas to a form short enough to be useful in a speaking outline. The essential problem with writing actual sentences that use pronouns and prepositions is that the mind automatically puts you in a reading mode—moving the eyes horizontally right to capture the idea. This slows you up and takes time away from your jury eye contact and your rhythm of "look down—get the idea—bounce up and start talking."

To understand how to design your written materials for the eye to function that way, let's go to the world of television, which is surely the most efficient communicator these days. The teleprompter was designed knowing that the human eye can grab three to four words at one time without having to move sideways to read them. Teleprompters roll words, through a series of mirrors, directly in front of the lens of the camera, allowing the speaker to look directly at you, the viewer, and appear as though he isn't reading but just talking. Actually, he or she is reading words that roll up before them, yet there are never more than three to four words on a line so the eye does not have to travel across the page. Therefore, they can make and keep eye contact with you.

For the same reason, all of your notes should be designed so that you, too, don't lose eye contact with the jury. Don't put down more than three long or four short words at most (two are best). Use only essential, descriptive ones—nouns, verbs, an adjective for color. Then you don't have to shift into the horizontal mode of reading from left to right. If you can see more than three words on a line, you will automatically feel impelled to read and think before you can speak again. If you see only clue words that don't make traditional "sense," your mind is triggered to grasp those words and use them to form a catalytic thought for you. Writing sentences, phrases with prepositions and pronouns or anything that looks horizontal impedes your forward momentum and your thinking.

Make Your Outline Visual

The traditional forms of punctuation were designed for reading traditionally written words. As you read, your mind pauses for commas, hears a louder tone when you see an "!," and raises your inner voice when you see a "?."

But you need some new markings when you use an abbreviated outline form as a springboard for oral presentation.

What you need are a series of symbols or signals to tell you—in advance—what's coming and how to deliver it. You need to know that the next thought is important, that the list of words you see will culminate in a major statement or that in the next section you must shift gears and change the mood from a cool, logical one to a softer, more intimate one. How?

By designing a set of visual symbols to alert you, when you see them, to deliver the next words or thought in a different way. Like a road map using symbols with a legend, these clues should explain in advance what's coming up. We all respond to different visual stimuli—spaces on a page, shapes, contrasting colors, accents, indents, underlines. Find yours and develop your own system of visual shorthand to signal the other dimensions of your outline words—to remind you of their relative importance, their intrinsic drama or what you're leading up to and how to deliver them.

Headlines

Topic headings or themes should be written in block letters or capitals. Choose your best format, handwritten or typed, and find the shape that has an imperative in it for you.

Place it on the page as outlines are usually written. (The old school habits still work.) You can use I, II, III or A, B, C to define them further. It's also useful to write the theme or general idea of each in the margin, although your A, B, C headlines deal with specific topics. Then you can see, at a glance, what each section is about and where your themes are.

Lists

A vertical list is an automatic organizer. As soon as your eye sees one, you know that there are several points connected to each other that explain or pertain to a headline or topic heading. Suggestions:

- Remember the two to three word-on-a-line rule.
- Indent your lists to separate them from the headline.
- Use numbers or "•" (bullets) before your words.
- Be sure to use action words—nouns, verbs or adjectives that instantly capture the main thought.
- Omit all prepositions, pronouns and extraneous descriptive words—just the rock-bottom essence words are needed.
- Keep the list consistent—all ideas should have only one line so they look like the same general length and importance. Don't interrupt the rhythm you see.

Underlining

Underlining works, but not as well as you think. It's like a car with only one gear. There is no implication of nuance. How loud is the underlined word? How is it different from the next underlined word? Does the accent mean *loud* or does the underline mean *important*? Heavy? Thought provoking? Memorable? Therefore, you may want to make different underline symbols like =====versus _____ versus ☐. Decide what each symbol means so you can instantly recognize and respond to it when you see it.

Colors

Using colored pens to write out certain kinds of thoughts is an extremely useful tool. If you decide that blue means explanation, red means key points in the case, green means points of law, orange means emotional concepts and so on, you can give yourself a visual spur to presenting your ideas with the proper weight, mood and style. You can either write the words themselves with colored pens or, if you prefer typewritten copy, use them to underline or box words in.

Something else you can do with color is to use yellow magic marker to highlight the whole word or mark lines in a transcript. The color is transparent but it lifts that line out of the rest. Orange works on the yellow pads.

Choose your colors based on your emotional response to them and use them for the various impacts on your consciousness, and therefore your presentation, as you see them.

Spaces and Indents

Words are usually written just as you see these words you're reading now.

What happens to you as you read these words? Did you read them more slowly? Did you read them putting more weight on each word? How would you read them aloud? This device is excellent when you come to your key, big sentence or thought. It alerts you, slows you down and tells you right away to deliver it differently.

Another really effective device is to insert more than the usual amount space between ideas and to indent even further, like this:

A   major   thought   is   really   seen
when   placed   this   way   on   a   page.

To identify the key sentence still further, box it in, use color and/or underline it. The major point here is that your eye sees this sentence jump out of the page and tells you that you're heading towards a big buildup and a major delivery.

The Typed Versus Handwritten Word

How do you learn best? By writing something out yourself or by reading something typed or printed? Decide what mode suits you best, what helps you remember, what triggers you. Then decide whether to write your outlines out yourself or have them typed. You might like the combination of basic outline typed and then going over it using your own special symbols using color, margin notes or any other personal way eloquent to you, to distinguish one idea from another.

*   *   *

To sum up: You need visual catalysts, not only words, to help you add emphasis, feeling and verbal order to your thoughts. You're writing on the jury's brain to organize and explain your ideas so clearly that the jury can understand them. Unless you can see and absorb them instantly yourself with some logic and order *before* you deliver them, much of what you say can go right past your crucial audience.

TECHNIQUES OF PRESENTATION

Now that you've prepared your opening statement, what techniques are most effective to deliver it—and to an audience already overloaded with the many forms of sales and persuasion that assault them daily?

Twentieth Century communications are fast, simplistic, multimedia presentations with quick-hit images and a great deal of visual reinforcement. Juries, like the rest of us, have been permanently imprinted with these forms of communication. They come to the courtroom with those audio/video rhythms beating inside, unfamiliar with and unwilling to follow a slowly evolving, unfolding solo message that simply presumes their interest and attention.

In order to reach them and make them stay with you, to both listen and remember, let's turn to the world of performance and communications skills. There are a variety of techniques to make your opening statement deal with and conquer the short attention span, the conditioned audience resistance to oral presentations and to help juries process and absorb complex information.

Beginnings

The opening moments of your presentation are crucial. Not only do they set the personal tone for how the jury will meet and feel about you, but that is also when the jury decides whether or not to get interested in what you're going to tell them. Let's not forget the basic truths about "getting-acquainted-with-a-stranger," the phenomenon we talked about at the beginning of the chapter. This is the jury's time to take in all kinds of information from and about you. Therefore, your first moments need thought. The jury is ready, waiting and curious, as "guaranteed-attentive" as they're going to be at any part of the trial. They're wide open for impressions and information and will use all those instinctive judgment skills we discussed earlier. So, you must be very clear at the start, not only about the content of your statement, but also about your style and the personal impression you wish to convey to them. Perhaps the hardest part is just getting it all going.

Getting Started

Did you ever have to push a car? You know how much power you need to get it rolling at the beginning and then how much easier it gets once that immovable object has forward momentum? Getting up off that cold counsel's chair, wending your way to your opening spot and starting your presentation is kind of like pushing that car, except that it happens fast—like charging all burners in a spaceship at once and saying "Go!"

There are several forces you need to marshal, several kinds of energy you need to make flow. There are your own adrenals that need to get up to speed. There are the jury's attention and energy which need to be focused on you and then moved to start walking down the path with you. There's your mind, reaching for the organization and the specific words of your message. And there's your self-confidence, that deep inner voice you want to hear, that says, "You can do it; you're terrific; wait till they hear this!" But that may be easier for me to write than for you to say. . . .

Stage Fright

That old bugaboo "stage fright" keeps more people in thrall than they'd like to admit.

Stage fright is actually born by measuring yourself against some mythical perfect performance and developing anxiety as you imagine how far short you'll fall. You focus on what others will think of you and lose sight of the end product—what the jury will hear and learn.

The best antidote is to continually remind yourself about what you're doing and what your end product should be. Get lost in the action and let go of the image. And remember—this isn't *Hamlet* and no one knows what your lines are supposed to be. You can alter, falter, fix and change with no one the wiser. What power you actually have as you stand before your anxious, needy audience with a head full of goodies to give them!

Psych Yourself Up at the Table

Before you get up, say a quick checklist to yourself.

• What do you want to accomplish?
• What simply, are you going to tell them about?
• What overall feeling do you want to convey (warm, serious, analytical, folksy, wise).

This will help you focus tightly on your goals and your material, giving you a quick send-off and banishing a lot of general floating anxiety.

Some lawyers sit still before they get up to do the opening statement and hyperventilate. They take a number of very deep breaths, hold on to their clasped hands or squeeze against the table or chair arms very hard. It sort of thrusts them into a higher level of energy very quickly, and nobody knows that they're doing it.

Tell Yourself You're Good

Mustering self-confidence at this highly charged moment is sometimes hard to do. But it's crucial to get yourself in this frame of mind *before* you begin so you can start at the top of your form, rather than reflecting on how well you did after you've delivered your statement. Just say, "I know what I'm doing. I'm prepared. I've done this before. The jury needs me to explain this to them."

When you walk up to begin your work with this much conviction, you can then ease up and present your opening statement in an easy, soft or casual manner if you like. But you're ready; you know it's showtime and you mean for the jury to hear you.

Walk with Assurance and Purpose

Gather your papers, get up and get moving briskly, with minimal wasted motion, looking purposeful and energetic. Looking disorganized and unsure at this stage bodes ill for the jury's first impression. If your case warrants it, or the previous statement has been all fire and bombast, you might want to change pace by walking deliberately and thoughtfully, as a contrast, if it suits your style.

Take Your Space

How you "take the stage," how you carve out your turf and take command of it, how you take control and settle in is very visible and very affecting. Decide where you're going to start, go there and put your notes down. Then take a beat to settle down. Don't start talking at once. Just make eye contact with the jury, and wait a moment to get total attention and silence.

Take a Breath

Use the baseball pitcher's technique of focusing concentration by taking a breath just before each pitch. That moment of silence, that breath, not only helps you tighten the iris of your inner vision, it also helps the jury settle down to listen expectantly. It heightens the attention and the suspense. Find that magic moment of expectation and use it.

Don't Get Too Close

Wanting to reach out to the jury on a personal level, many lawyers get too close to the jury at the start. But the jury isn't ready. And it's too soon.

Give them a chance to get to know you first. Show your warmth and informality in how you tell the story; simple words, colloquialisms, identifiable visual images. But preserve their privacy, their territory, till you've earned the right to come closer by getting to know each other better.

Don't Pace

When you begin your opening statement, the whole body goes into high gear as a result of the surge of adrenalin. This has different effects on people and they respond in different ways. Some people stand absolutely stock still and hang on until they feel safe enough to leave the podium, but some people start off with fidgeting or a lionesque pacing right away as their adrenals charge up and spill over. This can create a bit of a problem, since pacing at this point is distracting.

The jury is working very hard at the beginning of an opening statement to understand and recognize you, and also to try to get what it is you are saying. They cannot also absorb much movement, like pacing back and forth. The amount of movement in pacing and the heightened energy level seen and implied are too high a gear for just getting acquainted. You need to move into the jury's consciousness at an easier pace. Also, pacing can be misunderstood. It reminds people of anger (irate fathers, rejecting bosses) or of anxiety or restlessness. Visually, it looks almost like you're wiping out what you just said.

If you're a pacer or a fidgeter, stabilize yourself at the beginning of the opening statement by leaning on an inanimate object such as a piece of furniture, the side of the counsel table or the side of the podium. Find a place where an inanimate object will ground you. You can press very hard on your hand or against the side of an object and no one can tell. This serves to charge you up and stabilize you till all systems can get focused and operate. Once you get your mouth and head in synch, and you feel really good, you can trust yourself to walk away, because the movement will be quite natural, and it will be commensurate with what you're saying. You've also given the jury the chance to take your measure while you're standing still.

Say "Good Morning"

This nice, generic, courteous greeting has several benefits. It's people-sized, not oratorical. It's recognizable and therefore disarming in such a ritual environment. It's an informal greeting that says something about you. It's a recognition of the jury. One lawyer I know who uses it says that the jury sometimes answers back, especially if you do it whenever you address them, throughout the trial.

Introduce Yourself

How you say your name and what you're doing there is very important. Do you slur it? Say it too fast? Use Bob or Robert? Are you "attorney for the defendant," do you "represent John Doe," or are you "Bob Jones, John Doe's lawyer"?

People are interesting about names. Are you part of the great majority that says "I'm really bad about remembering names?" This has to do with inattention and the fact that we focus much more on a person's face, voice and demeanor than on the amorphous, abstract combination of syllables that identify them on paper. Yet getting your name before the jury clearly is not only important, it's useful as an ice breaker.

Help the jury remember your name, and take step one toward showing them who you are, by making something of your introduction. If you have a complex name, spell it out with a side comment like, "I know you're trying to imagine the spelling," or "I've always had to do that because it's a hard one to pronounce." If your first name is Fauntleroy, have a little fun with it. Let them imagine having that name. Use some humor. "I haven't been called that since some major fights in the schoolyard. People call me Roy." If your name is unusual, you might like to talk of how distinguishing it is and that, although you hated it as a kid, it's rather nice for it to be so memorable now, as an adult.

You could mention the ethnic roots they can hear in your name or that the anonymous "John Smithness" of your name has always made you work harder to be "that John Smith." Use the possibilities available in this first step of getting acquainted to make a three-dimensional statement out of your name, your approach to yourself and to them.

How can you warm up the atmosphere, at the beginning, when you introduce yourself? Try using some throwaway lines at the beginning to say things about the bad weather, last night's baseball game or the fact that the little league team that all of you have been rooting for in your home town has finally won. These gestures unify, touch something of common interest and give a little warmth and dimension to you and your case.

Introduce Your Client

The words "plaintiff" or "defendant" do not register on the jury at this early stage. They aren't even sure what they mean. Don't be the "attorney for the plaintiff." You're "Joe Doak's lawyer." Identify yourself with the qualities and character with which you will imbue your client and the issues of the case. If you represent a major corporation, that's always hard. "I represent the people at Mega Corporation" or "the folks who make Yummies" or anything else you can do to humanize that stereotypical, skyscraper boardroom image they see. You might want to stand near, even touch your client, especially if he or she is a criminal defendant.

Do not ask your client to stand. Most people do that badly. They look and feel embarrassed and don't want a spotlight right at the start when there's nothing for them to do.

If you are a plaintiff's lawyer, then you have something very good on your side. It's easy to identify with a human being. It's easy for the jury to identify with just this one person who's out to fight the giant company. You may want to think how to introduce your client by name. Is he James Smith? Is he Jimmy Smith? Is he Jim Smith? Is he Doctor James Smith? What do you wish to emphasize most about him? His credentials? Dr. James Smith, who has now lost his hand and cannot be a doctor anymore?

You should think about using the name as an additional persuasive tool, and what you are going to call him through the rest of the trial. What if your client is a criminal? How close will you be to him? How do you point him out? Do you introduce the two of you as a package and then walk toward the jury and describe the rest of what is going to happen? How much unity do you wish to make early on?

The same thing is true for corporate defense lawyers. You need to be serious and professional, but you might want to think in terms of trying to make people see that whoever it is that's speaking for the company is really a person speaking *for* the company rather than *being* the total company. That also allows you to be identifiable as an individual.

Respond to Opposing Opening Statement

Don't pretend it didn't happen. If you're second, we must assume your opposing counsel's opening statement has had some effect on the jury. Notice it. Make some benign comment about it, if its appropriate, and then go on to do your thing. Show the jury that alternative points of view are the essence of the trial. Point up another style and another approach—yours. Bounce off the points your opponent made by wrapping them into a key phrase or concept and then use that to go forward into your side of the case. Don't belabor this, however. Use it only to start telling your side of the story, unless that would spoil your planned opening.

Change the tempo and energy level. Notice your counsel's final lines and where the jury's emotional level is. Stand up prepared to change that. Think of making them turn over a new leaf when you begin and making them see you as a distinctly different person with a different style and approach. Make it clear. Wipe their slate clean as you begin your statement. Be sure to wipe out visuals, if plantiff used any. A note of caution: Don't start by being negative or argumentative. Don't hurl epithets or degrade opposing counsel. The jury gives demerits for that. Rather, point up the differences in the case by your wisdom and skill. Let the jury downgrade him or her.

Affirm the Jury's Role

The pitfall many lawyers fall into is to be too product-oriented, to launch themselves into the classic opening statement too soon, "and the evidence will show . . ." "and you will hear . . " "and we will argue . . ."—without first welcoming the jury to the courtroom and the process of the trial.

It is very meaningful to the jury to be a jury. They take their job very seriously. They like to have someone else, the supposedly jaded lawyers, recognize that what they are doing is wonderful, important, timeless, universal. Giving jurors recognition, not only of their power, but also of the honor of the office, and that you know they will discharge it well, is a vital piece of information to convey. It shows your approach to the law, your respect for the idea of the trial and the jury system. And it tells them you notice and respect them.

Set the Tone

Not only do you need to clarify the issues and the story, but you need, right at the beginning, to set the tone for your case. At what level will you pitch all your presentations and examination? Somber? Thoughtful? Philosophical? Emphatic and emotional? Down-home folksy? Clearcut and factual?

Whatever approach you plan to take must be made clear and consistent right at the start. The style you begin with, from the moment you introduce yourself, is what they will come to expect from you throughout the trial. That's the level at which they will listen. That's the approach they will take as they respond to and think about your part of the case. Therefore, think hard about it and determine what that style is, but first be aware of what your natural style is. Don't design an acting job for yourself. Look for flavor and nuance. Get in touch with and actually label your sense of how to try this case. Find the adjectives that characterize what is needed. Then be sure this decision is integrated into how you begin. It's your best launching pad for showing them what attitude to take.

Establish Your Theme

Clarify the issues by stating your theme early. The jury wants first to know the essence of your side of the case as you will try it. Paint it in broad strokes, with primary colors. Save the details for later explanation. Use clear, simple concepts; be short, direct and concise. That can easily tune the jury into the heart of the matter. Make it as simple as, "This is a case about . . . and whether . . . What's really at issue is . . . ."

Tell Your Goals and Concerns

Don't just focus on the facts of the case. Humanize your job. Ruminate about the case, why you care, what's at stake, why it matters. Share what you were thinking about as you prepared, what you wanted to be sure you could make clear. Tell how you were thinking about the jury; of their job, of what they needed to hear from you in your opening statement and what their eventual decision would involve. The above points are in direct response to some of those original jury needs I mentioned—"Who's my leader," "Who'll help me understand what this is all about?" and "Why is he or she doing this?"

Tell Them What Your Statement Will Do

Give them a reason to listen. Analyze their job and what they need to know to do it. You should then tell them how your opening statement will help them do that.

"You need to decide if Sam Jones really acted illegally. To do that, you'll need to know what the law says, how such a business normally operates and a great deal about what actually happened and what Sam Jones really did. Well, let me tell you how you'll find all that out. Let me tell you what we will show you to prove our side of the case and help you make up your mind."

Make them look forward to your presentation as you explain what you'll tell them about. Give your agenda, your table of contents. Show how you've organized it and what they'll hear from you. Telling them where you're going and why they should listen ensures that they'll stay the distance; otherwise, they don't know what you'll cover and why they should continue to pay attention.

Explain Courtroom Procedure

Along with the facts of the case, the jury needs to know what a trial is like: what they will see, what the format is, the chronology and so on. It may surprise you to know that juries really misunderstand the courtroom procedures they see during the course of a trial. And this can be much to your detriment. For example, jurors know that the two lawyers will fight with each other. When a lawyer stands up to object, they believe that he or she is panicked and thinks he's losing, that what the opposing counsel is getting from the witness right now is dangerous and he doesn't want the jury to hear it. That makes the jury watch the judge's ruling with glee and then become extra-attentive to what will be said next, particularly if the judge overrules your objection.

Explain the procedures that will take place during the trial in simple, personal terms. "You will see me or my opposing counsel stand up and object, and wait for the judge's ruling. This has to do with the rules of how we are permitted to conduct a trial." Or, "You will see us go to the bench for a conference. That's because . . . ." Or, "You will see me place objects into evidence and I will show you precisely what that evidence is." When you tell the jury what odd procedures they may see, they will secretly think, "Hey, he told me about that," when the procedures occur. It makes friends.

Don't Say "I'm New at This"

Remember that old song "This is my first affair so please be kind?" That's the essence of what you're asking for when you get up and tell the jury you're inexperienced. It's a plea for sympathy and understanding and the jury wants none of it. They need you to do your job. Well. Dependably. Securely. Telling them you can't, or may not be able to deliver develops annoyance and signals them to not place too much faith in your skills and presentation of the issues. If *you're* broadcasting your insecurity, you tell them not to have any faith in you, either. The jury wants to look forward to how you'll handle your case and how you'll help them. Telling them up front that you may not be able to do it well becomes a self-fulfilling prophecy. They'll sit in critical judgment on you, concentrating on how you're messing up, expecting you to fail. Even if your knees are knocking, stand up and make them believe you know what you're doing. You'll begin to believe it, too, as you act it out.

Presenting the Subject Matter

Unify with the Jury

When you first walk into the courtroom, get a feeling that you are all in this together. For the length of this trial, you, the jury, the witnesses and the judge are bound together in a most unique experience. Feel a closeness with them. Feel as though perhaps you are an elder tribesman here. You have taken this trip before, so it's easy for you to turn around to help. Don't feel so distant from them in your head, because it will change your delivery. Feel connected and close.

Try to imagine the lives of the people in the jury. What would you have in common with any of them? Find something to like or notice about each of them. It will change the way you deliver what you are saying. It will develop a kind of friendship with them and the concept of your being an elder, but still definitely a part of their tribe.

Try to include references to this kinship in your opening statement to let them know of your sense of connectedness to them.

Involve your Audience

Although you may not always think of it this way, a trial is actually a performance. It is a play. It has spectators and actors, and you are one of the actors. You must involve your audience. The problem is that the very nature of an audience is passivity, watching someone else do something. This can encourage dropping out of the proceedings entirely. In addition, there is the fact that it's hard to keep their attention, since only a small percentage of the brain is automatically involved in listening, while the rest is up for grabs. Therefore, you must hook the jury and keep them with you.

In what way can you keep the jury involved, interested, always on their toes and personally feeling what happens so that they will care at the end and come up with a verdict for your side? One of the challenges of opening statement is to get the jury to care. You cannot get them to care by browbeating them or saying, "You should!" That sounds parental. You cannot *tell* them that your version of "fair" and "justice" must be their version. You must, rather, engage them in their own sense of what's right so *they* will see that justice has not been done, and therefore they will want to be sure that justice will be done now.

Your skills should be used to show them what is just and unjust. By dramatizing, by humanizing, by making the issues poignant and clear, they can begin to get involved in the story and begin to care. You must find ways to help them relate to your side, to be concerned about what happened and to want to right it. But remember, you must step outside of it. You're a conduit, a messenger, a catalyst. You are a dissector who picks up the facts of the case and shows the jury what's at issue, what's right and what's wrong. But you cannot, by *your* passion and sense of outrage, heat them up to your level. Let them come along as you unfold the case. Get them involved by thinking about what reaches people and makes them care.

Make Words Visual

It is terribly difficult for people to tune in and understand when you talk in abstract terms. Remember your arithmetic classes? Unless you were mathematically inclined, it was very difficult to find a reason to relate to symbols, figures and abstract concepts. If they can't catch on to the principle being discussed or relate this point to something they already know, most people tune out. But visualizing helps people tune in, since there's something concrete and tangible to latch onto, to imagine and to think about. They'll stay with it while you extrapolate and make a principle or a concept from it.

To visualize something, you must use words and images that are quickly clear, that have feelings in them, that are sensory experiences with color, shape, and size. "It was a big building, a huge building." Or, "It was a beat-up, rough, old truck with the fender falling off and the paint all peeled, and obviously well-worn tires, and one of the windshield wipers wasn't working. And as he bore down with his dirty windshield, unable to see . . ." See what happens to you as you read this? You suddenly see that truck, completely. Compare that with, "The motor vehicle was proceeding westward on the main thoroughfare, and as the other car approached in the opposite direction going easterly . . ." The jury not only hasn't gotten a clear picture of what in the world you're talking about, but they are put off by these two removed objects that are moving on a board somewhere. Every part of the trial should be made visual to help the jury *remember*. Since they can't write notes, and aren't informed about the law, they can't always see the relationships of the points as you make them. But they can remember a picture or an image, and you can keep recalling them, especially in final argument.

By making your words create visual images, you appeal to the right, rather than the left side of the brain. You play upon everybody's instincts and feelings, where decisions are actually made.

Emphasize

Emphasis is another technique to help the jury note and remember the important points. Think about how many experiences they undergo during opening statement:

• getting introduced to you and the other lawyer;

• getting to know you and to make judgments about you;

• getting used to their surroundings, their new job and the formality of the trial; and

• trying to sort out and understand the facts and cast of characters.

Seeing these diverse demands on the jury's attention should make you realize how much you need to emphasize and underline the key issues in the case and to find ways to make them more memorable.

The most common ways to emphasize are:

• repeating of a word or phrase;

• pacing—slowing down or speeding up to make everyone notice;

• modulating your voice, harder, softer, more thoughtful or more weighty, to make the jury lean in and notice that this is different and important. Let your voice reflect the subject, its importance and quality.

• creating a catch phrase or a metaphor that you can use again and again to refer to an act, a fact or an object.

• recapitulation—summarizing the key points you've just made in a quick review.

Since there is so much material to cover, and it's all new, your ability to make priorities and emphasize what's important in terms of events and concepts is vital. You need to help them keep the trial, the facts and your point of view straight. Don't assume they will catch it all with one explanation.

Use Topic Headings

Tell the jury about your progression. "Now let's turn to the day in question." Introduce each subject by heading. Recap before you go on. Make transitions as you change the subject. Be scrupulously clear about the differences between topics and descriptive details. If you wander off, bring them back with you, deliberately, by announcing what you're talking about. Don't just jump to another subject. Clear order in your presentation, with headlines to keep the jury aware, helps them to think and remember as well as keeping their attention.

"I Want You to Listen to. . ."

In your desire to point up certain important issues or make the jury notice some anticipated testimony there is a tendency to say "I want you to listen to Mr. X." This can breed resentment. What is your relationship to them that they should care what you want? Why should they do what you tell them to do? Of course you don't mean to be so overbearing but that's how it can be received, and the last thing you want is a resistant jury right from the start. Try these instead:

"When you hear X you will know why . . ."
"Listen for . . ."
"Notice how . . ."
"Pay particular attention to . . ."
"Y's testimony is important because . . ."

These accomplish what you want without intruding. Your

needs, your ideas can become the jury's more easily as you alert them to what will be helpful to *them* rather than to you.

Don't Patronize

It is very difficult to keep from sounding patronizing if you are trying hard to explain everything to the jury, because the image begins to grow in your mind that they're not smart: "They don't understand this." "They won't understand that." "If I have to explain *this* to them . . ." Well, the image is wrong. They're smart enough. They're just not lawyers!

You must guard against explaining things too simplistically and becoming patronizing in your explanation. From the beginning, the jury is feeling very sensitive, since they already feel so inept about what is required of them and what is about to happen. They are concerned about the fact that they are being called upon to make judgments in an area in which they feel insecure. They feel unknowledgeable when they see how much they don't know, how many things you must explain to them. They hope they'll get it.

Therefore, explain with enthusiasm. Think to yourself, "Now they'll know what that means," instead of, "All right, let me back up and wait for them to catch up to me." Explain something by saying, "There's one of those legal words again. Let me explain it because you may not have come across it." This not only gives you permission to explain, it lets the jury think, "Of course we didn't come across it," or, "Of course we don't understand it."

If you use buzz words or phrases like "This is an unfamiliar term," "This is a technical term," "This is a legal term," "Let me just spend a moment explaining it" the jury has the right to feel "Well, of course, I would know it, too, if I was a lawyer. It just hasn't been in my experience." These little phrases excuse your explanation, so that you sound simply benign and helpful, rather than patronizing.

Do edit and question your words in advance. But even with the best of intentions we're all fallible, so be alert. Listen to yourself when you're talking, and be aware of how you explain anything. Assume jurors can and will understand, as adults, if you make it clear. Don't puree it; just cut it into bite-sized pieces.

"It's Simple"

"You see, this case is very simple." Whenever you use the word "simple," you've created a challenge for the jury. You are saying "Look, don't you get it? It's simple!" The implication is that if they don't get it, they're not too smart. When you, the lawyer, says, "It's simple," that means *you* understand it and expect they should, too. The problem is that what's simple to you isn't necessarily simple to them.

Remember when your mother or older brother said, "It's so easy—why can't you do this?" But it wasn't easy, because you couldn't do it. And it made you feel twice as stupid, since others seemed so able. Challenging the jury with "it's simple" could let them know they're inept. And no one loves *that* message.

Instead, say something like, "Let me break this down into a few clear, basic ideas." Tell them you mean to reduce something, to give them only the heart of the matter. Don't tell them how you want them to perceive it. Just *make* it simple.

"What I Say is Not Evidence"

There is a major pitfall related to that classic phrase used in opening statements. You are supposed to explain that what you are saying is not evidence. Of course you mean not bona fide, acceptable testimony. But the jury thinks that means, "Then don't listen. It's unimportant," "It's not useful." or even "Not evidence? Then it's not true!" The only thing jurors know about the word "evidence" is that it's serious, connected to the courtroom, connected in some way to trials. So "evidence" sounds like the right stuff, the serious stuff. They think, "Evidence is what we'd better listen to." When you say "This is not evidence," to them that means "Disregard it."

Therefore, when you say, "This is not evidence," qualify it. Tell them what that means. Each time you explain something, you let them know that you want to dispel the mystery of the trial and you want them in on all of it. The implication is that you trust them enough to explain everything. It means you feel that the most in-formed jury will come up with the right answer—yours.

" . . . And the Evidence Will Show . . ."

Any phrase repeated often enough without change is irritating. Don't set up a litany. It negates what comes after it. Use some variety. Create synonymous phrases like:

- "First you'll hear . . . Then you'll hear . . ."
- "You'll also find out about . . ."
- "Other testimony will tell . . ."
- "As you hear witness X testify that . . ."
- "You will learn that . . ."
- "We plan to show you . . ."
- "We will prove that . . ."

Variety in your speech keeps the jury alert and adds vigor and interest to your statement.

Sympathetic Role for Defense Counsel

There is a special obstacle to surmount when you stand up in any case in which there has been a personal injury or harm done to a single citizen or a group of citizens who are identifiable to the jury, and you represent the opposite side.

The pitfall is that you become lumped with the perpetrator of the deed. It becomes difficult for the jury to separate you from your client. Your challenge is to let the jury know that you are a human being too, who can also feel great sympathy about what happened, as they do.

Therefore, you must first establish yourself as one of them, a person who can perceive the tragedy, who also feels bad that the accident happened, as everybody does. If you let them know first that you feel as they do and understand their feelings, you can then carry them with you to the next place.

Tell them something like:

You actually have a hard job to do here. Mr. Jones has lost a leg and that's very sad. We all sympathize and understand that. I'm sure you do, as I do. But that's not the issue before you in this case. The law asks you to decide *why* it happened, *who*, if anyone, was at fault, and then to decide if anyone should be responsible to *pay* for the loss. I know it could be hard to transcend your natural sympathy in order to look only at the facts, to do your job coolly and objectively and to keep your eye on the issue, not the person. But that is actually what the law is about, what this case is about and what your job here requires.

This approach not only clarifies what they'll hear and decide, it also shows that you are understanding and sympathetic as well. It gives you permission to try your case on the facts and not look too heartless.

Use of Visuals

Lawyers are quite accustomed to using visual aids in their examination of witnesses. It is rarer to see them using tangible visual devices in opening statement. Yet there are tremendous benefits to using them right at the beginning. Let's explore the ways in which visual aids are helpful to the jury and your presentation of the case first, and then we'll talk of the specific ways to use them in opening statement.

When you describe anything to a jury only orally, they will use their imagination and their own frames of reference to "get the picture." They will imagine their own versions of the diagram, design or image you are telling them about. But none of their images will match each other, or, most importantly, yours. Therefore, in order to be exact and clear, you must use visuals to explain to the jury all at once so that everyone knows exactly what you want them to know, and will visualize them correctly whenever you talk about them.

Another major incentive to use visuals is that it empowers the jury to learn on their own. Recognizing the passive state of the jury, one of the greatest gifts that you can give them during the trial is a clear and active job, like being able, on their own, to look at a visual and decide, see, absorb and get a clear image for themselves, not because you told them about it. They will become involved in trying to understand and recreate the event that you are describing. Until that moment, they have been totally dependent on you as the only source of information. You have all the power. You give them your information when you want, how you want and in the form you want. Once you have made or shown a visual and let the jury look at it on their own, they have control and power, too. They have options; they can look at the visual when *they* want to and/or they can look at you. They can compare what you say with what they see. They can go back and check out what they just heard with what they thought about before. They can change their minds based upon what they see in the visual. But it's entirely up to them. It treats them like grownups, giving them activity and making them participants.

Visuals are memorable and much easier to recall than words. They remind and reinforce every time you show them again. The major danger in using visuals is overload.

You must be careful not to give the jury any more information than you can explain at a time. Show the information a piece at a time and explain it. Giving the entire piece of information, a fully delineated chart loaded with information, is confusing and defeating. Each juror will look in a different corner of it and decide what that's supposed to mean while you're busy trying to describe the one place you want them to look.

The particular benefits of using illustrative material and visual devices in your opening statement are succinctness, interest and clarity. They will help you:

- state major themes;
- list key issues;
- show the general perameters of the case;
- visualize the key facts;
- illustrate what happened;
- create devices the jury can recall;
- set up visualizations that will be used throughout the trial;
- indicate your zeal to make things clear;
- keep interest at a high level as you deliver a varied, multi-media presentation;

- present you as an interesting, energetic, analytical, clear-thinking leader who will always get to the heart of the matter.

Enough said. Just be sure to get a motion *in limine* for permission to use visuals in your opening statement. (For a full, comprehensive discussion of all aspects of visual aids, from choices to methods and effects, see Chapter 8—Visual Aids.)

*   *   *

PRESENTATION STYLE

Non-Verbal Communication Skills

Along with the content, the methods of delivery are an integral part of the message. Many factors, verbal and non-verbal can color and alter what you mean and what you say. Here are some thoughts and suggestions on how to enhance, clarify and add to your opening statement.

Everybody uses the words "body language," but I'm not sure if people really understand much about what it means anymore. In the most general terms, it's all the non-verbal things you express, what you do with your body, with gesture, space, movement, posture, stance, with your hands and eyes. It's important because these can become much more eloquent than your words. Your body language is a physical extension of what you're really thinking and is visible and recognizable to all of us. It is spontaneous, unedited and often a betrayer. Although you sound like you're totally confident, people will watch you twist a paper clip in your fingers or jiggle one leg while you sit or give other telltale signals that all is not what your words convey. But let's concentrate now on the positive uses of non-verbal communication and how it can make you more effective and eloquent.

Gesture

Gesture is actually visual punctuation. That's all it's for. It is to aid and abet, to underline and emphasize, to engage and point up what you're saying. It is almost as though you are so moved by what you are saying that the mouth and the words are not enough. Your physical energy must pour out into your arms, hands and body, into getting closer or perhaps thumping the table. The origin of and the impetus for the gesture is the message. It is centered in what you wish to get across.

How you perform your gestures comes from a curious and interesting variety of experiences relating to your childhood. Your gestures will most often reflect what you saw your parents do. If you come from a Mediterranean family where there is a great deal of arm waving, arm waving is for you. Therefore, for you, forms of physical expression are a comfortable thing. You've always seen it. It's always been permitted, so you will always do it naturally. But if you come from a Northern European or Anglo-Saxon background, you may be rather circumspect about how much physical movement you use to express yourself; it may be more difficult for you.

Be true to yourself. Do not suddenly try to put on a gesture-jacket and think, "From now on I have got these six wonderful things in my repertoire and I will do them." Unless they come from you and are comfortable to you, they will not work at all. The jury needs consistency. Deviations from your natural style are the things they pick up.

Try a short exercise to illustrate this point. You are talking about trees, or about something that is round or something very murky. Right now pick up your hands, and in front of a mirror, show how you would describe something like that. What do your hands do? How would you show "He was horrified as he picked it up"? How would you do "The conversation went on and on"? Discover your instinctive gestures. See how they can really help the jury visualize and remember.

But gesture also has another vital connection and that is as underlining, as emphasis. In order to help the jury remember or notice, you might say, "And there are three points to be made, ladies and gentlemen," and as you explain the three points, you move your hands on each of them, perhaps with three different gestures. Then you walk and say, "Now let's take the first point." You have visually made the jury turn the page. It helps them to see the organization of your message.

Be careful not to overdo. The overdoing often comes from an innate sense of patronizing, trying too hard and believing they don't understand. Rather, see if you can discover what gestures are natural to you. Then tune in to how hard you have to work to explain this point and give no more energy or extra help than that.

Hands

The most eloquent aspect of your body, after your face, is your hands, because they are the most mobile. Letting them just dangle gets talkers anxious. Therefore, the most common complaint I hear is "What should I do with my hands?" What is natural to you? Is your natural stance with your arms at your sides? With one hand in your pocket? Do you notice that you're the kind of person who crosses your arms over your chest? Are you a finger pointer? Do you keep a pencil in your hand and point at the jury with that? What prop do you normally feel comfortable with? A clipboard? A pad? In what form are your notes held?

Since the hands are the most eloquent, don't point while holding anything. Pointing at someone looks punitive or judgmental. Shaking a finger for emphasis makes them feel slightly childlike, and you, parental.

Putting your hands in your pocket can call up images of Jimmy Stewart and the old cowboys or a kind of rumpled Clarence Darrow or Spencer Tracy. It establishes a kind of easy, relaxed format. For very tall or physical people, it sometimes can be disarming and makes the jury feel a little more secure. Don't make the mistake of clasping your hands behind your back, because that is a tense gesture. It's rather militaristic and suggests that something is being repressed.

Stance

Standing with your weight equally distributed makes you look inviolate and strong—on solid ground. It can also make you look stubborn, very powerful, sometimes macho or challenging. It's not a very conversational look.

Standing with your weight on one foot is very disarming. It's a more relaxed posture. You are actually off balance and allowing yourself to be so. It makes you look softer, more vulnerable, like you could be pushed over. Yet, it might be a disarming position you'd want to assume from time to time, depending on how powerful your client is and what other images you are trying to present. Crossing one leg over the other as you lean on the podium is obviously very relaxed and informal.

Although a relaxed stance can disarm the jury and show a softer you in order to dilute what may be a very tough personality, it can also dilute a very strong delivery. You should choose how you stand, but be knowledgeable about its total effect. Use a strong, solid stance for incontrovertible facts. When dealing with a serious issue that is intimidating in itself or dehumanizes you, you may want to take a more relaxed physical position at that time. The same is true if you want to be more personal and intimate. But when you do relax, remember not to slouch, slump your shoulders or cave your chest in. What that slouching posture can do is make you look apologetic; it does not inspire confidence. Abraham Lincoln became President that way, but until you can do everything else he did, it may not take you very far.

Eye Contact

Eye contact simply says to another human being, "I see you. I notice you. I care about you. You are important in the process I'm now doing. What I say to you and what you think, matters. That's why I'm looking at you." It gives the jury power. It enfranchises them. It gives them identity. It does another thing, too: It shows you are investing yourself, saying, "I'm committed."

When you look at somebody, he or she looks back at you. So at the same time that you are saying "I see you, and you're important," you are also saying "I will let you see me. I will let you look at me." It is a vulnerable gesture, in that you are allowing the jury to get to know you. Since you do want them to see you as an intelligent, thinking, caring, hard-working person, you must commit yourself, as a human being, to them.

It's important to look from one person to another. As you make eye contact with each one, you link them together as a group, and they each feel equally important. Such contact develops an energy level of its own. It creates warmth and a kind of commitment from them to you. It reaches out. It includes everyone. It gives everybody color. It gives you a chance to check up on what they are noticing, or if they are noticing. And, particularly in the opening statement, it helps you get their measure and begin to know them. What's their tempo? Are you really reaching them in the way you want to?

Energy Level

Sometimes it's difficult for you to gauge your own energy level. It is hardest of all to get a feeling for it when you are doing the opening statement. You're tense and working very hard. You don't yet feel the jury. You don't yet have your special jurors—the ones who are always paying attention, the ones that smile at you, that nod and give you the feedback. Later on, you get your energy charge from that. But right from the start, keeping your energy level high—which includes how fast and loud you talk, how involved you get in telling your story, how active and engaging you are—helps keep the jury's interest and energy up.

You need to give them much of your commitment, your drive and desire to get them involved. It's your case and so far, they're uninformed spectators with no idea of how this will come out, if they even care. But, starting with your opening statement, see if you can hear yourself, see if you can distance yourself enough from what you are saying to discover whether your energy is now going, down, down, down, or whether you have a tendency to be rather monotonous and project yourself on a single level. Find where you want to vary your energy level, based on what you're saying, what's soft and low, what's high key, where you change gears and why. Energy can be high and intense while you speak softly. It's all in your level of commitment to communicating to the jury.

Use of the Lectern

Close your eyes and imagine yourself sitting in any audience. On the stage there is a lectern and a speaker walks in with a sheaf of papers and plops them down, adjusts the microphone, clears his throat and begins. What are the images that come to your mind? You are bored before he begins. The conditioning about a lectern or podium can be a major pitfall in presenting your case. The jury conjures up a great number of associations from their past experiences of people who have stood at lecterns with long, fixed lectures. So, by itself, the lectern carries many negative images. Just think about who stands behind them? Preachers, teachers, tellers, righteous folk—someone who wants you to do what they say, to recognize that you're deficient and they will tell you how to fix it.

The lectern has another negative image: a shield with most of your body hidden behind it. (If you are short, you are lucky to get your nose seen above it.) It means, subliminally or subconsciously, that you are protecting yourself, that you are not as vulnerable as the jury or anybody else, because you have this shield. The shield says, "I am an expert. I am allowed in this special place. I cannot be touched. I will tell you what I want to tell you, when I want to tell you. I am protected."

Another disadvantage is that the lectern makes you stand still and, therefore, lowers your energy level. It makes you look serious, pompous, rigid and unfeeling. It becomes much more difficult to transcend to that place held by a leader, a helpful teacher, a guide, and a friend. Behind the lectern, you are a powerful person, formal, unavailable and hidden.

Therefore, it is important to use the lectern as little as possible, if you're allowed that discretion, and to use it dynamically even if you must stay there. If you're in a jurisdiction where you must use the lectern, put your notes on the lectern but stand to the side of it. Go back behind the lectern from time to time, to create contrast, to think or to look at notes. Go there to become more powerful and forceful, to look more factual and serious. Use the implied weight and objectivity of the lectern; it will do that for you.

Step out from behind the lectern whenever you wish to say something that is more personal, ruminative, thought-provoking, deeper, insightful or touching. Get out from behind the hidden shield and say, "I'm here, all of me. I'm trying so hard to get close to you, for us to have a meeting of the minds." If you must use the lectern, be creative with it, because it is such a hard image to transcend.

Movement in the Courtroom

As you know, jurisdictions in many parts of the country are vastly different; even in the same city, courtroom procedures differ. If you are allowed to move in the courtroom, it is one of the very best attention getters.

Remember that the jury sits in a passive state. They have no idea that the trial process takes so long. Perry Mason took only an hour. They think it should all be done by then, and be fun all the time. But remember, Perry Mason was not only edited, it was written to be 100 percent interesting and exciting every minute.

Wouldn't it be nice if your trial could be edited and only the good stuff handed to the jury? Since that won't happen, you must become their surrogate physical energizer. It is important for them to see you move around. They are always more interested and challenged when you move. The background behind you changes. Your movement gives them a feeling of energy, like the beginning of something new. But there are choices to make and consequences to think about. When do you come toward the jury? Where do you stand in the room? How much is too much movement? Are you secure enough to walk back to the lectern to see the next thing in your notes, and how should you approach that?

The jury gives you permission to do many things in the courtroom, if they are basically natural or familiar-looking. In other words, the movement must fit what you are talking about. Wanting to read your notes, walking over to read them, standing still while reading them and then walking away is all perfectly digestible. The jury understands that and it's fine. It would be difficult, however, for them to accept movement in which you arbitrarily walk during an emotional statement or walk towards the table and surreptitiously thumb through your notes while you are making a key point. They see that, and it makes them extremely uneasy. They are much happier if you straightforwardly, non-verbally indicate, "I need to see what is in my notes right now, and I need a minute to think." That's fine.

Many lawyers take time out by asking the judge's permission, "If I may, Your Honor, I'd just like to refresh (or collect) my thoughts," as they go to their notes. The jury accepts that pause if you don't look uncomfortable; if you look as though you are in such charge of things that you can give yourself a little recess, without being nervous, and then pick it up again. They admire that. They hate the nervousness you betray by trying to hide the fact that you are groping for the next thought.

So movement must be consistent, but it must also be eloquent. The jury sees everything you do, and if you are uncomfortable, pacing from sheer nervousness, they know it. Therefore, be aware. Use movement, but use it with judgment.

Spatial Relationships

There is another key issue in how the jury sees the trial and the lawyer. This influences the prejudices they can develop about the lawyer in relation to the witness, the case and to themselves.

It is the issue of space and spatial relationships in the courtroom.

The jury has a keen sense of territory and you need to earn their permission to invade their space. If you are an informal, hale and hearty, friendly person, you would probably instinctively get a little closer to the jury because that is how you feel about people and the style that you would use for your presentations. If that's not you, I would stay back from them and allow them their territory. Give them your respect for their territory, for their own space, and also give them a chance to see you. In either case, work your way up toward greater intimacy and the jury's "space invasion" slowly, just as you would in real life.

In considering spatial relationships, you should look at the courtroom in which you practice. You should try to decide what are the best sight lines. Where should you stand in the room in order to be seen best? Is there glare from the windows? How does it vary at different times of the day? (This might make it hard for the jury to watch you without falling asleep if the glare hurts their eyes.)

Where are the places that they will see you but will not see much activity behind you? Locate the doors where the bailiff goes in and out or people arrive and disappear and avoid these. Find places in the courtroom that allow attention to remain on you. Stand over to the side for a while and cause the jury to turn their heads to you. This allows them some movement and demands some energy from them. Then, for variety, you can move back into the center again.

Spatial relationships should be in tune with what you are saying: closer for closer feelings, farther off for objectivity or conceptualizing. Go to another place when that part of your statement calls for it. Integrate and choreograph where you stand, how near or far, based on what you are saying.

Because the center of your space before the jury is the most important place, save it for your really key points. Take the center ground at the beginning. Take it at the end. And there are several times in the middle where you might want to recap what you were just talking about by moving to the center. During your presentation, use the more oblique, angled areas in front of the jury for ruminating and considering. Physically write on this "stage" which is laid out before them. Think through and place the first part of your statement, the second part and the third part. Go to three different places that put you in a new relationship to the jury and your material each time. It becomes logical, then, to go back to them every time you want to refer to that point to reinforce it. Use space as an artist arranges his canvas—and use the light and color in the room to enhance your presentation.

Walking and Talking

One of the greatest ploys for covering a moment in which you want to get your thoughts together is to walk from one place to the other. It looks very learned and purposeful. It also re-energizes you. It clears your thinking because your whole body is activated and "charges" your head.

When delivering the opening statement, it is important for you to always speak in paragraphs and for the jury to know when each section is over. One of the best ways for them to see a conclusion is to change your position as you say, "Now let me talk about another aspect of the trial." As you say that, you walk away, taking some new ground, and are now in a different place. It is a visual signal to change from one subject to another, and the jury remembers it better. You are helping them organize your material visually, not only verbally, as you speak in outline form.

Movement can also color what you're talking about. Suppose you're standing far away, and now you want to finish up with your final paragraph. How about walking forward toward the jury, saying, "So, ladies and gentlemen, this will be a hard trial. Very much is asked of you, much is asked of me, and I hope . . ." As you walk forward, there is a great sense of sincerity. Walking toward the jury—getting closer—implies a more personal, intimate approach. Use it only when it applies. The motivation and the appropriateness must be apparent before it's acceptable. Be sure to stop and stand still to deliver important lines or thoughts.

Of course, there can be too much of a good thing. Beware of extraneous walking or pacing and too much movement. It gets very distracting and irritating after a while. Only move when it will further explain or enhance what you're talking about or as a vent for your energy. And don't forget: the other half of walking is when and where you stop. That's powerful and very noticeable. Use it. For fuller information (see Chapter 9—Non-Verbal Communication and for ways to develop skills, see Chapter 10.)

SPEAKING AND LANGUAGE SKILLS

Given all the other aspects of how you will communicate to the jury, oral presentation is still the major form by which you will reach them and deliver your message. The skills you develop should deal not only with how you present this and the techniques for making your delivery interesting, but should also deal with your choice of language and an understanding of what words can do.

Making Language Clear

Language means instant understanding if it is used well, and if it uses terms that are acceptable and comfortable for everyone. Words are exact. While movement and other forms of non-verbal communication can embellish words but leave them open to individual interpretation, words will state facts and concepts exactly, and we all instantly understand the same meaning.

Once we know a language, we expect its words to be factual and clear to us, making an instant image which is shared by everybody. We depend on them to be easily processed, moving us along in our comprehension. We don't expect to get stuck and are challenged and concerned if we don't understand. The major problem with language in the courtroom is that lawyers have become so ac-

customed to the legal shorthand learned in law school that they
have forgotten the language everyone else speaks. It is simpler,
from force of habit, for you to use those shortcuts. The trial puts
you in that frame of mind and you often forget that juries don't understand. But it's a serious matter and needs attention.

The problem is to find a common denominator vocabulary
that everyone can understand. You will probably recognize the
most blatant and obvious law words, those fancy Latin ones, as
legalese and will try to translate them for the audience, if you are
alert to the importance of doing this. But let me warn you: There
are a great number of other words that are also not clear to the
jury, sophisticated words *you* might use but which are not in the
average vocabulary.

Here are some examples of unfamiliar and misunderstood
words.*

prior	prudence/prudent	infer
subsequent	insinuate	diffuse
relevant	extrapolate	pursuant
relative	interpolate	antedate
magnitude	proximate	divisive
erroneous	stipulate	malleable
foreseen	salient	anachronistic
credibility	demise	rotund
deem	facetious	blatant
submit	decelerate	dichotomy
impute	epitome	censure
thereon	indolence	complacent
thereupon	variables	conjecture
thereby	acquiesce	

*All of the following lists and examples come from from an excellent study
by Robert F. Erhard and Veda R. Charrow "Making Legal Language Understand-
able: A Psycholinguistic Study of Jury Instructions": published in the Columbia
Law Review, Volume 79, No. 7 (November 1979) and from "A Workbook in Legal
Writing" created by Charrow and Erhard of the Document Design Center of the
American Institutes for Research in the Behavioral Sciences, Washington, D. C..
They also appear in "Effective Writing for Law Students" by Charrow and Erhard
published by Little, Brown and Company.

Overstatement

In an effort to be extremely clear and persuasive, speakers are sometimes given to overstatement and redundancy, which often sound pompous or verbose. Temptation to overstate develops habits of using two words when one will do:

personal opinion
next subsequent
honest opinion
positive benefits
each and every
any and all
aid and abet
full and complete
final and conclusive
absolutely and completely

How To Simplify

To further simplify language, consider the following words and phrases you can change by using less complex synonyms in more common usage:

Difficult	*Simple*
accord	give
adequate amount	enough
administer	manage
afford	give
aggregate	total
allocate	give or divide
applicable	that applies
as to	about, relating to
assist	help
attain	reach
attributable to	from, by

Difficult	*Simple*
be required to	have to
by reason of	because of
cease	stop
commence	begin
consequence	result
constitute	make up
deem	consider
effectuate	carry out
exclusively	only
expiration	end
for the duration of	during
for the purpose of	to, for
for the reason that	because
furnish	give (provide)
give, devise, and bequeath	give
has the option of	may
heretofore	until now
indicate	show
implement	carry out
in excess of	more than
initiate	begin
in lieu of	instead of
inquire	ask
institute	begin
in the event that	if
issue	give
I submit	I suggest
maintain	keep, continue
necessitate	require
obtain	get
omit	leave out
on behalf of	for

Difficult	*Simple*
on or before	by
on the part of	by
originate	start
per annum	a year
portion	part
preserve	keep
prior to	before
proceed	go, go ahead
procure	get
promulgate	issue
provided that	however if
pursuant to	under
retain	keep
render	make, give
represents	is
request	ask, ask for
shall	must, may, or will
solely	only, alone
sufficient	enough
submit	send, give
subsequent to	after
said, same, such	the, this, that
terminate	end, finish
to the extent that	if, when
utilize	use
with regard to/respect to	for

Unclear Legal Terms

There are many legal words whose concepts are misunderstood even though some of these words are in common usage. They do not stand alone and require explanation and amplification to be useful symbols for the jury:

beyond a reasonable doubt
preponderance of the evidence
contributory negligence
burden of proof
scope of employment
proximate cause
stipulate
evidence
punitive damages
recovery of damages
I submit
hearsay

An example of how to make a legal concept simpler:

There is a type of negligence that involves the behavior of the plaintiff, rather than the defendant. It is called "contributory negligence." If a plaintiff is negligent, and his negligence helps his own
injury, we say the plaintiff is contributorily negligent. A plaintiff
who is contributorily negligent cannot recover money for his
injuries.

Become sensitive to your own speech patterns. Edit your
word choices, scrutinizing whether they are readily understood
and the best choices to carry your message.

By using words that are instantly identifiable for the jury, you
are also showing your desire to make them understand, as well as
your essentially common background with them.

Show Examples of Facts

Words of exact measurement, like square feet, yards, inches,
pounds are totally inexact in the jury's mind. None of us has a clear
sense of distances and sizes and confusion reigns as each juror conjures up his or her own version of what you mean. In order to make
such references instantly clear and precise to all, when you know
you will refer to such measurements, go to the courtroom and
measure out the distances or spaces that correspond to your de-

sired description. Then, when you refer to them, you can pace off or refer to those tangible, visible areas right in the courtroom to give the jury a precise picture of what you mean. "It's twenty-four feet away, ladies and gentlemen—as far as from this table to the back of the room." Or else bring an object to show exact size. "It was only six inches long—as long as this pencil."

Technical or Legal Language

Use words that are explicit and clear, but not technical. When you use technical words, "lawyer words," or words that are outside of common usage, you not only lose your own credibility and a kind of warmth and togetherness, but you also lose the jury's attention. When you use a word that's not clear to the jury, the next ten words go unheard. They stop listening at the unintelligible word and start thinking about it, trying to figure it out, imagining how it's spelled and what it might mean. While they're ruminating, they're not listening to you. Then, when they plug in again and try to follow your ideas they're even more at sea, and that may finish their comprehension or interest. Be aware of a laymen's understanding and always have synonyms or explanations ready.

Colloquialisms

The use of colloquialisms in the opening statement is a good way to get the jury to feel that you are one of them and you will be easy to understand. It's a relaxed, unstarched way of talking that translates from real life. But only do this if you're that kind of person. Don't get folksy if it's not natural.

Any time you can use language that makes the jury recognize you as one of them, that makes them hear things that are familiar in another context or that simplifies an idea or fact, the jury will be much more comfortable and receptive.

Rhythm and Phrasing

Since you have to rely so much on talking, in the opening statement you need to create as much nuance and interest in your speech as possible. Therefore, notice what kind of cadence you speak in.

Do you speak in rapid bursts? Do you speak in short, choppy phrases that interrupt the flow of your sentence? Is there a rhythm in your speech that sounds singsong and becomes predictable? Do you speak in the same size sentences all the time, sentences that become lulling and mesmerizing, an invitation to sleep?

Your speech rhythm can have great value in pointing up, emphasizing, underlining and making exciting any aspect of what you are saying. If you start out slowly, figuratively with a walk down the road, and then take the jury by the arm and begin to walk more rapidly, and then begin to jog and then suddenly stop dead and say, "Look!" they will remember that "Look!" much more than if you were to just walk them through the story and then, casually, as you keep walking, point to the sign and say, "Look."

Phrasing, making groups of words go together, is also vital. Make an effort to find phrases that become memorable and can get lifted out of your statement and used again. Whether a phrase is humorous, or has a surprise combination of words, whether it's eloquent, pictorial or alliterative, you would be surprised how much of it the jury will remember. They will begin quoting it and using it to describe a particular issue, just as you did.

If you can characterize an act, a person or an event in a phrase, that phrase is something you can refer back to several times, and the jury will be pleased as they remember and recognize it. It becomes a neat, finite package that you and they can pull out from the general morass of words to refer to something specific in your joint, newly-found shorthand.

Take, for example, an opening statement in the case of an accidental death. What if you make a little litany, a little phrase, that you create and repeat:

> He drove down the road . . . and he never saw her.
> He stopped at the red light . . . and he never saw her.
> He started his motor, and turned into the street . . . and he never saw her.
> And even when he hit her . . . he never saw her.

Can't you feel how arresting, how effective that is? See how much more powerful the statement becomes each time you come back to that same phrase. This demonstrates another use of rhythm—repetition.

Repetition is reassuring because the jury not only can grasp it, but they also recognize the rest of the sentence as they listen. They become more and more familiar with it. It becomes theirs, they can say it with you, internally, knowing they can predict what's coming. Setting up a rhythm with the repetition of a phrase, a word or the length of a sentence that is heard again and again is one of the most memorable and hypnotic things you can do, with words. Not only is it compelling but it also develops and confirms a point of view—your point of view.

How to Use Silence

The opposite of rhythm and phrasing is knowing when to stop. Speakers often have a problem with that. They're afraid that stopping might look like they forgot what to say next.

Since television delivers such a seamless message, we all fear "dead air." Also, most people who deliver oral messages are so highly charged that it's hard to shift gears, let alone come to a complete halt. It's difficult for speakers to realize that, as eloquent as all of their great words are, silence is equally, and often more, eloquent. Eloquent because it not only gives the audience a chance to stop and think, it compels them to do it.

When you are busy delivering a message, the jury is busy absorbing it, as much of it as they can get, and you're both moving at quite a pace. It is therefore invaluable for them to have a pause in which to consider what just took place. Not only for the relief of not hearing a voice, but also for a chance to ruminate, to think, to put together and savor what just happened. To consider and evaluate what they think of this or that idea. It is vital for the lawyer, then, to know when to stop.

Whenever you deliver an eloquent statement, a challenging statement, a shocking statement—stop. It makes the jury know that what you just said was important, simply because you stopped. It makes them know that they should be thinking about this now, simply because you're giving them the time to think. You're leading them to ruminate on it. It also makes a space between what has just gone before and what comes next, so they know *that* was important, and they will remember it before they turn their attention to the next subject.

Silence used in connection with rhetorical questions is another wonderful teaching device. Just say, "How did it happen?" or "What could he do? What would occur to anyone on that night if they were standing on that street corner?" and then stop. Let them answer silently. You have engaged the jury with your question. The seconds you wait will not only let them come up with an answer in their minds, but will tantalize them as they wait for *your* answer. Since the essence of a rhetorical question is that you will tell them what you mean, silence engages and promises. You become both an instigator to action and a savant.

Use of the Voice

It is important for you to listen to your own voice and consider it an instrument you can play. It is the message carrier. It is what becomes eloquent when used well, or difficult to listen to when used poorly.

There's only one person on earth who hears your voice like you do and that's you, since you're the only one who hears your voice inside your head. Everyone else hears it when it has left your vocal chords and has gone into the air and the outside world. Therefore, it's hard to be objective. but there are some basic principles to follow.

Make it Audible

Be sure your voice is loud enough. Be sure you can be heard. Look at the wall behind the jury and make your voice hit that wall. When you stand in the courtroom, that wall will become an imperative, a tangible thing for you to throw your voice against. That image can make your voice loud enough to be heard by the people in front of it.

Breathe

One of the most common things that people do wrong with their voice is that they "sit" on their vocal chords and don't let them vibrate. We are supposed to breathe in and then speak on the air as we breathe out. The vocal chords vibrate on that air and your voice is its fullest and richest then. Yet many people speak after the breath is gone. Your vocal chords rub against each other, which can make your voice sound hoarse and tired, or raspy and harsh. While it may be hard for you to learn new breath control, think of it in terms of breathing when you change a thought. If you breathe in with a new idea, it will help you to send that idea out on air and feel it as you exhale, which is what makes the vocal chords vibrate naturally as you talk.

Nuance and Feeling

Nuance in the voice is very important. You can enlarge your voice to make it forceful and compelling, then soften it to something that's intimate and more personal. Depending on what it is you're talking about, you can sound insincere if you talk about sad or touching things and use exactly the same tone you did when you described the number of computer errors you found. Be careful to make your voice reflect what you're saying.

One way to do that is to visualize what you are talking about. Imagine the scene you are actually describing. Imagine that story as if it is happening. Imagine the person you are talking about. Imagine those numbers in the cash book and the shock of opening the book and discovering that there was an embezzlement. Imagine the accident, the victim. Imagining the scene helps create color and nuance in your voice; it gives you the stimulus to vary and alter the pitch and tone almost subconsciously; and it makes you much more interesting.

Pitch and Tone

Pitch is something you want to think about. Many people's voices are pitched a little too high. Women, especially, worry about this. It is easier to listen to a lower voice, and it is worth some effort to develop this. A lower pitch sounds more credible and important. It is something that you might strive for, since it makes easier listening for the long haul of the trial.

I don't often recommend voice lessons because it can take a long time to make changes. However, if you are aware of a difficult problem, such as a nasal twang, a rasping voice, a flat monotone or a voice pitch that is difficult to listen to or understand, you might feel self-conscious and you should seek professional, individual help. Generally speaking, however, there are some exercises you can do with your voice to help yourself find out what the jury finally hears. (See Chapter 10 for exercises to improve voice production and interest.)

*   *   *

In opening statement, you are in total control of what is said and how you say it. You have infinite choices. Opening statement is an untrammeled time when you can address the jury and reach them, affect them, set up a relationship with them directly. How you do this has much to do with the way they will feel about you for the rest of the trial and how strongly they will believe your half of the case.

Remember the jury's needs. Every time you get up to address the jury, run through how they feel. Be clear about what they need to know and give it to them.

Clarify your role and be sure the jury always understands what you're doing and why. Give them the information they need clearly and succinctly to follow the trial knowledgeably and attentively. Remember that they identify with the witnesses, and it is your job to see that you give them some way to identify with you. And most of all, remember the stereotypes they bring into the courtroom and that every time you get up you must transcend them.

You can plan your case brilliantly, with much time and care and previous research and deep understanding of what the theory of the case is, but in the final analysis, the way the jury will judge the case has a great deal to do with how they feel about you and what you tell them. It is, in essence, a visceral and emotional response to a cerebral, orderly, sometimes technical process. And that dichotomy is the challenge: for you to cross the legal canyon to be a person to them as well as a lawyer. Opening statement is the first and best chance you have to do that.

4

DIRECT EXAMINATION

"Will you state your name for the record?"

This line usually begins the direct examination. You can imagine the rest of the process: witness in chair; lawyer behind podium or counsel table, near jury box or standing clear; court reporter typing; judge writing; jury listening.

Ideally, the story of your witness' case unfolds smoothly; the jury understands, recognizing what's important to remember and ends up liking and believing your witness and you.

That would be true if everyone followed your script.

What really happens much more often? The witness rambles; the pace of the story is sloppy; the lawyer interrupts, backs up, and fills in or carefully and imperceptibly nudges the witness. The opposing lawyer leaps to his feet and interrupts with objections. The jury gets bored, confused, doesn't follow and won't remember.

Wouldn't it be great if, instead of conducting a direct examination, *you* could do it alone? If you could stand up, look the jury in the eye, and say, "Let me tell you exactly what happened"? Then, in a careful, orderly, interesting, dramatic, succinct fashion, you would proceed to do just that. They'd listen, understand and be persuaded in no time.

The fact that a lay person is given the responsibility means that the bulk of the trial is conducted through novice, untested narrators. Not only are they unskilled, they can't even tell their story

177

naturally. They may only speak when you, the lawyer, wind them up with a question. This stilted technique for giving the jury information adds a number of problems to the jury's perception and understanding of the major information in a trial.

In order to understand these problems, to discover what else is going on during a direct examination and to help you include these additional factors in your preparation and performance, let's look first at some basic issues facing the lay witness, the lawyer and the jury as they enter direct examination. (See Chapter 6 for a discussion of expert witnesses.)

ISSUES AND INSIGHTS

The Witness

Before a witness was a witness, he or she was just a person. Therefore, some insight into the basic human condition and what happens to it as one becomes a witness is of great value.

Everybody has had fantasies of "knocking them dead at the Palace." We've all seen those remarkable performers who can take an audience, put them in their pocket and strut off stage, straw hat fluttering in air.

A witness is thrust into the spotlight just as a performer is, and sees himself and his role in the direct examination in just that way. He has an image of how smooth and terrific he's supposed to be when giving a performance, how much poise he would like to have, how dignified he'd like to appear when speaking seriously of serious matters. The problem is that very few people *are* good performers and very few people have ever had much experience as performers. Even if they've tried it, they've probably been uncomfortable, nervous and embarrassed as they portrayed the third angel from the left or even stood up to recite in class, all eyes on them.

Witnesses' concern about how they will appear, especially in this ritual environment, often overwhelms what they will say. A number of such concerns, together with the risk of losing the case, causes what they're talking about to be affected by a subconscious stream of thought that starts as they prepare for trial and continues to run in the courtroom, at the same time they're listening to your questions and trying to respond. Here's what some of their subconscious fears are:

"I'm Afraid I'll Forget the Way We Talked About It in Your Office"

Witnesses know that the sequence, as well as the individual facts, are very important; therefore, their anxiety level is very high, because they are not accustomed to doing this and to retaining so much information in order and without notes.

"I'm Worried About the Consequences of Making a Mistake and Being Unable to Take It Back"

They know a mistake will make them look bad. They keep worrying about whether things are happening the way they were originally planned. They can't stop and ask you, either. Witnesses develop preconceived ideas of how their testimony should be fashioned by your preparation of them, and they're trying to measure up to that image.

"I'm Performing Before a Jury Who's Evaluating and Judging Me. Will I Get Everybody to Believe Me?"

They know that there must be clever techniques to convince people and that they don't know them. Their sense of watching the jurors out of the corner of their eye to see if they're being persuaded, and imagining how they're receiving the testimony, adds to their anxiety and detracts from their giving full attention to delivering the answers. Also, people often respond to questioning by looking, and even feeling, guilty. Anxiety doesn't help.

"What Impression Will I Make On People Who Have Nothing Else to Do But Scrutinize and Listen Only to Me? Will They Like Me?"

From early adolescence all of us worry about the impressions we make. We rarely give ourselves the benefit of the doubt, either. We all seem to carry with us forever that list of "unacceptables": nose—too long; body—too fat; voice—too high; hair—too thin; complexion—the pits, and so on.

Sitting in the spotlight, the witness knows that the jury will notice how he sits, how he looks, what he's wearing, whether he fidgets and how well he speaks. Not only are they rating him in very vulnerable areas, they're tapping into that universal basic insecurity: "Am I likeable? Do you like me?"

"What if I Have to Go to the Bathroom? What if I Need Some Water? What if I Sneeze and Need a Handkerchief?"

How normal human events are handled in a place of ritualized behavior is another cause for concern. The old reliance on instinct or past experience doesn't work in a courtroom. This raises the anxiety level both about the "right way" to do things here and about what effect the "wrong way" will have on the watchers.

"I Hope My Lawyer Thinks I'm Doing It All Right"

In direct examination, witnesses also feel that they are being evaluated by the lawyer who has prepared them. All people set up authorities they allow to write on their "report cards" in life. "Will I measure up to what my lawyer has carefully rehearsed and planned with me? Will he approve? Did I pass the test?"

"It's Up To Me"

Witnesses also know that it's up to them. Lawyers transfer their own anxieties to the witness as they emphasize how important it is to remember the format and the caveats they give him. The witness feels responsible but incapable in such a strange setting, doing such an unusual thing.

"The Cross-Examination is Coming"

Witnesses have a nervous anticipation of what the cross examination will be like. They know it's coming. The sword of Damocles hangs over their heads. Each word they utter is something they know could also be used against them.

If the witness is the defendant or plaintiff, there's a major consequence here: the great risk of personally losing. For all witnesses, there's the fear of loss of face and the concern about doing things badly. They've seen as much Perry Mason as everybody else has, and they're wondering what kinds of clever thrusts and parries the opposing lawyer will leap out of his box with. How will they counter this attack, since they may be digging their own graves with the responses they have already made?

"Will I Be Tough Enough for the Cross Examination? Can I Stand Up To It? Will I Remember? Can I Really Stand by My Story?"

People try to avoid adversity and conflict. Everyone knows that every fight has a loser. Everyone hates to lose—especially in front of an audience. Witnesses worry about a strong professional, the cross-examining lawyer, as an opponent in the ring. They worry about how emotional they may get: can they handle their own anger—or his? They're very concerned about getting into a duel with a skilled, experienced adversary. What does it take to win this verbal battle of wits?

"What Does the Judge Think?
Does He Believe Me? Does He
Approve?"

The ultimate judge/parent sits wrapped in the flag, hand on
the Bible, overseeing the witness, expecting purity and goodness
and all the attributes we are taught to attain in the best of all possible worlds. This is an atavistic set of anxieties—in a sense, the basic
and ultimate test. The witness feels a deeper, hidden pressure,
that his past behavior and present performance are being judged
by the elders, by people in authority, not only by his peers. The
law, the state, the government is testing him. And way back, in the
back of his mind, the witness probably hears some old tapes of his
parents' judgment as well.

"This Is It. This Counts"

The witness is keenly aware of the seriousness of the trial and
of what's at stake. This anxiety makes it more difficult for him to
keep straight something that was really very simple. Now, suddenly, with all these other factors playing in his mind, what
seemed so clear in the lawyer's office becomes extremely complex.
As the witness sees it, he has only one chance to tell his story which
will become part of the record and he may not do it very well. And
further, a life, a fortune, or a good name rests upon the outcome of
his testimony.

The Jury

Jurors take their job very seriously. For almost all of them, it's one
of the most memorable moments of their lives. They want to do it
well and judge fairly and wisely. Since most of the information
comes to them through testimony given by witnesses, but ex-
tracted through questioning by lawyers, how they perceive the
questioning process, as well as the players, must be examined.

As a group, the jury basically sees the act of questioning as, at
least, manipulative, if not downright aggressive. They have already
experienced it themselves, not only in the voir dire but in their
own lives. They know how impotent they felt being questioned

about a job or a traffic ticket. Therefore, they have great empathy for any person who sits in the witness box, all alone, next to the judge's bench, beneath the star-spangled banner and the seal and flag of the state, being interrogated and forced to reply. And, along with that heavy responsibility, they recognize that there, but for the grace of God, go they. This witness is only a lay person, just like themselves, asked to do a very hard job.

"What Kind of a Person is the Witness? How Do I Decide?"

How does a juror evaluate what he hears and sees? Basically, he uses the same gut feeling everyone does when meeting someone at a party or talking to a salesman. He listens to an inner voice ask, "How does this person strike me?" He senses, "He's too pushy; she's too talkative (aggressive, stiff, or self-conscious)." He responds viscerally, not logically, and hopes his instincts are right. But since he's done it that way forever, he trusts them over his mind.

"Can I Really Be Objective? I Know I'm Supposed to Listen to All the Testimony Fairly. But What if I Like This Witness Better Than That One? How Do I Stay Open-Minded?"

Everyone lives with a series of stereotypes and prejudices. It's hard for anyone to suddenly abandon his preconceived notions about ethnic groups social status, kinds of work and eduational levels, and sit with a clean slate as he gathers impressions and makes judgments about the testimony. Jurors know this and worry about it, since they're trying very hard to be impartial and fair.

"How Do I Feel about the Questioner?"

How the lawyer handles the witness tells jurors what kind of person the lawyer is. What is your approach to the witness and, indirectly, to the jurors, who identify with the witness? The jury now has an opportunity to judge some of the lawyer's background and morality. Did your parents teach you to be polite? Are you a respectful, sensitive person? Do you seem gentle by nature? Or are you cold, hard and formal? Do you look at and notice the witness? Are you making him comfortable? Do you have a sense of humor? Are you easy to talk to, accessible and agreeable? Are your questions clear and human or stiff and lawyerly?

All of these qualities come through as jurors watch the lawyer in this aggressive and telling process. The spotlight is focused squarely on *both* the lawyer and the witness. The jury's response to the testimony they hear is filtered through their judgment about the questioner.

"How Would I Feel Being Up There?"

The witness' anxiety is transmitted to the jury. They become uncomfortable, since they recognize and empathize with human feelings and empathize with the witness's nervousness, self-consciousness, stage fright and feeling of being in the spotlight. It's something that doesn't happen very much to them, either, so their anxiety rises in direct proportion to what they sense is present in the witness. When they see this, their attention span and ability to listen to facts and details fall sharply. They become much more involved with thinking, "This poor guy, I hope they get him off the stand soon. I can't stand it." They become much less involved in, "So then what happened, and why?"

"I Feel a Little Suspicious about What the Witness Says"

Since jurors feel that the examination process can be a manipulative tool used by the questioner (the lawyer), many of the answers can be suspect. In the back of their minds lurks the thought, "Maybe the witness is just saying that because he feels pressured." Maybe the lawyer told him what to say. Maybe the lawyer (you know how lawyers are) is getting him to say these things so cleverly that with a little flim-flam; the facts *seem* to add up, (but they may not, really)."

"This Could Be Boring and Hard to Follow"

People's attention spans are shorter now than ever. Also, they are preconditioned to the fact that oral presentations are notoriously dull. Just sitting and listening reminds them of school—not a great experience for many people, unfortunately. Also, lay people don't usually speak in an organized fashion. Most people are just not good story tellers. If you remember back to your Uncle Jake and your Aunt Fanny and how difficult it was to listen to some of their endless, rambling tales about what happened to them on their last vacation or the family's Christmas, you will recognize that it is a human failing. Most people don't think in dramatic terms, in headlines, in paragraphs. They just speak as events occur to them.

It's very hard for the jury to gather information through oral presentation only and make sense of what's important and unimportant, especially from someone who does not, on his own, underline, make dramatic pauses, emphasize or recap. The jury knows this and worries not only about being bored and irritated, but about not paying attention and missing important information.

"I Can't Really Understand the Witness"

Oral presentation is a learned skill. Most people speak poorly and witnesses are surely no exception. Many witnesses speak inaudibly, too slowly or too fast. How hard it is, then, for the jury to sustain concentration on the main issues you're trying to bring out.

Witnesses can't be heard because they're not accustomed to projecting their voices. As they become more anxious about the answers, their subconscious tendency is to let the voice fall, to mumble, hopng they will sort of slide through, thinking, "Maybe only a few people will hear or notice this part; maybe it's okay." When they are very definite about what they mean, they speak up and speak clearly. The jury notices this and it colors their judgment and memory of the testimony.

"How Can I Remember What's Important?"

Another problem for the jury to resolve is that words and phrases are hard to sort out, to organize into facts, to arrange according to priorities and to remember when delivered orally, only once. That is part of what you're asking the jury to do—to accumulate facts, dates, times, directions, sizes, shapes, colors, events in sequence and to rank important versus unimportant, details versus headlines and memorable moments versus discursive background.

In the course of this examination as you get your witness to lay out the elements of your case, the jury must edit and underline. The amount of material, especially details, is a source of great concern for them. Will they be able to sort it out and remember it all?

"Of course, the Lawyer Will Make His Witness Look Good"

Juries expect you to try to sway them. The jury sits down expecting each lawyer to put the best face on his or her story. They expect you to slant questions and get answers that will only favor your witness and your case. Therefore, they're always a little suspicious of a direct examination. They know instinctively there's another side to the story. They subconsciously filter and question some of what is being said at the same time that you are eliciting what you think is a series of definitive statements. At the back of their minds they wonder, "What is he *not* asking?"

The Lawyer

As if the witness' fears and the jury's expectations were not enough to handle, what inherent problems face you, the lawyer, in the process of direct examination? What concerns affect your presentation and your ability to listen and improvise?

"What Will the Witness Do on the Stand?"

You have a very careful plan of what you will say in what order and for what purpose. However, the witness is essentially unpredictable and can't be counted on to follow it exactly. This creates tension and anxiety in you as the questioner, for, although you go in with the best of all possible intentions (nice orderly questions and good themes well laid out), you know from the begining that you're going to have to back up and fill in. You're going to have to deflect and build anew. You're going to have to recount, recap, find the thread again and carry it back in the right direction. All of these demands upon you make the natural flow of questions very difficult, because you have to keep listening, evaluating and critiquing as you go.

"I Mustn't Lose Control of the Testimony"

Witnesses are bound to ramble, get ahead of the story, get the facts out of order or forget. You want to control that. At the same time, you want to control what the cross-examiner can elicit from your witness. This need to control the witness and maneuver him down your path can be very damaging to you because the jury can see you doing it. Not only do they resent it, but if you are too manipulative, they will suspect both you and the testimony.

"I Have to Ask, Listen and Think"

It is very hard for any human being to listen to answers, while, at the same time, thinking ahead to the next question and thinking of the consequences of what has just taken place. Your need to constantly decide whether you have already gotten enough information out or whether you should continue to question on a point causes tension and distraction. It sometimes makes your performance look too tight, cold or unsure.

"I Already Know the Story and the Answers to Every Question"

It is very hard in direct examination, to affect genuine curiosity about each question and answer when you have been over it many times before. How difficult it is to ingenuously ask, "What is your name? Where do you live? What is your work?" When the jury and everybody else within earshot knows full well that you know the answers to all of these questions. Nonetheless, a kind of curiosity and interest must be sustained throughout the direct examination. It not only keeps the witness talking in a fresh and interesting manner, but keeps the jury involved.

"Direct Examination Is Not My Favorite Part of the Trial"

Direct examination is nurturing, nourishing, currying and supporting your witness, focusing the spotlight on him or her. Therefore, it often doesn't feel like much for a trial lawyer.It makes you much less visible. The role feels weaker and softer, not like the adversarial cross-examination. It's a much subtler form of communication than advocacy. Many lawyers really don't like the direct examination because they don't feel like they have done a great deal visibly.

It's a great challenge to be nurturing. It's selfless to set someone up so *they* look good, and to do it so adroitly and subtly that your role is not noticed or appreciated. It's the same role as parenting. It's helping a kid ride a two-wheeler or letting go so he can walk alone. The pleasure is vicarious. In direct, the witness is the star, the one who does all the telling. The lawyer stands aside cheering him or her on from the sidelines, and it's not in the nature of litigators to be the cheering section. They like being the quarterback.

*   *   *

So there you have it; a view of what everyone carries with him or her into the direct examination, the hidden scenarios being played while the external behavior looks like just another part of the trial.

Now that I have laid out many of the difficulties that get in the way of a witness, a juror and a lawyer, let me give you some techniques to circumvent some of these already existing problems.

DEVELOPING THE DIRECT EXAMINATION

There are two phases to your work in direct examination: What you do to prepare yourself and your witnesses in advance and what you do with them in the courtroom.

The pre-trial process with witnesses is a grace period in which you can move very far toward insuring a well-presented and executed examination with few surprises in the trial, resulting in a solid, intelligible story which is well-expressed and fully absorbed by the jurors. But it does require some additional insights and skills to reach the witness and to teach him or her.

During the examination itself, there are many questioning techniques that can help overcome both the witness' anxiety and the juror's skepticism or inattention. Here, too, we will perhaps cover some new ground and some new ideas. My intention is to deepen your understanding of what makes people listen and how they perceive what they hear, as well as stimulate you to enlarge your repertoire and add some new material to your own familiar trial techniques.

Preparing the Witness

The essence of good witness preparation is developing rapport and establishing a working relationship with your witness. You must make the witness understand what he or she is doing and how you'll work together. He needs to understand that testifying in court is a way to actively take the jury with him on a re-enactment of the particular events of the trial to help them understand the story. This would then include teaching him the most effective ways to tell his story, giving a thumbnail sketch of how juries feel and what they need, as well as explaining the basic format of a trial and where his testimony fits.

This background information is crucial if the witness is to become a willing, useful participant rather than a wind-up toy. It is step one in helping the witness overcome his anxieties by giving him purposeful action in concert with the lawyer, rather than infantilizing him into a passive role, making him submit to just being reassured, shaped and led by the lawyer.

This will go far toward making him a more interesting, energetic, thinking witness in court. You can help allay some of his fears by getting him actively and knowledgeably involved in working toward the jury rather than making you his only starter and energizer.

We all do better when we know where we're going, what we're doing and why. If you help your witness understand some of the concepts you know about how juries listen and what they need, the witness will feel more grounded in reality and will bring his best efforts to bear. He will be able to tap into his skills to try to reach some tangible goals. The more active he becomes, the less vulnerable he will feel and the more he will think with you and understand. You must include him.

Remembering how I described the witness' thoughts and anxieties, let's first set about dealing with them. How skillfully you do this can not only assure you of solving these problems, it can also draw your witness into a closer, more cooperative relationship with you.

Handling Stage Fright

The best way to handle fear is to identify it, state it and discover what it is and why it is there. The worst way is to say, "There's nothing to be afraid of, " "It's really easy," or "I'll be there—don't worry." When you do this, a witness' guilt and embarrassment about feeling inept are enlarged by your seeming unconcern and your trivializing of his anxiety. This separates him from you. It doesn't unify or help calm his fears.

Why not begin by explaining the essence of stage fright and that everyone, even you, has it? Stage fright comes from the fact that everyone carries in his mind the image of a "ten"; everyone thinks there is a perfect way to do a performance. Therefore, the witness' fright revolves around how far short of that perfect mark he assumes he will fall; how bad he will be, as opposed to the ephemeral creature who can do it "perfectly." So you need to start out by saying something like, "No one can present this perfectly because there isn't one right way or one right kind of person. There are many ways to do it, each equally effective. Probably no one can really do this job any better than you because *you* are an expert on what you know about yourself, about your life and about what happened in this case that you are asked to testify about."

Help the Witness Express What Scares Him Most

Ask the witness to tell you what he anticipates, what he imagines. How will he feel about sitting in the witness chair? What is he most worried about? You can then give him direct and explicit answers if you encourage him to tell you first. Create an environment in which such truth-telling is safe. We are all embarrassed to admit weakness, and we all avoid doing it. You must make a non-judgmental space available for him to be straight with you.

It might be helpful sometimes to take the witness to the courtroom. Show him what a courtroom looks like, give him a chance to see where the jury sits so that, on his own, he can begin to imagine himself in this setting, rather than walking in and being shocked by the dark wood, the judge's bench, seeing where everybody sits and how boxed in he might feel in the witness chair. It's reassuring to be tangible, to let him imagine and even mentally rehearse the reality of testifying. It encourages him and helps him to see what the environment will be, and it allays the fear of the unknown. Remember: A scared witness is an unthinking, unconvincing witness.

Make the Role Clear

Remember the jury's mind-set (See Chapter 1). Give your witness specific insights into jurors' needs and anxieties: their need to know, remember and understand; their anxiety about making a decision, about being fair and right; their dependence on the witness to tell them what happened.

Explain what the witness is doing for the jury when he answers your questions. Emphasize how important it is for him to keep thinking about the best, the clearest and the most interesting way to tell his story to the jury. Ask the witness to put himself in the jury's place—what would *he* want to hear and how would *he* feel. Explain the role of the witness as a clear and succinct source of information and how hard it is for the jury to remember and understand. Explain how you'll practice asking questions with him, getting all of the facts in order, so that the witness will learn to feel comfortable with this way of telling a story.

Explain the Organization of the Testimony

Tell what the categories are; show how you are going to go from the witness' personal history to a section dealing with the general background of the event, to a specific description of the event itself, and so on. Mention that you will do recaps about A, B and C if you need to and let him know what that process will be. Then lead the witness through the direct examination several times.

Show How You Will Keep Testimony Organized

Give support by telling the witness that you will help keep him organized. Explain that as you listen to his testimony, you can see what's missing or confusing. Describe how you will introduce each new subject or category to help keep him on track by saying, "Now let's turn to this subject." Show how you will move him to focus tighter on the details by asking more questions about an issue and that he needn't worry about telling everything in the first answer. Show how you will support his storytelling.

Handling Loss of Memory

Tell the witness you know he'll try to keep it all straight, but that sometimes people forget. "If you forget something, remember that I'm listening. I'll remember to ask you about it." That should help to allay a key fear.

"Your Honor, I Object"

Every time the opposing lawyer stands up and objects, it feels like a direct attack on the witness. He thinks, "I've obviously said something wrong, something that's out of line, something that's not supposed to be said." He doesn't really understand why the opposing lawyer is objecting. Feeling guilty and defensive, he thinks, "It's me. I've made a mistake. I don't know what the consequences are if the judge says *"Overruled'* or *'Sustained.'* Which direction should I go now? Was I doing it right or wrong? Is that a warning?"

The witness has no obvious options or instant answers to these questions. He only knows that there are many pitfalls in this battlefield. At any moment he may fall into any of them without knowing how to get out. Explain to your witness what objections are for, why opposing counsel makes them and how to feel about them. Show him how to handle the continuation of his testimony if the opposing counsel objects and what you will do. Show him how to wait in a relaxed manner while both of you argue it out.

Let the Witness Experience Your
Interrupting Him

Interruption implies that a witness is doing it wrong or isn't being responsive to the question. This is a jarring experience and leaves lingering worry. Therefore, go over it with him. Tell him why you are doing it—he might be talking too long, or off the subject. Show that interrupting lets you stop him and re-route the testimony and that it's helpful, not judgmental. Let him find out what it feels like so he doesn't feel insulted. Say something like, "Excuse me, John, there's a lot of information here. Let's take it apart and deal with one piece at a time. Let's begin with . . . "

Teach the Witness How to Speak
Loud Enough

This is a difficult concept. People speak at only one or two levels. Most people's experience is to speak in conversational tones to others who are fairly close to them or on the phone. The other level is shouting to someone far away or screaming in anger. That middle place of addressing a group, in a quiet room and at a fair distance, is almost unknown to them.

Show the kind of voice power a witness needs by suggesting he think of hitting the wall behind the jury with his voice. Tell him to put out enough energy to feel like he is hitting that wall or hitting behind you. That tells him about how loud is loud enough and makes the wall a visible reminder to hit and speak out. Practice what you'll say if he's not loud enough in court.

Get Them Used to Being Alone

Always practice with the witness in a chair quite isolated from anything else, as he will be in the courtroom.

Don't sit your witness next to your desk or a table. This gives a false sense of security and protection and will not help him prepare for his isolation in the courtroom.

Stand quite far away from him, with empty space between you. If you must stand behind the lectern, or sit at counsel table in your jurisdiction, practice that way with the witnesss, showing him how he will feel responding to you in such circumstances.

Teach Him to Talk to You, Not the Jury

The witness should look at the lawyer, because that's what most people expect. It's natural and recognizable. If you throw me a ball, I throw it back to you. The dialogue goes from you to the witness and back again. If you ask the witness a question and he turns to the jury to answer, it looks like a performance.

Don't Give General Instructions

Be careful not to say things like, "Talk faster," or "Don't talk so fast," or "Don't talk too long on this subject." These are vague generalizations that only cause anxiety. They are not really clear enough. How much is "faster"? What is "too long?"

Rather, be very specific and say, "Why don't you give it to me in small sections. First, tell me only about the size and shape of the room. Wait for me to ask you before you start describing the next part."

Clear, specific directions will make a witness begin to understand how to lean on you as the questioner, rather than hoping he is not talking too long and worrying about it. Being vague only raises the anxiety level. It doesn't give the witness any clear direction to follow. Take apart the sections you are going to talk about, describe these to the witness and show him how you are going to call for them. You will cut down on his garrulousness by reminding him that you will ask him to fill in if there's not enough information. You will also pick up on something that may be unclear and ask him to clarify. This will reassure him that he needn't try to tell too much.

Don't Over-Direct

Since a direct examination means that you really want your witness to talk, be careful not to give him too many negative directives. The witness may end up by giving you two-sentence answers and you will not be getting the kind of narrative that you really want.

Don't give him a list of do's and don'ts or cosmetic stylized techniques. He'll be afraid he'll forget, or that he can't do it without practice; this will only serve to make him more anxious.

Creative Criticism

Try to be positive. First tell the witness what he's doing *right*, before you tell him what's wrong. Remember criticism is meant to be *creative*, to fix something. Be sure to give the better way, and reasons why, rather than a dictum. The witness can fix it if he can understand and if you make him feel your faith in him that he *can* understand and do it differently.

Teach Self-Editing

Tell the witness to tell less. Explain that people lose interest if you tell too much that's unfamiliar. They can't follow. Remind him that you'll decide, that you'll ask him for more if you need it. Teach him to listen hard to your questions and really try to answer what you asked, not to tell all he knows at once. Explain that the jury knows nothing about the story and is basically not interested in knowing too much. The witness needs to orient them first, to give them the overview. Then you will move him into the specifics and then go into detail. Suggest he tell the process, not the details, until you ask for them.

Teach the Use of Demonstrative Evidence

Get the witness familiar with the exhibits and demonstrate how you will use them. Get him used to getting out of the chair and going to the chart or other exhibit. Show him what diagrams he will participate in and the clearest way to do this. (For more on witnesses using visual aids, see Chapter 6 on expert witnesses and Chapter 8 on visual aids.)

If Your Witness is Unusual

Suppose your witness is handicapped, old, hard to understand or very different from most people. Juries will notice. It may affect how they hear the testimony. You need to decide how this issue can affect the trial and then discuss what, if anything, you plan to do to get everyone past it.

It's best to enlist the help and suggestions of your witness. (For example, how to deal with getting the witness to the witness box if he's blind or how you'll communicate with a deaf witness and how to explain that to the jury.) Explain why you want to get it out in the open—that sometimes people assume one handicap means the person is perhaps incompetent in other areas. Handicapped people have lived with the knowledge of this stereotype for a long time and will know just what you mean. A handicap, being fairly unusual, also gets jury attention unless you can be open about it and help the jury get used to it and set it aside.

Make a plan to deal wit this problem head on, and enlist the witness' ideas. Make clear what your goals are: to show the witness' ability to handle the handicap completely and how he will do it in court, and to show his competence and self-sufficiency in order to lay these prejudices to rest. (For further suggestions, see the section on techniques for handling unusual witnesses on the stand, page 217.)

Videotape and Replay

Helping prepare the witnesses by videotaping them and then letting them see themselves is an excellent way to instruct. It encourages them because they will discover that they don't look nearly as bad or as nervous as they thought they did. They will get over the initial shock of hearing themselves questioned and then hearing themselves talk. It can help show that they need to speak up or they need to have more energy. It's a much more effective way to help them than for you to simply tell them, "Speak up. Be more forceful. Be more direct here." Letting them see for themselves removes you from a negative role and makes them feel less manipulated and criticized. It gives them more of a sense of participation. With the use of a videotape replay and your objective insights as you both watch, they can fix some of the things they themselves see as not being effective ways to tell their story.

Be prepared for the fact that people are initially shocked at what they look like. Help them get past this by telling them that television adds at least 10 pounds to everyone (it does!) and they're really much more attractive and so on. Otherwise, they'll never get past it to hear what you want to tell them.

*   *   *

To conclude: Witnesses are deeply concerned about the actual examination and what will happen as you begin to work with them. Be sensitive to this, and be aware of the fact that men, particularly, have trouble admitting fear and letting someone, epecially another man, tell them what to do and how to behave. Their response to women lawyers is easier—not so threatened and defensive—but there may sometimes be a stereotypical credibility gap with regard to a woman in authority. In either case, ignoring how they feel will not help you prepare them.

Get to know your witness. Working through some of these conditioned attitudes and anxieties can draw him closer to you, make him much more cooperative and aware and make the two of you a much more effective team in the courtroom.

THE EXAMINATION IN COURT

This is the big moment. The time to put all your plans into practice, to create the stuff, the fabric of your trial.

Since first impressions are so important, I've divided this section into "Beginnings," which deals with getting started and the options and pitfalls you encounter there, and "Questioning Techniques," which will take you through the rest of the examination. Before I do that, let's get into the right frame of mind by reading this first hand-account from a juror about her perceptions of witness examination.*

> Listening to testimony being drawn out of witnesses is not so clear-cut as I had imagined it to be. I guess I had thought from what I had seen in the movies, that a lawyer zeroed in on one point, and when the witness finally shouted 'Yes' or 'No,' then the lawyer would say to the jury, 'You see! She had left the store by that time so she couldn't *possibly* be guilty of taking the money!' It doesn't go that way at all.
>
> Frequently a point was so belabored it was lost. That was our rationale for asking each other questions. To our credit, no one passed judgement, maybe because we couldn't figure out who was lying. We had also come to realize the need for a jury to be made up of several persons -- so there'll be at least one person concentrating at any given time.
>
> Imagine, for a moment, nine disembodied brains hovering over the chairs in the jury box. One brain is wondering if it's still snowing so he can run his plows that night; another brain is thinking of what the substitute teacher should be working on with her second graders. Another is confused over the matter of $56.64 void on the cash register that the defense lawyer keeps going over; two brains are fighting sleep and another is trying to decide whether one of the lawyers wears a hairpiece. That leaves three minds following the proceedings, and they may not agree on the point being made. (One day we each took eight-minute periods to pay attention so that at least one person was alert during the afternoon.)

---

* From *Barrister*, published by the Young Lawyers' Division of the American Bar Association. Copyright ©1979 American Bar Association. "What It's Like to Serve on a Jury" by Joanne Duke Gamblee.

Beginnings

The law of primacy, which deals with the impact on people of what they see and hear first, needs to be particularly remembered as you introduce your witness to the jury. Therefore, the beginning of any direct is very important, not only for the witness' impressions, but because the jury is most attentive and judgmental then.

The Jury Watches Your Relationship

Since you have known and worked with him, how you handle the witness will give the jury clues about how you feel about him, and therefore how the jury should feel. Handle the witness with respect, warmth and sensitivity. The jury will not only like *you* as a human being, but will see that in such a nurturing and supportive environment, whatever the witness says must surely be exactly what he thinks and feels, since there seems to be no pressure, only approval.

Support the Witness

Remember that your witness needs reassurance, especially at the start, to feel that he or she is doing it right, that everything is going according to plan and that you are pleased and want him to keep on going as he is. Give the witness a safe environment in which to operate.

In other words: "Give before you get." If you give reassurance, understanding and reinforcement through the form of your questions and behavior, the witness can give back what you want to hear with his best effort.

- Nod your head as if to say "That's good. That's right. I understand." The jury also gets the same message.
- A pleasant facial expression looks welcoming.
- Use warmth and softness in your voice.

These gestures of support not only help the witness, they help

the jury answer the question "What do I think of the questioner?"
They tell the jury you're an empathic, thoughtful person and
they'll like you for it. It also flavors the first part of the exchange—
the witness' personal story—with warmth and humanity.

Get Closer

Spatial relationships are a most eloquent, non-verbal aspect of
communication, important in every part of the trial. Standing
closer to the witness at the beginning of a direct examination
implies your friendship, your support, your desire to be helpful,
your lack of fear of the witness (if he's a criminal), your respect, and
your commitment, It implies you're with him—that you support
him. The jury sees your relationship and responds to your obvious
regard for the witness and so does the witness. He feels your
support.

When you come to the section of the examination that deals
with the event itself, moving back and letting the witness seem to
be on his own shines more focus and attention on the substantive
part of the testimony. It not only implies, but visually tells the jury
that the witness is telling his story with no help or manipulation
from you. This is *his* story, told *his* way.

If you like to or are required to use a lectern, step to the side
and in front of it (if you're allowed) for a greater sense of intimacy,
warmth and informality as you begin your questions. (For further
discussion, see Chapter 9—Non-Verbal Communication.)

The First Question

Even asking something as simple as a witness' name and address is an introduction. It gives the jury a feeling for you and the
witness. Therefore, avoid saying, "Will you state your name for the
record?" This is as cold and distancing an opening as you can possibly give and is very startling to a witness. Until this moment, he
has been calling you Jack, and you've been calling him Joe. Too
suddenly, you take on the role of interrogator under the guise of
courtroom procedure. This creates formality and anxiety in the
witness and, since it sounds like a ritual, it makes the jury sit back

and observe the form, rather than getting involved with the person.

Therefore, expain this formality both to the witness and to the jury by saying, with some warmth or a smile, something like, "So the jury will get to know you, will you please tell us your full name." Or, "Would you please tell us your full name?" Or, "Let's begin by asking your name and address and something about yourself." Now the jury hears that you have begun by creating an environment for the witness. You are a thoughtful person and you have gotten the dialogue going informally.

Do Something Personal, If Appropriate

If it's your style, you might even reach out with "Good morning," "Are you comfortable?" or "Can you hear me all right?" especially if the witness is very young or elderly or hard of hearing. Some lawyers use these first moments to create a dramatic introduction. Jerry Spence, the colorful Wyoming trial lawyer, uses a most direct, emotional approach. He asks his plaintiff-client in a personal injury case:

Q. How do you feel?

A. I'm nervous, Mr. Spence.

Q. Why are you nervous?

A. This is my trial.

Q. Do you want the jury to believe this is an important day for you?

A. Mr. Spence, it's the most important day of my life.

The Witness' Background

Many lawyers race through this perfunctorily for the facts. Yet this is a gold mine! This is the part the jury can really relate to. The witness becomes more conversational and interesting, since he's dealing with the one subject he feels comfortable with—himself.

He'll get the momentum of his communication going because you're helping him get past his pre-conditioned fears The jury can look behind the witness box into life experiences they can all relate to. And they can see you as a person grounded in the real world with an understanding of the basics of life.

Get the jury interested in the witness by giving them a mini-soap opera of his life. Everyone loves stories and can identify most of all with what it takes to come through life—to survive and to follow the paths of school, work, kids, family and hardship. Find the most human aspects—working his way through school, starting a business with $100, a widow who brought up three outstanding children. Let the story come out through easy, informal questions and stay interested in each answer. Draw a human-scale portrait of your witness.

You can also help further authenticate the witness, since many lay witnesses also have expertise in their background which would enhance their testimony.

*   *   *

The essence of how you begin a direct examination, then, is to see it as a debut, an introduction to a watchful jury ready to make several snap judgments about you and your witness. Once you're under way, there are a number of other concerns to be addressed. The next section, Questioning Techniques, addresses these concerns and gives suggestions about keeping the momentum and developing clarity and interest.

Questioning Techniques

Where to Stand

Where you stand during the examination can affect both the witness' delivery and the way the jury responds to the testimony.

Very often lawyers tell me they like to stand to the side of the jury box during their examination. They feel this causes the questions to sound as if they came from the jury. It also causes the witness to look at the jury and gives the lawyer a chance to discover whether the witness is speaking loud enough for the jury to hear him. All of this is true, and it is sometimes useful, but there are some other points to consider when you plan to do this.

Jurors can also be distracted because they cannot see the lawyer or the interaction between the lawyer and the witness. Then, too, it is very difficult to ask the jury to focus totally on one person, someone who may not be very eloquent or charismatic. It is more interesting to watch a dialogue between two people than to see only one person and hear an amorphous other voice. Also, if you stand at the far side or at the back of or behind the jury box, you may make the witness feel abandoned, as he sees you becoming a part of the jury, drawing away from him. You might factor these thoughts into your decision about where to stand. It is more interesting to give the jury an opportunity to look at two people: to see you, to get the lift of your energy and your commitment, and then to see the witness answer.

Therefore I suggest you control yourself and how you ask in order to make your witness star. If you ask open-ended questions, a springboard for a full witness answer, you will not detract from the witness if you are visible. You will not take over center stage if you ask short questions that get him to talk. You will be a participant, not a competitor.

Moving closer or backing away should also be done in relationship to the subject matter. Your measurement here is to think of how you would have this conversation in a room. When would your instinct tell you to get closer? What part would you want to hear coolly, objectively, from a more removed place? When are you a part of the dialogue and when should the witness show how he handles it alone?

There is one other area to consider. Where you stand should also be measured against the physical placement of the jury box. How far away is it? What does it make the witness and the jury do? Where is the sun? Will it make the witness strain to see and hear you? What other statements are you making by choosing to distance yourself from the witness if you move around? Are you denying your connection? Are you comfortable with what is being said? Spatial relationship is a powerful hidden persuader.

The Lectern

The rigidity and formality of the lectern mitigates against the warmth you'd like to convey as you examine. But, many jurisdictions require using it. Use it as an instrument (though it hums but one sound); choose when to come out from behind it and step forward (softer, more intimate, a closer look at an issue) and when to let the issue itself ring out from behind the lectern or step back and make the witness look like he needs no help. A good compromise is to stand to the side so you can see your notes and still not look so formidable. Leaning on it also shows relaxation and informality.

Sitting

If you must sit at counsel table to examine the witness, my suggestion is to move out of that jurisdiction . . . it's a most difficult way to create rapport with the witness. The counsel table is a real barrier. You look inquisitorial, removed and powerful, and your own energy level is compromised and can flag.

The focus must be on your voice, your language and your body language and hand gestures, when appropriate. You must ask and explain clearly and motivate your witness to respond with vigor and interest. Learn to use small hand gestures to emphasize or embellish your questions. Sit up or lean forward to show interest. Sitting back shows a lack of interest and concern or a removed attitude. Be most aware of your own energy level and fight to maintain it and to keep your voice and your questions alive and interesting in order to keep the jury listening, and your witness responding in a lively fashion.

Hold Eye Contact
During Entire Answer

Eye contact with the witness shows commitment and concentration.

Ask, and then really pay attention to the answer. If you look down at the next question, fiddle with your notes or lose the energy between you and your witness, it is an invitation for the jury to lose their interest, too. It also looks rude. You have just asked a question but the answer seems so unimportant to you that you are already looking away or down at your notes for the next question. When you don't actively listen you give the signal that a canned answer is coming. This makes the jury question whether the response is a genuine, open, extemporaneous answer or a rote response to your signal. But most of all, if you are not interested, why should they be? You also discomfit the witness when you do this. You signal to him that his answers are not important and this will interrupt his flow and his concentration. Look down at your notes *after* the answer. The jury understands and is willing to wait.

Notice the Witness' Voice and Energy Level

Can he be heard? Is he mumbling? Is he talking too quickly? Too slowly? Most of all, is his energy level falling so that he is getting downright boring?

It is your job to feel and notice when that happens and then to encourage the witness by saying, kindly, "I wonder, Jack, if you could speak up a little. I think it's a little hard to hear," or "I'm sure that this is a long examination and it's difficult for you to keep answering these questions, but can you keep your voice up?"

Use a little introduction to the directive, because all by itself, it sounds like a punitive parent to a child who has just done something wrong. If you simply say "Will you speak up," "We can't hear you," or "Will you keep your voice up," you startle the witness and make him wonder. "Have I just been very boring, have they forgotten or have they not been listening?" This creates anxiety. So, explain with your voice and your words that everything is really going fine, but at the same time, suggest that "Mr. Smith, I'm having a little trouble hearing you. I wonder if you would raise your voice a bit—thank you."

To slow a witness down, try: "The court reporter is trying to get all this down and keep a record while we're both talking and that's really hard to do. Could you talk a little slower, please?" And smile.

A special word of caution: People have a tendency to be imitative, like chameleons. Be careful that a laid back witness doesn't pull *you* down and that you don't mimic *his* lowered energy level without knowing it. It happens to everyone. Be aware. Notice at what tempo and in what gear *you* are conducting the examination.

To elevate the energy level for either of you, speed up your delivery, walk, change positions, or change voice level; all of these signal a revitalization of the action. Through example, push the witness into a higher gear.

Really Hear the Answers

Listening (being passive) is very hard when you're actively involved in questioning. Your action-arrows are going away from you and it's difficult to shift gears and let action-arrows come toward you and take them in before you send out another question

Let each answer be the catalyst for the next question. Let the answer be the springboard that triggers the way your next question is asked. See the process as a tennis game in which you keep serving easy shots for your opponent to hit back. You go where his ball lands. If you don't listen, you may very well miss a key point or a graceful lead-in to the next question.

Link your Questions to the Previous Answer

Use a part of an answer, the actual words, to form the next question. Your questioning then looks seamless, smooth and non-manipulative. It feels almost as though the witness is giving a monologue, rather than being set up by you to talk about a certain subject, right now, in this way. This technique makes your question sound like a continuation of what was just talked about. Use it with discretion, not as a formula, but it does encourage the witness to continue, since you are using his or her words as a subliminal signal to him or her that you approve.

Q. What happened then?

A. Well, it was 3:30 in the afternoon, just before I was getting ready to go to the post office. I always go to the post office at 3:30 with the packages I have to get out.

Q. The packages you have to get out? What are they?

A. You know, big manila envelopes with sales material, confirmation of orders . . .

Q. This confirmation of orders, tell us about it. How does that work?

Be Flexible

One problem with careful preparation is that you very often become inflexible in how the story should unfold. This makes it hard for you to depart from the list of questions that you have already prepared in order to improvise when your witness departs from the planned text. While designing the examination based on what you need to make your points is necessary, you risk becoming too rigidly committed to your plan, your notes, your way. This sometimes prevents you from listening carefullly and being able to change direction.

Rigid adherence to a plan can make you look inattentive to what is being said. It prevents your following up on a new thread and gracefully bringing it back, and causes too much reference to your notes and not enough attention to the action in the courtroom.

Make the Progression of your Questions Logical and Orderly

Organization makes it easier for the jury to follow. In television and film (which is where most people now learn new information), the logical progression for introducing an idea is to start with a long shot, which is a picture of the whole scene, to establish the background or overview and to orient everybody to where they are. Then you go to a medium shot; the camera draws in closer and begins to focus attention on one aspect of the scene. Finally, you go to a close-up to see all the details of that aspect once you've been introduced to the subject.

In an examination, introduce a subject by going from an overall view to one aspect of the story. Do this by narrowing the iris to a tight-pupiled look at one key issue. People have been trained to think this way, not only because television has been teaching them

visually for the last thirty years, but also because it is a logical way
to look at or listen to anything. "Tell me all about where I am first,
then tell me what's happening. What's the background for the action? Now let me draw closer. Single out one point of interest. Get
me involved before the details. Now closer still. What are the
names of the players? What exactly are they doing? What is his
hand holding? What kind of gun is that? Is his finger on the trigger?
Did he *pull* it?"

Asking your question this way is not meant to be a rigid pre-
scription. The opposite technique, that of starting on a closeup of
the shocking moment and then pulling back slowly to reveal the
rest, has tremendous dramatic impact. Think of it pictorially. See
the effect. The body; the collision; the whole street. However, this
approach must be used with consummate skill, since you will, in a
sense, have blown the climax. Why you might do this and what
more you can do with it than the cooler, slower, inexorable
zooming-in technique must be carefully thought through. Both of
these are visual experiences for the jury, and powerful ones at that.
Once you begin, you must be consistent and not disappoint their
expectations or play with their responses.

Make Transitions from One
Subject to Another

It's important to know how to move from one subject to another, how to move gracefully instead of just dropping an idea like
a hot potato and then "turning the page" without giving the jury a
chance to make a transition. Use topic headings: "You've told us
about your family and your business life, Mr. Smith. Now let's
move on to the day of the collision."

The transitions should be graceful and smooth, but they also
serve another purpose. They let the jury know that it is time to
stop thinking about this and start thinking about that. So, as you
change from one subject direction to another, tell the witness and
the jury at the same time by saying, "Now let's focus on the day in
question," or, "Now, let's talk about what happened after the whatever." This gives everyone a chance to change gears, to go to the
next paragraph on their mental typewriter or to start a new page.
It's terribly important to help the jury derive this kind of organiza-

tion and order out of testimony because they're trying to group information into sections, segments, paragraphs, so that they can recall it again at the end of the trial. It's also important for the witness to know where to go next.

Transition sentences also help bridge a pause. You may want to think for a couple of seconds about whether you now have got enough and want to move on to the next subject. If you have paused first, then explained that you are now going to another subject, everyone knows why.

Another way you can gracefully move from one subject to another is to physically change your place. Such a change visually lets witness and jury know that you are now talking about something new. Move to another area. Or, put down your notes and walk away from the podium. Or go back to the counsel table, look at your notes slowly, calmly, and then walk away. Or pick your head up and say, "Now, let's turn to . . . "

You can even make a transition with your voice, like a fresh start with some new energy. It helps everybody to perk up and pay attention to the next thing that's happening.

Ways to Interrupt

One of the most difficult problems is a garrulous witness who goes on and on, making one endless sentence of something that should be delivered in small portions. The problem, of course, is that if you interrupt the witness, you are doing something that in real life, you are not supposed to do. Everybody's been taught not to interrupt, that it's rude. Interrupting can also show impatience. It seems critical. It makes people think, "Oh, what is the witness doing wrong? That's not what the lawyer wants him to talk about."

Therefore, interrupt with, "Excuse me," or "Let me interrupt you for a moment," or any other word you like from normal, not legal, vocabulary. "I know you want to tell us all of this, but perhaps it would be easier if we just focused on this for a moment."

Flag the jury that what has just been said is so important you need to focus on it. "Let's pause there, Jack. Exactly what direction were you walking when you first saw Mr. Brown? What you are describing is complex and important. Let's take it apart a little."

Be non-critical. "Just a minute, Elizabeth. This is very familiar to you, of course, because you have seen or done it so many times, but perhaps you should take it apart for us and describe it in more detail. For example, would you tell us more about . . . " Or, "Could you explain that to us in layman's language?" This approach reins in the witness non-judgmentally. It also doesn't make the jury think you are criticizing the witness, but rather that you are being helpful, want to know more or are trying to be a little more detailed or clear.

Another good way to interrupt is to move in and pluck some of the witness' words. Take whatever words you've just heard and say, "Just a moment. You just said 'red ink.' That's very important. Let's stay with that just a moment, may we, please?" Then ask a more focused question.

With all of these interruptions, not only are you saying, "Excuse me," or "Would you wait just a moment," but also giving a reason to the jury why you have interrupted. Interrupting with sensitivity and with a reason removes the chance that the jury will see you as manipulating and maneuvering the witness to say the things you want him to say, and shows your sensitivity towards people's feelings.

A word of caution. Juries hate many interruptions. Sometimes they're not all necessary. You can also let the witness finish his narration, and then go back with a spotlight to get the omitted details with specific questions. Be sure, if you do that, that you re-orient the jury to where you are and what you are focusing on.

How to Use Silence

Everyone is afraid of silence. It looks like you ran out of words, got lost or just plain forgot. Yet the single most arresting, compelling technique in oral presentation is to slow down, lower the voice and just stop talking.

With the advent of television, everyone is afraid of "dead air." Wall-to-wall talk is an assurance that a person really knows a great deal, isn't at a loss for words and isn't going to lose the floor. Daring to pause is very noticeable because it's so rare. It also commands rapt attention as the jury waits to see what comes next.

Let the impact of important answers sink in. Stop. Take a breath. Let the jury consider and think about a key point that has just been made. Emphasize the points by repeating the answer or asking the question one more time for clarification. You can use body language here. You can walk a little closer, perhaps, or you can stop, turn and walk away, even toward the jury, turn around again and say, "Let me understand you. You said, '_____.' ?" This action makes the jury notice and remember. The fact of the physical movement visually underlines what has just happened.

A pause linked to a gesture, such as putting down the paper or your notes, taking off your glasses, taking a breath or taking a step toward the witness, makes the jury stop and consider what has just happened. Pure silence is extremely effective.

Do not take it for granted that the jury understands each of the important points when they are made. These points are important to you because you know what the rest of the trial is about and what your final argument is. They are not yet important to the jury, so you need to underline and emphasize them, especially since the delivery from a lay witness is often not eloquent.

Clarify Language at All Times

It's surprising sometimes to discover that many of the words you and I may use all the time are not in common usage. Lawyers speak a special brand of shorthand to each other and it becomes vernacular to you. Many sophisticated words are outside the ken of many jurors.

Therefore, take heed. Don't let unclear words go by. Catch any statements whose meanings are not instantly apparent. Go back over them and ask again, or state that they are not clear and ask for clarification. Watch for technical language or language that comes from the specific work world of the witness. Help the jury by asking for an explanation. The best way to get the jury to understand is to say, "Just a minute, Jack. Will you go over that again? I'm not sure we really understand what you mean. What exactly is a flange? Will you describe what that is? Can you draw it for us?" Ask anything that will help the jury understand what the witness is describing. It also puts the witness on notice that he is moving off into something that is either too abstract, too technical or too large for the jury to understand all at once.

Be careful not to say, "Tell the jury what that means." You are then saying that *you* know, but the dumb jurors don't. You must walk a fine line between patronizing the jury—pointing out their ignorance and separating yourself into a league with a knowledgeable person—and pretending that you don't understand the technical matters of the case. Jurors expect you to be informed, yet they don't like to feel at sea or know how much they don't know or understand. Therefore, using "tell *us*" instead of "tell the jurors" softens that issue and reminds them that before this case, you were a mere mortal who didn't know what a flange was either, and that's why you know it needs more clarification.

Don't use technical or legal language in forming your questions. It encourages the witness to use it, too. Not only is the answer useless, since you just lost the jury, but it may also confuse the witness about how you want him to talk—simply or technically. If you use legal terms in your questions, you run the risk of turning the jury off. You distance yourself from them. And you, as the identified guide and teacher, have just moved off into your own world and reminded them that you are a lawyer and they are not. "When did you exit from the motor vehicle?" and phrases of similar ilk are too commonly used by lawyers in the courtroom, and are just as commonly decried by jurors. You can talk plainer than that. . . .

If legalese slips out, or even if you wish to play super-lawyer and put legal terms in to show your competence and expertise, stop and explain what you mean. That does the double duty of demonstrating both your knowledge and your sensitivity to the laymen, the jurors and witnesses. There is also a matter of style here. Some lawyers are more formal and like a little distance on occasion and a feeling of respect for their "differentness" from the jury. Be consistent with your basic persona *but* be careful not to patronize as you explain, and don't forget to explain.

Use Short, Simple, Direct Questions

In an effort to guide the witness, you can sometimes create very complex, convoluted wordy questions. For the benefit of witness and jury, the very best open-ended questions to stimulate direct and fulsome answers are short, simple and classic. Who. What. Where. When. Why. How. Describe. Explain.

This not only guides the witness to
but also helps the jury stay interested
where you're going. The most effective
just a person to just another person,

The Use of Notes

In any witness examination, cons
not commandments carved in stone. Write and underline the key
categories or subject headings. (see chapter 3 for more on notes.)
List buzz words and one-word action words underneath them, so
that you know that these are the places you want to go. But see
your notes as flexible, mobile, so that if you really are listening to
the answers of the witness, you will still be able to get to these key
stops, although they may need to be rearranged somewhat, depending upon what the witness has just said.

The jury gives you permission to look at your notes *after* the
answer. They know you're working. They know you've prepared a
certain plan. You are supposed to have done your work and they
give you extra points for being prepared. If you surreptitiously try
to peek down at your notes while the answer is being given, you
will give the jury the impression of either rudeness or anxiety, because they see you trying to plan ahead, worrying about where to
go next.

You will look much more relaxed and at ease if you can take
the time to listen, look down in a very deliberate way and very
calmly pick your head up and form your next question. That looks
as though you are in total control. You're not easily flappable. You
know exactly where you are going and you needn't clutch for the
next question. Hold your ground. Don't look or act nervous or lost.
Take your time and think. It shows control.

Objections

This subject is pertinent throughout the trial. Read it here as
a guide for how to handle your opposing counsel's objections when
you're the direct examiner and also how to object to your opposing
counsel's line of questioning.

Jurors do not understand objections. All they know is that you
and your opponent are going to fight with each other. You are each

try to discredit the other's witnesses and each other.
the jury hears objections, it only signals one thing to them:
and your case are in trouble—you are in danger of losing on a
ertain point. They think the lawyer is thinking: "Oh, oh—don't let
him talk about that. That would be disastrous for my case." Then, if
that's so, what was going to be said next was obviously very important information. The jury doesn't know what objections are about.
They don't understand what point of law you are citing. They see it
all as a win-lose situation.

When there is an objection, the jury listens judgmentally to
the judge's ruling. They look to him to see who shall live and who
shall die. It looks punitive. Then they pay unusual attention to how
the "losing" lawyer takes it and what is about to be said. That's why
you should explain what objections are all about in opening statement so the jury will understand.

You signal the jury by the way you make objections. Be careful about jumping up in an agitated or angry way. This confirms the
jury's belief that you're in trouble. Take your time. Stand up slowly
and calmly. Think about this as a point of law, a simple interpretation of the rule book. Be careful to explain your objection, not with
disdain or in a patronizing or angry way, but as a point of information about which you disagree.

Be prepared to look at the judge and the other lawyer as
though you're just interested in clarifying a point. No problem. No
danger.

After the ruling, take your seat with no outward emotion
showing. Nothing was at stake, just the rules of the game, and it's
not a big deal either way. The jury will let it pass easily.

If there is a repeated issue to object to, keep your cool. Let
the other lawyer get all upset. You keep explaining in a low-key,
pleasant manner what the problem is. The jury will feel you're
much stronger and on solid ground. Also, you're obviously very
smart because you know this inside thing.

Choose your shots and don't belabor. The jury loses patience
and hates repeated interruptions. To illustrate this point most
graphically let me tell you a true story about an occurrence in a
U.S. Central District of California Court. In a direct examination of
a product liability case, after repeated and heated defense attorney
objections, a *juror* stood up and said to him, "Why don't you sit
down and be quiet, we want to hear what this man has to say!"

Another important point. Don't accept the judge's ruling, if he has ruled against you, by saying, "Thank you, Your Honor." That's phony and the jury knows it. We all hate losing. Who are you kidding? Judges hate hearing that, too. It's so *humble*. Just take your lumps quietly and sit down looking none the worse for wear, if you can. Save the fury for later, outside the courtroom.

Don't Say "Strike That"

You're human. You're fallible. You make mistakes. The common courtroom jargon of "strike that", however, is resented by jurors. To whom are you addressing that directive? To the court reporter. A worker the jury easily identifies with. The subliminal judgmental response from the jury is, "That's rude!" It's too curt and arrogant a phrase, one you'd never use to your secretary. Therefore, try, "Let me re-phrase that," "Let me start again," "I'd rather put it this way," or "Would you please strike that?" Juries really notice!

Visual Aids and Demonstrative Evidence are Crucially Important

The jury has been drowning in oral presentations. Now they must get lost in that dullest of dialogues—a lawyer asking and a lay witness answering. They have gotten no other information except through the tone of your voice and now the tone of voice of the witness. Tonal quality can be as unmemorable and as unnoticed as words that vanish in the air. Even more important is the fact that anybody's description of any event, fact or object is open to endless interpretation by everybody else. If you want to talk about something and be sure that you, the witness and the jury are all starting from the same place and that they all know exactly what is meant and what is being described, you must have one static image that everybody can refer to at the same time. The choices are many but the most important choice you must make is to use some form of illustrative device to increase the jury's attention and the clarity of the testimony. Be sure you have trained your witness to be involved in the description by utilizing him at the blackboard, the photo, the chart or the projected image. The jury will believe his testimony and remember it if *he* is the "show and teller." Get your witness up to explain and make it clear. If *you* show it, it could seem manipulative and questionable. (For a full explanation of visual aids and how to use them, see Chapter 8.)

Sensitive Issues

How to Handle Emotional or
Shocking Moments

This is a key issue because it demonstrates your sensitivity and also strongly colors what the jury can take in and absorb.

If you enter the portion of the examination in which you know there will be tears, gory details, a discussion of death or trying emotional moments surrounding the event itself, warn everybody in advance. Warn not only the witness, but the jury as well. Let them hear that something is coming. Let them know that you recognize in advance that this will be difficult, even for you.

Say something to the witness like, "Now I know that this next part is going to be a difficult thing for you to discuss. It's difficult for all of us, but it is necessary. You're only human and we will understand if you cry, or have to stop for a moment. That's all right. We understand." You've shown you can anticipate how it's going to feel. You've given your witness permission to be fallible on the stand. And essentially you have warned the jury, "That's what may happen, but you understand, don't you? Be prepared." This helps what could be a very tense time and lets the witness move on without as much concern about the fact that he may break down. It shows the jury your concern for the witness and for them. You can also use non-verbal techniques in such an event. Show by your tone of voice, by a change of pace, posture or physical position that you're cueing the witness and the jury about what's coming. This is a subtler way, indicating that you know the jury will understand and rise to the occasion on their own.

How to Handle Personal or
Embarrassing Questions

Be aware of the fact that asking very personal questions is different from what people normally do with each other. Acknowledge your humanity, the difficulty of asking and answering such questions and the intrusive nature of such questions. Change your pace and your space and use your voice to let us know the subject is intimate. You're sensitive to it. The jury notices and appreciates this.

Handling Unusual Witnesses

If the witness is older, disabled, very young, obviously very unattractive, very big physically or culturally different (an accent), anticipate how the jury will respond. What stereotyped views can you expect?

Think what would be appropriate behavior for you, the lawyer, in relation to some of these issues. What do you want to defuse or neutralize? What do you want to point up? It's also important to think about what is seemly behavior for you, from the jury's point of view.

If you deal with someone who has an accent, be sure, at the beginning, to mention it in some fashion, "Where are you from originally? How long have you been in America? How did you get here? Why did you come? Did you have family here?" You might thereby answer some questions on the jury's minds like, "Is the witness a burden to the U.S.?" Tell the witness how well he has learned English or something that is complimentary, but let everybody know that the witness may be difficult to understand, that he or she will need patience and understanding.

For someone who is disfigured in some fashion, stand closer to show your ability to see past it. In no way patronize or sound as though you are speaking to someone who is less entitled to respect or more helpless than you. Speak forthrightly and respectfully, but as one adult to another and with some energy and vigor.

We are sometimes uncomfortable around handicapped people worrying about their feelings and the right way to behave. Showing the jury how you handle them as people *and* handicapped or *although* handicapped, helps relieve some tension and gets their minds off it so they can listen. If you want to be sure that the disablement or disfigurement will in no way make the jury question the competence of such a witness, then, once you begin, you should stand farther away and let him be on his own, presenting himself with energy, force and courage, so that the jury gives him twice as many points for being competent in spite of this problem.

If you are dealing with a witness who has some form of disabilty which would cause him to have difficulty getting into the chair, anticipate this in advance. Discuss with the witness how he is going to get into the chair most comfortably, and then do it in a most matter-of-fact way, with some pleasantness, letting the jury see it. Don't hover. When the person is finally settled, say something to the effect that, "You have obviously gotten yourself in and out of many such situations before. I hope you're comfortable. Now let's begin." In other words, you allude to the fact that this person does this all the time, and that it has nothing to do with his competence as a witness, unless your case wants to emphasize his injury.

The issue of handling older people is a very important one. In our youth-blinded culture, older people often live lives of loneliness and experience feelings of irrelevance. Being singled out and spotlighted on a witness stand can be a unique and remarkable experience for them. "Look, everyone's going to listen to *me,* for a change. I'm important. I have momentary clout. I matter." Therefore, the possibility arises of wanting to talk, to tell too much or to become disorganized in their rush of words and their excitement about the attention they're being paid. Interrupting them and focusing their testimony is a delicate matter and must be handled with sensitivity and dignity. Just direct them in small pieces, in short, specific questions that progress, but not too slowly and indulgently, through their story.

In general, be careful to be gentle with older people, but do not be patronizing because it questions their veracity. Do not be overly solicitous. That is insulting. The jury would rather see you be respectful, pleasant but totally normal in order to give them the chance to feel like a peer with someone who is older, rather than indulging someone who seems to be slightly incompetent. Remember to notice your jury. Are older people on it? How would they like to be treated?

In dealing with a young witness, you might try to pick up a chair, sit down and question that way so as not to appear so overwhelming, dominant and formal. Be careful not to be too solicitous lest you awaken questions about the young person's competence to testify.

The rule of thumb, then, is to show and discuss differences up front since the jury surely sees and responds to them. Point out what's different. Indicate subtly by your behavior toward the witness or actually explain, if you need to , that this has nothing to do with the person's ability to testify, think, or remember. Then let it go and begin the examination.

*　　　*　　　*

Direct exmaination of a lay witness is a segment of a trial that has within it all the dangers of human fallibility and human frailty. The process is one in which a group of lay people watch a layman being probed by an expert. This gives rise to judgmental decisions by the laymen (jury) about the layman (witness) and the expert (lawyer) that often have nothing to do with the facts of the case. Rather, they are colored by the behavior of the performers. Therefore, when you can get a clear understanding of how the witness feels and what his or her needs are, what the jury needs and expects and what your own stresses are, you can smooth the way to a more successful direct examination. Before turning the page, stop for a moment. Put yourself in their shoes. Try to pull up from memory your own first steps into a courtroom. Remember how nervous you were? Remember what you worried about?

In gaining increased sensitivity to the witness' needs and the jury's feelings and pre-conditioned responses, you will avoid seeming manipulative, overbearing or intimidating. Most importantly, you will go far toward making your direct examination clear and memorable.

In direct, just see yourself as a conductor creating an environment in which the witness (soloist) can "play" his or her story to the best advantage.

5

CROSS-EXAMINATION

"Counsel, you may cross-examine the witness."

In the best of all possible worlds, cross-examination should make the jury begin to question or doubt what was said in direct examination. It should:

• redefine the story, or add ingredients or perspectives missing in the direct exam;

• be used to impeach the witness's credibility, knowledge, or version of the story by pointing out inconsistencies;

• get you helpful admissions or concessions from the witness;

• be used to introduce new or additional evidence that is helpful to the jury's understanding of the case;

• cause the jury to dislike or mistrust the witness and to admire the clarity of the cross-examining lawyer's points and point of view;

• make the jury feel that the cross-examining lawyer is closer to the actual facts, has more knowledge and information than the opposing lawyer, and sees the total picture in a much fairer way;

• cast a shadow on the opposing counsel's credibility and forthrightness, since he or she left out points that are now being brought to light;

• preview the closing argument;

• star the lawyer as witness for his side by the way he frames his leading questions.

So much for the best of all possible worlds. Now let's discover what really happens, what can go wrong and why.

ISSUES AND INSIGHTS

To gather some new information about cross-examination, to discover the many overt and hidden issues and to gain insights into why they're there and what they mean, let's take a deeper look at the jury, the witness, and you, the lawyer.

The Jury

If the underlying job of the jury is to sort, sift and then decide, they need help. They need to find key, telling points in the evidence and testimony that can substantiate their conclusions. They then have a foundation for their decision(s), and the courage to bring in a verdict.

Cross-examination is crucial. It puts to the test the jury's most recently acquired facts. This helps them accept or discard those facts based on your skillful additions or subtractions. So, what they need is to focus, to hear your discrepancies, differences and new information clearly—with as little extraneous "noise" as possible.

However, the jury has fascinating, pre-conditioned expectations about a cross-examination that prevent it from being an unmarked slate on which the cross-examiner can write.

One of the few things they know about a trial before they walk into it is that they are going to watch a fight between two lawyers. They are excited about that because we all like a little conflict when we ourselves don't have to fight. It's wonderful to be at ringside, to watch a fight done verbally so there's not much blood spilled and to see how cleverly the two lawyers are going to try to do each other in. The jury knows it—subliminally perhaps—only through the good offices of Perry Mason, but they really expect it. What other stereotypical ideas do they bring with them?

*"Watch the Lawyer Take Apart
Everything the Witness Has Just
Said. He Will Be Tough and
Really Push the Witness
Around"*

They expect the cross-examiner to be aggressive and hostile toward the witness. Under attack, the witness will be manipulated and trapped into making a confession or admission. The jury's expectation of what will happen gets in the way of their hearing the new information coolly and objectively. They don't know whether it's true or not, since their feeling about the atmosphere of pressure in cross-examination makes them question the genuineness of the answer.

*"The Poor Guy, He Must Be So
Nervous. I'm Glad It's Not Me"*

The juror identifies with the witness as another lay person, unskilled in the ways of the trial and the courtroom. He imagines his anxiety about the ensuing duel. Unless he's a very unsympathetic witness, the jury starts out feeling somewhat defensive about the process of an uneven struggle—a professional going after a layman, someone like themselves.

*"Listen to That Lawyer
Maneuver"*

If the jury identifies with a witness, then the lawyer is not like the rest of "us folks." The lawyer, doing very special things, manipulating and going for key points in his own inimitable closed-question style, is backing the witness into a corner, until the latter can't do anything but admit, "yes, yes, yes." This makes the jury see the lawyer as a powerful, aggressive person with no other human attributes showing. This colors what they hear and take in. They think, "Anyone would break down, get confused or contradict themselves when they're brow-beaten like that."

"Who's Right?"

The jury needs to know what to believe, especially if they like the first lawyer. The lawyers will argue (they've seen the movie). The other lawyer will obviously disagree with the new facts or line of questioning. Is it really about the facts or is it just his job to argue? This is America, where people rarely sit back and view a fight impartially. We're a nation of sports lovers, conditioned to take sides, to pick a favorite. We don't usually watch a contest without caring who wins. Imagine what happens to the jury's ability to sort and sift facts objectively as they watch a sparring match.

"There's More to the Story. I Hope I Understand"

Knowing the cross-examiner is reaching toward some essential points and feeling the need to know them too, jurors become anxious that they may miss the essence of the cross. The cross-examination is so pointed, so product-oriented, it becomes a challenge to the jurors to see if they can catch on and understand. They are also on their fact-finding mission and really want to gather another point of view to help them make their decision.

The Witness

The following issues are useful to understand from two points of view: Read them for insights into how a witness feels toward you as you cross-examine him. Read them also for insights into your own witnesses' problems so you can help them be better prepared for their own cross-examination.

"Counsel, You May Cross-Examine"

The witness is on the alert, filled with anxiety over an attack from a well-prepared professional. "Here he comes to get me," he thinks. This causes the natural juices to flow unnaturally—a short circuit of the adrenals, as it were. He turns the corner from the relatively relaxed mental process of telling and describing a story to a friend (which was the mood of the just-completed direct examination) to a view of a battlefield with the enemy, in splendid armor, charging toward him at full gallop, lance at the ready (or is it a Sherman tank he sees?) No matter. The picture is danger and attack. This causes all his concentration, his preparation, his newly-found confidence to vanish and he is, for the moment, uptight, unthinking and vulnerable.

"What Will He Go For? Can I Answer It?"

Although you've prepared him for the possible issues opposing counsel may bring up, the witness is on his own now. He does a quick retrospective. "What did I say that he'll use against me?" He worries if he dug his own grave somewhere. The mystery, the suspense of what subjects will now be dealt with, what weapons the lawyers will use and whether he, the witness, will handle them correctly, increases his anxiety and consequently decreases his ability to think and speak extemporaneously, at the top of his form.

He may also feel basically guilty and wrong because the implication of the cross-examination is that he goofed up somewhere and gave some fodder to the the cross-examiner instead of being clever enough not to. And his own lawyer can't tell him whether that is so or not, nor what, exactly, is coming.

"What Does This Mean? Where is He Leading?"

Often, because the cross-examiner begins in a fairly aggressive and rapid-fire manner, the witness becomes confused. As the witness gets confused and starts fumbling, he tries to second-guess the lawyer and give answers that he imagines will counter the offensive. Because the witness expects to be attacked, he looks at every question with suspicion, trying to find ways to counter it. Rather than clarifying or diluting the attack, this often leads to the greater problems of inconsistency and self-contradiction.

"No One Can Help Me Now"

Not only the element of surprise looms before the witness, but also a great sense of aloneness. "I'm on my own and can't ask anyone's advice about how to answer." This sense of vulnerability and isolation heightens all the other responses and diminishes his sense of personal power.

"But I Told the Truth!"

Scared to death that now the opposing counsel is going to really get him, the witness becomes naturally defensive, a very human response to being attacked. After all, everything he said was what he really meant, what he really saw, what he really thought and felt. Now somebody is going to come along and say, "Wrong. Not true. You're lying. There's a piece you're leaving out; why don't you come clean and tell us everything?" Although the witness is intimidated, he starts thinking of a response to the attack. The first one is to become defensive. Feeling defensive causes the witness to look guilty, to sound nervous and tentative, although he really *is* telling the truth.

Defensiveness often reads like guilt to an observer. It is interesting, if you look at videotapes or even watch trials from this point of view, to see how witnesses change in the moments when their own lawyer sits down and the cross-examining lawyer gets up. Their body language betrays it. They shift in the chair. Hands grip the chair arms. The backs get a little stiffer. They clear their throats. They lift their chins a little bit. You see them sort of getting themselves organized and ready for the onslaught (which the jury notices too, by the way).

"Don't Think You Can Push Me Around!"

Different people handle hostility differently. Some counterpunch and fight back. Some fold, acquiesce and meekly let themselves be pushed around. This has to do with their previous history and conditioning and we'll talk more of it next in witness preparation. For now, let's focus on the possibly aggressive response to the cross-examiner.

"I'm as tough and as good as you are," begins to run through the witness' mind. When he gets into fighting stance, cool and objective thinking and careful responses disappear. The issue becomes a tug of war, a win-lose competition with anger rising in the witness as the lawyer pushes harder, especially since the lawyer is experienced, has planned his moves and can often outmaneuver the witness.

"I'll show him who's tough," can often prevent witnesses from handling the cross-examination well.

The Lawyer

It is sometimes difficult, particularly for male lawyers, to conduct a direct examination, because it doesn't feel like anything is happening. But the cross? That's "show time!" Cross-examination, because of its more flamboyant nature, is often misunderstood. It also has built-in pitfalls for the lawyer, the most common being over-aggressiveness. But there are actually many other subtle areas to explore.

"Just Let Me at Him"

The temptation to "make a kill" in cross-examination is very great. There is visibility and the thrill of performance. There is excitement. Obvious skills are displayed. There is power. You can box a witness in. Your closed questions force the witness to answer with absolutely no recourse. There is cleverness and a chance to show your knowledge. You move into high adversarial gear, fighting back against the testimony and the other lawyer. All these things tempt you to make a great aggressive show in cross-examination.

But remember, the jury sees this from a totally different point of view. Not only do they expect it, they can see you as a bully—"ganging up" on a fellow lay person, someone like themselves. In that moment, they discredit much of whatever you got the witness to say. "Of course the poor guy said that. Look how the lawyer

backed him into a corner and scared him to death. He got so confused, he didn't know what he was saying." As a consequence, the
good points you scored pass unnoticed. The jury gets so busy picking sides and feeling defensive about how the witness got so
discumbobulated, that they forgive him for much of it and don't
fully absorb what the witness said.

"The Direct Is Over. Here I Go"

Unlike the softer, underplayed approach of the direct examination, the force and intentional attack of the cross-examination set
up a great contrast between both lawyers' behavior in the mind of
the jury. They can quickly dislike the cross-examiner because they
don't basically understand the format of the two different styles of
questioning—open and closed. They see only one nice guy and one
killer. If the direct examiner has been particularly warm, friendly,
charming and outgoing, the contrast of a cold, analytical, aggressive cross-examiner will turn the jury off and turn them against
whatever is being uncovered.

"I Must Control the Witness and Not Let Him Get Away From Me"

Even as you read this, imagine telling that to the jury, out
loud. Yet is is a fact and a main component in your cross-
examination. Witnesses who bicker or want to explain each answer
or try to deal only with facets of your question make you lose momentum and dilute your effect. How can you hide what you're really doing from the jury? How can you not let your manipulation
get in the way of the jury's clear perception of the witness, the new
testimony and even of you?

"You're Lying, Little Old Lady!"

How do you get up and say "you're lying" when the witness is
handicapped, old, or in some way unusual, with a built-in sympathy factor? Our culture and family training teach us to handle certain people with a kind of deference and sensitivity. How do you

get the jury past this emotional pre-set and into a cool, cerebral response to your facts regardless of their natural sympathies toward a unique witness?

"I've Got to Whittle Away at This Point"

Often a key issue in the testimony must be gone over, harped on, circled and homed in on again and again. But, unless the points made by the cross-examiner are clearly organized, outlined and led up to so that the jury can readily absorb and follow, they have no idea why the lawyer is harping on a particular point. It doesn't make any sense to them if they don't understand the overall plan or why the lawyer thinks this particular piece of evidence must be clarified, dissected or changed. It seems arbitrary. Sometimes it seems nasty or picky, an irrelevant detail and very unimportant. It also gets boring very quickly. Unless the lawyer makes it extremely clear where they fit and why they matter, pursuing small nitty-gritty points may eventually make you lose their benefit because they become irritants to the jury.

"There's Not Much for Me To Do Here"

I have just made a case for the jury's expectation of fireworks, hostility, aggressive manipulation, adversarial exchange and general excitement. Suppose you have only one or two small points to make. Suppose you decide not to cross-examine. How does that seem to the jury? They are not only let down, they suspect you don't know what to do and are in some sense beaten. This can strengthen the effect of the direct examination. And yet, you really don't want to do much on cross. A problem of misunderstanding by the jury can exist here.

"This May Be a Long and Detailed Cross"

Although you have much to cover, the jury doesn't give you carte blanche with unlimited time to make your point. Juries (like most people) have a rather short concentration span. Remember, this is a world permanently imprinted by television. An average news story is one and one-half minutes long. Given this condition, although you have many points—what should you cover? How long can you keep the jury's attention? What can you leave out? When do you quit?

*   *   *

To sum up: The expectation of what a cross-examination will be like affects both juror and witness adversely. The clear refutations and fine points you wish to bring out can get lost in a rough sea of aggressive behavior and an overly controlling cross-examiner. The anxiety around loss of control, both for the lawyer and the witness, heightens the possible missteps on both sides. The jury's prediliction for identifying with the witness can alter how and what they hear.

It's time to find some new techniques to counter these problems.

BEFORE THE TRIAL

Preparing the Witness

Here again, as in the preparation for direct examination, you can do a great deal to give your witness insight into the process of cross-examination and his possible reactions to it. You can help him live through and overcome some of his natural responses. You can give him techniques and information to be able not only to withstand but to actively respond to a cross-examiner with credibility and strength.

Explain Cross-Examination

Witnesses have the same stereotypes about cross examination as jurors do. They got them from the same source from which most laymen learn about trials—movies and television. Therefore, not only is their anxiety level very high, but they really don't understand the subtler purposes of cross-examination.

Talk to your witness about the form and substance of cross, about what the opposing lawyer wants to accomplish and why. "He doesn't necessarily want to kill you or make you seem stupid." Explain how the additional admissions he gets from the witness will bear out his points in the case and that he tries to make the witness his tool to do this.

Tell Him What Points You Expect Opposing Counsel to Cover

Since you know the possibilities and basic themes of the case on both sides, share with your witness what subjects to expect in cross. Show him what admissions opposing counsel will probably want to get from him and what main areas he will probably harp on. Tell him what opposing counsel needs, and why.

Share the Way You Cross-Examine

Tell him what *you* do, how *you* prepare, what's on *your* mind when you get up. Explain how you see the opposing witness and what you're thinking as you question and attack. This not only gives your witness insights into how his adversary, the opposing lawyer, thinks, but it also becomes a basis for all the rest of your witness' preparation. He believes you really understand the experience and can help him.

Help Him to Understand the Psychology of the Jury

Explain what jurors need from cross-examination. Tell your witness the jury will see him as one of them—with some sympathy and understanding—especially if the cross-examination gets very aggressive and hostile. Remind him of the good old American custom of rooting for the underdog. The jury sees the unfair battle. Explain how that will get in the way of their hearing the testimony. This gives your witness courage and a sense of connection to the jury. It can help his attitude and presentation.

Talk to him as well about juries enjoying a witness who holds his ground. They need to feel conviction and sure-footedness in the witness, or they will get nervous and doubt him.

Help the witness to understand that the jury does not see the fine points of the testimony in the same way that the lawyers do; that they often get a rather general picture of who's winning; and that if the witness can be helped not to feel so defensive during cross-examination, but can stand his ground and answer calmly, much of what he says in direct will still have credibility. It doesn't all have to be washed away just because the opposing counsel sounds so powerful in the cross-examination.

Discuss the Psychology of the Cross-Examined Witness

Talk about how it feels to be alone, isolated and the object of an attack. How does one gird one's loins for a personal attack by someone who is skilled, uses a mouthful of technical words and knows his way around the courtroom and the law?

Discuss with the witness the fact that everybody feels like that.

Let him understand that different people, like different animals, react differently when they're attacked or feel cornered—some choose to counter-attack, some retreat. Both work with different results. Explain that you'll explore with him how he will feel and how he might react, and that you can help give him many constructive ways to respond.

Explore the Idea of the "Victim Mentality"

A witness often goes into cross-examination imagining himself to be a victim about to be ganged-up on by a bully. This not only scares him, it weakens or confuses his best instincts.

Find out about your witness. Ask how he feels when he watches a fight and how he feels about this one. Find out what happened when he was attacked in the past (family, work, etc.). Discuss how a lawyer's attacks might make him feel. Show what happens if he feels like a victim: he gets defensive, looks guilty, sounds weak and so on. Don't be judgmental. Just open the discussion around the issue that people often respond this way and begin looking for clues about how your witness will respond.

How People React to Aggression

The women's movement has raised many questions. It has opened people's minds to the range of behavior and fields of endeavor available to women as they transcend the old stereotypical images of seemly feminine postures in society. It has also done this for men, raising questions about the traditional macho role being the only, or at least the best, way to be a man. The old images remain deeply ingrained, however. The old responses reappear with Pavlovian regularity. The age level tells us how often, but people repeatedly fall back into old behavior patterns and hear the old tapes when threatened.

It's important to think through this information as you consider what a male or female witness feels. Each responds very differently to aggression and the basically aggressive act of being cross-examined.

"Be a Man"

The aggressive counter-response to an attack is what's expected when one man confronts another. That's the learned behavior, the conditioned reflex of our society: "Be a man! Stand up and fight back!" It's important, however, to remember that many men hate to fight and feel intimidated by overt aggression. Their childhood experiences taught them that they could lose or get beaten. Their nature may recoil from conflict and open hostility. What range of behavior is left for them in response to being attacked? Based on the traditional male pattern, it is painful for a man to fold, to back away in front of a jury of his peers when he knows "be a man" means "fight back." How embarrassing! The thought that "they see me as a weakling" turns off his power to think and fight back on points or issues, even quietly. Instead, it puts the witness into reverse gear. "Retreat." "Don't argue." "He's making a fool of me." The witness loses the momentum to "play his own game," to move into the mode he can fight back with or to find an alternative.

Instead, he submits. He allows. He lets the cross-examiner move into his area of vulnerability, and he ends up destroying his own testimony by his passivity and despair.

"I'm Only a Woman"

Only recently have women seen role models for several kinds of female aggressive, fight-back behavior. The newly emerging competitive sportswomen, the television heroines who conquer adversity and the real life achievers are showing women options and styles of how to let their natural aggression and competition emerge and be expressed. Yet many women have still not tried it very often in their own lives. Therefore, such thoughts as "How do I fight? What will I sound and look like? Should I? Could I?" are deeply ingrained resonances that come to the surface as women on the witness stand are confronted by a fight.

Now, multiply this by the adversary being a man. What's the prototype? Who does a woman see as she is confronted by the cross-examining male lawyer?

Father, first. "What would he think? Be a lady. Behave nicely."

Perhaps the lawyer reminds her of fights with her brother, who often won just by sheer muscle. "Let's not tangle with *him*. I can get hurt."

Perhaps she thinks of her husband. What lessons has she learned about fighting with him? Within her family, where it's safe, she'll try to argue. She may dissolve in tears of anger and frustration at the inability to get her point across. Perhaps she screams. That involuntary, out-of-control sound somehow feels like a substitute for exerting physical force and power. She may feel pent-up rage without being able to express it, building the desire to be physical, to hit or fight back. But she hasn't learned how to throw a punch and has probably never experienced resorting to some form of aggressive physical release that has been a natural part of a boy's growing-up.

At the least, arguments with her husband are probably not noted for their cool and logical, cerebral and stylized form on either side, the form she is now confronted with by the cross-examiner.

What about lessons in aggression learned from Mom? What did she teach? Women's roles in the family traditionally have been peace-maker or supporter-helper-encourager, cheering from the sidelines as the men go forth to do battle. Mom's life patterns often demonstrated how to accommodate, not fight, when confronted by aggression. Even if she told her daughter to act differently, she couldn't show her how.

Given all these atavistic roadblocks to women expressing natural aggression or anger, or even learning how to fight back, what would most women witnesses do when confronted by a well-prepared, on-the-attack male lawyer? Would their behavior be all that different against a female lawyer? Although the female witness is more comfortable with her own kind, and the issue of physical aggression is not there, the woman lawyer is still an authority figure, representing and committed to opposition. The witness knows the lawyer is a professional, with experience in doing battle and the intention to do so.

Of course, these are all generalizations but they're meant to raise your awareness of the pre-set attitudes possible in your witnesses. These issues for men and women are important to consider because they can pre-condition and color how witnesses will react to the sheer aggression of cross-examination as a system.

Find Out How Your Witness Will Fight Back

It's important to get to this subject fairly early. Yet, since it's a sensitive one, it must be done sensitively and openly, explaining why it's important. In order to find the most natural, comfortable mode for your witness to handle the cross-examiner, explore your witness' attitudes and experiences.

Start with family experiences to uncover attitudes toward fighting back. For example, where does he or she fit in the original family's structure? Younger kids usually get bossed around by older brothers and sisters. Your witness may have learned to fight back or to play it safe and retreat. Older siblings often dare to be more aggressive, to beat up or intimidate the younger ones. Ask if he fought back physically, or was aggressive as a kid. If so, your witness may become really belligerent when the cross-examiner attacks.

If he's a fighter, don't turn him off. Use and redirect his energies. You may need to show him some of the pitfalls of unchanneled counter-attack, how the jury sees it and what the opposing counsel can do. But show him how to direct his energies to his head—to listen hard and try to see where the verbal punches are coming from and what they mean.

On the other hand, he may have learned to fold as a younger brother, seeing himself in a hopeless situation. This doesn't mean he won't fight back in this situation. He may just need you to give him a safer environment to fight from: a very clear picture of what will happen, how he can fight back and if he has a chance to win. People who don't normally fight back need to be taught some options that feel good to them, that fit their style, and that will also feel effective before they'll take a chance. Tell your witness that you will teach him techniques to use for opposing cross-examining counsel and that you will give him an opportunity to try them and to practice.

The same things are true for female witnesses. Find out how they feel about fighting back or being cornered and find techniques that feel right to them.

Effective Preparation Techniques

Now that you've oriented your witness about what to expect, it's time to instruct him or her. One of the most difficult aspect of teaching witnesses is to reassure and encourage at the same time that you're criticizing. How much is enough? What are they really grasping? Can they remember it until the trial? What will sustain them during the actual cross-examination? Here are some ways to help witnesses absorb new information and explore some responses to the cross-examination.

Role Play All Situations

The best way to get past fears and to instruct or change behavior is to find out what you naturally and instinctively do first. You need to experience and experiment with the witness. Role playing the direct and then the cross with a witness lets him experience the trial at first hand. He finds out how he answered, how it felt, if he did anything unacceptable and so on. And you get a chance to see his basic instincts at work so you can help him, not generically, but specifically.

Videotape and Replay Is the Ultimate Teaching Tool

If you can, try videotaping the role-playing. It's so much more effective than just letting the witness take your word for things. It can give a witness great confidence as he discovers he doesn't look nearly as nervous as he felt. He will see his own gestures and answers, and you can then talk about how this will affect the jury and what else one can do. A word of caution: Help him get past the usual shock and concern about how he looks and sounds on TV.

Television adds pounds and flattens features, since it is more horizontal than vertical (look at the shape of your screen.) Also, your lighting is hardly network quality. Be prepared. Your witness will surely talk about it.

Take the Witness to the Courtrom

Everyone's imagination runs rampant when they're nervous. Ground your witness in reality by showing him the actual courtroom. Then, to help him work through the cross, recreate the shape and space of the courtroom in your office as well as you can to help the witness imagine himself in the actual trial scene as you role play.

Teach the Witness How to Sit in the Chair

Body language, as you know, transmits more than words. Seeing how anyone "takes his space" gives the jury additional information about the strength and calmness of a witness.

Let your witness try sitting in the witness chair to find out how he fits and to see how he looks. The best way to sit in a chair to give an impression of security and confidence is to sit about 3/4 of the way back in the seat, with the upper back leaning against the back of the chair and the hands relaxed on the chair arms. Sitting all the way back looks rigid, tense and very proper; sitting on the edge looks anxious and strained. Hands clasped in the lap look parochial and clutching; this can also lead to distracting twisting and fidgeting.

Tell the Witness to Look at and Answer Only the Lawyer

If the witness looks at the jury while testifying, they will believe he is evasive or speaking for effect, not out of honesty. In direct and cross, the witness is talking to the lawyer; he is asking the questions that the witness is answering. The witness should see the jury as spectators, not audience.

Handle the Feeling of Isolation

The witness needs to experience his sense of aloneness in advance. For this part of your preparation, start to role-play by setting the witness up in a chair in your office. Place the witness as far as you can from you, unsupported and alone, with no furniture between the two of you and with no other props in front of him such as a desk or table. Really make him experience the idea of being in the spotlight. Let him feel alone, exposed and vulnerable. It helps bring to the surface any insecurities he may feel about this. You will then see and hear whether or how this total lack of physical support affects his performance as you cross-examine him. Keep this arrangement through all your role playing. Give the witness the idea that although he feels vulnerable, he is protectecd by your thorough preparation. Explain that you're monitoring what the opposing counsel is doing and that your ability to object will help him; remind him about your re-direct when the other lawyer is through, to help you fight back and pick up any pieces you need to.

Show Them the Worst That Can Happen

Place yourself behind a lectern as a lethal cross-examining lawyer, all cold and diabolical, or come charging out at him full of accusing voice and gesture. Be as threatening as you like, to show the worst of all possible worlds in order to let the witness find out what would happen if his worst fears were realized.

This becomes an excellent base on which to build. It smokes out the demons and lets you and the witness see his natural tendencies (aggressive, passive, defensive) if he's really attacked. Then you can show ways to recover and reassure him that he can handle it and how to do so.

Getting Back Some Power

The witness needs to feel he can take back some of the power, that he needn't automatically cede all power to the cross-examining lawyer, even though the lawyer looks so strong. Tell the witness that there are many things he can do to give himself a chance to recover. Begin by having him create a visual image in his mind of gently but firmly pushing the lawyer back whenever he feels assaulted. Show him how to take a breath, sit up and regain some of his own forward momentum.

De-personalize the Opposing Lawyer's Attacks

"He is not attacking you as a person." Show your witness that he is one of the major impediments to the opposing lawyer's developing the case his own way. One of the predictable ways any lawyer convinces the jury is to say that what he, the witness, said is not true, because the lawyer wants more credibility for what *his* witnesses will say.

Give the witness a small motto to say in his head, such as, "It's not you, it's what you're talking about," or "He's attacking issues, not a person." This helps the witness focus and concentrate and not internalize the attack. It helps him tune into the subject being argued about. It gives him sharper listening skills and supplies some bolstering and support when he feels hurt or especially vulnerable. It also helps him see the cross as part of a scheme, what lawyers do to all opposing witnesses and what you'll do to the other side, too.

Show Counter Techniques

Let me start by saying you should never teach unethical, evasive tactics to pretend ignorance. Your witness must speak the truth. But do tell your witness he can stop the lawyer in several ways. For example, he can get the lawyer off his rhythm of "Isn't that correct," and "Isn't it a fact," by saying, "I'm sorry . . . would you repeat your question." In a complex question, he can ask, "Which part of that question do you want me to answer first?" Teach him how to qualify his answers and explain, and not to be so willing to just give in and follow the leader. Answering more slowly to stop the momentum is also useful.

In such a moment, even if it's only a moment, the witness has taken back some power. Now he's stopped the flow; he's become active by questioning and doesn't feel quite so much on the receiving end. It gives the witness courage and energy and lets him get the feeling that it is possible to participate. The jury notices this counter move and sees it as strong, alert and trying to be clear, not obstructive.

Of course, I'm sure you will tell him not to obfuscate, since the jury will pick that up very quickly, and the judge can also come down on him. But show him how not to answer until he understands and that he can slow the pace if it's too oppressive. (It's like hitting a lob back in tennis until you can catch your breath.)

Teach Your Witness to Listen
Thoroughly and Critically

It is human nature to try to anticipate what the cross-examiner will do next and what the questions might be. Many witnesses don't really listen but answer what they think the question is about.

Role-play and show your witness what's in a question. Show

him *your* techniques for hiding the real meaning of a question and then teach him to take it apart, to think in what direction the cross-examiner is going and to be very aware. Help him learn to listen and answer only the questions asked—no more.

The best technique is to cross-examine him and then stop, asking the witness to tell you what you asked and what you really meant. This sharpens the ear and makes the mind connect. Of course, you understand about teaching him to amplify, describe or qualify his answer if he needs to. But first the essence is good listening skills.

Don't Be too Critical

People are their own worst critics. If you focus too much on all the witness is doing wrong as you role-play, it will discourage him and panic him more.

Rather, start each critique with the good news. Find the thing he did right, the instinct that worked. You must show your faith; encourage him to feel that he can handle the cross and that he *can* understand before you start expecting him to add new moves and think with new insights.

Videotape and replay provides its own criticism. But even if you don't use that, critique by objectivity, picking out the principles, the reasons things do or don't work and point them out first. Avoid saying, "Look how you did this," or "That was wrong." Rather, you should say, "See what happens when a person does that," or "The jury might think thus and so." Then there's more room for him to hear, digest and try based on a concept rather than just trying to fix a bad performance.

DEVELOPING YOUR CROSS EXAMINATION

Now, let's change gears and talk about you, the cross-examiner. No more Mr. Nice Guy, figuring out how to be supportive to a victim. Move into your toughest, most adversarial inner self and come out of the corner a fighter. But if you've been reading and agreeing with me so far, here is one of the most dangerous pitfalls of the trial: Cross-examining as a fighter, an attacker, visible to the jury as the heartless manipulator/lawyer they all expected to see.

This is not necessary. Let's discover some new ways to fight, to do your job as cross-examiner more effectively and more persuasively and not to hit the pitfall of overt aggression.

The secret of a good cross is to get the jury involved. Like a good detective story, you must intrigue them and get them to follow the clues you drop along the way. They will stay tuned in and listen attentively as they work to discover where you're going. You must first establish a line of questioning that makes them ask themselves, "What is this all about? Why is he asking that? What's he getting at?" Then, as you continue, each question begins to reveal what your thrust is. The more you uncover, the more interested they become until they can say "Aha!" almost before the final answer.

You must also help them to move from visceral, instinctive judgment to a more distanced vantage-point where their cerebral and analytical judgment takes over. Therefore, you can't set yourself up as an adversary against a layman, the witness. They will stay with feelings and take sides with the witness and, consequently, won't hear the testimony.

Remember, the jury expects you to attack. They'll look to your body language to tell them about your intentions. An indirect, lateral or circuitous approach, rather than a frontal one, is necessary so they can't see you coming, head-on, to do battle. Rather, you need to focus the jury on the facts, the points, the new information gleaned, just letting it all unfold with no hands showing. You must wield a sharp and skillful scalpel—"Look, Ma, no hands!"—so no one sees you cutting; they just see what you uncover.

Beginnings

How you begin the cross sets the tone and the jury's attitude toward how you and your examination will be perceived. It's the old "first impressions" issue again, but this one is even more consequential because of the pre-conditioned image the jury carries about what cross-examinations are like and what they're supposed

to accomplish. Therefore, thoughtful care should be taken to prepare what you'll do first. The beginning should allow the jury time
to see what you're doing and how, to be surprised, drop their
guard, clear their minds and get intrigued as they see you haven't
leaped out of your corner fighting. Then they should get involved
in the material, hearing it critically, analyzing where you're going
and finally leaping ahead of you toward your carefully planned
conclusion.

Lift the Jury's Energy for the Cross

The jury is often bored after a long direct examination. Seeing
you get up may really glaze over their eyes and minds as they con-
template more talk and more questions (especially if the witness is
boring). Generally, you should move into position energetically,
with enthusiasm and purpose. Arrange your notes, put them down
and settle into your spot. Take your space. Wait for a beat or two
after you're in place to get all attention focused on you. Make eye
contact with the witness. Take a breath and begin—lightly, and
with a lift, which will be reflected in the jury's renewed attention.

Make a Transition from the Direct

Take the time to make a separation between the direct and
the cross. Let the other lawyer's voice and images die down.

Notice the atmosphere at the end of direct. What do you want
to do? If it's somber and sad, you can't jump up full of energy as
though you didn't hear what just happened. Come in on the same
wave length but then build up and away from it.

If the direct ended very forcefully, with an emotional crescendo, take a few moments to let it fade away. Say nothing. Get up
and get yourself positioned. Put your notes in order. Look confident, take a deep breath and start out on another tack. Show the
contrast between you and the direct examiner.

Feel the ambience. Think about how you can make a new and
individual statement, taking the jury under the arm with you as
you go.

Start Subtly

A successful cross is a subtle cross. Let nothing in your body language, your voice, or your energy level betray that this will be an attack. Approach with humanity, without judgment. Just begin by introducing yourself pleasantly if you like or suggesting you'd like to discuss a couple of points.

Don't Try to Develop "Rapport" With the Witness

The jury has a nose for phony friendliness. Remember they're still looking for the attacking cross-examiner, one who is ready to leap up and say, "You're lying!" They know this is your opponent. Don't give them reason to doubt your sincerity throughout the whole trial by affecting exaggerated warmth at this point. Rather, be courteous and considerate in your approach, with a clear understanding that you come from the other side and that your points will be made because of what you know and because they're true. Show dignity and integrity even if you dislike or don't respect the witness.

Don't Patronize

Telling the witness he can interrupt you if he doesn't understand or if he needs a glass of water implies he's stupid or weak, or that you anticipate your questions will be so obscure and complex he'll need an interpreter. This is often seen as patronizing and transparent by the jury.

Don't Say "I Just Have One or Two Simple Questions"

Unless that's actually true, the jury will quickly see this as a ploy and secretly call your bluff as you launch into a full-sized cross. There are other ways to seemingly put the witness at ease. This one becomes blatantly clear very soon.

Start by Sorting Out

"Let's see if we can agree on a couple of points." This is extremely disarming and gets the witness and the jury off-guard. It also helps sift out what they don't need to consider in order to focus the jury's attention more sharply on what *is* at issue.

Use Small, Simple Questions First

Let the jury and witness believe your seemingly simple curiosity. Get the examination going by asking benign, clear, short questions of the witness. He will feel secure if you start on safe, neutral ground, discussing a relatively minor point, before you get into deeper and more controversial waters. This also helps the jury change gears and start following your direction.

Get the Jury Involved Early

The jury doesn't really understand the end product you want from cross-examination. If you want them to follow your clues to the big admission, then you must help by tuning them in early to the general direction in which you're heading, and then showing them why you're going there.

Intrigue them. Begin asking questions around a certain focused area that you name. It makes them sit forward and ask, "What's this for?" Then uncover the pieces bit by bit, but make them keep adding up toward a point pretty quickly so that they grasp it and want to see you go on. Alert them by using topic sentences so they see what the subject matter is.

The Use of the Lectern

The lectern can be a symbol of power, individual strength, distance, formality, coolness and objectivity—as well as of the courtroom process itself. It can be played like an instrument as you decide when to go behind it, what moving out to the side of it means or when you choose to leave it.

For your "benign and friendly" opening, you could move to the side of it (if you must stay in contact at all times in your jurisdiction), as a symbol of dropping the barrier or reaching out—person to person. If you can, move about the courtroom and leave the lectern altogether, so you are seen as unencumbered, out-in-the-open (literally), relaxed, at ease and in control.

Go back behind the lectern when you begin a more serious, accusatory line of questioning. It stands for factual objectivity and looks like the law. This separates the benign from the meaningful and lets the jury know when to move into a more attentive gear.

You might like to establish the lectern as your beachhead and use its cold formality to intimidate from the beginning, never leaving it except to show documents to the witness or to go to an exhibit. In any case, be aware that the lectern affects the jury's perception of what's happening.

Approaching the Unusual Witness

There is a fine line to walk here. The jury must see your sensitivity to the situation but you mustn't fawn or patronize. If you do, they will accuse you of insincerity. They know your job is to cross-examine and they expect you to do it. However, if you must cross-examine such a witness, you must put to rest the jury's fears that the witness is too weak, old, incapacitated or vulnerable to be a credible candidate for your questions. If you can't, the answers you get are not worth much. So handle the witness with respect and regard for his comfort, but also as a capable adult who can and will rise to the occasion.

If the witness is a child, you have to deal with the jury's instinct to defend him against a bully, as well as the possibility that they will not put much credence in a child's answer. Explain what you're going to do. "Just a few more questions, Billy," and be sure your cross will be fairly short. You might try sitting in a chair in front of him to reduce the size and power image. Again, don't be cute or fawning. Imagine you're talking to another child on your block, asking what else he knows about your broken window (you might get carried away if you imagine him as one of your own.)

Show respect and an understanding of his strange position. Show your interest and curiosity about getting some more facts, and a willingness to scale down your rhetoric but *not* your goals or your task. It requires a delicate hand on the reins.

Don't be obsequious as you ask if a witness is comfortable or if he can hear you. You might suggest a way you'll question him to get past some major obstacle. For example, if he's blind in one eye, offer to stand to one side. Explain any other unique arrangement you plan to make. If the witness is deaf, say hello to the interpreter. After that, handle this cross like all the others, with perhaps greater sensitivity to the stereotypical image of the killer cross-examiner, but still as a thoughtful professional doing his work.

If You Have No Cross, Explain

Juries really expect to have opposing lawyers question a witness to get both sides of the story. They don't understand the fine points of why you choose not to. "I have nothing further" can make them misunderstand. They may think you can't think of anything or are too defeated by the direct to even try. In an opening statement you might mention that you will not cross-examine every witness because . . . . Then, when you don't, they are already alerted.

When called on, give a short one or two line explanation, like "I don't need to ask anything else at this time," "There is no need for a cross-examination now," or anything that comes to mind that says you deliberately did this because it fits your master plan, and that they'll hear more from you later.

Another way to do this is to say, "We represent the XYZ Company. The witness is an expert on points 1, 2 and 3, which have to do with the other company's case and have nothing to do with my case. I need not question this witness."

If there is more than one defendant, mention, in opening statement, that you will not cross-examine all the witnesses, since they don't all bear on the issues of your case. Then when that witness is on the stand, the jury will understand when you say, "I have no questions for this witness. He does not bear on my case."

Organization

In your zeal to "get at him" you sometimes lose sight of the contrast between your clear laser-like sight lines drawn directly to the issues or key points of the case and the jury's wide-angled view of a very busy, information-laden and unfamiliar landscape, often out of focus. They see only the forest. You have to point out the individual trees.

Therefore, how you organize your material is extremely important. Always begin by asking yourself, "What do I want to accomplish? How can I do that?" Not only should you select what you're going after, you must decide how to get there. Leaping up over buildings to jump directly into the middle of a busy street is dramatic and attention-getting, but be sure the jury sees where you came from so they'll appreciate your leap. People do follow a natural path to learn something new. They need orientation, encouragement to take the steps, a road map, and time to stop on a corner to look back where they've been and be sure where they're going before they move on.

Tell the Jury What You're Doing

Juries often miss the point. They are totally unfamiliar with the file. They do not know all the nuances and details of the case. They've never heard the case before and they don't know what else is coming up afterwards so as to be able to make connections. Since they are trying to gather all this information, which is given orally, it is often very difficult for them to follow and make sense out of one part or another of the testimony unless you lead the way.

Plant each issue firmly and clearly in the opening statement and use those phrases again as you ask the questions on cross-examination. Then the jury can connect with what you said at the outset of the trial, when you told them which issues you were going to bring out and they know why it's important to listen to them now. Unless they know why you are pursuing a line of questioning and where it fits in the whole scheme, the testimony will have little value.

Put Your Questions in Order

It is extremely hard for the jury to know what you have planned and why you planned it that way. The points must be underlined and clarified and put in continuous order for them so they can relate the new testimony to other points that have been made previously and, finally, remember what you want them to remember at the end. You must develop each point logically and in order. Use simple chronology as you develop a point; use time, day and date references, and do this visually, writing them down, or continuing to remind the jury so they can follow. If you're out of sequence, tell them, "Let's go back to the first time. . . ."

What Are the Differences?

One of the most significant ways to make cross-examination meaningful is to establish a clear contrast between what was said in direct and what is being said now. State the subject. Describe the issue. Show the discrepancy or the omission in the testimony. Relate it to what has been said before. Unless the jury sees a difference, your points are lost. Be sure to remind the jury, through your questions, what was said and how that differs from what is now being said. They can't remember without specific reference points.

Remember to Recap

As orderly as you think you're making your points, the jury is most often "at sea." Help by recapitulating what was just brought out, subject to the restraints on repetitive examination.
Example:

And when you saw that car go by you at 75 miles an hour, you also saw the driver waving out the window, didn't you?

Put it in order for the jury before you go on to the next point. Use the outline form of topic sentences to define or list the points you're covering. And as you finish an area of questioning, recap

what you uncovered to help the jury remember details more
clearly.

Example:

> Now let me understand this, Mr. Pepper. After you saw him hit
> her, you didn't try to stop him, did you?
> You just told us you didn't call for help either, did you?
> You didn't even call the police, true?
> You just watched it and walked away, right?

Use Visuals for Clarity

For a powerful effect, try to use the same visuals that were
used by the direct examiner if you can. Using the opposition's
charts to show digressions, dichotomies and inconsistencies makes
a very strong statement. You didn't write on it, the witness did and
so did his lawyer. And yet, they were leaving out certain parts of
the story or another point of view which you can now add. It becomes much more condemnatory because it is their own material.
And you can alter the visual image left in the jury's mind by the
direct.

Or you can create your own visuals. Write on a blackboard or
flip chart to help the jury see exactly where you're going. They will
participate with much more attention as you use another dimension to clarify and question. Draw the same diagram again, if the
direct examiner has removed his, showing the same beginning
with another point of view and another ending. (For more on the
use of visuals, see Chapter 8.)

Use Comparison

One of the strongest, clearest ways to show the difference in
testimony is to use comparison, and the best way to do that is
visually.

Example: In a case involving conflicting testimony about the
times or dates, make a list and show what was said on direct and
what you can extract now. In a case where the issue revolves
around when an illness began and if a specific event caused it, you
might want to contrast the health of the patient and the events be-

fore and after a certain date that might have led up to the illness. List all the dates on a time line—adding a description next to each date as you write it. It stands still and continues to testify cumulatively as you gather further information.

Just remember that anything that is organized to clearly define the norm and is then made visual gives the jury a basis for evaluating severity, deviation from regular patterns, differences between one statement and another and the contrast between the direct and the cross.

EXAMINATION TECHNIQUES

Questioning the Witness

Effective questioning techniques should make you feel and look like a wise, fair and conscientious person on a quest. Opening a door, you let the jury discover what's inside by shining a spotlight on it. Then, nudging them, you point out the new discovery to the jury, saying, "What do you think of that? Just look at this. See what I mean?"

Don't Feel Hostile Toward the Witness

Feel secure enough in the idea that your points are so clear and will soon be so well made that you don't need to be angry or lean hard on anybody. Believe you have the facts and the logic on your side. Allow the witness to hang himself. Don't march up to the cross-examination table with a noose in your hand. You will get in the way of the testimony and the jury will make it a personality contest between you and the witness, which you will usually lose, since you're a pro and the witness is a layman. Remember what the jury expects. Surprise them.

See the cross from another perspective. You don't need to "wring" admissions from the witness. Rather, see your job as a clear and thoughtful analyst. Feel that the facts must inevitably come to light because you will deftly seek them out. The facts will do their own work on the jury. In our culture it's bad form to "gang up," it makes you look weaker, like a bully.

Don't Become Irate Too Soon

Uncovering obviously misleading statements or misinformation tempts lawyers to jump up and down with righteous indignation. Resist! You rob the jury of its need to get involved and feel irate on its own. Don't vent the jury's anger for them. Be sure you understand the great value of keeping the jury engaged. Let the jury do their work. Let *them* get angry. You must be the catalyst, the dissector, the agitator. See yourself nudging them with your elbow. This will help you to ask your questions with the correct tone of voice. Remember, the goal is to be sure that the *jury* sees it. Underline. Repeat. Show them your massive self-control, being so provoked and yet not losing yourself. But be sure they get the point of what the testimony is showing.

Know When to Move in

Judge Thelton Henderson of the Northern District of California says:

> Cross-examination is like a boxing match. You spar and circle around until you find an opening. Then you go in and deliver your flurry of punches and then back off and spar again, looking for another opening.

> Be sure that not every sentence has a punch in it. Save those for the openings you see and for moving in. Otherwise, circle around looking for the opportunity to get aggressive. Keep the lead-ups lighter and more factual.

Remember to Listen

Be careful that while you are busy testifying, presenting your closed questions and setting up your short, "Yes-or-no" answer pattern, that you don't forget to listen. When you're driving for your points you can get so charged up that sometimes you hardly leave room for the witness to actually answer yes or no or for the jury to even hear it. It can look like a one-way steamroller and the jury begins to doubt what's being said. And you may miss a cue, inadvertently dropped by the witness, that can take you off to something new or give you a short cut to where you're going.

Maintain Your Eye Contact

That's almost become a cliche. There are many reasons to keep doing this, but let's analyze why it is important in this part of the trial.

A direct gaze intimidates the witness. It helps set up the rhythm and control that you're looking for. It keeps the witness focused and concerned as he feels you looking at him. It becomes harder for him to play with his answers. Your eyes seem to say, "I *know* and I'm watching you." A clear gaze, unflinching, makes you seem on solid ground. It also helps you keep your own thoughts more focused. It energizes you as your opponent stays visible to you.

Another reason is that you have ample opportunity to watch his body language to know when you're hitting a sensitive spot. Look for fidgeting in the chair, changing position, clearing the throat or swallowing, change of pace, lowered voice or nervous hand gestures as signs of insecurity or tension.

Be Careful of Your Body Language

Are you a finger-pointer? It's an attack signal that looks like everyone's parents accusing or teaching them a lesson. Just open your fingers and use the whole hand instead. Watch pointing with a pen. You're not writing. Put it down. It looks like a school teacher taking notes.

Be careful of your witness' space. Don't intrude on it. Close-up physical presence heightens the look of aggression and belligerence. Stand back so as not to be misunderstood. Of course, in case you have good reason and decide to attack, just turn these techniques around and use them. But always evaluate the pros and cons. (For more on space, body language, and gesture, see Chapter 9.)

Watch the Use of "Legalese" in Your Questions

The jury resents big or unfamiliar words for the witness and for themselves. They know the witness probably can't understand them and it looks like you're showing off or like a put-down. Make your language simple and clear, not only to get a full answer, but because if the jury doesn't understand, what's the use of your question?

Try Not to Get Into a Legal Battle With the Other Lawyer

The jury finds legal battles really tedious. You exclude them. You interrupt the flow of the examination. The jurors are thoroughly disinterested, tune out and resent it. Consider this when you pick your fights. Also, be careful about being nasty, calling names or casting aspersions on the other lawyer when you do fight. The jury really hates that and thinks it's unprofessional. When the opposing counsel objects, don't look at him. You give him too much importance and credence. Look only at the judge and speak only to him or her. (See Chapter 4 for more on handling objections.)

Be Careful of the Litany

Use many variations of "Isn't that correct?" and "Isn't it a fact?" Do not continually repeat one phrase. After a while it can become very tedious and irritating for the jury to listen to. It loses its power and sounds terribly predictable. Find a number of alternatives and use them interchangeably, such as "Didn't you?" "You did do that?" "That's true, isn't it?" "Right?" "Yes?"

Still another way to get yes or no answers is to start a question with "Wouldn't you agree with me that . . ." or "Would you agree with me that . . ." The word "agree" has a positive tone and makes a temporary colleague of a possible hostile witness. The jury is very surprised to hear that you can both agree on anything.

Use your own creativity to find other phrases that will do what you want. The entire examination will sound more alive, spontaneous and interesting, like you are pursuing information, not fitting something into a mold. By the way, don't use the "Is it not true?" form of question. The answer is too ambiguous—"Yes (it is not true)," or "No (it is not true)," or "Yes (it is true)."

Also note that "Isn't it a fact" as an opening to a question is much more argumentative than "Did you see," or "You saw . . . didn't you?" You flag your witness to bristle, to become defensive and to resist answering you right from the start when you use the former question.

The Drive for "Yes" or "No"

Although it is classic to ask such closed questions that the witness can only answer "Yes" or "No," there is a problem with that.

The witness won't do it.

Witnesses are on the alert against being boxed in. If your question is too ambiguous the witness will want to explain or qualify. Often the problem is in your phrasing of the question. Question them in short, bite-sized pieces and cover only one point at a time. Be sure your questions are answerable with yes or no. Don't push right away; first re-state the question. Show how reasonable you are. Be careful about saying, "Just answer the question 'Yes' or 'No.' " Juries dislike that. It's curt, discourteous and looks very aggressive and unreasonable as well as showing you're afraid of a fuller answer.

If the Witness Persists in Avoiding Answering

The jury takes points away from you if you bicker with the witness. You're supposed to be smarter than he. Keep your cool. Be graceful, forceful and final. Just ask your question again gently and say, with no rancor, "Now you can answer that, can't you?" or begin by saying "Let me ask it again." If he changes the question in his answer say, "That wasn't quite the question I asked you, was it?" Repeating the exact same question, not changing any words, several times, alerts the jury to what's happening.

What's most important, if the witness is avoiding answering

you, is to make the jury see it. The witness will lose points because the jury will think he has something to hide, or that he's playing with them, hoping to fool them. But be sure to make the jury aware of what's happening.

I saw Wyoming attorney Jerry Spence do a masterful job on a cross-examination after repeated stalling and rephrasing by a witness. He wrote and identified his question on the board saying "That's the question I asked you." Then under it he wrote and identified the witness' rephrased question saying "And that's the question you were answering." Then, looking at the witness, he said quietly, "Now you can answer *my* question can't you?"

Don't Ask the Judge to Direct the Witness to Answer

Try not to do this if you can help it. It looks like you can't handle it and you're going home to get Mommy or Daddy to help. If the witness is out of control you might turn to the judge and say, "Your Honor, perhaps the witness doesn't understand that he must answer the question."

Interrupting a Witness

The extremely verbal and eloquent English barristers rarely interrupt a witness in cross-examination. They let the witness run on and when he's finished they say, "Are you quite finished? Perhaps you didn't understand my question. Listen to it again . . . Now will you answer *that* question?"

If you wish to interrupt, you might say "Excuse me" and repeat the question. If he continues, you might interrupt again by saying "I'm sorry, did you hear my question?" (Yes.) "Did you understand my question?" (Yes.) "Then will you please answer it?"

In all of these situations, be sure that as you discipline that witness, you let the jury know he is being shifty and evasive by showing them what question he didn't want to answer. But never lose your self-control or composure. *He's* doing something wrong, not you.

Don't Just Drop It

It is important to pursue and stay with the witness till you get a reasonable facsimile of what you want. Dropping it like a hot potato looks bad to the jury; it looks like the witness beat you. A sense of timing is vital. Try some of the previously mentioned suggestions. If you're still hitting a stone wall, find a way to save face by saying, "I see you don't want to answer that. Perhaps you'll answer this question," and then go on, following your original question about that issue by asking a series of smaller ones that circle the area till you can go in for the key one again or just move off.

Hanging on too long becomes irritating and underscores your defeat. Get a feeling for how much is enough before it gets tedious, and when to move on, which keeps your momentum and control. Even if you change the subject, move into it deliberately by showing a transition, not just silence.

When You Get Hurt by a Witness' Answer

Sometimes a witness on cross really gets you or his answer hurts you. To keep your cool, and to keep the momentum going, you might say, "Let's talk about that." This makes it sound like you're not at all worried but are ready to dig in. Start by bringing up something simple that you can agree on or that has already been agreed on to reverse the witness' negative response. Then keep going and build into another subject where you're on solid ground. Don't just stop dead and try to change the subject. That makes you look like you just got beaten. An excellent retort on such an occasion, or if the witness argues with you, is a line Professor James Jeans of the University of Missouri Law School uses. Put them away with, "Well, that's for the jury to decide."

When to "Kill" the Witness

Sometimes the jury *wants* a lawyer to punish a witness, to do their work for them. If the witness is a discredited person, if he has shown duplicity and dishonesty on the stand, or if his reason for being in court is an unacceptable act towards society in general, then go get him.

Your moral outrage as one of the good citizens of your community and as a spokesman for us all is not only in order, but will get you points. There are many ways to do this:

• Distance yourself physically. The lectern, that symbol of righteousness, is the perfect place for you.

• Shake your head in disbelief or nod with cynical expectation at the answers.

• If you've got a short fuse, let the jury see your controlled anger. Breathe in deeply, look off into the distance and then continue.

• Be careful not to go too far. Keep your dignity.

• Remember, *you're* the *good* guy.

Persuasive Uses of Evidence

Since you see tangible evidence in terms of its factual significance, your focus is often on being sure you get it admitted and figuring out when and how to use it. But there is another interesting area you may not have thought about—how to use and handle the evidence itself for its dramatic value, to make an emotional impact on the jury.

The Printed Word

You should understand the power of the printed word in the eyes of the jury. Everything that happens in the courtroom that is not printed is happening before their eyes at the moment. Oral testimony feels improvisational and transitory. Although they've seen and watched it happen, basically the jury thinks that it's probably a little malleable. It happened this way, at this moment, with these people. Tomorrow they could say it a little differently. Different people could make it sound different again.

The one thing that is totally objective to everyone is the printed word. It is timeless. It stands all by itself. Nobody can change it. It feels like it's carved in granite. It stands still, a much truer truth than anything they can only hear. So whenever you introduce the printed word (documents, letters, books), know that it carries with it extraordinary weight. It comes from another time, another place, and it has lasted until this moment. It is accepted by the judge. It is *bona fide* evidence. It can also carry greater weight if you make a big show of presenting it and putting it into evidence. Then, when you read from it, it sounds sonorous, ominous, much more important than anything anybody has said to date.

Impeachment with Depositions

When you use the printed word, such as depositions for impeachment, there's a need for caution. The jury has no idea what a deposition is. They've never seen one taken. They don't understand the process. They've never heard the word and they do not understand the importance of it, so its weight as prior testimony is lost.

Therefore, before you try to use a deposition as an instrument of impeachment, make a word picture so the jury can really understand what it is. Make it serious and important. Through your witness, create a total picture of the scene. The most telling aspects are:

- You remember you came to my office to give a deposition?
- You were protected by your lawyer, who was there with you?
- Your lawyer prepared you for the fact that you were going to do this?
- I told you that you could stop me at any time and ask, if you didn't understand something?
- I told you it could be read in court?
- A court reporter took everything down?
- You swore under oath, at the beginning, just as you did today, to tell me the whole truth?
- You read it and signed it?
- This is your signature, isn't it?

Show the jury there was nothing nefarious about it, no coercive plot. You didn't manipulate him in a dark corner and squeeze a confession from him. Rather, in the clear light of day with his lawyer present, the witness said all of these things, swore to them and signed the deposition.

As the jury hears this description and visualizes the process, the deposition becomes ten times more powerful. Now the jury really understands its significance. They understand how objective and serious a deposition is and that the witness understood it all when he swore to what he said. Think through what the jury doesn't already know whenever you bring up damaging evidence.

Who Should Read from a Deposition?

Should you let the witness read from the deposition or should the lawyer read it?

When the lawyer reads from the deposition, he can color it. He can speak with emphasis and imbue the words with a great deal of meaning. Of course, the jury knows that; they know you'll overdo it a little and make it more dramatic if you can. Your reading it gives you great control, but be careful how you do it. The jury understands. Yet the lawyer's reading is clearly a more powerful and dramatic delivery, accenting exactly what was meant.

What happens when the witness must read the damning phrase himself? When he can't wriggle out from under it? There is something quite fascinating about watching a person hang himself with something he said earlier, which he is now powerless to change. It becomes, in a certain sense, a purer truth. If he mumbles, you can draw the jury's attention to it. Say, "I'm sorry. We couldn't hear you. Will you speak up and say it again?" Be sure, as you approach the witness, that you don't get between him and the jury. Let them savor every last moment, just as you do.

You can also combine both: Set it up, let the witness read it, then you recap and re-read it for more emphasis, as you take it back before you put it away. Make your choice as to who reads based on the material and the witness, and what you feel will create the most tellling effect.

An interesting suggestion is made by Michigan attorney Ed Stein. He arranges to have the original deposition, the one admitted and marked with the court's stamp, to be available on top of all the admitted documents at the beginning of his cross. Then he uses that very document, which he shows to the jury, stamp and all, to impeach the witness. It gives an extra punch.

The Physical Handling of Evidence

Objects you place in evidence give the opportunity for dramatic eloquence by the way you handle them. The additional statement they can make by your use of non-verbal techniques can have a much more memorable effect than just the fact of their existence.

Do not matter-of-factly pick up any object, whether it's a gun, the condemning forged check, the coroner's report of the accident victim or the pictures of the collapsed building and simply handle them as objects. They have within them as much power as voices and people, if you handle them correctly. Think in advance of what this object is. What did it do? Why do you place it in evidence? Decide how you want the jury to feel about it. This is emotional confrontation time. This is the real thing, not description. This is tangible, living proof of what happened, what it really looks like. Often these are objects people have never seen up close before. They have horror and fascination and repulsion in them.

Handle such objects differently from the way you handle your notes or anything else you've just been holding. Take a pause. Pick it up slowly. Bring it to the bench carefully. Don't talk for a moment. Build a little suspense. Pronounce your wish to place this object in evidence with some weight, with a different tone of voice from anything you've used before. Handle it in such a way that the jury is keenly aware of it and that it makes a visual impression. Then turn and show it first to the witness and then to the jury.

Let the Jury See

One of the greatest problems in relation to evidentiary material is the fact that the jury rarely gets a good look at what it is you're talking about. This greatly reduces the value it could have for you. If you haven't really shown them what the evidence is up close—what a deposition looks like, what the signature on the contract looks like, the gun, the crumpled piece of metal that comes from the ladder which caused a man to fall and break his neck—

then the trial is all hearsay to them. When the jury is excluded, they feel frustrated and finally remove themselves and become less involved. When you let them see or touch, their own senses, and their imagination go to work to enlarge and deepen the impression you wish to make.

The Right Moment

When you first design your case, think through what are the most dramatic, tangible pieces of evidence you have. Build your examinations knowing what the right moment would be to bring them forth. Think of impact, of the effect it will create, and that the evidence will then continue to be visible to the jury. It can continue to testify on its own and remain eloquent or useful as comparison with or reinforcement of what they hear. See your evidence as having the potential to breathe new life into a possibly tedious or dull examination.

*   *   *

Whether it is in direct or cross examination, look at all your evidentiary material as an ally, another witness. In our visually oriented society it can be worth a thousand words.

The Ending

Even with all you've done before, how you end a cross-examination leaves the most lasting impression. It flavors the testimony and shows us who feels he's winning. The importance of the ending therefore calls for some careful planning.

End on a High Note

This cannot be emphasized enough, since the jury really doesn't understand all the ins and outs of a cross-examination. They have some idea of what you're doing. They may hear a few of the points you wanted to uncover. Most of all, they don't know whether the witness has hurt you or not. Only you and your opposing counsel know that. So if you keep your courage up, look as though what happened was exactly what you wanted to happen and sit down quite delighted, they will assume you won that round.

One Chicago lawyer writes a series of one-or-two word cues for points he would like to bring out, and keeps his pen next to him. As he finishes each question and the witness answers yes or no, he checks off a point on his list with a flourish. Then he checks off the next one, and the next as he gets each answer. As he aims his last question and gets the answer, the lawyer makes his last check with a big flourish and say, "No more questions, Your Honor," and sits down with a smile. Although he may just have gotten killed, he looks totally satisfied and the jury assumes that whatever points he made, even if they weren't terribly clear to the jury, were just exactly what the lawyer planned. He won. And that's the right image for finishing a cross.

Don't Just Fade Away

Don't let the jury see you fumble. No matter what happens, keep your energy and your self-assurance up. Be very sure when you come to the end that the jury feels you're a winner. Don't stand there, hesitating, running through a few more questions in your mind or your notes and then hesitantly say, "Umm . . . ah . . . , no more questions." Sit down with a very definitive, "No more questions, Your Honor" and a sense of satisfaction.

Don't ever stop on a sustained objection or where the witness has won the battle. Always keep one safe line of cross-examination, carefully prepared from the deposition transcript, to finish with. Always find a way to save face, even by picking up the last admission and repeating it, as though it were a gold mine of information.

Plan Ahead

Know your last line. Building to a climax is something you do before you start. If you know where you wish to end, back-track to figure out how to get there.

A steady build to a climax is the most powerful way. Be sure you've got the jury with you so they can almost anticipate what's coming. Sometimes a Beethoven-like climax of three key punch-line cymbal crashes is possible. Use it if you can—the echo reverberates for a long time.

So you never saw the red light, did you?

No.

You rode right through that intersection, didn't you?

Yes.

The only thing that finally stopped you was Nancy—Nancy's little body, flying through the air when you hit it.

Sense When to Get Off-Stage

If your questioning takes another turn than you had planned and you're going great guns, quickly evaluate if *this* might not be your ending. Don't rigidly adhere to an earlier script. Your momentum and consequent climax may do much more than one more line of questioning. Feel the dynamics of your cross. Feel the moment. And, as Irving Younger always reminds you, beware! Resist! Don't ask the extra question, the one-too-many. With it you may watch the instant disintegration of your whole edifice. Know when to stop and get off stage.

*   *   *

After all this advice about form and style and structure and content, go back and think about the cross-examination as the sum of its parts.

It's not just dos and don'ts and techniques all strung together. Even if your points are logical and correct, the key ingredient is feeling: how the jury *feels* about what they heard and how they thought you and the witness felt.

Like every part of the trial, the cross-examination is a performance for persuasive effect, as well as for the getting and giving of information. And, like all performances, your cross should have a beginning, a middle and an end. It should have drama, intrigue, and suspense. It has villains and heroes, conflict and resolution, but most of all, it's a great performance that totally captures the audience. Think of how to capture yours.

See your cross in its totality, choreograph it, design it from start to finish:

- How do you begin?
- At what level of energy?
- What mood will you bring?
- Where are you going?
- What are your major points?
- Will the jury know that?
- Where is the drama?
- How will you show it?
- What is the climax?
- How will you get there?
- How will you end?

Cross-examination is a test of self-discipline: to be at a high level of adversary attack, and at the same time holding back so that the jury can catch up as you step aside to let them see, too. Save most of your histrionics for final argument; in cross, just stay cool, strong and insistent, and get the facts.

6

EXPERT WITNESSES

An expert is a person with superior knowledge in a given subject, superior to laymen, that is. We all assume that an expert, by reason of education and experience, has achieved a certain level of recognition, acclaim and power in his or her particular area and we basically respect their expertise.

When one thinks about experts, the images that come to mind most often are doctors, engineers, scientists, economists, researchers and academics. But you are an expert, too. A lawyer is an expert on the law and trial procedure, and in the case of expert witnesses, that creates some problems. Each of you comes to the joint task of working together in a trial with certain pre-set conditions. You come together with individual and personal agendas, specific needs and a high level of investment in your own professionalism that are often inimical to and competitive with each other. Therefore, the scene is set for some difficulty in communicating and coming to a common agreement about how the expert will do his job for you in the trial.

ISSUES AND INSIGHTS

Whenever people meet to accomplish a task, there are two levels of consciousness and behavior: what should be and what is. How we *behave* connects with how we should be. How we *feel* is connected to the basic truth, to how we really *are*. Problems and conflicts arise in direct proportion to how close or far apart these two vectors are and how well the parties involved are aware of and deal with both of them.

When a lawyer and an expert witness begin their work together it's exceedingly important that you, as the prime mover, are keenly aware of what the personal plots and sub-plots are for both of you, far beyond the basic needs of your case. In order to get the best effort from anyone, you need to understand why he or she is there, what he or she wants and needs and the best way to satisfy those requirements before you begin asking for what *you* need. Let's not forget that you, too, have many agenda items surrounding the trial.

The Expert Witness

An expert is, by definition, someone who has achieved a certain level of recognition, acclaim and power in his or her particular field. But in a trial setting, he walks into a situation in which he is no longer the most powerful person, the central figure. This is a problem. It creates internal concern for his welfare and status and a sense of competition for power. The stimuli for these feelings are many. Let's look at what worries him, and use an M.D. expert witness as an example.

Loss of Power

Coming to you from his or her own research lab, operating room or office with a busy staff doing his or her bidding, the doctor's self-image is formed by sweeping down the hospital corridors, in a long white coat and with a flock of interns trailing behind; it is an image of total power wielded unquestioningly. He sees himself teaching university classes definitively, delivering papers to learned societies, attending exclusive meetings and receiving awe and respect automatically from lay people, professionals and patients. Now he walks into your office, sits in the receiver's chair on the other side of your desk and is required to listen to you, another person with authority, describe *your* area of expertise and explain what *you* want *him* to do. Result—competition with you for territory, autonomy and ownership of expertise. The visual image that stimulates this is interesting to think about.

Territory

Imagine an expert walking into your office; your comfortable milieu, your surroundings, with your telephone, your desk with all your papers and appointments on it, your books, your secretary, your bibelots, images and diplomas on shelves and walls, and probably some displays of your acclaim and accomplishment. All of this signals to the expert that he is in somebody else's power base. For the moment, the expert has lost his cave, the surroundings that constitute his territory, that make him instantly recognizable as the central figure, the person in power. It causes him to feel a little unprotected and to want the prop of *his* office and *his* environment to establish that *he's* somebody, too. That set of signals and the attendant feeling of momentary loss and lessening of power before anybody has even begun to talk is disturbing to a person who is quite accustomed to the nested, secure, visual reinforcement of the fact that he is a person of accomplishment.

Independence

He's accustomed to making his own decisions, initiating ideas and being the final arbiter of his own professional actions. Therefore, he feels some concern about his autonomy. He needs to feel ownership of his expertise and is very defensive about anybody trampling on or moving into that territory in any way. He's reluctant to take advice. Usually very senior, he's not accustomed to being in areas where he's not an expert and where his judgment isn't the last word. Therefore, he finds it difficult to take advice on anything, particularly when you, a layman, are dealing with his subject.

Professionalism

There is a great concern for professionalism. Expert witnesses continually bring up the fact, in my work with them, that they know that their testimony can be and probably will be reviewed by their peers. Therefore, they are very concerned about accusations of being less than totally professional; of having their research questioned; of being accused of unreliable or incorrect statements or methodology; of leaving gaps in what they say, which can be interpreted as lack of knowledge. This brings a measure of anxiety to their testifying and a set of concerns quite different from what the lawyer has in mind. Their need to protect themselves and their reputation, and not compromise their intial purpose in this world, which is to be *the* expert in their own field of endeavor, makes it much less important to them that you may want them to be more succinct or not quite so detailed in their answers.

Manipulation

They're very worried about being manipulated by the lawyer, both in preparation and on the stand. Experts are uncomfortable being in a situation over which they don't have much control, like a trial in which they need to be a respondent rather than an activist.

If you think about an expert, the reason that you've chosen him at all is that he is generally an inner-directed, creative individualist, a ground breaker, a kind of intellectual entrepreneur who has tried to deeply understand and question what's known or to find out something new and then proceed to prove it against somebody's opposition. In a trial, those traits are diluted and compromised. Not only must this independent spirit talk only in response to your questions, which is the only way he can tell his information, but he will also be challenged severely, sharply and aggressively by another lawyer. In both situations he has to sit on a chair and only respond, rather than taking over and describing the situation in the way that he wishes. This obviously causes a certain level of anxiety and concern about whether or not he can remain in control of what he cares most about; his reputation as an expert and as an esteemed member of his profession, as well as his basic predilection to be independent and a self-starter. This anxiety will cause resistance. It will cause him to think very carefully about what he will and will not say, how he will commit himself and, consequently, how he will listen to you—in preparation and in trial.

*   *   *

The expert's concerns about lawyers and the trial breed resistance and defensiveness, creating an environment that is not the most fertile for cooperation and supreme effectiveness. What about the lawyer's needs and concerns about experts?

The Lawyer

The bottom line is—you need them. Experts serve several important purposes in your case, so the choice to use one or not is less than discretionary. Yet they pose some problems for you, both in their preparation and in their performance during the trial. Just as we looked behind the facade to see where the expert's inner conflicts with you lie, we should look at the other side of that coin to discover if you have any hidden resistances to them.

You Need Them

The lawyer needs an expert to corroborate his theories of the case and to make objective statements based on a superior knowledge of the subject in question. He also needs the expert to give an overview, with some definition and background, to the jury to show what's normal and, therefore, what went wrong. Experts can also prove a witness' contention. Since the individual witness is only a layman and somehow involved in the case, he can have personal needs or specific goals of gain or personal protection. The expert brings objectivity and personal removal to a case and thereby adds great weight to what you're trying to tell the jury.

However, this feeling of needing and being dependent on an outsider in your case makes for some discomfort and possible resentment. You are the captain of your trial and naturally would not want to accommodate and cede territory to anyone, especially someone who may thwart your plans and your script of how the trial should go.

They Have Independent Opinions

A big problem is that the expert may not be willing to go as far as you would like. When you, as a trial lawyer, bring an expert in you have a pretty clear image of what you want him to corroborate, what you hope he will state, what kind of foundation he can lay for you upon which you can then argue the individual merits of your case. However, that may not be what finally happens. You will need to adapt; to get what you can, select what is useful and let go of the rest based on what the expert indicates he will or will not say.

Lawyers Need Control of Their Case

An expert is often unwilling to take instruction from a lawyer, yet you know what you do and do not need in court from an expert. The difficulty of explaining and getting agreement on the information you need and how you would like to present it is another area of concern. You know the pitfalls, where you do and do not want the expert to go, but we have already discussed their independence and resistance. You already understand what your counterpart in the courtroom is going to cross examine him on and how much that could hurt you. This agenda must also be made clear to the expert, but then you can only hope that his ego won't get in the way, so he'll trust and believe you.

Experts Are Not Communicators

Experts are often, very often, pedantic, technical and boring to laymen, especially when they talk about their own fields. Their fields do not usually require charisma or the ability to persuade. In their work, the persuader is facts. And the more the merrier. So that's their reflex response to "Tell me about that, Doctor."

They have no knowledge of the jury's needs or mind set. They do not understand, as you do what sways a jury in one direction or another, or keeps the jury's attention. Their main goal is to explain in great detail, in their own occult language, what they know and care about greatly. They've devoted their lives to their field. They love it and understand it. It doesn't often occur to them that other people not only do not understand, but really don't care, or could even be bored by it. So, they can go on at great length in this loving monologue about drafts and graphs and numbers and cells, never even looking up to see that the jury has long since fallen asleep.

"Now on the supply side of the equation we have a monopsonistic effect while on the demand side we have a . . . zzz . . . zzz . . . zzz."

Experts Don't Self-Edit

I hear so often from trial lawyers that not only are expert witnesses garrulous and boring, but is is difficult to stop them once they get on a roll while sitting on the stand. This creates problems for you, as you try to re-route or simplify them. It begins to look manipulative to the jury if you interrupt the expert too often.

Yet experts cannot or will not hear how to self-edit or clarify the facts. They feel threatened if you begin to tell them to "make this simpler," or "make that shorter." What is "simpler"? How much is "shorter"? "How could I possibly make this simpler or shorter when the jury obviously will not understand what the basic structure of the cell is?" and so forth. Getting your witness to speak simply and succinctly (mostly succinctly) and to self-edit in lay language before they even get on the witness stand, can develop into a minor tug-of-war for this reason and end up in real problems on the witness stand.

*   *   *

What we're looking at is two people who need to work together but have basic agendas that do not mesh. This chapter will deal with finding a middle ground by gaining some new insights, understanding the expert's needs as well as your own and finding ways to respond to both. We'll explore how to prepare an expert witness and learn what techniques make him most effective in the courtroom. Then we'll give some techniques for direct and cross examination of an expert witness in trial.

PREPARATION OF EXPERT WITNESSES

Given the above list of concerns and the strange places where the agendas of these two people—the lawyer and the expert—clash, it is a challenge to find new, creative and psychologically insightful ways to help an expert witness finally do what you really need done in your trial. Here are some ideas for bringing the expert more solidly onto your team and preparing him more effectively for trial.

Ways to Begin

First impressions matter. They can set the tone for a relationship. Starting out on the right foot with your expert requires a little more thought than the usual instinctive way you meet people. Since there is work to do, developing some plan for your approach can help you arrive at a more productive understanding more quickly.

Understand Them

Before you even see the expert, you should first sit and think about what his or her emotional and professional needs are to get some deeper understanding of what he or she brings into your office and into the courtroom. Decide beforehand what ways you can adapt your methodology of preparing any witness to take into account the things this unique witness needs from you.

• You must give the expert a sense of his own territory in relation to the trial.

• You must give him visible respect for his knowledge.

• You should create the forms of his trial presentation together.

• You need to include him in your decisions and always explain what you are doing and why.

• You should establish a friendly, professional rapport as between colleagues and peers.

• Beware of and listen hard to his or her concerns and then deal with them; do not dismiss them or say "Trust me."

First Moves

To begin with, don't meet him or her in your office if you can avoid it. It smacks too much of your territory. Rather, meet in a neutral place —a small conference room in your workplace or a comfortable and informal environment away from work, like a club. You might even think of going to his or her office.

Offer coffee, something to eat or drink. This relaxes both of you. Being aware of his or her physical needs and comfort is one step in showing your sensitivity, respect and friendliness. It may surprise you to discover that extending yourself in this direction is an extremely important touch. Giving you a chance to be a host casts you in another light than just the hard-driving, product-oriented no-nonsense lawyer-machine. That little homey, personal touch reminds us all of the kitchen table and being fed and nurtured, and creates an environment that is conducive to good talk. (An excellent idea for depositions, too, by the way.)

Do some small personal warmup as you begin your discussion with your expert witness, some general getting-acquainted, unfocused kind of small talk that gets people to know each other a little better. Talk of the news, weather, vacation, family or anything that's more personal and less goal-oriented.

Making him or her feel a little more comfortable gives you an opportunity to observe the expert's behavior. Is he or she reserved with you? Does he seem tense? Does she seem garrulous, competitive or shy? Open up a few general areas of discussion before you begin discussing the trial.

Ask Before You Tell

In order to find a more open communication channel, don't tell first. Ask. What does he anticipate about the trial? Has he been in a courtroom? If so, what kinds of experiences has he had? Discover how uncomfortable the expert has felt with lawyers he has worked with before. Find out his predilections about how he likes to behave on the stand. What is his image of the courtroom, the jury, the judge? This will help you to get an idea of where the problem areas are.

By asking, you show your concern for his comfort and well-being as well as your interest in his participation in the trial and his needs. Put him at ease with your willingness to discuss them and your desire to understand.

Don't shortcut this warmup and sail right into, "Now the essence of this case is..." It will cause him to remain with those basic problems mentioned at the beginning of the chapter; you may not uncover them and he may never get to see you in any other light

than as an impresario, conducting and manipulating the cast of
your opera, getting everyone in line to do your bidding.

Give before You Get

Before you can ask for or get something, it's necessary to give.
That's a basic rule of thumb in all communications, but most particularly in this area, where the expert is concerned and on guard.
Give acclaim for his knowledge and expertise. Give some reassurance that you are aware of what his professionalism requires and
that you will not compromise him or exceed the bounds of the
things he cares most about.

Tell him you need his help. Make him feel important to your
case. Explain that you are illiterate in aerodynamics. "Help me to
understand this." That entreaty puts him in the mode of explainer
and teacher as well as giving status and a sense of esteem and
territory.

Explain Your Needs

After your reassurance is given, it then becomes easier to explain in very basic terms what the issues are, the needs of the particular trial and your assessment of what the jury's responses could
be. If you explain it to him not only in terms of the basic issues of
your trial but also in terms of what you can predict about the jury's
responses and what you need to convince them, it will help him to
move towards you as a more effective guide and expert.

Testing the Expert

It's important that you evaluate the expert before hiring him
or her on several counts. You should look at not only his expertise
but also what he is willing to say and how well he can say it.

Robert F. Hanley, the nationally acclaimed litigator from
Denver, who has been chairman of both the ABA Litigation Section and the National Institute for Trial Advocacy, suggests the
following:

Bring the expert in as a consultant first, not as a witness. Have him
or her make their own evaluation of the issues at stake and come up

with an opinion. If it's against you and they know what they're talking about, you settle! If they find a theory, it's theirs; they own it and will fight to the death to protect it.

Bob Hanley also suggests putting the expert on videotape to see how he comes across. Then, after he develops his theory and you judge his overall performance, decide whether or not to hire him.

Get Him on Your Team

Having hired the expert, you now need to build motivation and support. In order to get his acquiescence and willingness to follow your lead, get him actively involved on your team: let him see himself as an important part of the outcome. Develop some loyalty, some concern for the case, for the implications of the case and most of all, make him see how important he can be in the case. Give him your confidence. Let him know at the beginning how much you rely upon his willingness to be a part of this team. Tell him you value suggestions (at least you will listen, even though you may not always use them), but at all times let him know that he is more than just another cog in the machine. This will go a long way toward getting his compliance with some of the things you will suggest later on, because he will feel that you are both on the same side instead of competing with another. Remember, it's *his* opinion. Show your respect and how you'll help him tell it.

Where Does He or She Fit?

You have to make it clear exactly where the expert's information fits into your theory of the case. It is not enough to isolate that segment of the case that deals with the expert witness and his testimony. It doesn't make him feel part of a team, nor does it help to understand the full impact of what he is going to say.

Involve the Expert in Designing Testimony

The key to getting good expert witness testimony is to get the expert willing to help, listen and take the suggestions you offer. Since there is resistance to direction and a sense of ownership of his or her knowledge and expertise, it is difficult sometimes to find a way for you to design and critique the methods of presentation in court. The most effective is to make him feel like an active partici- pant, involved in designing his testimony, from the beginning. This also gives him the sense of importance and territory he is look- ing for.

Once you and your expert are agreed on the theory to be proven, involving the expert in designing his testimony will make it, and the expert, most effective in trial. However, this can only be done if he is given an orientation and fully informed about every aspect and problem of the trial and how he will affect it, as well as a deep understanding of the audience and how people learn and listen.

Explain the Jury's Needs

Explain the psychology of the jury to the expert. Describe the needs of the jury. What do they need from someone who describes an aspect of the case? What are their concerns about not understanding?

Explain how people feel unsafe in an unfamiliar environment where they are exposed to their own ignorance or inability to catch on quickly and learn, and how this fact turns them off. If they don't understand, it makes the rest of the testimony useless because they don't want to pay attention to something that doesn't interest them or lets them know about their own inadequacies.

Explain the jury's inability to assimilate a great deal of tech- nical data, especially when it is presented orally. Help your expert accept the fact that the jury may find it difficult to understand his field of expertise; that although *he* understands it because he has spent his lifetime in it, it's totally foreign to them, and that it will take some work between the two of you to make the jury understand.

Clarify His Role

Present your expert with the role of teacher, guide and clari- fier for the jury. If you explain the jury's learning problems relating to oral descriptions, to technical, difficult, unfamiliar data, to organizing information, to picking out the salient points and remembering them at the end, you will have gone far towards explaining why it is necessary for the expert to think carefully about the methods by which he gives the jury information.

Explore His Teaching
Techniques

Ask him to remember how it was when he was a young student, with no information on this subject. Make him see it, feel it and know *that's* the jury. But they're not even interested, as he was. Therefore, make him think about how to begin the process of preparing an orientation lecture for a beginning group of students in his field, hoping to recruit them to become involved in his work. What would be the best way to give them an overview of what this field is about and what the subject is? How would he capture their interest? How would he then focus in on the specific subject he'll discuss in the trial?

Ask him to describe what he would put into an introductory or survey course. How would he present it? What would he tell the students first? If you put him in mind of this process, not only will he then begin to understand the jury, but as he talks, you can begin to pick out how to organize your direct examination questions: how much background to lay down, how to describe it, what else they need to know and how your expert teaches. This is why it is valuable to get an expert witness experienced in teaching, not just a researcher or practitioner.

You need to add more ingredients to this thinking. Unlike the students in the expert's introductory survey course, who have already elected to take this course or need to understand it, the jury has absolutely no reason to be interested, except as it helps them to understand the case. Since they also expect his testimony may be boring and obscure, he must find ways to make everything he says relevant to the trial in order to stimulate the jury's interest and to keep their attention.

Presenting this teaching role as a challenge enables you to discuss the kinds of teaching techniques the expert has used that are successful and to find others that you think will be useful.

PREPARING YOUR EXPERT FOR
DIRECT EXAMINATION

Teaching Presentation Techniques

Now that the two of you are rolling down the road together, you have developed enough rapport to go into the instructional phase of your work. The fact is that most experts have very few ideas about the most eloquent and most captivating ways to present their material. Therefore, with the proper introduction about the fact that you know what makes juries pay attention from experience, you can suggest several techniques to the expert to make the material more understandable to the jury. If you have presented the previous points well, he will now have a good understanding of who his audience or "class" is, and will be much more willing to hear about some presentation techniques that work in the courtroom. Your previous explanations also improve your credibility as the "expert" in the art of getting the jury's attention and acceptance, since you've shown you know them and therefore have a basis for suggesting what works best in the courtroom.

Use Videotape and Replay

As a way to accelerate the expert's understanding of the jury's needs, exercises can be done in which you role play an examination and videotape it, then let him watch the replay to see what he has just explained and how. He will very quickly see, now that you have given him the mental set of the jury and what his audience really needs, what works and what doesn't. He can then, on his own, be able to critique himself and begin to internalize some of the suggestions that you're making, and he won't feel like you're too critical or telling him what to do.

Self-Editing

It is never useful to say to any expert (or to anyone else for that matter), "Don't take too long; don't explain this in too great detail." Those are very vague generalizations. All it does is raise their anxiety level. "How much is 'too long'? " "How much is 'enough'?" "What is 'detail' ? "

I have a special motto for teaching people how to self-edit. This is what it says:

TELL THE JURY WHAT <u>THEY</u> NEED TO KNOW;
NOT ALL THAT <u>YOU</u> KNOW

It means: Don't give them all the information you have on any subject. Give them the kinds of basics that will help them understand the issues in the case — what the jury needs to know.

If you explain this well, it becomes the objective measuring stick by which your expert can control himself (or by which you can gently critique his performance). This guiding principle will help him to shorten, simplify, clarify and edit even before he speaks. This gives the expert a purpose, an end product, a listener to keep in mind for measurement and evaluation.

Simplify Language

You must be sure to keep the language simple and recognizable. Keep interrupting your witness, as you practice, whenever he gets into the technical language stratosphere so that he becomes aware of this on his own and can remedy it instinctively. Remember, what's gobbledygook to laymen is mother's milk to him. Be especially aware of the fact that, in your preparation of the case, many of those words have become mother's milk to you, too! Remember the jury and where you were before you ever heard of femurs and bytes and oligolopolistic markets.

Giving Technical or Abstract Information

Most people stop learning new and challenging things when they leave school. They stay on at jobs they already understand and that don't change. Their experiences of being exposed or embarrassed in school whenever they couldn't understand cause them to be unwilling to try too many new ideas later on. High on this list are technical data and abstract concepts, since it seems like nothing in the jury's past experience carries over into these areas.

However, people can open themselves to abstract and unfamiliar things if you start out with something familiar that they know. If you say, "like turning the wheel of a car," they have an instant image because they've done that a thousand times. They're on safe ground, and now you can add something new and slightly unfamiliar to it. Being on safe ground at the outset, they'll still stay with you because they believe they can follow and understand.

In explaining a process, always try to liken it to a process that everyone knows and can quickly imagine or identify with. That makes jurors feel confident and interested enough to continue. They'll be willing to follow you down an unfamiliar road and try to understand more.

Use familiar processes as examples and then add differences, one at a time. Since they already know the part they understand, these changes become interesting.

Process—Not Detail

Everyone can understand processes. This is, indeed, a technological age, and we use enough "things" everyday to grasp fairly quickly what makes things work. Problems arise, however, when you add too much detail.

Labeling parts that do not matter; using terms that don't sound like anything a juror can even imagine spelling; using foreign words not in their vocabulary and telling them details that they don't care if they ever know are all invitations to shutting off the master switch. Detail is often overkill, yet process is interesting, graspable and demonstrable, which brings me to the next key area—the use of visuals.

Teaching Use of Visuals

Visualize and Demonstrate

Knowing some of the problems jurors have with understanding and relating to complex material, the best clarifier in the world is some form of visual reinforcement or demonstration.

The major reasons to use visuals are:

- To make an expert's material clear to all at once
- To synchronize and focus what everyone's thinking about

• To make graphic, easy-to-recall images out of complex information

• To separate and list the components as an aid in sorting out, understanding and remembering.

But there's still another important reason to use visuals with an expert; that is the effect it has on him or her.

• He's out of the chair, actively involved in doing something.

• Handling visual material curtails some of the endless stream-of-consciousness talk that experts indulge in.

• It raises the energy level of his testimony, both for you and for him.

• It focuses his presentation; he can more readily see what he needs to explain.

• It forces him to be clearer and more succinct as he looks at the chart.

Visual demonstration gives the jury something else to look at, something that unfolds before their eyes, something that relegates some power to them.

Another reason for using visual aids in expert witness testimony is how it helps you. It's a form of looking at your notes:

• You see what needs further explanation as he writes on the chart or board and can immediately refer to it.

• You see exactly what the jury's image is of the issue and can more critically evaluate what is clear and what is not.

• You see what he has not yet explained and where to go next.

Let the Expert Do the Demonstrating

Let the expert draw the diagram, unless it's very complex. If it is complex, you might want the initial diagram prepared before the trial, but then have the expert label and identify every portion of it as he describes it. If you wish the diagrams or charts prepared in advance, use overlays—slick transparencies on which the expert can then draw and add his own interpretation, description, analysis or identification. Finished overlays can also be designed and prepared in advance and used to add information one at a time. But keep your expert actively involved with the visual aids in the courtroom. He is the teacher. It also makes his testimony much more energetic and interesting.

Choice of Visuals

Introduce him to various visual aid formats and get him involved in choices (overhead projector, video, charts, blackboard). Inasmuch as possible, your expert witness should not use slides. Turning out the lights is an invitation for everybody to fall asleep, and you lose your audience totally. Also, a slide is not malleable; it's just plain there. There's not much you can do with it except point. You can't add information and you can't keep one slide on too long.

Instead, with the lights on, let the expert witness handle, write and explain either on a board, chart, using an overhead projector or with a live demonstration. There is much more dynamism in his explanation and in the jury's participation.

But let's not unleash a monster here. There are very real techniques for making effective use of visual aids. If your expert is also a professor, chances are he has used just a few traditional visual forms like slides and a blackboard and has also developed some deeply ingrained classroom habits, like a tendency to abbreviate or scribble.

Do a demonstration in which you show good and bad usages of visual aids like overloading information, illegibility, etc. It goes a long way toward helping your expert to voluntarily want to do things better, because he sees the techniques that will or won't work in the courtroom. Let him get comfortable with new techniques and practice them. You can also use this time to further analyze the content.

Show Your Expert How to Diagram

Visuals are only valuable if they are self-explanatory. Teach your expert how to draw a clear, straight horizontal line that connects the object he is describing out to the side of the blackboard.

Then teach him to write on that line. Teachers' tendency to assume you understand as they scribble an abbreviated something down the side of a blackboard causes the jury to have to stand on its ear. If it isn't instantly self-explanatory to them, they can't look at it later and understand, so after a while they just give up.

Make Him Print Rather than Write

You and I both know about doctors and their famous pre-cription-pad penmanship. The writing is designed for us *not* to understand. That's the same handwriting you will probably get on the blackboard and, lo and behold, the jury will not understand it either!

Never Abbreviate

The jury must be able to look again and again at the visual and understand it each time. Abbreviations of unfamiliar terms recall nothing. Spell out each identifying label.

Don't Overload

Give only as much information as you can control and explain at a time. Then add and explain some more. Accumulate data as you explain it. Have it all together at the end, not the beginning. Putting it all down and showing it at once and then asking the jury to hold back while you try to make them focus only on point one as you try to explain is unrealistic. The jury will, as we all would, look at everything, at their pace, and try to understand it all, without benefit of your explanation.

Be Aware of What the Jury Can See

We often forget other people's sight lines when we get involved in explaining. Teach your expert to point by standing to the side of the board or chart, rather than standing in front of it. Remind him to step away as soon as he has drawn or labeled something so the jury can see. Go to the court and find out how large the letters and images should be to enable the jury to see clearly.

*   *   *

The use of visuals is crucial to any good expert testimony. To get a full understanding of the effect of visual aids, techniques for use and the pros and cons of possible formats read Chapter 8. You might even suggest your expert read it, too.

PREPARING YOUR EXPERT FOR
CROSS-EXAMINATION

As far as the substantive issues of the expert's testimony are concerned, those which will be fodder for the cross-examiner, I feel confident that you will deal with them most ably. Let me suggest some points relating to style and substance for you to help the expert.

Insights and Techniques

Be Aware of His Apprehension

The most important thing to remember in preparing an expert for cross is his high level of anxiety about being found wanting or being denigrated in any way. Remembering his professional concern about being judged by his peers, you should know that he may be unusually defensive, belligerent and/or too embarrassed by a very competent cross-examiner to sustain his end of the fight.

Remember His Competitiveness
With You

The expert also feels he has something to prove to you. He hardly wants to come out a loser in that little joust, so he will have some additional anxiety about the cross as he imagines you watching him possibly falter or let you down.

Discuss His Concerns

It does no good to clap him on the back and say "No problem." Open the path for him to share the real concerns he has. Adults, especially men, are conditioned to have great difficulty admitting weakness, incompetence or insecurity. Help your expert discover and talk about what he or she anticipates and what the concerns are. This gives a freer, more open basis on which you can help and prepare your witness.

Discuss the Possible Issues of the Cross

Learning to fight back by being fully prepared with counterclaims, explanations, qualifications and corroborative material around specific issues not only helps the witness to be prepared to handle them in court, but gives a greater feeling of security in anticipating what can happen in cross.

Practice with Role Play and Videotape

Nothing tells the truth faster about how your expert will sustain cross than to put them through a grueling, hostile, attacking cross yourself. Taping it gives you both a chance to review, analyze and consider alternate plans and more pointed answers. It also gives the expert opportunities to banish some anxiety as he or she practices and becomes more comfortable and secure. Be sure to put the expert in an isolated situation, near no furniture, and that you stand far back or attack them in this position. (See Chapter 5 on Cross-Examination for additional ideas on preparing witnesses for cross and more insights into how they feel on the stand.)

Courtroom Tactics

Show Confidence as Cross Begins

Tell your expert not to break his stride or visibly change his demeanor as the cross-examiner gets up and begins. He or she should give the impression that what he said on direct, in the comfort of that role, is what he always says and will continue to say on cross. No change. No gearing up for the onslaught. No deep breath, digging in the heels and waiting. Just a calm, even demeanor and a clear, straightforward look at the cross-examiner.

Take a Break, if Needed

If your expert feels anxious or at a low energy level, tell him to ask for a drink of water, saying he has been talking for a while or to say, "Excuse me" and quietly blow his nose. This doesn't look nervous; it simply looks like he has been talking for a while or needs to blow his nose. The effect, however, is to give the witness a break and a moment to re-group. It also breaks the intensity of the cross-examiner's concentration, as he must wait till the activity is completed. The witness can also re-arrange his position in his chair and get more comfortable.

Teach the Expert a Secure Position

Sit about 3/4 of the way back on the chair, then lean back against the chair. Putting hands on the arms of the chair prevents gestures that look tense (like crossing arms over chest or clutched hands.) Visible hands on the chair arms are the most relaxed-looking posture.

Keep Eye Contact

Everyone watches to see who flinches in an argument. Be sure you work with your expert on maintaining eye contact with the cross-examiner, especially when he or she answers.

Learn to Listen

Careless listening causes assumptions about where the cross-examiner is *probably* going with a question, rather than hearing specifically and exactly what is being asked. The expert then runs the risk of answering too much, being inaccurate or sounding evasive. Teach him to wait until the question is finished, then take a beat and think before he answers.

Take Apart the Question

In order to be sure he understands, as well as finding a moment to collect his thoughts, teach your expert to clarify the question. Technical questions are often complex, and asking multi-faceted questions is common in cross. This is an extremely important point, since the cross-examiner has certain goals in mind and in order to get admissions he will try to over-simplify an issue. Teach your expert to listen critically to see if and how that question, stated as it is, can be answered.

Tell Them Not to Bicker

Know the weak points of the testimony; teach him to admit immediately what must be admitted and not to quibble. Your expert should be taught to be above petty squabbling. He loses face and substance in the eyes of the jury if he lowers himself to a quarrel. Teach him to keep his cool. He looks strongest that way. Suggest that he answer any disagreement or confrontation or need to qualify his answer by explaining to the lawyer and/or the judge why he can't answer that question the way the lawyer put it. The jury can then hear *why* he is not answering, rather than coming to their own conclusion about "he can't" or "he's afraid to."

Breaking the Yes–No Pattern

The expert needs to tell the jury that sometimes research, science and the laws of probability cannot be absolute and therefore, a definitive one-word answer is useless and not true. Say, "This is too complex or too serious an issue to be reduced to such simplistic answers. One must explain what other factors exist."

Teach him to use two or three word answers, such as, "It can be," "That's possible," or, "Perhaps so." These two- or three-word answers interrupt the opposing lawyer's momentum and the rhythmic litany. It saps strength from the cross. Of course I hear you saying, "The judge will instruct him to answer yes or no." But if the judge does that at the entreaty of the cross-examining lawyer, the lawyer has already become weakened in the eyes of the jury by badgering the expert and needing to ask the judge for help. Your witness has gotten his point across as a reasonable person.

Remind Him of Redirect

If the cross-examiner is trying to get him to admit something that he can't agree with completely, tell him to answer "yes, but. . ." and try to explain and that you will help him get his answer completed when you come back. Explain that if the judge stops him, you'll know to ask him to complete his answer on re-direct.

"You're Getting Paid, Aren't You?"

This problem looms over almost every cross of an expert. The idea is to make the jury think he'll say anything for money. The issue here is to clarify what he's getting paid for. If asked, tell him to say, "I'm paid for my time, not for my opinion." Then, if he can, let him elaborate on being paid for his time as a consultant and an expert, just as he is paid for his time in the lab or in the classroom. That's his work, just as the cross-examining lawyer is being paid for *his* time. "It is my professional integrity and expertise that has formed my opinion, not money," is the answer to that question.

If he can't get it out on cross, ask him on re-direct. This is a very important point for the jury to understand. Don't let it lay. Pursue it and clear it up in your direct, before it's even asked in cross, in order to make the jury feel confident about his integrity and his opinion.

"You were Prepared by a Communications Expert, Weren't You?"

Try this:

I stand on my record as an expert in research, which you've already heard, and that's what my conclusion is based on. However, I have rather poor speaking skills and I know this is rather complex material to explain to lay people. So I did everything I could to make my testimony accurate and clear. Since the jury can't ask, I must anticipate what will be the best way to tell them. I felt I needed to find good teaching techniques because an understanding of my findings is vital to judge this case. Therefore, I went to an expert, a communications expert who did not tell me *what* to say, just the most effective, clearest and most succinct way to say it.

Another way:

Every witness is prepared by their lawyer. You prepared yours, too. There is a big difference between a courtroom of lay people and a laboratory where everyone understands me. I wanted to be sure I got down to the basics that were needed in the courtroom. As all of us would do, I went to an expert.

*   *   *

Let me conclude by reminding you that before you begin your preparation of your expert witness, put yourself in his position. As an expert, how would you like to be handled? How would you like to be asked to play in someone else's arena? Try the role on yourself to get a sense of the expert's reluctance, suspicion and competitive approach toward being handled by a trial lawyer. Then, give him your expertise, your knowledge of trial dynamics, the lexicon of how to make juries understand and your experience in handling direct and cross. Ask for and listen to his concerns, especially about handling himself in cross-examination. Be sensitive to putting him in the role of student after his years as teacher. Develop a feeling of camaraderie between you, of colleagues and team-mates. Show enthusiasm and curiosity about what he knows. The world is so full of a number of things, it's always interesting to take a condensed mini-course in someone's expertise.

DIRECT EXAMINATION OF EXPERT WITNESSES

What the Jury Expects

In order to present your expert well, let's look at the audience. The jury has a number of assumptions and expectations as you begin your direct examination.

The jury, working from stereotypes, sees the expert as smart, aloof, and outside their experience. They have a conditioned com-

posite of pompous, unreachable doctors, absent-minded professors, mad, intense scientists, and vague, enigmatic or nit-picking
researchers. Their expectations pre-condition how much they wish
to hear and assume they will understand. Here are some of those
expectations:

Unintelligible

The jury expects not to be able to understand the expert. Obviously someone with a Ph.D. from a university who teaches a subject that you probably flunked in high school or never even took at
all, must be outside your own ken. The first assumption is that he
will be too technical, too difficult to understand. They also don't
expect that the expert will care very much whether the jury understands or not. They expect to be talked down to, to be patronized
or to have the whole thing go over their heads. So their first response is quite negative in terms of anticipation and willingness to
learn and understand.

Boring

The expert probably will be boring. This conclusion stems
from the jury's past school experiences. The number of teachers
that taught you badly, or that went on and on at great length about
something that seemed so dull to you, extrapolates and magnifies
itself into this expert being the ultimate one of those teachers and
therefore, surely uninteresting.

Who Cares

Most jurors feel that there's really no need to know this information in their daily lives. Who cares exactly what the inner structure of a ladder is? How should they know if the operation on a leg
was done correctly? Who could absorb those tables of economic
statistics? They do not have much motivation to try very hard to
understand the expert witness's testimony.

Should I Try?

They do have some feeling, however, that the expert's testimony has great bearing on the case and, therefore, they should try to absorb the information. However, given the uphill battle of how hard it will be to understand, and how boring the expert probably is, they may or may not stay with him or her. Some jurors really are curious and interested, but for the greater majority, chances are that conscience and curiosity will be superceded by the anticipation of dullness or the difficulty of following the expert testimony.

Who's Really an Expert?

Although you spend a great deal of time finding the right expert, that kind of qualitative information is generally over the jury's heads. They can hear degrees and names of institutions, but they have little or no basis for comparison and generally no knowledge about a given profession. Therefore, they end up not knowing just how good, famous or prestigious your expert really is.

Fear of Ignorance

People are often afraid to try to learn something new. They would sooner turn off and not listen than be confronted with their own inexperience or lack of ability to learn. They must be given a feeling that the expert believes they can and will understand. Some of the expert's enthusiasm about his subject must be transmitted to the jurors, so that they will really want to follow along or be affected by the desire of the expert to explain to them. They need, most of all, to be in a very safe environment and to feel confident in order to learn.

A Biased Witness

The jurors generally suspect that the expert will say what the lawyer who called him wants him to say. They're really canny about this, because they understand that there is a win at stake here. There is a point of view, and obviously the lawyer will not call somebody who does not share his point of view.

Admiration

Generally speaking, most people look up to researchers, scientists or professors. They admire their degrees and what they know. This is true for experts on both sides. We usually feel such people are above money, and should testify for the good of science or justice.

*   *   *

Your direct examination should be designed to handle all the aforementioned concerns, objections and suspicions. Always test your planned questions against these issues to see if you have taken them into account. Here are some ways to transcend the jury's resistance and involve them in your examination and your expert's testimony.

Qualifying the Expert

The qualification of an expert is a much more complex task than you think. Basically, it's a credibility contest. What you think is meaningful to the jury and will impress them is generally not meaningful to them. They do not understand the significance of what is described in the qualifications.

Juries do not know how professionals operate. Prestigious societies, appointments and journal articles have absolutely no meaning to them. They don't know how professors are chosen and, by and large, which are the most prestigious institutions in a given field. They don't know what it means that your expert presented a paper or the significance of ten articles he wrote.

They therefore cannot assume that an expert is an expert just by those words alone. They have very little knowledge of how to compare how good, smart or professional these experts are as opposed to other people in the field. They have very little experience, if any, with any experts in this field, so they do not have much reason to know which expert is particularly good, more qualified or better than another. They are impressed, but in order for you to make your points well, they need to become truly impressed. The jury needs to be reached in ways quite different from what professionals normally think of as an impressive resume. An impressive resume is meaningful only up to a point. It makes an expert unique and different, but not yet very different from any other expert.

Here are some ways to organize and present the qualifications of an expert so that they will be clear and carry weight with the jury.

The Qualification Matters

Judges try to get you to rush through the qualifications. Don't! The jury has never met an economist. They don't know what he does or how he can help them. Take the time to present his relevant qualifications. Don't let the judge bully you. Explain that the jury needs to understand why he is an expert and how his expertise will be used. Don't accept your opponent's offer to stipulate to his qualifications. The moments you spend impressing the jury must last through some upcoming heavy seas to make that opinion last. Make that happen.

How to Begin

Make the qualifications relevant to the jury, right at the start. Ask your expert on what, in general, he is prepared to provide evidence and an opinion. Then say, "Let's review your qualifications to give that opinion." Make sure you select and the expert describes the specific areas of his expertise. Explain exactly how that expertise will be brought to bear in providing his opinions. This will let the jury know immediately why they should listen. If they see that they are being asked, in a sense, to judge if this expert is important enough and knowledgeable enough to give an opinion, they'll listen hard.

Don't Overdo

Be spare and circumspect in what you choose to cover in qualifying. Since the jury is primed to hear an important, objective opinion they want to get on with it. Don't be unmindful of the jury's attention span and use up all the good time of total attention at the beginning. Make your qualifying section pithy, pertinent and interesting, but not lengthy.

Categorize the Resumé

We are all, by nature, deeply interested in ourselves. We can get interested in others if they're fascinating, charismatic people, if they have an unusual story or if it's in our self-interest to know and pay attention to them.

Therefore, the long litany of dates, degrees, names of institutions, courses and publications that usually follow the lawyer's question, "Tell us about your education, (background, professional career) Doctor," is bound to bore the jury and disappear into a fog. It doesn't make a dent. Who cares about Dr. X in 1957, 1963 or whatever?

All that the jury can absorb are the kinds of experiences that have made him an expert on this subject. They need the list telescoped into digestible concepts, categories they can understand and relate to. These categories can become organizing receptacles into which you put the variety of accomplishments under a specific heading and which can then accumulate weight that is meaningful because it's organized and digestible.

It is very difficult for anybody to collect and remember the data of a resumé orally. Since you don't want to use visuals (although some lawyers do use an overhead projector with an edited resume), present the resumé in organized groups or paragraphs with topic headings. When you first look at the resumé, group together everything relating to education, faculty appointments, publications, awards and so on. Then present each area with a preface announcing the category, "Now let's talk about your education" or "your awards" or "the societies you've been invited to join."

Condense the Resumé Yourself

A number of trial lawyers do some of the testifying to shorten the process. They will say things like, "I see research projects A, B, C and D. Tell us more about why you did that" or "What were you working on?" Or, "Well, you went to this university and that university, where you specialized in subject X and graduated with three degrees in such and so. How did you develop your expertise in your field of concentration?" That helps the professor or doctor list his or her university credentials succinctly (since they usually do this at much too great a length). You have gotten the basic information out, and can then point up what was significant about his or her education. Example:

You: Tell us how you developed your specialty.

Doctor X: Sixteen years of research, paid for by grants from the American Cancer Society, plus four appointments to faculties.

You: Why did that happen?

Doctor X: Because I was the only one in the field.

Compare that with, "I taught and did research for sixteen years." If you do some of the editing in this manner, putting the spotlight on the most unique aspect of that piece of their background and asking the expert to elaborate on only one thing, it's much easier for the jury to understand and assimilate what you're saying, and to assimilate it with meaning. Also, by listing a group of achievements, you can create impact by sheer weight of numbers. Then, as you single out the best and use it as an example for further clarification, the jury will extrapolate from it, and think, "That means all of those accomplishments have similar stories to go with them."

Another reason to do this is everyone's predilection to tell too much, especially when we talk on our favorite subject—ourselves. This technique focuses on what is necessary and eliminates the chaff.

Impress by Explaining

Think through what you really want the jury to know in order to impress them. What aspects of the career of this professional are most meaningful or bear most on the particular points that you wish to make? What activities, grants, articles or writings show that this expert is an expert in the particular field which bears on the issue in question? As you choose from his resumé, you need to ask

yourself, "How is this useful? What happens if the juror knows
this? Why is this important? How will it help the jury believe him
and/or reach a verdict?"

Expertise in a field can become apparent to the jury when you
talk of prestigious academic appointments, elected memberships
in honorary societies, institutional grants, publications in learned
journals or the length of time that he has been in any part of this
field. However, before you introduce any of these subjects, you
should know that the jury understands nothing of how any of this
comes to be and why any of it is prestigious or meaningful. They
think you can join the American College of Surgeons like you join
the National Geographic Society. So, before you introduce any of
these subjects, let them find out how one qualifies. Ask the expert:

- How many members are there in that society?
- How do you get invited?
- How many are chosen each year?
- Who presents papers at a learned society meeting? What are
they for?
- How many times have you been invited?
- Who gets appointed to a faculty and why?
- What's a medical journal for?
- Who reads it?
- What types of subjects are covered?
- Why are you invited to write those articles?
- Who addresses medical meetings?
- How are they chosen?

Lawyer: Who gives papers at these meetings, Professor?

Expert: Only people doing innovative or ground-breaking research are invited.

Lawyer: How many of those papers have you given, Professor?

Expert: Seven.

The jury then begins to hear exclusivity. "Isn't that the only
research grant ever give by the XYZ Company, Dr.?" Prestige becomes clear only when you ask the expert's relationship to any of

these accomplishments and what they are to begin with. Never assume that the jury understands that only one person is chosen each year for the National Academy of Science Award, and that that one person is chosen from a cast of thousands. Unless all of this is made clear in advance, sheer membership or the sheer weight of 16 publications or a list of degrees has no meaning whatsoever to the jury, who have long since tuned out on what sounds like a boring resumé.

Protect Their Professional "Humility"

You remember being told when you were a kid not to brag, show off or blow your own horn. Unfortunately, too many of us took that to heart so much that it was difficult to find our self-confidence when we grew up. As damaging as it may have been, it's still a social convention and the jury grew up knowing it, too.

Therefore, you must find clever, subtle ways to brag for the expert, to give him a graceful way to talk about himself. Not only because many professionals feel a little reluctant to present themselves in a self-aggrandizing manner (although they may very often feel that way), but also because the jury may be a little repelled by a recitation of: "and then I wrote . . . and then I was chosen . . . I am the one and only . . ." Find ways for everyone to get comfortable telling and listening to self-praise.

Ask all of the questions dealing with their glorious accomplishments by prefacing them with, "I know it's very difficult, doctor (or professor), for you to describe some of your accomplishments; most people are loathe to do that. But in order for the jury to know of your competence, and what some of your accomplishments are, let me ask you to put modesty aside and tell us about your professional achievements." But be careful. Just letting your expert rattle off his achievements will make the jury as bored as you are with someone else's home movies. You will lose the chance to impress them.

Tell the jury why it's relevant; preface each gold star with a reason to listen. Limit the qualifications to those most relevant to the testimony the expert is about to give. Find out what would make the expert feel comfortable to go on about this. Take the onus of making him boast upon yourself. Continue to make the jury understand that the expert is humble and reluctant, but you, the lawyer, are pressing him to explain all of this.

Humanize the Expert

One of the few things that will impress the jury is your making the expert witness a human being. Therefore, the story of how he got to be an expert, why he was motivated and how hard it was to become a doctor, an economist, a geologist or a physicist, is of much greater interest than a list of his societies. It humanizes and allows for more personal involvement between the jury and the expert.

Therefore, look for the stories. Find out as much as you can of his early life: The reason it took seven years for his Ph.D. is because he had to work his way through graduate school; she always wanted to be a doctor, like her father; his greatest goal is to create the ultimate safety device for cars to protect humanity forever; a friend or relative was hurt by a defective product and he decided to spend his life creating safe ones. These humanizing factors in an expert's early life and career decisions are identifiable to a jury. They not only make a good vignette to listen to, they draw the jury closer to the expert as a human being.

Show the Expert's Dedication

"When did you decide to be a doctor?" "Why did you specialize in this field?" "Who influenced you in your field and how?" "Were you the first person in this field and why?" "What are your goals?" These questions add a personal dimension to all of the accomplishments and make them much easier to listen to. But there's another important benefit. It tells the jury that this person is extremely motivated. Asking him "Why do you testify in this case" can help carry them through the stumbling block of the cross-examiner's question, "You're getting paid to do this testimony, aren't you?"

Questioning Techniques*

Clarify the Listening

Since the testimony is generally heavy going, help the jury listen for specifics as you question the expert. Always give the goals before you ask for an explanation. Start each line of questioning by letting the jury in on why they should listen. What are they about to learn? What effect does this have on their understanding or on what actually happened in the case? "Now, about how a widget is made, Commander." Never assume that they know why you're going on to the next point. After you have made your point, recap what you asked him and what they just heard, so that with each step you get short bursts of information. Never assume the jury has gotten it all the first time around.

Listen as a Juror

Try to hear the testimony of the expert with the jury's ears. Stop him whenever the words get too big, when the concepts get too involved or when he's gone into too great detail too soon. Go back over certain points that would be unclear if you were a juror listening for the first time.

You have a problem here because in your preparation of the trial you have become something of an expert yourself on the technical data that your expert is now presenting to the jury. You, too, may forget how you felt as a lay person a year before, when you knew nothing about how to build a skyscraper. So listen with very sharp ears and keep going back and taking apart the complexity of the technical information as if you were a juror listening. This is very important, because your habit is to listen as a lawyer to see how your case and your plans are progressing. Do that, too, but add a fifth gear—how the jury will understand this. (I know, I know . . . but who said being a trial lawyer was easy?)

---

*(See Chapter 4 for additional direct examination techniques.)

Use Those Visuals

Get the expert to the blackboard or other visual aid as soon as possible. Having explained the strength of the visuals and how he will work with them, you should be the best judge of when things are getting too wordy and when you need to perk up the jury's interest by asking the expert to get up and demonstrate. Notice the light, size of writing and the voice level, etc. at the board and fix anything that's not right by saying, "Could you write a little larger, speak up, etc."

Also understand when to let him sit down again. Having presented things on the blackboard, it is interesting for him to then go back to his seat in the witness box and reflect upon what he has said and come up with his conclusions. That allows the jury to look from him to the blackboard to make the comparisons, and to follow what he means, which allows them to stay much more actively involved. Remember to suggest he sit down when he's done writing and talking about the diagram. If, after he has explained everything on the blackboard, he has nothing more to draw, he can look very wooden as he stands there, even if he's a physical type and likes moving around a little.

You can also use the ploy of letting him sit down and then go back to the blackboard again to point to his diagrams in order to explain his final conclusions. That gives the conclusion even more strength and emphasis, because there is now a visual reinforcement of what is being said. Remember the interest generated by movement in the courtroom.

Progression From Familiar to More Difficult

People can dare to explore something new if you start them with something familiar. Begin with a familiar, simple process, something in their own experience, when you want to explain a complex or technical matter. Then extrapolate. "It's like a . . . , but it differs in this way." Keep the jury in safe territory and keep coming back to familiar similes.

Help your expert witness to do this by saying, "To clarify, Dr. So and So, that is it like a . . . ?" "Can you give that to me in more familiar terms?" "Can you explain that so that I as a layman would understand that a little better?" "You know, Dr. X, you're an expert. Is there a simpler way to describe that?" Then you keep reminding him about what you had both already planned in advance, which was to start with much simpler processes.

Don't Patronize

Never say, "Will you tell the jury." That's patronizing and sounds as though you and he already know, and only the jury is stupid and uninformed. Always say, "Tell us," or "Would you please explain," or "I don't understand," or "Can you help me (or us) with that particular technical term?" and so forth. Don't focus on the jury as the only people who don't understand or the only people who need an explanation.

Interrupt and Re-route

Learn to interrupt or re-direct if he gets off the track, which experts often do. As I suggested in the earlier chapters on direct and cross, everybody knows it's rude to interrupt, so you must learn how to do this so that the jury won't misunderstand your interruption as rudeness, manipulation or broadcasting to your expert what you want him to say. Explain to be sure that everybody sees your major motivation for interrupting. "Excuse me, Doctor, there's a lot of information there. Can we please take it apart? Let's start with . . . "or "Just a moment, Doctor. You know, that's very technical. Could you go back and explain that again . . ." Use your humor: "Now you're getting me lost in that sea of numbers that always gave me great difficulty in high school. I still haven't gotten over it, so could you please go back and . . ." That kind of humanizing, reasonable approach to interrupting or directing the testimony makes the jury forgive you. It also recharges their interest since, if *you* noticed he was going on and on, they surely did. They'll be grateful to you for helping them out.

Be Careful of Your Own Language

Experts often like to show off with big technical terms that say, "I'm an insider and you're not." Sometimes they do it by force of habit. Since you're riding herd on this as you listen to the expert with the juror's ears, you'll surely notice, stop him and make him clarify the terms.

But sometimes *you* do it. Sometimes you've gotten so familiar with the words that *you* use technical terms in your questions without explaining or simplifying them. That tells the jury two things:

• You're an insider, too, and they're outside—and you're leaving them behind.

• You're showing off.

Now, I know you'd never do that! But sometimes it's irresistible or it's become a habit through your lengthy discussions of the case.

Another habit is to say, "Will you briefly tell us . . ." or "In short, what . . ." Both signal the jury that this next point is going to be boring. "Watch out! He's trying to push him along over this place. This will really be dull."

Also, don't say, "Tell us in simple terms." Say "tell us so a layman can understand." The first one says it needs to be simple for the jury to be able to understand; the second one says the jury can understand but you recognize that they're laymen—and so are you.

Moving Toward the Conclusion

A fine Seattle lawyer and teacher, Michael Reiss, has an excellent set of simple and logical progression questions that explain the process of the expert's investigation and research which led the expert and can lead the jury easily to a conclusion. About each issue to be investigated or opinion reached, he asks:

• What did you do?

• Why did you do that?

• What did that mean?

It is a clear way to take the jury and the expert step by step, chronologically, and understand the process used for the conclusion as well as the basis for the conclusion. You may need to ask for more detail after each question, but following this format is extremely organized and compelling. Be sure to recap the salient points and the testimony before you ask for the conclusion so that the jury remembers and sees how the conclusion will finally tie it all up. Then the conclusion has impact.

Asking for the Conclusion

Some lawyers like to ask the expert, at the outset, before they qualify him, if he has reached a conclusion and find out what it is. Then the qualifications explain who has made this statement and how credible he or she is. Some other lawyers like to ask only *if* they've reached a conclusion and go no further before they ask for qualifications, waiting to develop the theories and give the conclusion at the end. Still others qualify first, ask for the conclusion and then do a flashback. While there is no rule of thumb, I believe in suspense. Getting the jury interested by asking if the expert has a conclusion; not telling it, but demonstrating how impressive this expert is; building the suspense still further by showing how he reached his conclusions; and then, finally, using the conclusion as their last line, is probably the most dramatic way to do it and to sustain the highest degree of jury interest.

CROSS-EXAMINATION OF EXPERT WITNESSES

Insights and Techniques

The big problems with cross-examining an expert are the technical nature of your impeachment and your questioning, and how much respect and courtesy you should show to the opposition's declared savant. Of course, there are many other issues as well. Suggestions for effective cross-examination that take them into account follow. (For additional cross-examination techniques, see Chapter 5.)

Respect

Be sure to treat an expert respectfully. Don't negate the person or his stature, just his responses. If the jury sees you become too impatient, if they see you manipulate, if they see you interrupt

rudely rather than gracefully, they begin to question your upbring-
ing and your roots. They see your arrogance and judge *you*, more
than beginning to doubt the witness. Treat the expert with even
more deference than you would a lay witness because there is
something in our culture that says honor is given to people of accomplishment, and the jury should see you give the expert that
honor. Be careful not to put *him* down—just his ideas.

If, however, the expert is suspect, or has presented himself
pompously or arrogantly the jury would welcome your letting some
air out of his balloon, with dignity, of course. If you scramble
around in a gutter fight, some of the dirt gets on you. Therefore, be
clever, subtle and sharp, but don't get too abrasive or ugly. Show
the jury what the expert said that was wrong, not credible, not
carefully researched, not fully reported. Then they won't trust or
like him on their own.

Be Sure the Jury Sees the Point

Since so much of your testimony will deal with technical matters, don't presume the jury knows what point you're contesting. If
they aren't clear on what you're trying to do, they have every reason to nod off. So explain carefully what area you're analyzing further or questioning about. Send clues about what you disagree
with.

Don't Bicker or Nitpick

No tug-of-war with the witness. You're supposed to have
smoother skills than the witness and to know how to make people
answer you. Juries see your insistence on total control and only
"yes-or-no answers-no-matter-what" as petulant or a sign of slight
desperation. Instead of out-and-out battle, hold your ground, rephrase your questions, get agreement on parts of your question.
That all looks like a win. Arguing makes you look weaker.

Bob Hanley suggests getting admissions from honest
opposing experts and then letting your expert debate your
opposing experts' opinions during your direct examination. Find
creative ways to get at your facts. Rope 'em in, but no blatant
punch-out.

No Ambiguous Questions or Half-Quotes

A sharp witness can really do a number on this one. If you quote out of context and the expert knows the book—watch out! The jury will see you as cheating, and there goes the ball game. Ambiguous questions designed to trap the expert can also backfire as he describes why he can't answer that question, but can only answer certain parts, etc. Be sure you stand on solid ground when you ask a question. The jury expects you to fight the expert fairly—no tricks.

Add New Information

What the jury likes best is for additional clarification, insight, a new perspective and new information to come out of a cross. Building a new concept on some hard-won information they've just learned, through your cross examination, is a very strong weapon.

Adding to what they now know (albeit newly acquired) is much safer and more interesting to them than going off on some even more esoteric subject with the expert. Taking him one or two steps further and adding new insights dilutes what the expert said overall. It's one way of telling the other side of the story.

Of course, add totally new information as well as critically questioning what's just been heard. But do these after you tell everyone why they need to know it and what bearing it has on the case.

Create Doubt

Since so much of what experts talk about is difficult to understand, you cannot hope to make many major gains since the jury is always in danger of getting lost. But if you can create doubt—just enough suspicion that the expert doesn't know it all or that he wasn't totally candid and forthright—then you've done enough. Since the major idea is to make the jury question and doubt the expert, and therefore his testimony, you needn't go for a total kill.

Some body language to give this air of suspicion could be:

• Standing angled to the witness and looking towards him with one eye rather than frontally and forthright.

• Not keeping eye contact by looking at your notes as he answers. Do look at him as you question him, though.

• Using phrases like "Didn't you say . . ." or "Didn't you tell the jury" with some incredulous or shocked tone.

• Nodding your head as if to say, "uh-huh, that's just what I thought you'd say."

These must be subtle or you'll look nasty or arrogant. To create doubt, be sure that your behavior is above reproach and the points you bring out are clear. But be sure they are indeed questionable. Don't build up the jury to the letdown of a very minor win.

Don't Be Too Obseqiuous

"Could you please help me understand" with the appropriate gestures and overly nice tone works like a fingernail on a blackboard. The jury knows what you're after. Don't be a phony. You'll pay a bigger price in losing credibility than you'll ever get back from the point you made. Be your own person and do your job. The jury respects that you're not trying to fool them.

Using Technical Language

Some lawyers say they like to intimidate an opposing witness by showing how much they know. Let's face it folks—knowing ten or fifteen technical terms or three theoretical processes does not yet qualify you as an expert and would hardly threaten anyone. Actually, it might even stimulate the opposing expert to play a competitive game of who-knows-more with you and you would probably lose.

Use Their Visuals

If you can, dispel the strong visual images left by the direct examination by using their charts to show what's missing or to question their statements before you create yours. Then the jury will remember your additions and not the original images.

Juries Get Bored

Be careful how long you take for cross. If they've already been exposed to a long boring witness, it's hard to sustain the jury's interest for too much longer, no matter how clever you are. Be aware of the lapsed time and the time of day, how hungry and tired they are. Expert witness work is tough. Weigh how much good you can get out of a cross versus how much you can irritate a tired, bored jury. If the direct was very long and complex, you might ask for a recess. Try to pick your time for cross to get maximum attention.

*   *   *

In conclusion: The essence of examining experts effectively is to be aware of an expert witness' effect on the jury—prejudged and actual. How much can you do to make the subject palatable to the jury? What's the best way to handle it? How can you help the expert be clearer and more interesting? Most of all, how can you get the jury to listen and understand? Think of what approach the jury would like you to have to your witness and/or your cross-examination. What do they need to know? Do they know they need it? And be very clear about your role. You are an expert, too—about your case. Be sure everything you present actually helps the jury understand and be persuaded about your theory.

7

FINAL ARGUMENT

Final argument, rather than being a time of high gear advocacy, is a time of delicate balance.

One of the biggest errors made in final argument is usurping the jury's ultimate job and privilege, the thing they've been looking forward to all through the trial—making up their own minds. The kind of argumentative overkill that often happens in your zeal to persuade is seen as presumptuous and overbearing. It can turn jurors off so completely that they become passive, unresponsive and, ultimately, advocates against you. Let me explain.

In a play, a truly evocative actor rarely cries in a tragic scene. If he does, the audience has no choice but to sit back and observe him and his agony. They become voyeurs and spectators, not participants. The pain doesn't hit them, since the actor is already responding to it.

If, however, the actor does his job well, then he will dissect and lay out before the audience every detail, facet and nuance of the tragedy in such eloquent terms that he brings the audience to tears and *they* cry for the tragedy. The actor as a presenter, as a messenger, simply becomes a conduit directly into the audience's feelings. They perceive the tragedy themselves, they feel it keenly, deeply, personally and, in that process, almost forget it was the actor who made it happen. They are totally involved. They are the sufferers who see the injustice and feel the pain. And that's what lingers. Only in retrospect does the audience see how it was done.

Of course, I don't suggest that you make the jury cry. But in order to persuade them, to move them to your point of view, you must first involve them and make them care. You need to push them to find their own feelings and then, combining emotion with the reason that you provide, you have dealt with the two forces that make them decide.

The lesson of letting the audience rise to their own emotional heights rather than watching you rise to yours is a difficult one, but an especially difficult one for lawyers to learn when presenting final argument. After all, for you, final argument is the culmination and the climax of the trial. All your points of view will now be brought together. This is the time you must be most persuasive and convincing. It's also your last chance to address the jury. Therefore, there's a heightened sense of anxiety and push which, together with your inevitable extra energy and drive, translates very often into telling instead of involving, dictating instead of suggesting, and exhorting and proselytizing instead of convincing and persuading. This can create a backlash that causes the jury to resist rather than follow.

To change this common syndrome, let's look at some basic components of final argument: how juries make decisions, persuasive techniques, effective structure and some examples of good final argument tactics, to give you more options and new creative stimulus in your own final arguments.

HOW JURORS MAKE JUDGMENTS

It would be nice to say that jurors make judgments the way the law prescribes—with an uncluttered, unbiased mind. But the fact is that hardly anybody does. Or can. Generalizations, of course, are always vulnerable to individuality and exceptions. But, in broad strokes, this is how most people judge.

Early Influences

We make judgments based on our original ethical values: the parental, family and cultural influences that were the first voices we heard. They taught us what was right and wrong, acceptable and unacceptable, punishable and forgivable. These earliest tapes run in our minds throughout our lives, and they are probably the first things we think of whenever we judge anything. They may be superceded by what happened to us later on and the way in which we changed our minds, but the very first and deepest experiences of morality and judgment are the ones that we still bring to bear with great effect, particularly in a jury room.

Later Conclusions

People also judge by their own handcrafted individual morality and standards, by the additions and departures they have made through their own life experiences from those original ethical values they learned at their parents' knees. These newer standards have additional clout if a person has become disillusioned, if the things he or she was taught to believe in have turned out not to be so. If life has, in one way or another, betrayed him or her, then there is anger and disappointment and a forceful rejection of the systems he or she believed in. This disillusionment creates a dichotomy, an inner tug of war about which way to decide, about what *is* right and wrong. When a jury sits together, you can hear extraneous, unreasonable arguments that usually stem from this inner conflict of what people would like to believe and used to believe versus the other things that life has taught them.

Prejudices, Stereotypes and Pre-Conceived Ideas

These are very influential and they are, in many ways, the most dangerous reasons for people's judgments. They are based on a willingness to accept untruths and half-truths, on people's fear of finding out what else is also true. This comes from an unwillingness or inability to get past what everybody else is saying or doing. It comes from a need to disallow the strange, the novel and the different. Most of all, it comes from insecurity about making up their own minds about something that is generally unpopular or unacceptable.

Standing alone with our beliefs is a difficult experience for most people. It is simpler and less threatening to stay with the norm and go with the crowd than to raise your hand and say, "Wait a minute. Is that really true?" It is unfortunate that in most people's experiences they don't have much opportunity to find out more about people, to discover movements or ways of life beyond the general caricatures. We don't often question what we've heard or are willing to accept. This fact of human nature perpetuates prejudice. It washes over and often neutralizes the possibility that somebody could, perhaps, disagree and find out for himself.

First Impressions

People usually draw conclusions and develop attitudes toward a stranger within the first three minutes after they meet him. It goes back to the old days of needing to quickly identify friend or foe, but we all seem to have a need and a system for making some kind of snap judgment about people. The old animal instincts and the five senses provide us with clues to make those judgments and, since they're based on feeling, not logic, they're often very hard to erase. We change our minds slowly, and with real reluctance, about first impressions.

Personalities

Juries also make judgments based on their personal responses to lawyers, witnesses, plaintiff or defendant. It's unfortunate, but still a fact, that people develop predilections toward or against someone. If favorable, they are more willing to forgive him, to give him the benefit of the doubt, to understand, to smile away a little abberation or digression and, in the largest sense, to be more willing to forgive on a much greater scale. That's one of the reasons I keep emphasizing the ways in which the lawyer should not "get in his own way." The jury must be able to get through to the facts in the case, and not develop a need to thwart one lawyer or to reward his opposing counsel.

Identification

Jurors will feel closer to a lawyer or client who seems to share their own standards, background or life experiences, with whom they can identify and emphathize. This causes them to lean more in one direction than another. If they feel that a lawyer is arguing from a shared, basic point of view about life, then, although the opposing arguments in the case can be clear, decisions often revolve around who seems to see truth as they do.

Instincts

Gut feelings and visceral responses are a major factor in judgment and decision-making. When you consider that jurors do not know the law, what else can they bring to the courtroom? We rely on our instincts, those ephemeral guides that tell us how we're feeling and what to do, for most of the decisions we make in our lives. When we go shopping, even though we gather all the facts about price, suitability and comparable options, we still finally make our choices based on some inner voice that says, "I just like that one better."

Empathy

As the story is told and the events described, the ability of a juror to personalize, to feel like he was there, or to know how she would feel if she were there, is a most persuasive factor that makes a lasting impression. Jurors can then judge how *they* would act and their own life experiences tell them, "Yes, I would." "No, I wouldn't." "That doesn't make sense." "That's not how things work." The ability to actually experience, internally, what is at issue, to empathize and put themselves in another person's place, is something of which jurors are not consciously aware. Yet this process is human and universal, and it is a powerful inner voice in decision-making.

Comparison

Looking at the general norms of human behavior in any situation
and then comparing them with what actually took place in a case is
another major factor in jurors' decisions.

Everybody likes to feel "normal," which means doing the
usual, the predictable, the expected. Since a trial deals with an unnatural, abberant or unusual human event, one of the best ways to
judge it is to establish standards, to find out what people would
normally do or should do in such circumstances, to know how
things normally operate, and then to see how and why the behavior
in this case differed. This gives a basis for judging fault and
severity.

Wanting To Be Fair

Jurors take their job very seriously and try to come to a verdict in
as pure a form as they can. They know how they have made decisions in the past, based on emotion and instinct, and this concerns
them. They'd like to feel proud of the decision they make in the
trial and of their reasons for making it. They wish to fight against
baser instincts and unfair choices, and be fair, unbiased and just.
But they are, after all, only people, and when pressed they fall
back on the things they know best and longest and hope these will
suffice, although they keep struggling to justify and to find what
would be truly fair.

Leaning on the Law

Sorting out the facts of the case and measuring them against what
jury members think the law provides is another factor in jury decisions. In trying to be fair, jurors are trying very hard to add an ingredient they never used before, that is, the body of the law as it
has been told to them in the courtroom. They try to hear the story
against this measuring stick as the trial progresses. Matching the
story to the law, they then try to imagine what the law really means
and whether an action would be legal or not.

Therefore, one of the main reasons it's so crucial to be clear
throughout the trial, and to explain what the law actually provides

on the key points of the trial, is the fact that jurors are playing with concepts they may or may not understand at all, but they are anxiously trying to give themselves a better reason for their decision. The law is indeed the ultimate basis, but they need to understand it in order to use it.

Going Along with the Majority

What happens in the jury room is just a microcosm of what happens in life. Most people are followers. They are not accustomed to walking against the wind. Most people have not spent any time standing up for a cause, fighting against their neighbors or arguing for an unpopular thought. It's personally costly and they're just not willing to be exposed and vulnerable to the attack of the majority. Jurors are willing to knuckle under simply because they have run out of arguments after the second statement they make, or because they perceive that other people may be smarter than they are.

Remember that in voir dire, and even before, as they sat waiting to be called, the jurors did some natural bonding. They found out about the backgrounds and personalities of the other jurors. As the trial progressed, they began to discover who discussed, who analyzed, who was forthright and who were the leaders. In the jury room, they discover who is the best arguer, who won't let a situation rest, who likes feeling they're right. They have to measure that against, "Do I really want to stick my neck out that far for that long a period of time? Am I strong enough to fight?"

Most people want to belong and, unless they have a burning need or personal reason or they have had previous experience in disagreeing, it's very difficult for them to fight for an idea, especially if they're not rock-solid in their conviction.

Liking to be Liked

Dissenters can feel isolated, like an irritant, if they continue to disagree with the group. "Do I really want to disagree with my group and become unpopular?" Most of us want to be liked. As the deliberation time goes by, they hear annoyance from the rest of the jurors: "Gee, how many times must we go over that?" and "Oh, come on, it's time to go." Unless they can keep finding new arguments or have support from at least one other juror with a sense that they might prevail, most dissenters will fold. There are always jurors who start to disagree, but peer pressure finally makes them say, "Well, okay, I give in."

BASIC ELEMENTS OF FINAL ARGUMENT

What the Jury Needs

From the moment they first walked into the courtroom the jury has been made aware of how much they didn't know about the law and how much they needed to understand. They didn't even know what the judge was going to require of them or what the essence of the case would be. But one thing they knew: they would have to decide on a verdict. All they could offer were the instinctive processes by which they judged anything in their lives. Were these enough? To judge, blame and punish their fellow human beings based on their own life experiences and their personal standards?

When asked to judge, everyone wants to be above reproach. In the courtroom, particularly, they know that they're called upon to find the best in themselves, to be as clear and as pure as they would like to be in their judgments. It's based on a need to save themselves the pain of lying awake nights thinking "Maybe I didn't judge it right. Maybe I should have seen it differently. Maybe I was wrong."

So they need you.

The final argument is the time to:

- Support the jury and help them decide.
- Give them the reasons to blame.
- Help make them sure.
- Give them information that will muster their best judgment based on the facts of the case and the law.
- Make them feel strong enough to judge and punish.

To win, you must be able to assuage their doubts with solid answers, to show them logic and objective reasoning that will support their inclinations and to argue so convincingly that they are persuaded and finally agree, feeling that's their idea, too.

What is Summation

A Time to Review

Final argument is not only the time for argument; it is, first of all, the time for a summary of the basic issues of the trial, a time to look back in order to list and organize the key points of the case. It is a time to give the jury a base on which to hear your argument.

A Time to Unify

Closing argument is an important time to unify you and the jury as having shared an extraordinary experience. This is an opportunity for you as an advocate and a persuader to join with the jury and to be seen, not as an adversary manipulating witnesses, dealing with opposing counsel and "selling" the jury, but as a fellow human being, reasoning together with them. It is a time when they want you to be straight, to say what you think and feel and, in that process, to be seen as joining with them in the common, human goal of fairness and justice.

A Time to Involve

The jury must now, as never before, be engaged in participating, caring and being committed. One of the great dangers in final argument is losing the jury's attention. Here, as in no other part of the trial, it is necessary for them to follow the logic of your argument point by point. You must get them and hold their attention.

A Time to Explain

This is when the jury must hear and absorb the reasons why you put everything into the trial that you did. It is a time to tie up all the disparate pieces of the trial and the testimony in order to show the basic structure of your case and what that design was for. They saw many witnesses called, heard much testimony and were shown much evidence during the trial. Now you must explain why, what issues you proved by what you did, and why you did it that way. Anyone who can come at this point and show the inexorable logic of his or her trial plan and resultant argument is a very welcome guest.

A Time to Remind

When you began the trial and explained your theory of the case in opening statement, you told the jury what witnesses you would bring and why. You promised that at the end the witnesses would have proved all your contentions. Now it is time to show you kept your word, to remind them that you did what you promised and it turned out just as you said it would. You must show the self-fulfilling prophecies and how right you were in your predictions.

A Time to Organize

This is the time for the ultimate series of lists. Using visuals, blackboard, charts and outlines, you must help the jury put the facts in order. They need you to coordinate the issues and the proof, to put events and documentation in chronological order, to make sense of the morass of information and to organize it all into your system to prove your theory of the case.

A Time to Emphasize

Now you need to show what is most important and how it affects the jury's decision. It was difficult all through the trial for the jury to sort out and understand which points mattered and which didn't, which were the essential statements, what were basic issues and what was amplification and discourse. When you emphasize what to remember, what mattered and how to weight the many things they heard, they will be able to see clearly what to concentrate on and what to discard in their deliberation.

A Time to Compare

One of the best ways to evaluate what went wrong is to understand the norm. In final argument you need to show jurors the natural order, the usual process, in order to see the extent of disorder or wrong-doing by comparison. Only when they see the extent of the breach can they truly understand what and how much to punish. In final argument you need to ground them in the acceptable before you demand that they see what's unacceptable.

A Time to Clarify

This is when you must clarify the task that's before the jury. What do they really have to decide? At this stage their role is still vague. Major confusion and anxiety can exist around words like "guilt" or "damages," "reasonable doubt" or "burden of proof." The jury needs clarification about the essence of the law that is being tried in this case and how your facts and argument relate to that.

Although the issues to be proven in the case have been clear to you for a very long time, they're still brand new to the jury. Trying to relate what the jury has heard in the trial to what the judge says is at issue here, and being able to evaluate what parts of the trial make those points is very difficult. If they don't understand what points must be proven, they will make judgments based upon the wrong set of assumptions. So, it is up to you to be doubly sure that they really understand what they are trying to evaluate and what is not at issue.

A Time to Prove

This is the time to show you were right, to show how the end product proves what you said at the beginning and all through the trial, to show that the sum total of all the points you made fits our accepted scheme of good versus bad and of acceptable versus unacceptable behavior in our society. This is the time for you to bring in all the measurements people usually use to decide right from wrong and to show how those generally accepted concepts fit your side of the case.

A Time to Disprove

You don't profit from presenting only your half of the case. You must answer your opponent's allegations and theories. Since that's the basic fight the jury must decide on, you have to give

them reasons why he's wrong as well as why you're right. The
stronger your arguments about how your opponent has misunderstood the issues, didn't prove what he said was the case, or that his
case is at odds with what the law specifies, the stronger your case
becomes.

A Time to Transcend, a Time to Return

Defense lawyers ask the jury to transcend their sympathy and
emotional response to an accident or a tragedy and move into the
place in their heads that thinks, a place that can rationally judge
and decide what the points of law demand.

Plaintiff's lawyers ask the jury to use feelings, to return to an
older, more familiar and basic human view of the law as their
guide: the law of vengeance, of an eye for an eye and a tooth for a
tooth. They ask jurors to go back and dig into their feelings in order
to make a judgment.

Knowing jurors mainly make judgments instinctively and
emotionally but that they need to feel supported and sure
cerebrally, both lawyers need to explain what the points of law and
precedence are in order to corroborate and dignify jurors' decisions, but at the same time, they must deal with instinct and feelings as a valid reference and guide.

A Time to Reassure

Most of all, this is the time to show the jury your confidence
in them, to let them know you believe in them, in their desire to
do a good job and in their ability to understand and judge. Before
you challenge them to vote and to vote your way, tell them that
you know they can sort out the facts, that you know how much
they're committed to being fair. Show them your respect and your
faith in them as well as your security that sorting out the facts and
being fair will make them decide to vote for your side.

*   *   *

Final argument, then, is a time for you to explain and clarify,
to organize and underline, to recap and inform, to overcome and

persuade. But most of all, it's to help the jury make a decision and to support their instincts with the weight of facts.

You need to help them follow their judgment processes: the emotional one of empathizing with the person or cause you're arguing for and the cerebral one of the issue of law, fairness and logic. You must give them reasons and support for the decision they will come to. But most of all, you must give them the feeling that they are able; that they want to be, and can be, fair and just; and that through your analysis of what happened and what the law provides they will see what is right and act on it.

DESIGNING THE FINAL ARGUMENT

The final argument needs to be choreographed. As in all works designed to give a message, your final argument must contain the elements that make people listen. The jury, like any audience, must feel from the beginning that you are going somewhere they want to go. Your content and timing, your pace, and your intensity must compellingly move them to the inevitable climax with a resounding or thoughtful finish in order to be effective and to communicate. What do you do, then, to create a shape, to build around a form that will be eloquent?

How to Start

Create

The most important decision is to know that the final argument is your biggest performance and you need a vehicle in which to star, not just a platform on which to perform. The more crafted, thoughtfully considered and designed it is, the more you analyze what you really need and need not say; the more you know what quality you want it to have; the closer you feel to your jury and what they need from you—the easier your choice of form and structure will become.

Spend a little time listening to some inner voices about this. Let the right side of your brain, your instinctive, creative, imaginative self, lead you. List your facts and your issues. Then ask how they make you feel. What about them is most universal and compelling? Free-associate those elements with what color, texture, fabric, architecture, music, even food, they remind you of. Is it a meat-and-potatoes, around-the-kitchen table, red-checkered, homespun, garden variety issue? Is it a somber, purple-velvet, organ-music, lofty-ceilinged, dark-oak issue? Begin to shape and color your argument from these basic perceptions. The form, the language, the pace and style will fall into place naturally. That, after all, is the way you want the jury to hear you—naturally. Your argument should fit into their natural instincts about justice and fairness. Your logic should sound sensible and familiar to them. Your view of justice must be recognizable and comfortable for them to accept. Your conclusions should be as satisfyingly complete and inevitable as the last chords of a piece of music that definitively say "THE END (of course)."

Conceptualize

You need to see it all, first to conceive the overall plan, then to organize your elements and design a layout. It needs to be designed as a structure on which you can hang the points you'll make. As in a work of art, the form follows what you want to say and what effect you want to create. You need form to make a cogent, digestible whole, to be a proper container for your facts.

Begin by thinking through the elements of your arguments. Weight them. Which ones are basic, like primary colors? Where are the nuances, the subtle shadings? Find the vigor, the anger, the tension. What goes first and most of all, how shall you finish? List the elements. Now look at their qualities. Are they emotional? Factual? Abstract? Can you refer to more common human functions or experiences as analogies to make them clearer? Choose the style based on what you want to tell and how you want your jury to receive your message. How should they feel?

Design

Now—the design. What shape will this argument take, what form will it follow?

If you are a visual person, think through your final argument visually. You could start at the top left hand corner and wend your way in a serpentine fashion with built-in stops, exclamation points at key places, or idea-blocks that build and concept-shapes that connect, until you get to the end with a large bang or trail off with a controlled and thoughtful single note.

You can think of it in dramatic terms. What's the beginning? What gets their attention? Do you want to start by telling the most important part and then spend the rest of the story explaining that most important part, flashing back to its origins and moving ahead to its conclusions? Do you form the essence as the central pillar around which you will build the rest of your story like the spokes of a wheel, always coming back to your central theme?

Do you feel it in a narrative, horizontal form—starting with the beginning of a story and wending your way through it, explaining as you go along, stopping, digressing, looking more closely, analyzing more sharply, amplifying and building toward the inexorable conclusion?

You can see it in musical terms—A-B-A—(chorus-verse-chorus). Start with a theme—go to a "verse"—back to your chorus-like theme—to another idea—back to your theme and so on.

Content and Structure

The content of your final argument should not only be eloquent as you give it, it should also produce an echo in the jury room. What you talk about must be useful, either as factual subject matter or as an atavistic or emotional catalyst. It needs to create another dimension for your facts, one that compels and sustains the jury's reasoning. Here are some techniques for structuring and designing an argument that will make that happen. You might also use the basic elements of summation (pp. 319–232) as a checklist.

Give Them a Reason to Listen

The primary requisite in getting an audience to listen is to recognize everyone's number one motivation for doing anything—self-interest. They'll listen if it sounds like it's for them, if it's meaningful, startling, unusual, exciting, useful—anything they can internalize and translate into their own terms. They won't like it or listen if it's "good for them" (like hot cereal or sermons). They won't listen if it's abstract or above them or if it's in *your* self-interest for them to listen. They will listen only if they can identify it as theirs.

The opening of your argument must define why they should listen. Shock them? They want to know more. Show them they need and want this? They're with you. Cajole and seduce them? A warm, winning opening promises a good experience.

The essence is to tell the jury that you know their needs and that your purpose is to address those needs and help them come to a decision.

Establish a Theme

The most secure base on which to build your argument is to establish your version of what the case is basically about. "This is a story of greed." "The basic thread that weaves its way through all the events you've heard is responsibility, responsibility for . . ." "There was an accident, but Jim's not to blame."

Once you have set up your approach and the fundamental concepts you base your case on, you've got your home base. You've created an orientation for the jurors, a foundation on which you can build your argument. Coming back to it is reassuring; departing to explore one little avenue is understandable; tying it up at the end is fore-ordained.

Your theme can be a saying or a thought. It can be pictorial or conceptual. But it should embody the absolute heart of what you're going to argue. You can intrigue the jury by introducing your theme with a story, a quote, an analogy. You can say it straight out—bold and strong. But you must make it clear and put it into words—early.

Eliminate Unnecessary Issues

Tell them, and briefly discuss, what's *not* at issue to help the jury focus only on the important points of your argument. "There is no question about. . . That's not at issue here and requires no thought or discussion." Then, when you tell them what *is* at issue, you relieve the jury and give them incentive to focus and listen to the few main points rather than assuming they need to consider everything.

Use Recognizable References

Argue using concepts that are within the frames of reference of the jurors. This has immediate appeal and gains instant attention. The best way to determine what these concepts are is to study your voir dire questions and answers. Who is your jury? Where are they from? What is their work? What do they know about? Look for roots, for ethnic connectedness and what that group cares about. Look for religious affiliations and economic status and what concerns those issues bring. Be aware of educational levels and the kinds of references the jurors would or would not understand. Choose your language, analogies and examples with this particular jury in mind.

Humanize the Argument

Tap into human emotions and responses first, and then bring the logic to corroborate. You have to find a blend of getting a story out again, recapping everything that took place and then, after that, stopping at the key points and making the jury see how, cerebrally, in terms of the law, their judgment must be this way. But first, bring them there and keep them interested. Then give them the logic.

If you begin in an abstract manner, by exhorting them about what the law provides, you place them in an alien environment. It becomes very difficult for them to follow you, because they are already struggling to keep up and understand. Intrigue them, capture them with what they already know.

Explain Why You Care

What? As I write this I imagine you reading it and laughing out loud. "Sure, I'm representing the XYZ oil cartel with megabucks at stake and I'm going to tell them 'lawyering is what my mother always wanted me to do.' " But consider this:

The jury wants to see that you care. They want to see some passion and commitment. Yes, they want you to be totally professional, but they also need to know that you believe in your cause completely. Someplace, then, you need to answer these questions: Why do you care? Why does this matter?

The pursuit of an answer can be interesting and revealing to you. Do you really care only for the money? Do you care for the winning? For the competition? For your pride? For the excitement and the brinksmanship? Or perhaps you respond to the law—the principles, the process, the order law can bring. Maybe you like the ability to speak out and fight for justice, for the underdog or for reason. Perhaps it's to preserve the system of government. What finally makes you so impassioned?

Perhaps you see yourself as a gladiator, doing battle for a person unable to fight for himself. Maybe you see yourself as an analyst or interpreter whose excitement comes from understanding the essence of a problem and how the law can be used to solve it. Maybe you're a teacher whose excitement comes from deciphering the obscurity of the law for laymen like the jury, so they can use it and participate in the system too. Are you a truth teller? A pathfinder?

Whatever your reason, the jury would like to understand why any of this is truly important to you, and why you think it's important enough to fight for. You needn't be maudlin, but the thrust of your argument should include some inkling of why *you* got up such a head of steam. It would add immeasurably to your credibility. Remember—all through the trial you represented the U.S. government or the district attorney, a skyscraper or a checkbook called Universal Widget, maybe even a crook a.k.a. Mack The Dipper. Now you must also emerge as a person who cares enough to try to persuade the jury. If you don't, if you are truly erasable as an individual or only real as an extension of your client, they will vote based solely on how they feel about your client.

Remind and Clarify

Lawyers underestimate what the jury can understand and overestimate what they can remember. The most important ingredient, the spine upon which to build your final argument, is to sort out the facts; remind the jury of various pieces of testimony and why they matter. It is surprising, when research is done with juries, to find out how little they remember of the names of the players and what their parts were in the various aspects of the case. Studies show they criticize final arguments in which lawyers do not review important testimony.

Remind the jury who spoke. Describing witnesses in some way such as, "You remember the old man who came up, who had such difficulty getting into the witness chair? He described when he saw the so-forth and so-on," is helpful. Such a cue helps to fix in their minds what testimony you are about to describe.

Your recap and your argument also make the most sense when you sort out the facts in order, when you show what significance they had in the whole story and explain which facts bear out your contention. The jury does not know your plan. It all seems so clear to you that sometimes you move through it too quickly, without giving them enough of a chance to remember on their own and also to listen to why it's important. By the way, explain what you didn't do and why. Studies show that juries are often confused about why you didn't present corroborating evidence, for example, or cross-examine a certain witness. They notice and it nags at them. They appreciate your reasonable explanation.

Emphasize and Underline

In order to point up the key issues, use devices that make the jury take notice: "Just listen to this." "Think about that." "I want to be sure I make this very clear." "Just remember that . . ." "This is so important, let me write it out as I talk about it."

After you've done your outline and recap, unless you pick out the two or three most salient points to work with, you're asking the jury to carry the whole trial with them into the jury room. They need you to select the few pointed issues, the fulcrum on which the case rests, and for your argument to explain and support just those, in order to make a clear judgment.

Organize Your Facts and Your Argument

Outlines and topic sentences make order and a logical progression clear. Think of painting by numbers: First, outline the shape so they see the task, then fill it in with color and argument, then be aware of how you make a transition to the next point. The jury needs to see the logic in why you go there, or bring that up. It's not enough that it's self-evident to you. The steps and change of subject must be clear to them so that they can digest and let go of one point and turn their attention fully to the next instead of being left dangling as you abruptly close the door and start down a new thoughtway.

Visualize

Don't depend on words alone to help the jury recall. Use the blackboard to list and describe. Go back again to the visuals that were used throughout the trial. It's reassuring to the jury to see something old and familiar. Point again at all those charts and diagrams that were made. Explain what they've proved and how they were used. Anything you do that reinforces something that happened before is comforting. If you use something from the trial, it won't sound like it's your idea and as if you just made it up. Rather, it has even more validity the second time around, and you have the advantage of clarifying it further.

Visualize not only objects and diagrams but ideas and facts as well. Learning and recall are best if something is written down. You could write the questions at issue in the trial on the board, one at a time, or have them prepared in advance. State and show or write a question. "Was Larry at the scene?" Let the jury think. Then explain what is not true and why, even listing the reasons. Answer your question by writing *NO* next to each question as you deal with it. You have indelibly imprinted the answer to that question in their minds.

Writing the points of your argument, rather than just telling, adds cumulative weight as the jury sees your points pile up. They go over them in their minds as you speak and remember them again later. Visualizing fixes ideas in the mind and guarantees clarity and recall in the jury room. (For more on visual aids, see Chapter 8).

Clear Up the Technical Data

Using the scientific, technological and complex factual data you have brought to bear throughout the case requires some careful handling now. For the jury, any clarification would be a welcome addition. For you to refer back to some of those complex issues and key technical points and to explain them again in lay language, using the expert's data and charts, is both reassuring and valuable. You know exactly what you meant and can now extract only those points you want to reiterate and explain. It also helps that you can be easier and more informal in your discussion of technical data because you are not one of those "expert witnesses."

In recapping, explain what the technical data meant; use some of the terms again, explaining them in lay language. Then show how this information affects the case. It will help the jury assimilate what has been sort of hanging around in the air as a cloud of scientific jargon, some of which they understood and much of which they didn't. This is your opportunity to select and cite only those things that matter, those things they'll have to know in order to help convince them further. Caution: Do not cite your own new scientific data that was not already presented by an expert. Jury studies show jurors resent this and don't believe it. They wonder where it comes from and why you didn't bring it up in direct or cross.

Bringing up and clarifying the scientific and technical data again is very persuasive to jurors, partly because they feel it is objective and beyond human manipulation, partly because it was so hard for them to understand and partly because they feel that it obviously has some great bearing on the case or you all wouldn't have made such big fuss about it. They'd like to understand and use it, but they need your help to do so.

Anticipate the Judge's Charges

The judge instructs the jury when both lawyers are already through with their closings. By then it's too late for you to explain more about what his instructions mean to your case. Therefore—anticipate. Think through what his other instructions in the law will be, what aspects of the law he'll draw upon and what issues are pertinent to your case. Then preview them for the jury: "The judge will instruct you about comparative negligence . . . " Make sure the jury gets the basic idea in simple form, so they know how to relate it to your argument and the point of view you are presenting. With all due respect to Their Honors, judges are not all uniformly skilled at explaining things simply to lay people. Their often confusing or abstract instructions, without clear layman-like examples, can serve to dilute your argument as the jury struggles to relate what the judge said to what you said. So figure out what points of law are at issue and explain beforehand, incorporating that explanation as a reason for your point of view being the correct one.

Don't Make it Too Long

Be ruthless with yourself. Know when to get offstage. Be practical. Don't put on what's not useful. That doesn't mean a "just the facts, ma'am." You must have color, juice, flavor and feelings to serve a substantive, thought-provoking and engaging meal. But be careful about over-explaining; about lengthy prologues and about over-statement. Use visual reinforcement to cut down the words.

"Less is more." Be aware when, as well made and well-delivered as your argument may be, you have come to a place of overload where the jury wants no more.

First Lines

People notice most what is said first and last. When you begin to speak, you write on a clean slate. You are most welcome. The jury is at its most curious and attentive. Select a beginning that sets the tone and the theme for your argument. Capture their imagination and interest right at the beginning. You'll never have a better chance. You might look at how you started your opening statement and use parts of it, or evoke some of the same images again as a satisfying rounding-out of the whole trial. Just be sure that your opening lines set the tone as well as the theme of your argument. (For more on opening lines, see next section.)

Your Final Lines

Everyone listens to music, and, old music or new, there is a beginning, a middle and an end. One of the things I happen not to like about current popular music is that it never has a real ending. It dribbles off. After you've heard "Baby-Baby-Baby" 27 times, it just kind of winds down, fades away and then disappears for no particular reason except that the musicians have no more to say or simply ran out of gas. That's not how you should finish.

You need to end on purpose, with a flourish, or thoughtfully, but with a flair. Essentially what you are doing for the jury in final argument is putting something in their suitcase to carry with them when they go to make their decision. So the final lines matter.

Think through the essence of your argument. What are your main points? They should be repeated in the last paragraph. Tell the jury you're coming to the end. They will listen harder (not in relief, hopefully) with the expectation that you'll remind them of what you said at the beginning and give them your final message.

Let your last line be eloquent, a human statement the jury can relate to, meaningful, touching, accurate and wise. Let it go beyond the case and the law to a deeper level of understanding. Reach for an ultimate concept, a basic need, a universal truth. Use a quote, a saying or something from everyone's experience. Give them a sign, a talisman, a ringing phrase that echoes on. Don't exit too hastily. Your presence, even after you have delivered your final lines, causes the jury to continue to think about everything you've said. Stand still. Let them digest it. It's almost as though you are thinking it over yourself. Fold your notes, deliberately, slowly, completely, and then sit down. Let them linger over the thought.

DELIVERING THE FINAL ARGUMENT

How you deliver your final argument needs to be considered, and from three different aspects: what approaches you take to the jury and what's persuasive as well as what personal presentation techniques you can use to enhance your own style of performance.

Beginnings

Openings should always set the tone for your argument. Not only must the jury understand what course you intend to follow and what they will get, but they need to get involved in the reasons for your argument and to see that you know what they need to hear from you. They must also discover what your approach is to the process of persuading them. Do you really see them as capable, fair, responsible adults? They need to see how much room you will give them to make up their own minds. Will you deliver your argument manipulatively, oppressively, pushing them to your conclusion? Right at the beginning, they need to see your sincerity and commitment, as well as your structure and your style.

Since what you say first is so memorable, and must serve as the base or launching pad for your whole argument, here are some techniques to help you begin.

Don't Thank Them

Many lawyers begin their final argument by saying, "My client and I would like to thank you for being so attentive and listening to our case, and being so thoughtful etc." Thanking them seems like a gracious and ingratiating idea but juries see it as patronizing and presumptuous, invading their territory.

Think about this. *You* didn't invite them to be jurors. They have not come to the courtroom at your behest. They have come, and have sat through the trial, because they were summoned by the Constitution, the government and George Washington. They were doing their civic duty. They were paying attention because they were *supposed* to. That was their job. And *your* thanking them demeans it. After all, you're just another person, and someone who wants something from them, at that. What power have you to thank them?

Also, thanking them sounds like you assume they're already kindly disposed to your side of the case and are going to vote for you. It sounds like thanking someone for tomorrow's birthday present today. This gesture is often misunderstood. Don't use it.

Compliment Them

This is the answer to wanting to thank them: Compliment them on how hard they worked. Tell them you know, that you saw and appreciated how hard it was to just sit still and listen. If they've been especially attentive in a long, complex case, tell them how impressed everyone in the court was with the level of their attention and concentration. Everyone loves to be noticed and complimented and that's surely appropriate for you to do. Act appreciative and aware rather than grateful.

Do Some Bonding

Find a common denominator. Recognize in what way you are all connected. The trial is a really unique experience, much more so for the jury than you, but use that fact to make a connection. Open by looking back on what you've shared: "We have lived through a unique experience together." "Only we in this courtroom know what took place and how we felt." "All of you will go home and try to explain to your husband, wife, children and friends what took place here. You will be able to recount some of the highlights, or maybe what you felt, but only we, all of us who shared it, know every piece of what it was like." If you feel comfortable with it, you might also say, "It was a time of expressing citizenship for all of us, for me as well as you."

Remind Them of the Lighter Moments

Find various aspects of the trial that you and they could share together, almost as though you had all been away serving on a jury, because as you do this, you and your client become one of them.

Remind them of particular things that happened, of memorable human moments: times when someone dropped something, when the judge happily called a recess, when it was too late in the day and everybody had to stay over, when you were all so hungry or hot, when the tape broke down while they were watching the video deposition. It lightens the atmosphere before you go into your argument.

Of course, choose the right trial situation in which to do this. Personal injury or criminal cases do not lend themselves to this approach, but many other civil cases surely do and if yours is the unpopular side, you might want to present your most human aspects here.

Be Vulnerable

You might want to discuss with them the fact that sometimes it was hard for them to stay awake and sometimes it was hard even for *you* to stay awake. Tell them that they affected you, that when

they looked bored it made your job harder as you saw them thinking that the trial and the talk seemed interminable. Show your
awareness and your human side. If it's comfortable, use humor.
"After all, Perry Mason is shown in an hour with all the dull stuff
cut out," or, "You had no idea when you came in that I would talk
to you for three weeks, did you?" This is a way to soften the role of
advocate, adversary and proselytizer, to join them by saying, "It
was a fascinating and difficult time, not only for you, but for me,
too."

Don't Apologize

I often hear lawyers say, at the beginning of their argument:
"If there is anything I have done during the trial that might offend
you (or whatever) please don't hold it against my client or the
case."

If you did your job badly, the jury will surely hold it against
your client. Although he or she didn't try the case, yours is the only
version they got. You formed the jury's opinions; you did the presentation and the arguing. It's too late now to say, "Strike that." It
sounds like a cop-out and an immature shifting of responsibility
when the jury hears that. Don't do it. Just try your case so well that
it would never occur to you to even think it. But even if it does,
don't give them any ideas by mentioning it. Act sure. Not only will
they believe it, but you will too.

Don't Say "My Client"

By saying "my client," you are reminding the jury you're a
hired gun and not really involved in the case. Make the jury hear
your client's name and continue to connect it with concepts of in-
nocence. Personalize your client: don't abstract him. Decide at the
beginning what you'll call him or her and get the jury tuned in to
that person or group as the proponents or actors in the case with
you as their leader or explainer. Always keep the personal image
before the jury.

Show Your Faith in Them

Explain their job as you see it with the confidence that they are really up to it. Let them know that you assume they want to, and can be, fair and just, ethical and concerned. But be careful. Do not exhort them to "be fair." That assumes that they need to rise above themselves to *become* fair. It sounds like they are not fair in the normal, everyday course of their lives, and only because you remind them will they now suddenly rise to the occasion and become as good as they are supposed to be.

Don't Say, "This Case Is Very Simple"

If it was so simple, why did it take a week to tell it? The danger of saying "it's simple" is that to the jurors it seems very complex. Look at the sea of words, the legal talk, the evidence, the arguments, the cross-examination, the bench conferences, the objections, the technical details and the chronology of the facts. Simple? Maybe to you. But saying it distances you from the jury. It implies that if *they* don't think it's simple, they're dumb. You not only patronize, you imply that "simple" is the only way to see it.

Instead, simplify it for them. Encourage them to see its simplicity by starting out saying, "I know how complex and confusing many parts of this trial could seem to you—the objections, the conflicting testimony. But I think I can make it simple and clear. There are just three issues here. Just three." Now *you* have begun to simplify it for them rather than telling them to do it.

Don't Say, "This is the Most Important Decision You'll Ever Make"

Jurors consider that presumptuous. You don't know enough about their past lives or their future to say that. Be careful not to overstate. That backfires. Don't try to make them feel guilty. You know how much we all resent that.

Describe Their Task and Your Role

Describe what the basic issues are and what they have to decide. Share all this information in helpful terms, recognizing with them how difficult the job is now. They have a wealth of information to process. They not only have to use their instinctive judgment, but they also have to understand clearly what the points of law are, so that when they collect and sift through the data they will know what the law says about it. Theirs is the most correct and just decision when it is based not only on human instinct, but on evidence and facts. They want to do it that way. Knowing that the law is the most unfamiliar part of their task, tell them you will help them sort out the facts and the law.

Describe What You're Going to Do

Tell them how you will clarify the issues and the facts for them: "I will take the case apart into several sections and show you step by step what will lead to my conclusion." People always listen when they know what to look forward to. Give the organization of your final argument after you do your introduction. This can have many variations and be much shorter, but here's a basic outline you might like to follow:

- Your theory of the case is . . .
- You're going to show it by . . .
- You will prove witnesses 1 and 2 were wrong by . . .
- You will review the evidence by . . .
- You will show the essence of the case . . .
- You will explain how the law deals with this . . .
- You will show show why these facts add up to their verdict.

When you give them your table of contents and the intention of your argument, they will follow you much more closely and coherently, knowing what they will be getting.

Persuasive Techniques in Argument

Let the Jury Do Their Work

Don't be a teller. Be an explainer. Make it possible for the jury to join you in your conclusion. Don't give them their conclusion. Make it possible for them to agree with you, not simply accept.

The hardest task is to incite or persuade the jury without usurping their role. What choices will you make to be sure that the jury can get past you to see and get involved in the points of the case? Think of your never getting in their way. Think of standing to one side of them, almost, and pointing out something in front of them. Make the drama come alive, so that they hardly see your hand pointing. They are tired of people talking at them. There is a great natural resistance to being exhorted. No one likes to be told what to do. Don't take away their job. They want to feel they're deciding on their own.

Get Them Involved

Lawyers often present the ideas in final argument from their own point of view—neat, clean, well-packaged and logical. You want this efficient package accepted—actually swallowed whole. But that's like taking a puzzle out of your child's hands rather than giving the child a chance to stumble with it a little until he figures out how to do it. Because you know the case and you know it well, your tendency is toward errors of commission: too much show and tell, rather than standing back and letting the jury catch up with you and then walking arm in arm together.

To get the jury involved, make a point. Let them grasp it, drawing up beside you. Now, go behind them and push them forward again. Encourage them to stand still for a moment while you explain something more about your point. Tell them why you are going to explain what you do—what end product you are looking for. Don't march ahead of them like a drum major, assuming they'll follow, or stand and face them and deliver the Sermon on the Mount. Telling them how to think makes them passive, and they won't really absorb your material. They will just feel vaguely resentful, overpowered and over-sold. Remember, in our society sales resistance is one of our major developed skills.

Ask, Don't Just Tell

Asking rhetorical questions is another good way to involve the jury and to make what you're saying clearer. If you ask before you tell, there is an automatic response on their part. They try to answer the question. There is an implication when you ask the question that they should try to answer it. What it does is set up a kind of dialogue between you and the jury so that when you ask it, they think of an answer. Then, of course, they are anxious to hear what your answer is because, obviously, you're going to tell them what you had in mind and they assume it may be better or closer to the facts than their answers. Example: Suppose you began your summation with "Ladies and gentlemen, why was this law suit brought?" Can't you see how quickly this focuses their attention; how much more they want to hear your explanation than if you began "Now I'm going to tell you why I feel this law suit was brought?"

Involvement is especially important at the end of the trial, when the energy level is low and they are looking for leadership more than at any other time. Yet, at the same time, they're getting ready for your onslaught, your "pitch." Thinking of participatory techniques is vital.

Use expressions like "What do you think?" "What do we all do when we're scared?" "Would it be logical for such and such to happen?" These become a springboard for your argument, your explaining, your persuading. They also put the jury on your wave length because you have just put them in that scene and caused them to think like your client. They can begin to find human error and judge it, because they can see themselves in a similar situation. Just be careful not to overplay this. Remember the "Golden Rule."

Don't Separate Yourself

Take care not to emphasize the split between you and them. Saying, "you," "a jury," or "you, the jury," reminds them that you are the advocate and they are the decision-makers. The greatest strength in your final argument can be if you can make them think "we." If you can base your argument on the idea that we share a unique common bond, a heritage, a way of life, a way of doing things, which is what we depend upon when we ask ourselves to make judgments, you are much more persuasive. Be with the jury so that they will feel that your vision of life and theirs are the same. Find examples and analogies that show this, that cause the jury to feel unified with your way of thinking. Your arguments are strengthened as they recognize their own approaches to life and judgment. This bridges the gap between lawyer (with special knowledge you're going to perpetrate on them) and juror (a lay person dependent on you).

Show Them You Believe in Your Case

There has to be passion, commitment and zeal, not overwhelming, but enough to make the jury know you believe with a perfect faith. You must raise them to your level of conviction, and you can't do that unless you show how much you believe in your case. Jurors give many points for commitment. If they watched you fight for your side throughout the trial, this is doubly expected at the end, and is most persuasive.

One word of caution: Don't overdo. No obvious histrionic devices, no cliches. Affectation is transparent. Real conviction shines through. Create, don't imitate. Do it from the heart, not from the stage.

Pace Yourself

The biggest pitfall is starting out on too high, energetic or irate a note. If you begin at the same level that you're going to end on, you'll have no place to go. You will overwhelm and overpower them. The jury backs off from too much pressure too soon, and bitterly resents your pressure in telling them how angry to get.

If you start out furious or with a great deal of passion, what will you do for a finish? Use a megaphone? Remembering my description of trying to see and design a total structure, your opening

demeanor must be geared to the whole picture, the whole performance. Start at a normal speaking level. Your first job is to entice them to come with you and stay the distance until you get to
the fireworks or whatever ending you've designed.

Talk at Their Level

Talking over the jury's heads in abstract terms breeds resentment as well as boredom. But the greatest danger in final argument, aside from disorganization, overstatement and cliche-ridden
garrulousness, is talking down to the jury. Don't patronize a group
that you want to inspire to reach up and grasp your explanations
and your concerns. Respect them. Talk straight and talk about life
as *they* know it.

Handling Empathy

Admit to the natural sympathies jurors will have about an
emotional case. Let them know you understand that and sympathize, too. Tell them, "We all feel bad about this accident (or loss).
I do, as well as you." But then, point up their job: only to decide
about what the law asks. Tell them you know how hard this objectivity makes their task, and that it is difficult to transcend, even to
deny, basic emotions in order to focus on a cool, cerebral approach.
"But the law requires you only to decide about . . ." and so their
job is "to move towards logic and reason," "to move past feelings
and to think." Don't just clarify the actual points to be decided, but
show how they can lean on the law to strengthen them in their decision. They need understanding and support to bring in a verdict
against a sympathetic cause. Provide them with your sensitivity to
their concerns. Give them reasons and an excuse to leave their natural tendencies and find against someone, to feel sorry for a victim
and still punish or deny his requested verdict or damages.

Don't Attack the Opposing
Counsel

Jury studies show that attacking your opponent is a guaranteed loser. If you tried your case well, and right is on your side, it
should be beneath you to take a shot at your opposite number.

That's a sign of weakness and, as far as the jury is concerned, stoops to a lower level of personal attack and away from the loftier plane you want them to think on. Let *them* dislike him for not being fair or forthright, for being overbearing, aggressive or boring. Let them see it by contrast with your superior style, wit, intellect, personality and above-reproach behavior in the court. Show them what's wrong with your opponent's case; show what was not proven, where the mistakes lay. Attack the opposing issues and ideas presented, not the opposing counsel himself.

Performance Techniques and Style

You've all seen lawyers whose style you admire enormously. Enjoy, but don't try to copy them. Each of us is as unique as our fingerprints: different genes, different metabolism and different background. The only people you might emulate successfully (and actually have already, subconsciously) are your family. That's where you first developed your style. Even then, your metabolism, your experiences away from home and your later views of how you'd like to be seen have altered your style somewhat.

The big message here is that you have, to a great degree, already developed your style, and the jury has already seen it. It's yours, and it's the most comfortable and genuine way for you to be a thinking-on-your-feet advocate. You will have already presented that consistent style throughout the trial. The jury depends on you, by now, to be the kind of person they have gotten to know through the trial.

If you are a relaxed and informal person, then it is comfortable and necessary for you, even in summation, to argue in a personal, direct and informal way.

If, however, you are by nature formal, cerebral and thoughtful, your sincerity and clarity are what the jury expects now. Your thoughtful commitment will be for them as eloquent as the kind of relaxed and informal colloquialisms of another type of lawyer. Be careful not to suddenly try to become a folksy Andy Griffith in your final argument when all along you have been James Mason, or vice versa.

The essence of style is two-fold: be true to yourself and let the form evolve from the function. Let the material you're talking about and your audience's needs determine your delivery, not some arbitrary cosmetics from Column A and Column B. Polish who you are—don't create a persona for the courtroom.

Here are some further insights into persuasive presentation that you can use to enhance your natural style.

Space

As in all other portions of the trial, don't overlook the importance of placement as you make your final stand in front of the jury.

• *Center stage,* the center of the space in front of the jury, is the place of greatest strength and attention. Choose when to go there. It symbolizes power and absolutes. Using the absolute center for making the final statement in your argument does several things. It brings your argument to an obvious close. It has finality. It is also classic, in balance, in control.

• *On either side* is more informal; it's off center, off-balance in a way, and seems more vulnerable and softer.

• *Discussion or explanation* should take place slightly to the left or right of the center, medium close. Questioning, ruminating, discussing and describing should happen more on either side and can include walking or changing positions. Then, when you come into the center, it carries more weight.

• *Standing too far back* causes you to seem remote and different from the jury, formal and uncommitted.

• *Consider when you want to draw closer.* It's a noticeable intrusion, but also shows great emphasis. Reaching out to the jury is a metaphor for getting closer to the truth, the insights, the deeper places. It is the move of intimacy. Where in your argument do you want to talk personally, more intimately? Move closer then.

• *If your ending* is a small, soft, intimate one, you could use an off-center position, but use body language and your voice to let the jury know you're winding down and ending and then come into the center for your final line.

Movement

Walking to the blackboard or charts and walking and talking as you come back lifts the jury's level of energy and interest. Move to lift your own energy output as well, because the jury is so passive and the final argument, usually, is fairly lengthy.

Moving to another place is also punctuation. It causes the jury to finish with one concept and make another paragraph, notice a new phrase or idea. There are many ways to walk, talk and stop, and they should occur to you naturally. One way of repeating, for example, is what I call a double-underline. It's effective only if you can do it judiciously and with great subtlety. Say something. Turn away from the jury. Walk a few steps and then turn back to them and say it again. It makes a kind of visual impact; you said it, you moved and said it again. They can see two underlined phrases because you have drawn them in space.

Walking while talking is good for throw-away connections and transitions, but always stop and face the jury to deliver an important line. The stopping is another form of emphasis and getting their attention.

Eye Contact

We all get into the habit of looking at the most responsive, receptive or animated face in any audience. Be aware of where you make eye contact. Go to your "friendly face" for comfort, reassurance and the stimulus to continue, but be sure to include all eyes when you make a big point. Take the time to do it. It's riveting and flattering to the jury. It also makes you look very committed to your ideas and to them.

Gesture

Use gesture as punctuation to help underline the facts or give emphasis to an idea. If you're not a "gesturer," all the more reason to rely on movement or space to keep interest up. There are two great concerns about gesture in argument. The first is not to point your finger at the jury. It's a habit of many lawyers and, though you only do it as an intensifier, it looks like an admonition or an accusation.

The other concern is to avoid a single repeated gesture. It's very noticeable and can finally irritate the jury, as well as becoming so fascinating that they watch it rather than listen to you.

Silence

Don't forget the value of silence. The truth is that when you deliver your final line, you should let the jury think about it. Don't walk off. Stand still. Your standing still, silently, is an imperative to the jury to allow them to continue to consider what you have said. Once you leave, you have really turned out the light and pulled the cord. Remember the places where you want them to think. Stop. Be quiet. Let them consider. The impact of silence is true for the points you make all the way through as well, but when you get to the final line, it is time for them to agree, and it has to be very powerful. It is as though there were nothing left for them to do now but to say "yes."

Language

The use of language is a key issue too. Verbal images and word pictures are most memorable, but if you want to tap into the jury's sense of humanity, you should use colloquial, simple, familiar phrases, since you're dealing with complex points of law. Your words must interpret the unintelligible—"proximate cause," "contributory negligence," and "beyond a reasonable doubt."

How well you humanize and simplify these concepts will determine whether the jury can include them in their deliberations or only rely on their instinct and preformed prejudices. Create "quotable quotes" for the jury to remember. (For examples on simplifying language, see the section on Language in Chapter 3, Opening Statement.)

Repetition, Rhythm and Phrasing

There are other excellent techniques to help the jury to remember and also to sway them—the techniques of repetition, rhythm and phrasing.

You know how, when you sing in a group, everyone can chime in on the chorus, at least, since most of the singers have usually forgotten the verse. You sort of look forward to the fact that the chorus is going to come back again, because at least that's a part you know. There is something reassuring and reinforcing about the fact that it will come back again, isn't there? That's basic to all of us and it might be helpful for you to understand why it is such a useful device.

There is an interesting atavistic reason why repetition is reassuring. In all primitive art, one sees repetition; a figure is created and then occurs over and over, repeated on the surface of a piece of pottery, a boat, a shield. The figure can vary from one culture to another, it can be abstract or descriptive, but the fact of needing to repeat a figure is constant. What did it say to those people?

It reflected an understanding of their environment. People need (and still need) reassurance. To a tribe living in a hostile, strange environment, life was improvised. Each day could bring a new crisis, yet some things were constant:

The sun comes up in the morning, and it will come up again tomorrow.

The seasons will change, but it will become green again.

It will rain but then it will stop.

If you plant seeds, they will grow.

That kind of reinforcement reminded our ancient ancestors that there was a known, an already experienced outcome. Repetition speaks of a predictable conclusion, something to look forward to and depend on. In the midst of strangeness, from then to now, we all want something familiar to latch on to, to give us the courage to handle the new and the strange.

Think of a trial; it has a continual flow of newness in it. It is a constant challenge to the juror to absorb and deal with strangeness. Therefore, in the final argument, give reassurance in a number of ways; show that there is some familiar logic, reason or pattern that the jury can hang on to. One of the simplest forms of repetition, not only in terms of concept, but actually in terms of hearing, is a litany that gets repeated rhythmically. This is persuasive and memorable.

I have asked jurors about this, and when a lawyer has used a repeated phrase, an alliterative statement, a slogan, they are almost always able to repeat it with some pleasure. It's reassuring to them to "know the outcome," to recognize the familiar.

Therefore, if you set up such a pattern, the jury can anticipate the next time you are going to say it. You could stop and they could still fill in the ending on their own. For example:

And what did they do? . . . They ran . . .

And then, faced with that decision, what did they do? They ran . . .

And again, with many choices, what did they do? _ _ _ _   _ _ _ "

Sometimes repetition can be used with great dramatic effect. Suppose you were to choose the phrase, with regard to an accident victim:

And then, in an instant, she died.

You could begin to explain what events took place until the final moment, then pause and say, reflectively:

. . . and then, in an instant, she died.

Go to another place and explain what was happening to the people who would be deeply affected:

In her home, the phone rang, her mother turned, . . . and then, in an instant, she died.

Go to a description of what the victim was doing, what she was thinking about, where she was going, what was going to happen tomorrow:

. . . and, then, in an instant, she died.

This gives the jury the feeling of involvement because they wait for the next repetition, the drama of the inexorable turn of events; sympathy arises because, no matter what everybody else was thinking and doing, this event was about to take place, and then it happened.

. . . and then, in an instant, she died.

But repetition does not involve only predictability. It is also a creative use of language, of rhythm, and of musicality.

Rhythm taps into our fears and our deepest emotions as it makes us transcend from thinking to feeling and causes us to respond on a visceral, instinctive level.

Even, unaccented rhythms are calming and reassuring. Think of a ticking clock or a rocking chair and the rhythm they make. They are predictable, easily assimilated, therefore soporific and calming.

Uneven rhythms, however, are interruptive. They are not predictable and cause us to notice them much more. Think of the difference between the clop-clop-clop-clop of a horse's trot and the galumph-galumph of his gallop. Uneven rhythms have pulse and life, energy and drive in them. They are more startling and unstable. They can be frightening. (Remember the sound of those footsteps coming down the hall in scary movies. They were always uneven, da-dumm, da-dumm.)

The point is that rhythms are deeply affecting and, used as tools to enlarge your thoughts and your words, they can evoke remarkable responses from the jury.

Use of Notes

One major area of concern about the use of notes is to be free of them—to be able to just pop your eye down at them and then keep talking. Another key issue is that final argument depends so keenly on drama and performance that dry outlines of the facts do not give you what you need for eloquence. Notes can give you order and progression, information and facts but no visual cues to help you know how to deliver them. You need to see what's coming up on a page so you'll be prepared to give the proper quality and emphasis to key words and phrases, to know when to slow down for an important point and when to go into high gear as your argument demands it.

As you choreograph your final argument, be sure you add cues for all the nuances you want to build, and ways to see the headlines coming in your notes.

Help your performance by writing margin notes: "pause," "softer," "change tone," or "walk" to begin a new thought. Put key points in a box. Use spaces, colored pens, anything to help alert you to the quality of delivery required from each portion as it comes up.

Make your outline so clear to yourself that you can write it on the board at will as you imagine it. You might be inspired to do that as you present. Learn to pick your head up from your notes to begin new thoughts. Get free!

Particular attention must be paid to how you write your final line. You need to know it by heart, and how you will deliver it, because it is the thing the jury remembers the most.

DO NOT READ IT. You must make eye contact, pause and then deliver it. Your visual cues should help you build the entire argument to a climax so that your final line feels like a culmination and the jury can still hear it and savor it after you stop. (See Chapter 3—Opening Statement—for techniques on how to write effective notes and outlines.)

*   *   *

In summary: Juries know and see much more than you think. Don't underestimate them. They generally know many of the facts. They can understand how to apply the law. What they need from you is leadership. Lead them to a decision.

WINNING ARGUMENTS

And now, to the business of arguments themselves.

Along with choreographing your persuasive arguments and bringing out the facts that will corroborate the arguments, you must give the jury the kind of expiation they need to come up with a guilty verdict. They need reasons—almost an excuse—for punishing someone, for judging them and feeling powerful and sure enough to say, "You're wrong. I shall deny what you ask."

You must give jurors courage and reasons to say "No." They need to feel they can go home with a clear conscience after they decide. They're worried about living with the recurring thought. "Did I do the right thing? Is that what the law really meant? Is that what other people would do?"

To do this, you need to find ways to help them feel like an instrument of their society, to show them that the law really does represent what their society wants and that it objectively requires the same compliance from everyone in the same way. Give them the foundation of society's norms to support the decisions they finally make.

An effective argument gives permission. It gives a good reason for the verdict asked for, not only with corroborating facts, but also with a clear explanation of what the law provides so that jurors don't feel it's only their own judgment. Jurors need to know that they are simply carrying out what has been built into the Constitution and the laws. Remember, it's hard to punish or say no.

Since I keep telling you that one of the best teaching methods is demonstration, I have asked some of the many excellent trial lawyers I teach with to offer some examples of effective, winning arguments that have proven to be helpful to the jury's understanding, and convincing and affecting as well.

This section will use excerpts from real trial transcripts, often with the names of the participants changed. I have chosen some generic categories that many trials fall under, covering some basic issues. We will explore analogies, analyses, systems of explanation and some general suggestions for how to argue the essence of your case. The purpose is to stimulate your thinking toward some new approaches or to inspire you with an eloquent example of an approach you may already know.

Original Morality and Universal Ethics

One problem, in persuasive arguments, is polarizing too soon, before you get your whole idea across. In order to start out on a sound base that everyone can relate to, you need to remind the jury of some basic precepts people have always lived by—the basic, tribal concepts of right or wrong. Remember, the events that make up a trial are abnormal in the daily course of life. The jury needs to see the continuous norm in order to compare what went wrong. They're looking not only for whom to blame, but why.

How to begin this process? First, analyze the issues down to their most simple, common denominator components. What's at the heart of the matter? What's typical behavior in this type of circumstance? What's atypical? What are the basic reasons something

went wrong? Then dig in. Find out first how *you* feel—deep in
your gut, not as a lawyer but before that. Get into your own morality. Think about how your uncle, aunt, mother, father, grandparents, kids, college roommate, high school football coach or piano
teacher would react. What would they think about this? Ask them,
if you can, but knowing them as you do, see if you can imagine
their answers. Listen to those voices. They're much closer to the
jurors' than your own.

Now find where these beliefs came from. Ask yourself, who
teaches people that? Where would they see or hear it? Sunday
school? Westerns? Boy Scout handbook? Who are the good guys
and why do we think they are? What do the bad guys do that's bad?
Was it always bad? How can you explain why it was always bad?

My suggestion is to invoke the old laws, the old ways. Max-
ims, proverbs, folk sayings, Biblical quotes, fables—anything that
shows original moralities. One simple way to do this is to say, "My
father (grandfather, mother) used to say . . . " This always invokes
those durable, universal truths we grew up with.

Here is an example of how one lawyer tapped a jury's basic
beliefs:

> You know, when considering my final argument I played with the
> idea of going into the biblical story of Cain and Abel, Cain slaying
> Abel and saying, "Am I my brother's keeper?" I don't think it would
> be fair to do that, because Cain didn't do it in a court of law in front
> of anybody.
>
> But Ed tried to do it in a court of law and with lies. He tried to chop
> down his older brother. He wants to use an American jury to do it. I
> hope you won't let him, not because of any belief that brother
> should not turn against brother, or that the government should not
> encourage brother to turn against brother, but because he is doing
> it with lies and because his motives are to save himself, and because
> all sense of decency, of feeling for family have been driven out of
> him by fear, malice and desire for self-preservation.
>
> Ed does not reside in the Land of Nod east of Eden. He resides in a
> beautiful suburban home with his fashionable suits and he has the
> protection of his lawyers and now of the prosecution. And he does
> not have to answer the question, "Where is thy brother?" At least
> not in this world. . . .

Analogies

Analogies are an excellent device for clarifying a complex or abstract concept. Since they're usually a story or an example drawn from life, they have instant appeal for the jury. "Good—a story, this will be fun (or interesting or different.) Let's listen."

Analogies are fun for the jury to think about. By turning away from the case and finding a story that suits a basic principle, you cause the jury to transcend the particular issues of this trial in quest of a more familiar base for their decision. It's strengthening, as well as more amusing, to listen to. Analogies always provide a change of pace from the argument. Their best feature is the recognition at the end, when you connect the point of your analogy with the point you wish to make about the case. That moment is when the light bulb goes on and your meaning dawns on the jury. Analogies do that most effectively because they can extract a basic truth from a seemingly light-hearted moment. They can often provide a link to eternal verities by using an old fable, or something from classic literature that everyone knows or you can create an analogy just for this occasion, using something from life we all recognize.

Here is an example from Judge Warren Wolfson of Chicago who was an outstanding criminal trial lawyer before he went on the bench:

> Reviewing the evidence in this case reminded me of a personal problem we had. You know, for a while my daughter wasn't able to sleep unless we opened the closet door in her bedroom. She was convinced that someone was in there. No matter how many times we showed her no one was in there, she remained convinced, despite the facts. To her that someone in the closet was real.
>
> That is what the prosecution is asking you to do, to see someone in the closet, despite the facts and despite the proof.
>
> Fortunately, my daughter grew out of it and now she sleeps with the doors closed, and she sleeps soundly. Some people grow out of it. They accept the facts as they are, not distorted by imagination.
>
> In this case the government had a theory and it wasn't going to let the facts stand in the way of it.

Using a family-life analogy puts every juror directly into the story as well as humanizing the lawyer. He's obviously a nice married man with a universal kid's problem we all can recognize. The charm of the story is not only a relief from all the law talk, but it makes an accusation seemingly lighter and less hostile, though it is actually more lethal. While taking some of the heat away from the attack, it makes the point more strongly.

A word of caution: Always think through an analogy. How apt is it, in truth? Does it *really* make the right kind of instant image? Does the punch line clarify? Can everyone get it? Does it convey only what you meant and nothing more?

In an advanced National Institute for Trial Advocacy seminar, one experienced lawyer-student reached for an analogy in an exercise in final argument for a products liability case. Wanting to make complex machinery seem simple he said: "This equipment is just like your car." The instant image he called forth, however, was how often a car breaks down, the expense and inconvenience and frustration of getting a car fixed, and how powerless most of us are to fix it or to understand it. Not a great image for a product or for liability. So be careful. Use analogies but be sure that they mean the same thing to the jury that they do to you and that they deliver a clear message.

One lawyer I know doesn't use analogies unless he goes last, since he is concerned lest the other lawyer take the analogy and twist it around to suit himself or in some way make fun of it. This is possible, but I still feel analogies are an excellent way to teach, to clarify a complex concept and to get more than just your point across.

Questioning an Opponent's Use of the Facts

Juries resent your attacking the opposing counsel. It looks weak and desperate and to sports-crazy Americans, like poor sportsmanship. They want you to argue about your ideas, to clarify what's there and what isn't, what's important and what isn't. Yet, to help you get in a few shots, here are some ways to zing opposing counsel without falling into personal in-fighting.

From the legendary Irving Younger, famed attorney, judge, lecturer, and law professor:

> Ladies and gentlemen of the jury.
>
> You know what you heard and I know what you heard. It would be an insult to your intelligence for me to tell it all to you again. But as I heard my worthy opponent tell you what you heard, which didn't sound anything like it, I think I need to do some clarifying here. I need to take this opportunity to straighten out what we *all* really heard.

In describing the ways in which the prosecution has irresponsibly attached prejudicial meaning to a few words in a document, a lawyer used this:

> You remember reading Alice in Wonderland, the part where Alice points out to Humpty-Dumpty that he has taken a word—that's where Humpty-Dumpty was, in Alice in Wonderland—he has taken a word and given it the wrong meaning.
>
> 'When I use a word,' Humpty-Dumpty said in rather a scornful tone, 'it means just what I choose it to mean; no more and no less.'
>
> 'The question is,' said Alice, 'whether you can make words mean so many different things.'
>
> 'No,' said Humpty-Dumpty, 'the question is who is to be master.'
>
> That's all. The prosecution has taken a few words in this case, and the lack of many words, and has chosen to give them a certain meaning. We submit to you that the evidence and the lack of evidence showed that their decision is illogical and unreasonable. You are the final masters. You have the last word. You can take us out of Wonderland.

Credibility of Witnesses

The major issue in causing the jury to disbelieve a witness is to give them reasons why the witness would lie. We all understand lying for self-protection from the time we were kids (and even as adults). The problem here is the self-fulfilling prophecy. The jury knows you want to discredit the other side, and discrediting a witness seems like a good way to do that. So the reasons for lying have to be really good, logical and easy to understand. They have to ring a sympathetic and familiar chord in the juror to make him respond to your attack.

One good way is to ask questions of the jury. Challenge them to try to find a logical answer. Show the facts and let them mull it over. Often you don't have to give them the reason for lying. It can be self-evident, built into your question.

From a criminal case:

Why would Bill have anything to do with an agreement like this if he had nothing to do with Service any more? Why would Pancotto lie to the FBI? Maybe it doesn't make sense, but you know, four indictments hanging over your head can do an awful lot to bend your will. It can do an awful lot to make a man desperate. In this case Pancotto was willing to do what he had to do.

You don't have to belabor the issue. Sometimes just matching the facts of treachery with breaching a universal law, like family loyalty, is enough to cast doubt and cause the jury to be judgmental.

Now, I don't know how frightened or worried a man has to be to make him come into court and lie about his brother in a criminal case.
He gave three statements. He gave three depositions on I don't know how many other occasions. He received notice of a law suit for $21 million against him in February of 1967. Rumors and stories of criminal indictments started being heard but he says, "Well, I am not worried about the lawsuit and I wasn't worried about indictment." He did not have to be.

Calling personal character into question can make everything a witness says suspect:

You have a right to judge the kind of person who takes the witness stand and raises his hand to God to tell the truth, . . . [to judge] the kind of man he is, what he says and why he says it.

Or:

. . . Now, why would Ed . . . lie about that? It is not a terribly important matter in this case. He lied because that is his frame of mind . . . That is how his mind works, and if he will tell a small lie like that to you, he will tell a big lie. He will say anything if it fits in with what he thinks you and the prosecutors want to hear.

The opposite side of the coin is establishing your own witnesses' credibility. One of the best ways to do that, says e. robert (bob) wallach, a most effective and creative plantiff's attorney and teacher from San Francisco and Washington, D.C., is to point up the fallible, human imperfections in your witness and his/her testimony. Says wallach:

In a personal injury case, point to those aspects that are contrary to what the jurors would normally expect of someone trying to prove their own case. Emphasize your client's saying "I'm trying to learn to live with it" as being a fairer, truer answer than if he only used total negatives and pleas for sympathy. Make the jury think through what people might try to say and then show the honesty of your client by his being so open and not trying to only be prejudicial or dramatic.

Jurors expect you to only say the best things about your witness. Surprise them and make them see your level of forthrightness by pointing out human frailty and honesty. They will believe that more.

Visualizing Concepts of Law

Here is an example of reducing concepts to symbols to clarify choices for the jury.

Edward Stein, a very gifted lawyer and teacher from Ann Arbor, Michigan, used this excellent device. When most states used to follow the traditional doctrine of contributory negligence which provided that if a plaintiff was, to any extent, causally negligent, the jury had to return a verdict for the defendant. For example, if a plaintiff was only 5 or 10 percent negligent and the defendant 90 or 95 percent negligent, the verdict would be, in total, for the defendant.

Although this doctrine has been replaced in recent years in most states by the doctrine of comparative negligence, there is an important lesson in Ed's example. Not only did the jury need to understand the concept of contributory negligence (in itself a difficult one) but it also needed to know enough not to inadvertently apply a comparative negligence standard. Just talk alone could never insure that they would get the whole idea straight and understand its components. So he put this diagram on a board to make their choices visible, tangible and clear:

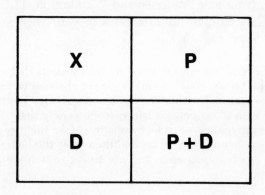

This diagram represents the four possibilities and combinations of negligence in a simple, two-party case. They are, starting from the top left, clockwise:

> X – No one was negligent.
> P – Plaintiff only was negligent.
> P&D – Plaintiff and Defendant were both
> negligent.
> D – Defendant only was negligent.

Stein writes:

> I would then explain it all to the jury and tell them that only in the "D" instance could they bring in a verdict for the plaintiff. I thus started out with a situation where 75 percent of the options would result in a defense verdict.

> This was much simpler and clearer than just relying on the judge's instructions. It allowed the use of a visual aid to diagram an otherwise amrophous concept. In one instance the jury, during its deliberations, sent out a question asking the judge to repeat, not what he

had instructed with respect to the law of contributory negligence, but what I had said was the law in the "P&D" situation.

Clarifying the issues of what the law provides is a key need for juries. Reducing verbiage to shapes or symbols and relationships helps everyone relate more quickly to the underlying principles and insures that you're all on the same wavelength. You can see how quickly the jury can focus its discussion around such a diagram. "Ask Ed what P&D provides" rather than "but maybe the judge meant . . .

Push yourself to diagram a difficult concept in your case. See how you can reduce it to symbols and talk from there, rather than drowning the jury in a sea of unfamiliar words which are not easy to remember or relate to.

Comparison

In summarizing the evidence in a case, the answer, again, is to visualize. You can bring back the charts and diagrams used in the case, or you can create a chart which puts forth all the testimony in order.

One important decision-making component is comparison: to compare normal behavior with the events in the case or to compare two aspects of what the testimony meant. An excellent example of both visually summarizing and comparing the evidence was provided by a fine trial lawyer I know.

He used two charts in a criminal case in which the defendant was charged with "assault with the intent to commit a felony, to-wit, rape." The argument dealt with mistaken identity. The charts were not introduced into evidence, but the information shown on them was. Permission was granted by the court to use them in final argument.

His challenge was to get all the information and testimony before the jury in a concise way so they could see where the inconsistencies were. He made some charts that compared the accusatory testimony of the plaintiffs with the information brought out by the defense which proved the young man in question was not even in the vicinity. He also wanted to show the circumstances under which identification was made, to further focus the jury on why the identity could be mistaken. Here's what he presented:

CHART I

DATE	10-31-1974	12-1-1974	1-15-1975	1-18-1975
TIME	11:30 PM	11:30 PM	7:00 PM	3:30 AM
PLACE	Screened porch, girl's apartment	Screened porch, girl's apartment	Window, girl's apartment	Bedroom, girl's apartment
PLAINTIFF'S TESTIMONY	KATHY: I.D. Time: 0 Seconds	LORRAINE: I.D. Time: 3-4 seconds through window KATHY: I.D. Time: 1 second on porch in dark	BARBARA: I.D. Time: 5 seconds side view of man's face through kitchen window	BARBARA: I.D. Time: 3-4 seconds of man in kitchen; 3½ minutes in bedroom
DEFENSE TESTIMONY	JIM: In Idaho	JIM: In Idaho	JIM: With his roommates in their apartment	JIM: In his apartment sleeping

The upper portion of Chart I shows the times and places that the witnesses claim to have seen the defendant around their apartment. The lower portion shows that at all times the defendant was someplace else.

CHART II

DATE	1-21-1975 Tuesday	1-22-1975 Wednesday	1-23-1975 Thursday	1-31-1975 Friday
TIME	Early afternoon, late after-noon	During the day	During the day	Afternoon
PLACE	Parking lot	Office	Office	Office
PLAINTIFF'S TESTIMONY	LORRAINE: Spots student in dark jacket in early afternoon LARRY: Spots student in dark jacket in late afternoon	LORRAINE and/or BARBARA: Shown picture of JIM	LORRAINE and/or BARBARA: Shown pictures	KATHY: Shown 12 pictures after being with JIM in office
DEFENSE TESTIMONY	JIM: In parking lot wearing dark jacket			JIM: In office 10-15 minutes with KATHY

Chart II shows the manner in which the complaining witnesses identified the defendant to explain the mistaken identity.

Can't you see how persuasive the technique of comparison is here? How clear and organized these charts make the events, names, dates and times for the jury?

The important thing to remember in using such a device, however, is not to give all the information to the jury all at once. To help do this, paste velcro strips across the very top and bottom of the chart above and below the print. Cover each vertical set of boxes with strips of plain chart board with velcro on the back so they stick to the strips on the chart, thus blocking each section of the chart. Set up your ideas, tell them what you're going to do and then, by pulling off the blocking strip, reveal each vertical comparison, one at a time. It's dramatic, easy to understand and has the added advantage of cumulative power as the evidence mounts up till it's all revealed. Give them a few moments to digest it again. Tell them, "Look at the evidence, ladies and gentlemen. Compare the women's story with Jim's whereabouts. Judge for yourselves . . ." and so on.

The charts, prepared beforehand, will leave an indelible impression and leave you free to elaborate and underline, rather than laboriously listing all the events yourself. Using a blocking technique, so you only tell as much as they can absorb and you can explain at a time, is very important and helps you persuade them. You can also have the basic chart prepared with the names, dates and subject, etc. and write in the details as you tell it.

Comparison, to be effective, must continue to exist beyond your explanation so the jury can get involved in doing it themselves. Just be sure that the scheme of your diagram is consistent and clear. Label the subject of each list, using the same kinds of nomenclature, symbols, and numbers for each. Also, I would suggest horizontal comparisons rather than vertical, when possible, since we normally read left to right and the eyes naturally go that way first.

Making Unpopular, Uncomfortable Decisions

Sometimes you need to ask the jury to be hard-hearted and turn against their basic sympathetic instincts because the law demands a seemingly cold and heartless choice.

I consulted on a product liability case involving a suit against a large company where, although there was grave personal injury, the statute of limitations for bringing suit had run out; this is what was in dispute. The defense lawyer was deeply concerned about how he could make the jury transcend the obviously pitiful state of the plaintiff and "go by the book." I suggested that, in order to use the law and rely on the law's dictates, one must explain the concept of laws: what laws are for and why they are structured as they are. You often forget that non-lawyers have never really understood the origins and the reasons for laws, only their prohibitions.

This was what I designed:

Start by describing the jury's dilemma: It sounds unfair and hard-hearted to deny the plaintiff the chance to try the case, but a law is a law. Ask if they've ever thought what laws are for and why this law seems so harsh and unbending, so unmindful of the individual case. Then say it would help if they understood this, and you'd like to explain. Tell them that:

> Laws are what any society says is acceptable behavior at a particular time. Laws change as society's visions of what's acceptable changes. Example: Two and three hundred years ago, hands were chopped off for stealing, witches were burned at the stake and insane people were chained to the wall. About 120 years ago, slavery was legal in this country. These laws changed as our communal morality did.

> Laws also change when they prove unenforceable and the society finally recognizes that: Remember prohibition? When laws do not reflect the way we really live, they change.

> We keep making new laws to protect the existing society's view of what's right for a community and how we should live together.

> Laws are also designed to protect individuals, to protect their rights so no one infringes on them. This makes it possible for each person not to have to fight his own battles every time someone trespasses against him, but to rely on nationally and locally accepted norms or laws, and enforcement to protect everyone.

> Now if laws are designed to protect individual rights, what's the statute of limitations for? Suppose someone tripped on a step going out of your house and sued you 12 years later because he often got a stiff neck. What objective evidence could you investigate, and what could anyone prove? It would mean your whole life could be lived on the brink of disaster waiting to see if someone could blame you for their problems, with no thought to when something happened

and no chance to investigate the realistic, probable cause and effect within a reasonable time.

What effect would the lack of a statute of limitations have on business? Suppose a suit was brought about an out-of-date, obsolete appliance or piece of machinery. Justice would suffer from not having enough available information to study, no existing models to compare and analyze, records long since destroyed, involved personnel dead or not available, and so on. If anyone could bring a suit at *any* time, businesses would need to protect themselves. They'd need to save endless examples and records of everything they ever made or did, as well as a giant contingency fund in case they would ever be sued and had to pay. Result? Much higher costs for goods and services as businesses cover themselves for these bolt-of-lightning possibilities.

Therefore, there is a statute of limitations that describes a reasonable time within which such suits can be brought.

And the rigidity of the law? The idea of no exceptions? Well, the law must be true for everyone, all the time, or it's not a law. If we could make up rules each time something happened, we'd lose our idea of equality and justice for all. It's like saying to your children, "Bedtime at eight, except if you can argue and talk me out of it." If you don't want your children to ride a motorcycle, but you make one exception, they'll do it again and say, "But you said it was O. K. last time." Therefore, we must stick to the letter as well as the spirit of the law or else anyone could think they could break it—just once.

By using well-known references and familiar situations, my goal was to give an orientation to the jurors about the all-encompassing or lasting reasons for laws and how the unique circumstances of this trial fit into an overall legal structure. It then gave them an excuse for an unpopular decision. Sometimes people learn best when you step back from a situation to see a total overview and to see where this fits, to give origins and bases first rather than close in on the details and become too specific and particular.

Damages

In personal injury cases, the most important things the jury needs to think about are not only what the injuries cost, but also what they will mean to the plaintiff in the future. That's a vague term, the future, and the arguments that become most persuasive here are the ones that can help the jury actually visualize the plaintiff's future life. Since they can compare it to life as they know it and hope to live it, this makes a deeper impression than just talking abstractly of sympathy, justice, and economics.

Obviously, during the trial the lawyer has drawn a poignant picture of the victim's limited, difficult life, going through his daily routine, perhaps with pictures or even a video documentary of "A Day in the Life." Now the challenge is to multiply that manyfold in the jury's mind as the plaintiff's future days roll on with no hope and no change.

An excellent and moving device was sent me by one lawyer, which makes the inexorable march of future years real and palpable. This chart was used in a negligence case where the plaintiff became a paraplegic.

THE YEARS PAST

That Dan Has Been in the Chair, Impotent, with a Catheter, No Control Over His Bowel and In Pain

1978	1979	1980	1981	1982

THE REST OF THE YEARS OF HIS LIFE
That Dan Will Be in the Chair, Impotent, with a Catheter, No Control Over His Bowel and In Pain

1983	1984	1985	1986	1987
1988	1989	1990	1991	1992
1993	1994	1995	1996	1997
1998	1999	2000	2001	2002
2003	2004	2005	2006	2007
2008	2009	2010	2011	2012
2013	2014	2015	2016	2017
2018	2019	2020	2021	2022
		2023		

With this chart displayed before the jury, the lawyer can pick out a year and talk about what would be happening then:

- 1988: unmarried, he goes to his friend's wedding;
- 1998: his aging mother dies and he has no one to care for him;
- 2003: he watches the neighborhood children grow up and go off to school, to lives full of promise while he sits in the window where life has passed him by, and so on.

If he's already married, you can spin out the years of no ball playing with his children, no camping with the Boy Scout troop, the financial strain of sending children to college with his limited earning capacity, his impotence and a married life without a fulfilling sexual relationship and more and more.

One of the most eloquent aspects of seeing these years listed is the sheer weight of numbers. Make the jury see how long his life will be—into the next century—and think about what quality it will have.

By the way, the chart was not introduced into evidence but there was evidence of the plaintiff's life expectancy in the trial and thus the chart met with the evidence. The court granted permission to use it during final argument. This is an example of creatively taking evidence brought out in the trial and putting it into a visual form that both reduces and points up the main issues.

Insufficient Evidence

Seeing how we can become suspicious without much substantive reason is another issue you have to deal with. Using a familiar, readily imagined situation can cause the jury to look beyond the details of this case to see a common failing in all of us and then to look back at the case with new insight. Here's an example from a final argument:

> Now, our hope is, and I think the law agrees, that you don't allow suspicion and innuendo to sidetrack your common sense and good judgment.
>
> Let me just give you an example of what I mean: Let's say you are watching a football game and I walk up to you and I say to you: "That game is fixed. It's a phony."

Well, the quarterback throws a bad pass, the halfback fumbles the ball, and the end drops the ball. 'Ah,' you are going to think, the 'game is fixed. It's a phony.'

Ladies and gentlemen, that statement was just in my mind because I made that up. I have no evidence that game was fixed or a phony, but what I did was plant the seed of suspicion in *your* mind. I had no right to do that and, in a trial, no lawyer has a right to do that.

Quarterbacks throw bad passes, halfbacks fumble the ball. It is a part of life. It is a part of the game just as some elected officials vote "yes" some elected officials vote "no."

In my example, if you are ready to believe or think that game is a phony, you are not being fair to the game, are you?

Your decision in this trial . . . is much more serious. There is much more at stake. This is no game. There are no instant replays.

James Jones doesn't ask for more from you because he is a public official, but ladies and gentlemen, he asks no less, either.

You know, when the government wins, and when I say "the government" I just don't mean the prosecution, I mean all of us, both sides of the table, everybody in the courtroom; we win not with any particular verdict but when the jury judges the facts fairly, when they follow the law, and when they do justice.

This is what James Jones asks and that is all he needs.

Giving Courage to Dissent

As I said at the beginning of the chapter, disagreeing is hard. We all like to be liked, to be accepted as part of a group, to play on the team. Furthermore, we don't practice fighting for unpopular causes very often so we can develop muscles of resistance to peer pressure. Therefore, dissenting jurors are not numerous, and crumbling under the assault of the group is more the norm than standing up alone.

To give jurors a sense of strength and independence, here is an example from James Brosnahan, a brilliant trial advocate and teacher from San Francisco: "When the government is insisting on conviction and you are really after a hung jury, you can try this one. I recommend it to you whenever you wish to strengthen the jury's hand to go against a commonly held belief or practice."

Ladies and gentlemen of the jury, Mr. Smith has been here, sent from Washington, for three weeks, insisting that the salvation of this country is dependent upon my client being pushed up to the jail house door and in. They insist that you convict. How independent are you as a jury on the question? I would like to tell you how independent you are, and it will just take a minute.

I was interested in the power of juries so I looked this up. It's a really interesting story on the history of your job.

In the late 1600s in England, where the jury system came from, the King had the power—imagine this—to tell a jury that he wanted someone convicted. And when he did that, they were convicted in the 1600s. In about 1680 a young man was brought in for rabblerousing and charged with a crime. The trial was held. The King made his wish clear. The jury heard the case. In the instructions the Court said, "It is the King's wish that this man be convicted." And the jury went out, and they were out two days, and they came back. The judge said to the foreman, "Do you have a verdict?"

He said, "I do." The foreman stood up and looked at him and the judge said, "What is your verdict?"

And the foreman said, "The verdict is not guilty."

The judge said, "I don't think you understand. It is the King's wish that there be a conviction in this case. Go back out and stay."

They went back out. They stayed two more days. They came back in. The judge said, "What is your verdict?" The foreman stood and looked at him—this is a true story—and said, 'Not guilty.'

Again out, again back. The circumstances the jury lived in were not good. Several of them became ill. Finally they were brought back in and an exasperated judge—for all they knew, they were going to be killed by the King—an exasperated judge said, "What is your verdict?"

The foreman said, "Not guilty."

And then, ladies and gentlemen, the words were exchanged that have made you what you are today, out of the contribution of those jurors who sat where you now sit.

The judge said, "And when will your verdict be guilty?"

And the foreman said . . . "Never!"

Transcending Prejudice

Sometimes a defendant represents a category or a position that is in direct opposition to popularly held views. Sometimes the jury has already been tainted with commonly held information that can prejudice them. One such case was *People of the State of Illinois vs. Brian Flanagan* tried in 1969 in Cook County, Illinois.

A member of the SDA Weathermen, Flanagan came to Chicago to demonstrate against the Vietnam War and also against capitalism and other establishment issues. The Weathermen's plan was that at some point the demonstrators would break and go wild. (Several days before, there had been a Weatherman incident in which there was violence, and the city was aware of this and really worked up against them.)

Richard Elrod, a corporation counsel and ex-football player, was acting as an observer of the demonstration for the police. As Flanagan, a Weatherman, was seen running, Elrod abandoned his role as observer and became a participant. He aimed a flying tackle at Flanagan and missed him, hitting a brick building, which resulted in his becoming a paraplegic. The prosecution wanted to prove that Flanagan hit him but the evidence showed otherwise. Given the temper of the times and the feelings about Weathermen, the defense counsel had to find a way to move the jury past their expected prejudice, into a clear place where they could judge objectively.

This is the end of the argument given for the defense by Judge Warren Wolfson of Chicago when he practiced as a memorable trial lawyer there. As you read it, notice the use of rhythm and repetition; notice the simple straightforward language, the explanation of reasonable doubt, the identification with the jury at the beginning.

Most of all, notice how Judge Wolfson states the possible prejudice and gives the jury courage and a reason to transcend it:

> None of us, I suspect, will ever be the same when this case is over. We have all been touched by a serious injury to Elrod; perhaps annoyed and angered with the events of October 11, 1969; but certainly puzzled about what actually happened. You can't know by the testimony and you can't guess.

> The State charged . . . with a knowing and intentional striking of Richard Elrod by Brian Flanagan. And they have to prove that beyond a reasonable doubt, and they didn't do it. They gave you testimony about everything but the charge in this indictment. And with all their pictures and their films and their skeletons—they didn't even bother to give you a chart or a map, showing you what they

think happened that day on Madison Street to Richard Elrod. They didn't because they couldn't; because they don't know. We offered possibilities. We didn't have to. It is not our job to prove how it happened. It is the State's job. And they didn't do it. And with this contradictory and confusing "possible" testimony, they have asked you to convict Brian Flanagan.

Now, you have an answer to that. You can serve notice that you won't be an instrument of vengeance at the cost of law and justice. You can serve notice that you won't be the knife that cuts the throat of the sacrificial lamb to satisfy the ambition and pride of others. You can serve notice that your interest is in truth and in justice, unaffected by appeals to hatred and fear. That kind of notice is true law and order. It is the kind that strengthens our legal system and makes it invulnerable to attack from anyone, no matter what the source.

These are difficult times, times of turmoil, times when it is important to keep a warm heart and a cool head. I suppose it is troublesome to have street marches, demonstrations, to have young people who shout their protests instead of writing letters to each other. But who ever said that maintaining a free society is easy? We made the choice a long time ago. The first law and order men were men who sat down and wrote our Constitution. They took some chances. And they made some promises. They said that people can assemble and utter their dissent and their disapproval, something Brian Flanagan told you he went to Chicago to do.

Things went wrong October 11, 1969. But it wasn't Brian Flanagan's doing. It wasn't his planning. Much bitter feeling came out of that day, feeling that young people somehow were our enemies, somebody to fear, even hate. I think we have had enough of that. It's time now to heal the wounds, to close that gap, because this is one country and one nation; and a nation that hates its young people has no future.

You can't solve social problems in this courtroom. This is one case, one indictment. And our job is to do justice in this indictment. And justice knows no generation gap. It applies to the young and the old, the rich and the poor, and to anyone, no matter what his opinions or beliefs.

So, if you have a reasonable doubt about the specific charges in this indictment—not about anything else that you think anybody else should have been charged with, but this indictment—the law demands a verdict of not guilty. That is not the lawyer making this demand. I have no right to make demands upon you. We have tried the best we can, within the framework of the law, in a calm, rational way, to offer you the evidence in the best way we can.

Soon the burden will be yours. Mr. Elrod's injury was a terrible thing. Violence is a terrible thing. How much worse it would be if the Prosecution tried to turn your natural distaste for violence into an unjust verdict, not supported by the evidence. That would be the worst kind of violence, because it would do violence to the law. And we'd all suffer. A verdict based on anything but the evidence in the case would be real brutality and no favor to your neighbors, no favor to the police, no favor to yourselves. If the injury to Elrod, as horrible as it was, were used to bring about an injustice, that would merely be heaping tragedy upon tragedy.

Many people today are wondering whether our system of law still works. And this is kind of a test. I think it does. And it will as long as jurors are able to put aside the irrelevant and determine a case on its facts, to put aside attempts, emotional attempts, to stir fear, anger and hatred. That is the way to get involved. Return a just verdict based upon the evidence. We can't have a decent system of law unless juries are willing to do that, to act without fear, prejudice, and hatred. I think you are going to do that. And that is why we have confidence in you. So, do the right thing. Do justice.

CONCLUSION

How to sum it all up?

First, let's agree that some people are born with a great gift to mesmerize and to tell stories. Even in your own family, I am sure, there is an uncle or aunt who can tell great stories with humor and insight, and you can't wait to sit down and listen to him or her. This ability has great power. Not only do you look forward to the fun as a storyteller begins, but you also know they can capture you and touch your feelings. Remember when you were a kid in camp, sitting around the campfire? Counselors could tell stories of great suspense and you could absolutely see it, live it and be scared to death by the time you were ready to go to bed. That's a real gift (although you may not have thought so at the time).

Some of those qualities are necessary in final argument. The spellbinder, the charismatic Pied Piper you've all seen in the courtroom, does succeed in taking the jury along and making them follow him to his conclusion. The bad news is that it's not a gift given to everyone. But there's good news, too. The good news is that it's not the only way and not the only thing that persuades.

Juries also respond to sincerity and succinctness, to useful analysis and orderly reasoning, to logic and common sense.

Therefore, if you're not a natural-born mesmerizer or revivalist preacher, take heart. You can develop and enlarge your ability to capture and persuade. It means trying new techniques: exploring, experimenting and then adapting them to your own style. It means reaching and stretching. It means taking a hard look at how you present final arguments now. Are they as effective as they can be? Do you feel the jury is with you? What does your gut tell you?

My suggestion for how to begin is two-fold: Focus in the right direction and be good to yourself.

Let's look at focusing first.

Final argument, at its best, should be so clear, so persuasive, so free of detour and pitfall, that as the jury listens they can only follow your logic to its inexorable conclusion for your client. The major issue is to think in terms of your audience. If you were the jury at the end of a three-week trial, what would *you* want to hear? What would *you* need to know? What could a persuader give you at this point to not only help you understand the facts but also to make you agree with his or her interpretation?

Consider the jury's needs. They not only need to clarify all they've heard and be convinced by your arguments, but to formulate in their own minds why they feel that way and to feel so solid in their belief that they could even convince some other members of the jury who might disagree with them. They have to carry into the jury room enough conviction, laced with enough facts and enough good arguments, that they can stand their ground and feel that they have come to the correct conclusion, both for themselves and in spite of other people.

Therefore, remember to give them clarification by organization, recapping, underlining and emphasizing so that they know that this point, brought out by these facts, finally adds up to this conclusion.

And remember—don't exhort. Don't tell them *what* to do. Tell them why.

Now, about being kind to yourself.

Your basic communications processes were formed in your house when you were a little kid. You come now as a sum total of many parts. Give yourself permission to be who you are. That's often a tall order. We are our own worst, unrelenting critics. We can instantly point to our unacceptable features; we seem forever aware of our weak and vulnerable places, those adolescent hangups that never seem to leave. That basic sense of self-conscious insecurity and unease mitigates against your being at your best as a performer. It can dilute or destroy your focus. My suggestion? Let it go. Be yourself—warts and all. Spend a moment with that list of "too much" and "not enough"; look at it, agree with it, laugh about it and then tear it up. That's who you are . . . Right . . . Now go on to the task at hand. Rev up *all* your energy and focus on reaching out and persuading others, not listening to that internal rumbling about your inadequacies in a bathing suit or a close-up. Wrong outfit, wrong activity. Better pack your brain and your soul for this one. Shape and size don't matter.

There's still another aspect of being good to yourself.

One of the biggest problems that gets in a lawyer's way during the trial is nervousness, particularly before closing argument. You feel, "This is it, this is the third act, my last chance." The major reason for your anxiety is that in your mind, you have an image of a "10," that there is one perfect final argument for your case. There is one best way to do it, guaranteed to win. When you slave over it, write it out, work and think about it, when you rearrange and reorganize and rethink it, you do it based on that mythical perfect "10": "This isn't good. There's a best." Your anxiety rises in direct proportion to how far away you think you are from that "10." Then, when you deliver the final argument, you give yourself a grade, don't you? It's still against that mythical "10," delivered by that mythical, perfect, ultimate lawyer.

I'd like to free you from that, It's a very harmful obstacle and the anxiety it produces diminishes your performance. The fact is, there is no "10." There is no nostrum, no recipe, no "best way." There are a limitless number of ways to do a final argument and there is no way to evaluate which is better than which. Your focus should be on your being as *effective* as you can be, not as perfect as you can be.

That's the thing to think about—what is most effective? What's going to get the jury? What's going to persuade them?

If you can let go of your focus on yourself and your performance, then you can make the jury primary. Until that time, your
agenda is you. You're evaluating yourself against the perfect "10,"
which is another lawyer, not against what the jury needs and
wants. Forget, "How would the ultimate lawyer do this?" and,
"How good can I be as opposed to him?"

Instead, from day one, think of "what will reach and explain
this to the jury? What do they need and want?" That's the thrust.
That's your stimulus. That's your focus. Then you will relax and
start working more effectively toward your real goal—to persuade
and to win. Ask yourself, then list, what you must accomplish in
final argument; what the jury expects and needs; what you must
dispel and what you must fulfill. Then decide how. Use my suggestions if they suit you. And then, give it all you've got and go get
'em!

8

VISUAL AIDS

"Seeing is believing." "A picture is worth a thousand words." These concepts are not just old-fashioned homilies. Research has shown that we get up to 90 percent of our knowledge from visual-sensory impressions and that these are the most memorable and lasting. The challenge is to understand these concepts in terms of the courtroom and to find ways to include them in your normal preparation of a trial.

The difficulties that may arise here have to do with unfamiliar territory. You are committed to and are most comfortable with words. The body of the law itself is written in words. You're accustomed to reading unintelligible, static phrases and adding your own juices to interpret, flesh out and eventually understand them. So your expertise and your learning mode is cerebral and verbal, not visual. Also, most lawyers know little, technically, about graphics, visual persuasion techniques and illustration, nor do they have much objective information about the emotional and intellectual effect of visual material on an audience. Therefore, imagining other ways to say, show or tell, as well as understanding the impact of alternative explanatory systems is foreign and generally unavailable to you.

Result: Since you wish to feel secure and in control in the courtroom at all times, many trial lawyers do not take advantage of a multitude of devices that could be helpful and much more effective in the courtroom. The goal of this chapter is to help you discover the world of visual persuasion and to see its techniques and potential much more clearly.

THE EFFECT OF VISUAL EVIDENCE
ON THE JURY

Take a piece of paper and pencil right now and do just what you will read. Ask friends, family, associates, and/or staff to do the same, as you read the instructions to them. No questions or looking at each other's papers allowed!

- Draw a line on the page.
- Now draw two squares on the page.
- Put three circles on the page.
- Place five dots on the page.
- Connect two dots.
- Connect two more dots.
- Now look at each other's papers.

Surprised? The chances are that there will be as many variations as there are readers of this book, and none of them may be what I was imagining as I wrote this. Let's sing a hymn of praise to the fact that the human mind is as creative as it is but here's the point this exercise makes: People absorb and interpret information which is given to them only orally in a limitless variety of ways, especially when they are unable to interrupt and clarify by asking what you mean. Even simple, easily imagined, universally known geometric shapes like squares and circles are open to endless interpretation based on everyone's totally unique, individual experiences and subconscious systems. That's what the jury does with your oral explanations. But using visual explanations in the courtroom has many strengths and much value for the jury and solves many problems for you.

Why Use Visual Aids?

Look at this chart and read the explanation under it.

Nuclear Weapons Chart. The chart above shows the world's current fire-power as opposed to the firepower of World War II. The dot in the center square represents all the firepower of World War II: 3 megatons. The other dots represent the world's present nuclear weaponry which equals 6,000 World War IIs or 18,000 megatons. The United States and the Soviets share this firepower with approximately equal destructive capability.

The top left-hand circle enclosing 9 megatons represents the weapons on just one Poseidon submarine. This is equal to the firepower of three World War IIs and enough to destroy over 200 of the Soviet's largest cities. We have 31 such subs and 10 similar Polaris subs.

The circle in the lower left-hand square enclosing 24 megatons represents one new Trident sub with the firepower of eight World War IIs. *Enough to destroy every major city in the northern hemisphere.*

The Soviets have similar levels of destructive power. Just two squares on this chart (300 megatons) represent enough firepower to destroy all the large- and medium-size cities in the entire world. (U.S. Senate staff have reviewed this chart and found it to be an accurate representation of the nuclear weapons arsenal.) (Reprinted by permission of William Morrow publishers, "The Trimtab Factor," by Harold Willens.).

Now imagine yourself trying to get this information across to an audience. How many words, numbers, lists and comparisons would you have to use to explain this information? How soon do you think you'd lose your audience? But most of all—could you possibly make the impact verbally that you can with this single visual aid?

Based on what you now know about how juries respond and listen, not only in court but through their television-conditioned responses generally, your major breakthrough as a communicator is to learn to add visualization as a prime source of information-giving and reinforcement. For your jury, visual aids have the following effects:

Accuracy

As we discovered on page 376, when you simply describe with words, everyone relies on his or her own interpretation. In court, when you try to orally describe an event, a place, object or an image, there will be as many pereeptual variations as there are jurors. Since the essence of what you are trying to do is to prove a point based on acceptance of certain facts, everyone must agree to the same set of facts. You want the jury to start with you at point A and follow you along exactly as you mean them to. Therefore, making facts visual insures that you're all talking about the same thing, and when the jury conjures up any image, it's the same as yours. But beyond accuracy, there are many other implications for using visuals.

Efficiency

Think about how long it takes you to absorb all the facts in a case when you prepare for trial, how much research you need to understand the basic issues, what technical data you need to accumulate and understand and how hard it is to come to the essence, the theory of the case.

Now imagine the jury that must hear only the edited version—and just once. How can you fill in some of those broad strokes with details or examples and still stay lucid and interesting? How can you give them an instant, in-depth, bird's-eye view? By using visual materials, the shortcut teaching tool that organizes, presents and demonstrates efficiently and distills information into usable form.

Empowering

Visual aids empower the jury. Consider the fact that the jury does not get any information except when you are ready to give it. All the information relating to your case is inside your head. You are the only source from which the jury learns about the case. Whether you are examining witnesses, presenting opening statements or delivering the final argument, the jury is totally dependent on you. They must sit back passively and wait for you to speak and explain at *your* discretion, not theirs. When you create visuals for the jury, suddenly they have a life of their own. The jury can now, independently, look at the visuals and absorb what they see. They have the choice of listening to you while they are looking at the visuals, or listening to you and then going back to check what you are saying or compare it with what the visuals say and mean. The effect is that you become not only more interesting, but also much more convincing, because as they lose their total dependence and see your intention to treat them as independent grown-ups and stimulate their thinking, your statements become *their* facts, not only yours.

Involvement

The jury has an activity quite apart from the one of simply, passively listening to you. They are actively pursuing information. This sharply heightens the amount of interest they have in what you're telling them because now they have something to do, and it decreases the ever-present danger of losing their attention. They get curious and much more interested in the next thing that's going to be said. They want to see how the story evolves. They want to see what else will be added to the visuals. They're learning. Whenever you use a picture, a diagram or a chart, you go from monologue to dialogue—a dialogue between you and an active jury. The interaction between your explanation and the jury's perception, interpretation and silent discussion or assent with you as you include them, is a new sound in the courtroom for them.

Clarity

Imagine yourself giving a verbal description of an object or a place. Not only does each juror create his own version of what he thinks you meant but each time you return to that image the juror needs to try to imagine it again. And nowhere is there assurance that his image is yours, or even the same as last time. This illustrates the importance of having a uniform image, so that everybody not only starts from the same place but, whenever you go back to your visual or your diagram, they all know where you are and they are all there with you again. They should be precisely and exactly where you want them to be, not where their own imagination might take them. It makes an instant connection to a past explanation.

Reinforcement

Visual aids are also very valuable as reinforcement because most people don't catch something the first time. They need to be able to go back and check it out again. Reinforcement is a key ingredient in learning and understanding, but there's more to it than simple repetition.

As the jury hears someone describing an event, they are not only evaluating what they are talking about, they're also trying to picture it. With visuals, they can look at the place where the event happened, imagining it in the proper setting. They see the product, how it was made and where the defect actually occurred. Then every time you talk about the defect they imagine it again, exactly, as they add their own experience to it. They can go through the intersection again and again, sitting in the very same car, experiencing the light changing and the car being struck, once the scene is made clear visually. But if you are simply talking about it, they may not be able to add their own information to yours, to dip into their own experience, to see what is logical and thus reinforce what you want them to believe and understand.

Comparison

Your visual evidence, especially if it's well done, can cancel out inaccuracy and also what has gone before. It can call forth comparison with what the jury knows from their own previous experience. For defense lawyers, visual demonstrations can give the jury a basis for comparison with what has been said before. Strong visuals cancel out the spoken word and persist in the mind. For plaintiffs' lawyers, they are a way of imprinting the jury to withstand the assault of the defense; a set of clear, well presented visual images remains alive in the jurors' minds as an internal argument against what the defense lawyer tells them. "But the schoolyard was right on the corner in that picture the other lawyer showed." One of the most effective techniques of persuasion is comparison with the norm or the fact.

Simplify Complex Facts

Product liability issues, lists of numbers, diagrams of technical data, lengthy contracts—all of these are virtually impossible to explain or describe without resorting to visual forms. This is true for any unfamiliar subject or anyone with very exact information. They take time to explain and aren't instantly recognized and absorbed. Creating demonstrations helps categorize and clarify what might otherwise be impossible for laymen to undertand and remember, especially if you are trying to explain it only once.

Visuals are More Compelling

Converting words to visualized images makes them come alive. In trying to make jurors understand and remember the exact words of a letter, a contract, a deposition or a confession, the mere recital of those words is like whistling in the wind. Making those words available visually lets the jury join in the impact or the import of a key word or phrase. Reading with you, seeing the crucial point reproduced for all to see, makes it easier and more compelling to follow. It also creates incontrovertible evidence that stays with them. Mere words, especially formal, complex ones which are merely read or said, are an invitation to tune out.

Visuals are Objective

One of your main goals is to convince the jury that what you and your client say is fact. Yet the spoken word is manipulable. Not only can one change its meaning by how it's delivered, but the jury's imagination can play with it as well. They may or may not hear everything that was said in the way it was given. They can also wonder about how authentic it is.

When something is on a piece of paper, it stands still, carved in granite. It has a special veracity that the spoken word never does. It looks much more objective. Also, hearing someone mumble or speak poorly as he tries to describe something doesn't have nearly as much credibility as clear straight lines of print, or diagrams cleanly or professionally drawn. They give weight to any argument.

Physical Activity is an Attention-Getter

Continue to remember the physical passivity and the resultant ennui of the jury. They are sitting still. If they have also to sit still and concentrate hard through their eyes and ears, on a static figure, they're putting out effort without recharging their batteries. You're their surrogate mover. Anything you can do that adds physical activity in the room is vital.

Remember when you were a kid in school and the door opened? Everybody's head snapped toward the door. You thought: "Thank God, something's happening." The same thing is true when you are grown up. An audience will automatically check to see when there is a disturbance or some other activity, a break in their passivity and physical paralysis. Allowing either you or your witness to walk, to point, to write, and seeing you move charts, change an image, flip a transparency, adds greatly to the interest of what's being told and said in the courtroom. It will also bring the attention of the jury to some new point of focus. When they look only at you they get a little glassy-eyed or look past you, because you already look familiar and it's hard to keep concentrating on one point.

Visuals are More Fun

Since much of what you do in the courtroom is reminiscent of the schoolroom, go back to another classroom image with me. Remember the excitement, the sense of anticipation when the teacher said it was time for the movie or the slide tape in class? There was the ritual darkening of the room, the moving of equipment, and the rustle of everyone getting comfortable in their seats, ready for the show. That never goes away.

As adults, we still get a charge out of any speaker interrupting the drone to go to the visuals. Our anticipation may be more in terms of getting more clarity and understanding than a show, but we still see the screen coming down or the TV monitors being turned on as an anticipation of entertainment. That's another reason visual aids work so well in the courtroom. Not only do we expect to understand more clearly, but the connection with past experiences says that pictures are more fun than just talking.

Visuals are Succinct

Knowing the natural tendency of trial lawyers to take off on a sea of words, this may not be such welcome news to you. However, from the jury's point of view, it's delightful. Not only the sheer change in the form of how they will get information but the fact that it's easy, quick and explicit gives still another reason to use demonstrative evidence. Keep in mind how hard the jury's job of understandng and remembering really is and how much they want to do it well. The fact that visuals talk fast and straight can make them feel most kindly disposed toward you. They also enjoy putting your voice in the background and letting their eyes take over.

Visual Images are Memorable

I've done research on what jurors remember at the end of a trial. It would amaze you to see how clearly they remember all the visual aids that were used: the charts, diagrams, blow-ups, transparencies, models and demonstrations. They can recall and even demonstrate or draw them again. What a valuable impact they have. You are creating a representative of yours to send back with them into the jury room.

*   *   *

In general, then, the effect on the jury of visualizing concepts or facts is that of a better, more efficient way to explain. They are a more objective truth, which is not so open to interpretation but can

stand alone. And they add great interest, focus and active involvement to your presentation.

SELECTING AND PREPARING
DEMONSTRATIVE EVIDENCE

How do you go about developing visual strategies? How do you
choose which forms to use? What effects are created by using one
technique or another? How do you say the most in the simplest,
most direct way? How do you make an impact in a matter of
seconds?

Although individual responses may vary somewhat, there are
some basic principles we all use to see by, based on common human needs and experiences as well as our orientation to the world
around us.

None of us, unless it is our profession, knows too much about
these principles. We just know "what we like," not necessarily
knowing why. You are about to become practictioners in using visual effects, so you need to know more. Here are some fundamental
guidelines you should know to help you understand and select
techniques for developing visual statements, whether they're simple ones you do alone or they're for use in guiding professionals in
the preparation of complex visual materials. Let's discover how we
look at visual images. We'll discuss people's innate responses to
color, shape, direction, contrast, composition, and design and the
attendant emotional impact of each.*

Balance

A sense of balance, symmetry and harmony is innate in all of us.
The most important psychological, as well as physical, influence on
human perception, is our need for balance, for having two feet on
the ground, fighting gravity and remaining upright with reasonable
certainty. Equilibrium is our strongest visual reference and is the
conscious and unconscious basis for making visual judgments.

The horizontal-vertical axis shows our basic relationship to
our environment. We adjust to variations of the central axis auto-

---

*Most of the concepts in this section as well as the illustrative diagrams are
excerpted or based on a book by Professor Donis A. Dondis called "A Primer of
Visual Literacy" published by the MIT Press, Cambridge, Massachusetts.

matically to compensate and continue our sense of balance. It gives us a sense of peace and well-being. Heeling over (tilting) in a boat while sailing, for example, causes us to automatically lean backward or forward and compensate, adjusting our own weight to keep the sense of balance. That axis is an unconscious constant and affects how comfortable or uncomfortable we are with what we see.

Therefore, anything that you want to seem orderly, stable, regular and instantly acceptable should have symmetry and balance. Yet beware of the fact that balance has no challenge in it and is, therefore, neither attention-getting nor interest-sustaining. It reassures. It registers and is done talking.

Asymmetry

The irregular and unstable create tension and conflict. They are disorienting and require effort on the part of the viewer to right them. Therefore, their effects are more complex. They are unexpected and demand notice. Discover how you feel about this:

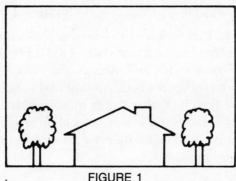

FIGURE 1

versus this:

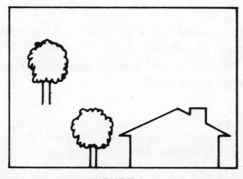

FIGURE 2

See how much longer you can look at Figure 2 than 1, how quickly you grasp Figure 1.

Therefore, any chart or diagram that is designed to create tension and surprise should not create harmony and symmetry. Moving off the axis creates intensity and greater challenge and interest.

Ambiguity

Our minds continually seek to create order and logic in all visual perceptions. Therefore, visual forms should not be unclear. They can harmonize or contrast, attract or repel, relate or clash, but they should be accountable to the horizontal and vertical axes we all use. Placing forms in a no-man's land of "almost" or "not quite" is irritating to the viewer.

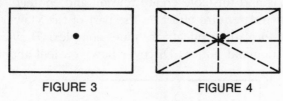

FIGURE 3   FIGURE 4

The dot in Figure 3 is not clearly in the center nor is it far enough off center to make a real statement. It fits no axis pattern, as shown in Figure 4. It's just unclear and visual ambiguity, like verbal ambiguity, obscures both content and meaning. Of all our senses, sight is the one that registers most quickly. It experiences and recognizes balance and interactions of diverse visual data, demanding exactness and logic. Be careful never to frustrate or confuse this unique function.

Placement

The vertical-horizontal axis area of any field is looked at first; it's where we expect to see something. Therefore, the dead center is strong, but harmonious and quickly understood, and not particularly stimulating emotionally.

Figures 3 and 4. (Reprinted from *A Primer of Visual Literacy*, Donis A. Dondis, Figures 2.26 and 2.27, page 28; The MIT Press, The Massachusetts Institute of Technology, Cambridge, Mass., with permission.)

The eye also favors the lower left-hand area of any visual field. In general, the lower half of any visual field dominates the upper half, perhaps because gravity means stability, or because the earth is tangible and the sky is endless. We use a common scanning pattern. We look at the center. That responds to the aforementioned need for a vertical-horizontal axis. Then we look at the lower left. Finally the eye travels to lower right. This lower left pull can be due to our western method of reading and writing, but its attribution isn't yet clear. Suffice it to say that it's true and you should know where the strongest and most compelling place to put a message is. Notice the effect these diagrams have on you, how comfortable or uncomfortable, pleasing or unsettling these images are.

Figure 5 shows calm, symmetry and harmony.

Figure 6 shows some interesting development but is still rather orderly and quiescent.

Figure 7 shows the greatest tension and surprise in its seeming top-heaviness and extreme assymetry. This is where the eye doesn't comfortably go and the mind doesn't find as much order.

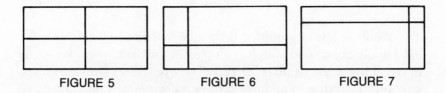

FIGURE 5   FIGURE 6   FIGURE 7

Simplistically, visual elements that are placed where they create viewer stress have more weight and ability to attact the eye than those that are balanced. Balanced designs are serene and easy to understand. Lower left placement, with its implication of eye movement to the right, is a more demanding form; it creates action yet is still felt to be orderly and strong. maximum attention and more weight are given to areas where we are least accustomed to looking—upper rather than lower, right rather than left.

Figures 5, 6, and 7. (Reprinted from *A Primer of Visual Literacy*, Donis A. Dondis, Figures 2.30, 2.31, 2.32, page 29; The MIT Press, The Massachusetts Institute of Technology, Cambridge, Mass., with permission.)

Grouping Interaction

Grouping shapes creates visual relationships. It creates a circumstance of give and take.

In Figure 8, the dot relates to the whole square field, but it stands alone.

In Figure 9, the two dots fight for attention in their interaction, creating comparatively individual statements because they are far from one another and consequently appear to repel each other.

In Figure 10, there is an immediate and more intense interaction; the dots harmonize and therefore attract each other. The closer they are, the stronger their attraction. They become a unit.

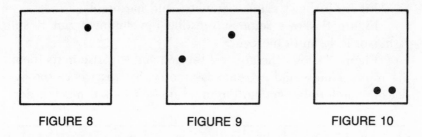

FIGURE 8   FIGURE 9   FIGURE 10

Another law of grouping is the effect of similarity. Unlike the old homily about odd couples—"opposites attract,"—in the world of visual literacy, "similars" attract. The eye relates like units more strongly. In trying to understand shapes, especially abstract ones, the eye and the mind seek similarities as reference points.

Therefore, when creating charts or diagrams that have two concepts, placing them in similarly shaped forms with similar colors or tones will automatically make us connect them as in Figure 11. Using variations of size, but similar shapes, underlines statements of importance or shows similar origins. It logically builds connection and cause and effect relationships for a stronger statement, as in Figure 12.

Figures 8, 9, and 10. (Reprinted from *A Primer of Visual Literacy*, Donis A. Dondis, Figures 2.49, 2.50, 2.51, page 33; The MIT Press, The Massachusetts Institute of Technology, Cambridge, Mass., with permission.)

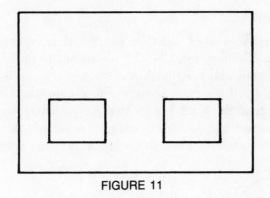

FIGURE 11

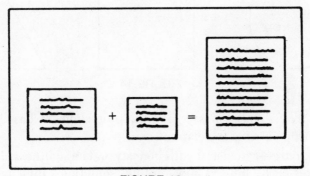

FIGURE 12

Using disparate shapes draws no conclusion.

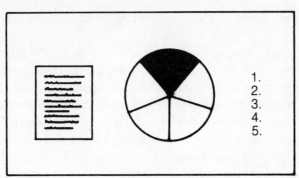

FIGURE 13

See how the dissimilar shapes in Figure 13 do not build on each other and make no cumulative, orderly statement. This makes the message much harder to follow.

Shapes

To be effective, shapes must be simple, clear, recognizable and memorable. The jury must be able to assimilate them quickly and see their intent and relationship.

There are three basic shapes: The square, the circle and the equilateral triangle. Each has its own unique character, characteristics and meanings, through association or simple general acceptance. We respond to these shapes in interesting ways.

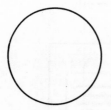  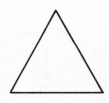

FIGURE 14

• *Circle*—endlessness, warmth, protection. It has embracing and encompassing associations.

• *Square*—associated with honesty and straightness. It is workmanlike, clear, limited and limiting, sometimes dull, but classic.

• *Triangle*—action, conflict, tension.

From these shapes, in endless combinations, we derive all forms.

Visually, shapes have more or less weight or dominance in direct proportion to their relative regularity and recognizability. Complex, irregular, unstable shapes increase visual stress, challenge the mind to understand and solve them and therefore attract the eye more. Yet, the use of regular, recognizable shapes or ones that balance each other is soothing, pleasing and easy to grasp and gives room to absorb another message aside from the shape itself.

Understanding what effects they have can help you choose in what shapes you wish to present your material and why.

Figure 14. (Reprinted from *A Primer of Visual Literacy*, Donis A. Dondis, Figure 3.13, page 44; The MIT Press, The Massachusetts Institute of Technology, Cambridge, Mass., with permission.)

Direction

Every basic shape expresses three basic and meaningful visual directions:

1. *Square—horizontal and vertical*

2. *Circle—the curve*

3. *Triangle—the diagonal*

Each of these visual directions has a strong associative meaning and is a valuable tool in making visual messages.

Horizontal-vertical

This is our primary reference in terms of well being, stability and maneuverability, not only in our relationship to the environment but also to stability in all visual matters, like architecture or any designed object.

A horizontal image in its most abstract form is a restful image, based on the earth, solid and at peace, while vertical images involve fighting gravity and imply energy, thrust and action. Therefore, a vertical image has challenge and tension within it, as opposed to a horizontal image. That's one of the reasons people love to look at the ocean and the horizon, and feel a little agitated when they look at a skyscraper landscape with its thrusting, vertical shapes.

Diagonals

Diagonals imply the opposite to stability. This directional force is the most unstable and, consequently, the most visually provoking. Its meaning is active, threatening and more upsetting. It has momentum and acceleration built into it, as opposed to the more static horizontal or straight vertical. On a stage, the diagonals are the most dramatic directions, cutting through the space and the placid horizontal-vertical axis, coming from far away upstage to downstage, and making a closer connection with the audience, in the longest possible line.

Curved

These directional forces remind us of repetition, encompassment and warmth, nurturing and softness. Think of the images curves conjure for you and of your response to them. Curved lines and shapes are best for describing softer or more repetitive concepts, circular in nature or in feeling.

All directional choices in visual communication have great influence on final effect and meaning.

In charts, showing contrasts like small versus big, one should use verticals (bar graphs, etc.), while horizontal and diagonal directions should be used to show activity like a trend.

Diagonals and strong, jagged, mountain-like shapes should be used for dramatic, active and forceful statements.

The most important thing to note here in relation to shape and direction is that the eye can be captured and directed with attendant impact or it can remain static, complacent and eventually bored.

Color

Color is loaded with information, creating dramatic, emotional responses, and is an invaluable source of visual communication. It works through common associations we all make from nature and our own lives. Although we all have some individual differences, generally these are the basic truths about our reactions to colors and the kinds of symbolic meanings we attribute to them:

• Although the primary colors are red, blue and yellow, the most direct colors and those that get the most positive reactions in graphic terms are red, blue and green.

• Both red and blue are the most affirmative, bold and appealing.

- Red is hotter, more exciting and connected with getting attention. It means danger (stop signs and fire engines). It means love and warmth and life. But when used with numbers, it says debit!

- Blue is calmer and more infinite (the sky). It means stability (true blue) or loyalty. It's also cooler.

- Green, such as emerald green, is also positive since it is connected with grass, trees, growth.

- Olive green is drab and negative.

- Associations make red and blue "good guy" colors and olive green and some tans and browns "bad guy" colors.

- Yellow means light and warmth. Between red and blue, it's strong; by itself or against white, it's weak.

- Orange, depending on the intensity and juxtaposition, can make a fairly strong message, but by itself it's weaker than red or blue.

- Earth tones, rust, gold, brown, are warm but more subtle and subdued than the clear primary colors.

- Pastels, pink, pale yellow, lavender, are young, light, soft and less consequential.

- Jewel colors, (purple, wine), are admirable, unique and regal, but they are also sophisticated and not so easy to relate to.

- Black on white is stark, formidable and dry. It makes no extra statement; it has no emotioinal appeal. It's factual, like a newspaper, it's not associated with pleasure and is neither interesting nor dynamic. However, knowing it looks like a newspaper could be helpful in reproducing photographs to show veracity. It adds no interest to charts.

- White on black is quite dramatic but hard to read. It looks trendy and is reminiscent of slick magazine ads rather than basic facts.

- Brown is warmer than black, but certain paler versions (tan, yellow-brown) have a negative association. Photographs printed in brown are softer and easier to look at but less "hard-news" looking. Chocolate brown on white is appealing, not quite as strong an image, but warmer and more sophisticated than black on white.

• Clear colors are simple, basic and uncomplicated. Grayed-off tones are subtler, more sophisticated and more restful but not necessarily attention-getting.

• The more intense a color is, the more emotional and expressive it is.

• Colors take on different meanings in juxtaposition with each other.

• Contrast, sharpness and variety of color are important for creating effects in charts and diagrams.

In a series of studies on babies, rooms using brilliant poster colors in graphics which were visible to them and changed frequently created alertness, while dull rooms with little or no color created lethargy.

Outline, Surface and Tone

To be most direct and effective in court, all images should be hard-edged, sharp and clear. Compare the blurred feeling of a watercolor with a brilliantly-colored poster or graphic. Which is more commanding?

Be sure you use strong dramatic shapes with clear outlines. Wavy lines or cross-hatching are negative images.

Glossy surfaces are perky, eye-catching and fresher, especially in white. Be careful of glare and reflection; check out the light.

Dry, flat surfaces are factual but duller. Be sure they're visually arresting in content. You don't have to be dreary to be factual. White backgrounds should be glossy or super-white or they will look dirty.

*   *   *

Reading through these principles should give you some basic guidelines that can help your decision-making process as you think through visual reinforcements for your examination or your opening or final argument. Since creating visual images is such a specialized art, use professionals, but stay involved so that your intention is clear to them and the end product truly suits your purposes.

BASIC CONCEPTS AND EFFECTIVE
TECHNIQUES FOR USING VISUALS

Concepts

Control the Information

The most important single mistake lawyers make and the one they make most often, is to overload visual aids with too much information all at once. When you do that, anarchy reigns supreme.

Once you show the jury anything, their minds go to work trying to figure it out. They will not dutifully wait for you to explain it, with your logic, at your pace. Any visual material is an instant challenge to each of them to try to understand it, since they know that you think it has meaning and that you want them to get some new insights from it.

The result? You've lost control. While you're explaining the first sentence or the upper left hand corner of the diagram, the jurors' eyes are all over the place, picking out the most arresting or the simplest bits, trying to make sense of everything and not listening to you at all. When you get to the end, they haven't been following and the chart is neither intelligible nor useful.

Therefore, you must control the information and only give one piece at a time—just as much as you can explain. Then you add the next point and talk, then the next and so on.

When using a blackboard or flip chart, draw or write as you explain. Then your material naturally unfolds only when you're ready to add it. There's immediacy and action in it and also control.

Use transparent overlays when using prepared charts. Separate the information into individual points, time lapses, chronology, additional information and so on. Show the basic premise on Chart 1, then flip transparency 1 over, talking and drawing on it, if you wish, or have it already prepared with additional information. Flip the next and talk. With each one you add another line, shape, color or point. At the end you have it all.

In either case, writing and/or adding prepared material, each time you add a point you pique the jury's interest anew. You challenge them to keep thinking, to stay active and involved. In order to control each piece of information you give, add the piece visually only when you are ready to talk about it, not before. Then, at the end, you are sure that they followed you, understood what you meant and that your visuals are effective because you let them in on the process of how the total information developed.

Let Them Look

If the idea of using visuals is to engage the jury, then hold still, be quiet and let them look. The initial impact of each visual should be arresting and get them interested. Learn to wait. Even the promise of adding visual information by going to a board is exciting. Build a little anticipation. It increases the appetite. Remember, a picture really is worth a thousand words. Use the visuals and work in conjunction with them. Don't overwhelm them or usurp their job.

For example: To show a blow-up, tell them what you're going to show them before you unveil it. Then, unveil it and wait. Let it sink in. Let the eyes roam and get adjusted for a moment. Then explain further. You'll get maximum attention as the jurors have satisfied their initial curiosity and are ready for an explanation.

Involve the Jury's Tactile Sense

If you're doing a demonstration, let them participate. Let them touch, lift, turn something, scrutinize. Pass the object around to all of them so they can add the sense of touch to those of sight and sound. It will make your demonstration much more effective and they will actually feel what it's like as they watch a demonstration or listen to further description and explanation.

Research Placement and Scale
Needed in the Courtroom

Go to the courtroom in advance and examine the sight lines from the jury box and the judge's bench. Experiment with the best place to put your screen, easel, blackboard or demonstration table. Don't guess. Sit in the jury box and look at the board. Check out the lighting. This is very important. Discover when the sun shines at the jury or at your exhibit. Nothing ruins a good exhibit faster than glare or murky light.

Check the size of the print you need to make all the words clearly visible and intelligible. Practice writing and drawing on the board and bring in a chart with printing to see relative size and ease of sight.

Be Sure your Visuals are Clear and Self-evident

Test your visual ideas on your family, staff or colleagues. See if they get the idea and can grasp what you mean as you show and describe. During the preparation of a trial you get very close to your material, and what seems simple to you may not be so simple to anyone unfamiliar with your case. This kind of "kitchen testing" is very valuable to give you insights into if and how your visual works, and what needs additional clarification.

Repeat Charts

Remember that reinforcement is one of the best teaching techniques. Once the jury is imprinted with an exhibit, bringing it back reminds them of your previous explanation and makes your points again.

Be Careful of a "Read-along"

Providing the jury and the judge with copies while you try to talk and explain is counter-productive. They're busy reading and drawing their own conclusions, or being confused, rather than listening to you and following at your pace. People can read faster than you can talk and will read ahead. You lose eye contact, control and the jury's attention.

Instead, pass around the original. Then collect it and make your presentation. Use an overhead projector or blow-ups so everyone can read along with you while you explain—all eyes on you and the exhibit. Then, if you wish, provide photocopies for further scrutiny and/or to send into the jury room later. Thus you're guaranteed that they got your point. Just be sure that, when you demonstrate, what you want them to see is enlarged enough so they can follow you as you talk, and that you isolate, by color, editing or underlining, exactly what you want them to look at.

Use Explanatory Exhibits as
Early as Possible

To keep the jury clear and imprinted with your visualization of the case, use your explanatory exhibits as early as possible, in opening statement. Each time you come back to them you reinforce those earlier concepts. Be sure you get them thinking your way right from the opening statement by clarifying with visuals. They last. This follows the law of primacy—being most attentive to and lastingly impressed by what you see and hear first.

Save Emotional Exhibits for
Impact

These work best at the proper dramatic moment. They depend on choreography, on building to a climax. They need setting up and a ready audience so that they become the culmination of a point being made. They should act as an exclamation point or a reverberating gong. Be well aware of their power and pick your time to spring them. Use them again in final argument to ring the reverberating chimes again. This follows the law of recency—remembering what you see and hear last.

Use Surprise

Keep your best exhibit concealed to use the element of surprise. Rarely can you match Perry Mason's tightly edited dramas, but if you have a dramatic moment, make the most of it.

You can either keep the exhibit hidden but convenient and available or build an element of suspense by keeping some large exhibit present but covered. What curiosity that breeds! Just be sure that when you unveil it, they don't discover a fizzle. You have to come up with something good if you build suspense. Beware of an anticlimax. Don't disappoint.

Techniques

Practice with Pointer and
Writing with Marker

You've watched people do it, and it seems simple, but it *is* a minor skill and requires a little work to get smooth and comfortable. The biggest mistake is getting in the way as you write or point. The other problem is to write or print in a straight line, especially down at the bottom. Be sure when you label a diagram that your connecting line between the object and identifying word description is connected and clear. Special practice sessions are especially necessary for using overhead projectors and writing on the transparencies.

Practice with Your Witness

In direct examination, you want your witness to show and tell for credibility, as opposed to cross where you're the one who "shows and tells" for control. If you point to an exhibit in direct and simply get your witness to agree, the jury doesn't believe it nearly as much as a direct hands-on demonstration by the witness himself.

Let your witness practice getting up from the witness chair (or facsimile in your office) and going to the board or diagram. Show him how to point, mark on the exhibit and get comfortable talking, standing and showing. Make him aware of the jury's sight lines so he doesn't get in the way.

Make the Exhibit Primary and
Visible

It is amazing to see how often lawyers get in the way of the judge or jury clearly seeing an exhibit. In your zeal to explain, you often lose sight of where you are and drift in front of the judge's or

jury's sight lines, getting between them and your prize exhibit.
This is a common failing and needs attention, since it's irritating to
a viewer to try to peer around you as you explain.

Use the Same Sets of Symbols
for Consistency

Don't write and print on the same chart. Do one or the other.
It looks sloppy, undisciplined, rather casual, and markedly lessens
the impact. If you write "Nov. 29," don't then write "12/2" as the
next date. Set up a system of visual symbols and stick with it con-
sistently for maximum effectiveness and clarity. There is a subconscious message of lack of concern or importance in sloppy or
undisciplined visual messages.

Mark Exhibits Clearly for Jury
Deliberation

Be sure you have self-explanatory tags on each exhibit you
send to the jury room. The jury forgets and doesn't often remember the context of each object, chart or diagram. Use big cardboard
luggage tags (like the ones used for camp trunks) so you can get a
full description on it. Don't think one or two words will suffice. Imagine how you'd answer their questions in the jury room: "What's
this?" "What was this for?" "What was this about?" Remember, exhibits continue to testify.

Keep Exhibits Organized and
Available

Nothing looks worse than messy, disorganized exhibits or
feels worse than the clock ticking while you get yourself together in
order to present. For example, if you're using charts, bring an artist's portfolio with all your charts stacked in chronological order.
Stand it against a solid object so you can pull out one at a time.
Mark with tabs on top showing names or numbers to help identify.
Practice this. Small exhibits should be in a box, instantly visible to
you for selection at the proper time.

*Handle the Exhibits with Dignity
and Care*

How you handle your exhibits shows the jury how true and how valuable they are. Their relative importance is broadcast by the way you lift, place and show them. There is also much drama and impact to be made from tangible evidence. (See Chapter 4 for further information on how to handle evidence and Chapter 5 on how to handle depositions.)

CHOOSING VISUAL PRESENTATION FORMS

Charts or slides? Videotape or film? Diagrams, chalk talk or a 3D model? How do you choose which format your visual presentation should use? The choices are many and therefore harder to make. Let me list the available and most often used devices and give you a quick summary and evaluation of their strengths and weaknesses and the situation in which each is appropriate.

Choosing the Message

First, you must determine what should be made visual in the trial. You, yourself, are the primary source for that information. Think back on your first learning to the facts of your case. What caught your attention? What did you keep coming back to? What convinced you? What was difficult to comprehend and needed work for you to understand it? What will be hardest to explain? What's most important to remember? Close your eyes—what do you see most of all? That's your main point—your big dramatic moment.

Make a list of all of the above. List next to each item the visual image that explains it best: a photo of the scene, a scale model of the structure, a diagram of the eye injury, a list of grievances and costs. Analyze what you're reading. Can you imagine how you want it to look, what you want it to say? List the essential ingredients, the key points you need to see for each visual image to be eloquent.

Now decide which can best be demonstrated and which can best be explained. What needs personal narration and what needs objectivity and overview? Can visuals embellish and enhance your narration? What help can you give your expert witness in clarifying for the jury? Cut your list down with this process until you are clear on what you will finally want to demonstrate. Here we come to an important juncture.

Choosing the Creator

Since your experience is in law, not in graphics and visuals, it's time to seek expert advice. Having narrowed down *what* you want to demonstrate and *why,* find an expert to tell you *how.* You may need only one session to eliminate some ideas, focus on others and discover the best way to say it among the choices that a professional can show you. It's fine if you can find one who's done work for the courtroom before, but any talented, experienced graphics creator, photographer or video producer can serve your needs once you're clear about what you want to say and what effect you want to create.

How to find one of these in your town?

Graphic Artists

There are national organizations of graphic artists whom you can call or write for local listings:

• The American Institute of Graphic Arts 1059 Third Avenue, New York, New York.

• The Art Directors Club of (name of city) in your area (listed in all major cities).

• Local universities usually have graphic design departments in the art, education or communication disciplines.

• Advertising agencies in your area always have a creative or graphic design department.

• The Advertising Club of (name of city). These exist in almost all cities. Call them for listings and recommendations.

• Word-of-mouth, the tried and true American way. Call colleagues or the local bar association to discover who does this kind of work or whom they've used.

Video and Filmmakers: Photographers

As far as video, film or photography is concerned, there are various ways to find one locally as well as national organizations to approach.

• Many ad agencies know commercial video studios whom they use. Ask for recommendations.

• The yellow pages list legal, medical and dental photographers as well as commercial ones. They also list print labs that make color prints, transparencies and enlargements. Shop a little.

• American Society of Magazine Photographers (205 Lexington Avenue New York, New York 10016) covers all kinds of photographers. They have a guide to business practices as well as a source book complete with examples of photographers' work. They have chapters and members all over the United States.

• The yellow pages list, under Television Films-Producers, or Films or Video Services, the film and video production houses in your area.

• Call your local television station. They often have a unit that services outside accounts or can recommend someone to you for film or video.

• Always ask for demonstrations of their work to help you decide on quality, sensitivity and professionalism.

How to Create Together

The secret to working with a professional is to feed him or her your information explicitly, clearly and succinctly, and then listen. Come in with a clean slate in your mind for him to write on. Don't tell him *how*, tell him *what*. Let him be inspired. Encourage him to think, to stretch, to find a new way. Don't be willing to settle for the old trite forms. But you must be well-grounded in exactly what you want to say and what effect you hope to achieve, and you must show him what corroborative materials you have gathered and tell him what could be available. Keep it a dialogue—the old adage of "you never learn anything when you're talking" will stand you in good stead here.

Remember, with all this you may only need advice on how to create the best visual statement. Often simple, do-it-yourself live presentations are the best solution. But even then, get good professional advice about how to do that.

Having said all this, I'd now like to make you a more knowledgeable participant in the decision-making process of choosing visualizing techniques. Here are the strengths and weaknesses of most existing visual media and hints about how to use them to best advantage.

Choosing the Medium

Let's start with three basic underlying principles:

• Form follows function. First decide *what* you want to say, *then* think about how you can best say it.

• The medium legislates the kind of message that is possible. All forms have built-in limitations and strengths.

• Different media forms have their own conditioned effect on us, by association, beyond the message you bring.

These principles should be often repeated and thought about in your decision-making. Now read about the formats themselves and see where and why you would use which ones.

Blackboard

Strengths

It's a familiar tool. It's immediate and live in the courtroom. It involves direct hands-on activity which is both interesting and adds authenticity. It's easy to involve witnesses in using it. It's horizontal—wide enough to make two lists for comparison or to illustrate more than one point. It's movable and can be adjusted so all can see or tilted to take care of glare. It's cheap and readily available. It's a good option for quick improvisation, as something occurs to you during the proceedings. Its do-it-yourself nature dilutes the rich-client image and makes you look more self-sufficient.

Weaknesses

It's erasable and not re-capturable. It can remind jurors of school and the assumption of boredom. You can look didactic or patronizing as you "go to the board." The usual green or black blackboards with white chalk are hard to see. It limits the option of using color. It depends on good handwriting or else it can be illegible.

Helpful Hints

• Use a white "blackboard" with a slick surface and colored magic markers, preferably blue, turquoise or green. It's a positive image, much clearer and sharper and more highly visible than the negative images of white chalk on black or yellow on green. These boards are easily erased for reuse. If your court doesn't have one, invest in it and use it at all your trials. It's worth it.

• Practice printing (unless you loved your Palmer method teacher and ended up with good handwriting).

• Go to the courtroom and analyze the sight lines to see how big you must make your letters and where to place the board.

• Design what you'll write in advance and try it on a practice blackboard to see how it looks and if it fits. Remember the previous section on placement and composition.

• Practice writing at the side of the board, not directly in front of it. Jurors read as you write and become irritated if you're in their way. So does the judge. The same is true for pointing at the board.

• Remember, in direct your witness should be the one to point out or draw the line of attack, impact or whatever, rather than you. This makes for credibility. Practice with him or her.

• Make your blackboard high enough so you don't have to scrunch down to write at the bottom.

• If you use chalk, bring your own. Be sure it's soft chalk. Hard chalk squeaks. Remember that sound from school? Ugh!

Blow-ups (Enlargements) of Pictures and Documents

Strengths

They increase the amount of information you can give the jury. An enlargement focuses and points up a particular detail. It helps visualize what might not otherwise be visible to the naked eye or to a group sitting at a distance. It allows everyone to see a detail at once, rather than pass something from hand to hand in the jury box. It can lift one element out of a wealth of unnecessary information and edit it out for closer scrutiny. It's exciting to get a close-up since our eyes can't do that. It's an authentic reproduction, not a diagram. A blow-up makes an ordinary picture or document visible to many people at once.

Weaknesses

Blow-ups or enlargements distort reality. They make one lose sight of the normal scale for comparison. You can forget the whole object or scene. An enlargement can disorient in terms of where something fits. If it's about the human body, an enlargement may be too gruesome.

Helpful Hints

• Make at least two photographic blow-ups for comparison and orientation. Give the jury a large normal view and then show a close-up or enlargement of a specific area. Sometimes this requires three pictures—an overview, a medium close-up of the object and then a tight close-up of the detail. Just showing an enlargement without orienting the viewer makes no point.

• Show a model in conjunction with the photo enlargement, if it's a portable object, so the jury can see where the detail fits. Show how it works normally and then show the problem in a close-up enlargement of the detail to explain it more clearly.

• Blow-ups need to be sharp and clear. Grainy, blurry versions only confuse. Get good professional help for this.

• A glossy surface may be a little slick-looking but it makes a sharper image than the dull matte finish.

• Be sure the easel you display on is very sturdy and is wide enough to take the chart board you've printed the enlargement on.

• Don't overload the easel with all your blow-ups. Use only the ones you need for this particular demonstration. Keep nothing else on the easel.

• Use a pointer only if the blow-up is large. If it is not, use your hand to point. It's more natural, more human and not as professorial or lecture-oriented.

Charts (Graphs, Diagrams, Outlines, Data)

Strengths

They are clear and concise visual explanations. Pre-preparation forces you to edit and distill information. Charts use professionally prepared lettering and images. They can create shapes and put facts in a visible order to be most effective. They use color to great advantage. Pre-preparation of materials allows practice and critique before the trial. They're re-usable and can be sent to the jury room in their original state, which helps the jury recall what you said about them. They're a primary and very welcome addition to the clarification process you're engaged in.

Weaknesses

They're already done—there's not much for you to do actively in court except talk about them. All the information is there at once for the jury to see, which makes it difficult to control where they look and what they listen to. They remind us of boring charts or graphs in textbooks or at school and do not have an automatically compelling character. If there are too many or if they are too elaborate, the jury gets a deep-pocket image, or an information overload.

Helpful Hints

• Feed information one piece at a time. To cover pieces of the charts until you want to show them use two vertical or horizontal velcro strips pasted on the chart. By attaching cut-up sections of blank poster to the strips, you can block out what you don't want the jury to see and control how much you tell at once.

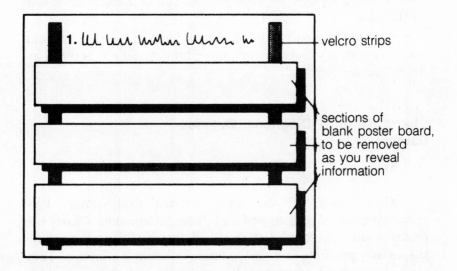

Example: In the diagram above, start by showing only point 1. Then pull off a strip which reveals the next point, and then pull off and reveal yet another, until the chart is completely visible.

• Decide what you want to tell before you show the next part. The great strength here is that you accumulate data as you explain and reveal it so the jury gets it all finally, but in bite-sized, digestible pieces.

• Make your charts flexible. In order to make them more responsive to your individual needs and to inject activity as well as to gain control over how much you tell at a time, use transparencies to add information. Start with a basic statement on a chart and add data in separate chunks by flipping attached overlays over on top of the chart, one at a time. The chart will end with a total message, and you can control the delivery much better. You can also write on transparencies with magic marker, so you can add data to the already prepared message yourself as you speak.

• Be careful not to drown the jury in charts. Edit down to what works and discard redundancies, or confusion will reign.

• Be sure you have just enough variety to keep the jury interested. It's hard to make one chart do all and to hope those sterile, unmoving symbols will sustain interest while you go on and on.

• Put the chart away when you move on to another point unless its message can continue to be useful. It wears out its welcome and won't be as effective when you bring it back in final argument or send it to the jury room.

• Put all the charts in correct order and number them, marking the tops so you can see them easily. Practice pulling them out one at a time and placing them. Nothing looks worse or less professional than a lawyer shuffling a deck of charts, spilling some and not getting them on straight.

• Be creative with your charts. Find interesting ways to make your concepts visual.

• For clarity and emphasis extract one concept and make a separate chart of it to make a vital point or to explain another aspect.

• Be sure the shapes you use are clear and memorable. Also, use the colors that affect the jury as you wish. Use the previous section on shape, color and composition as a reference guide.

Demonstrations

Strengths

Live demonstrations in the courtroom carry very high interest for the jury. They're dramatic and exciting. Seeing something happen right before their eyes not only provides great credibility and drama, but really proves a point. Using the very object in question, or a duplicate, makes juries tune directly into the problem, not the theory about the problem. Seeing how something works is far superior to hearing about it. Demonstrating the fallacy of a concept can be much more effective in destroying the opposition's point than just using testimony and argument alone. We trust our own eyes.

Weaknesses

Mechanical demonstrations may fail (as such things are wont to do sometimes), and then the fallout is very difficult to clear up. It may not be possible to make a really dramatic point; although it may be good and true, not everything is climactic or instantly understandable as mass public viewing. Demonstrating sensitive subjects like physical deformities is eloquent but can make jurors squeamish, unable to look. People are private, and a blatant public demonstration of a severe handicap can embarrass and turn off the jurors.

Helpful Hints

• Be sure you can really make your point as the demonstration is designed—with a flourish, not a whimper.

• Test everything to make sure it's fool-proof.

• Find the right height for the jurors to see your demonstration. Do they need it at eye level or should they look down?

• Be sure the light (windows, etc.) doesn't shine into the jurors' eyes and silhouette the demonstration. If need be, bring a portable light to illuminate it properly.

• If there will be a very loud noise, or smoke, warn the jury in advance. Otherwise your point may be lost as they react to the shock. However, if your point *is* the noise or the smoke, let it happen. Just give them time to absorb it and settle back down.

• If you have a model or a piece of machinery they can operate, or if you want them to know how heavy or light something is, ask the judge's permission for each juror to try it. It's fun and exciting for them and *very* persuasive.

• Looking through a microscope is also dramatic, but each juror might not see the same thing or understand what to look for. These demonstrations are done better as video, slides, and/or diagrams.

• Describe what you're doing each step of the way and explain each part you use. Write the parts or names on the board for reinforcement and for later recall in the jury room. Tag each part of your demonstration with the same descriptive, identifying names that you use in the demonstration and write on the board. This will help the jury recall during deliberation. Use names that are self-explanatory.

• Whenever possible, use comparison. Show a right way and a wrong way, a whole one and a broken one, what's possible and what's impossible. Otherwise you've only made half a point.

• Models work only if you give an orientation about scale. First show a picture, or film or video, of the original if it's too big or if it's unfeasible to bring into the courtroom. Then explain the scale and relative size of the original and the model.

Flip Charts (Large Pad on Easel)

Strengths

They're quick and immediate. You can write on them yourself or get your witness to write. They're easily portable. They create activity and directly involve you. You can save the pages and tack them up on a larger board in the background as you finish each thought and save it for re-use or to send to the jury room. They're easy to read (dark on light). They don't give such an instant reminder of school but rather of a more business-like environment. They look simple, inexpensive and direct— rather informal and home-made. As is the case with blackboards, witnesses can use these easily. You can use them to improvise on as a thought occurs to you that you wish to make clearer, or as something new happens in the trial.

Weaknesses

They do not carry the weight or the implied veracity of a prepared chart. They feel improvisational and temporary. They're vertical in shape and fairly small. Unlike blackboards, which are horizontal, they only have room for one thought at a time. No comparison is possible since you have to flip the page to give the next idea. The paper is soft so it doesn't sustain reshowing as well.

Helpful Hints

• Use colorful magic markers rather than spartan, dull black.

• Design your ideas in advance and see how they look and if they fit.

• Use transparencies as overlays for adding information rather than flipping away your basic idea when you turn the page and tackle a new point.

• Use these for small points or illustrations. They're not substantive enough for major statements.

• As with blackboards, practice legible writing or printing and learn to stand to the side so all can see.

Film

Strengths

Film is an elegant, sophisticated medium. We associate film with entertainment and pleasure as well as emotion or drama. It brings excitement and anticipation to the jury. Film makes beautiful pictures and it moves, which creates continuity and flow. It works very well to telescope time. It can be edited in advance for effects so that exactly what you want to say is seen, eloquently. It's in color, which is affecting. It can re-create familiar scenes or bring unusual, unfamiliar settings and activities into the courtroom. It's a very efficient and effective way to tell a story. It's a more easily portable technique for picture-taking outdoors than videotape.

Weaknesses

Pre-conditioned association makes film register in our minds as stories, as fantasy and fiction more than as reality. It's quite costly to make a film—more so than videotape. It requires much more artificial light indoors than videotape. For location shots, you can't see if you got the pictures until the film is developed, several days later. You must turn the lights out and darken the courtroom to see it (a conditioned invitation for a snooze). The projector makes noise as it plays in a confined space. It takes time to set up the projector and the screen and to darken the room, which can break your momentum. We all expect movies to be extremely slick and well done. We have highly developed tastes and expect professionalism; anything less is seen as amateurish and becomes much less effective. The jury knows you'll only show what you want to and that you can "fix it up." Therefore, it loses some credibility. Film looks glamorous and expensive—perhaps a damaging issue. You lose control of the jury totally since the film is doing the telling, not you. That transition is difficult, as you must get them back to seeing and hearing you, a mere mortal, after all the special effects of a film.

Helpful Hints

• Justify to the jury why you're showing a film. Can this be told any other way, or is this the strongest statement? Must the jury see the exact site, building, or street? Do you need "A Day in the Life of. . . .?" If you have good reasons, the film will work. If not, the jury will see it as a glamorous ploy without much merit.

• Use real people doing real things as much as possible. Let the plant foreman narrate and take us on the trip through the plant. (He'll be a witness, too, right?) Let the workers, not an actor, describe their machinery or at least work it with voice-over narration by a professional. Let the plaintiff go to the place of the event and describe it there, if showing it is an important issue.

• Be sure the jury understands who all the players are. Identify the important ones with their names and/or jobs by superimposing their names and titles as you see them talk or work in the film.

• Films should be fairly short—ten to twelve minutes is the maximum.

• Use only professionals, and heed their advice. Film-making is a technical and artistic effort of a very advanced nature. Be very clear as you give your input and ask questions, but let the professionals do their work.

• Create the whole film in a shooting script in advance and make all your changes then. Re-shooting is very costly.

• Find out about videotape. It's cheaper and quicker. The sprockets won't break as it's shown and it plays well through a couple of television sets easily set up in the courtroom in advance.

Overhead Projectors

Strengths

It's an inexpensive and convenient way to prepare visual information and show it to the jury. You can show it in a fully lit room. It creates instant charts, simpler and a little more homemade. Photocopied transparencies can be copied cheaply from books, papers and diagrams. Charts can easily be drawn on the 8" x 11" transparencies, with color. The information blows up to a large screen, visible to all the jurors at once. You can prepare a chart in advance and complete it as it's being seen during your presentation by writing on it. The transparencies allow extra activity and clarity, since you can fill in and underline what seems to be unclear as you go. You can write or draw in color on it as you present. You can leave a transparency on and walk to the screen to continue to point things out. It's excellent for use in showing words—contracts, depositions, and testimony. Its ease of preparation makes it possible for you to quickly respond to a new turn of events in the trial. You can write notes on the frames of the charts to help give you key points to talk about as you show them.

Weaknesses

The projector makes noise. It, and the screen, need setting up in advance or taking time out just before its use. It can be distracting work to run it. It keeps you from making eye contact with the jury. It's hard to keep the transparencies straight until you're quite good at it. The transparencies are a little harder to handle than charts. The thin plastic material is light and more informal-looking than prepared artistic graphs, charts and diagrams, and sometimes doesn't have the same visual weight and impact. The transparencies are not as eloquent in the jury room as charts. You cannot step in front of the projector or the screen, as you would get in the way of the projected image on the screen.

Helpful Hints

• Practice putting transparencies on the projector and writing on them to discover how to do this efficiently.

• Find an effective marking system to show the top and the consecutive numbers of your chart order.

• Organize a table wide enough to keep both the transparencies and projector on it, so you can reach them without much trouble.

• Practice going up to the screen to further explain a diagram. Use a pointer standing to the side so as not to throw a shadow or to obstruct anyone's view.

• Practice pointing to things on the screen while at the projector. Do this with your witness.

• Overhead projectors can be used very successfully to reproduce testimony overnight and thus show current excerpts to the jury. For greatest impact, excerpt and enlarge, underline or isolate the particular passage before you show it on a transparency. Always be sure to show the jury the original with a signature from the court reporter for authentication before you show the enlargement.

• You need a dark, clear image to copy from. Use a photocopy of material rather than the typed original. It reproduces better.

• Use pre-framed transparencies or ones with cardboard frames. They're neater, more rigid and you can write notes on the margins. There are also plastic frames you can re-use.

• To block light from glaring as you change charts put a piece of paper between each chart or turn off the light between changes, covering the dark time with dialogue.

• When you turn the light off between charts the eyes go to the teller; when the light goes on again, eyes switch back to the screen. Use a mercury switch to make it noiseless.

• Transparencies come in blue as well as clear, and it's a little less glaring. There are also negative transparencies that print white letters on a dark ground. These are very effective.

• To keep charts straight as you show them, put alignment pins on the projector as holders so you can drop charts with holes on top right on the pins. Then they won't move.

• Use a pointer on the transparency for focusing attention and for clarity. To focus or pinpoint one area, leave your pointer or pen right on the chart as you go up to the screen and continue to talk. It's best to use pointers at the projector for clarity; go to the screen for dramatic presence.

• To reveal information a bit at a time, place a blank paper under the transparency and block what you want to hide. Then pull the paper down one line at a time.

• Build ideas by flipping transparency overlays over the original basic diagram. Use colored print or colored marking pens.

• To prevent images from "Keystoning" tilt the top of the screen forward, or you can raise the projector high enough so it's shooting straight ahead.

• Don't forget the use of color as a very emotional ingredient and an effective persuader.

• Get professional graphics advice about designing your transparencies. These should be as professional, interesting, well thought out and visually appealing as charts.

The 3M Company can now take any photograph or other opaque printed material and make an overhead projector transparency of the same size or it can blow up a slide and make an 8″ x 11″ transparency of it in minutes, at their regional centers. If you send your material to a regional center it takes 24 hours plus mailing time.

Photographs

Strengths

They're real and believable, with nothing left to the imagination. They put the jury in a place complete with its visual imagery and recognizable forms, rather than an abstract diagram. They stand still (unlike film and video) to be studied and recalled exactly each time. They're not a very expensive process—even the enlargements. They are within our experience, associated with the truth, with newspaper reporting, with recaptured images, and with immediacy.

Weaknesses

They're generally small and must be enlarged to be useful or to be made into slides. You may need several views to make your point, and as you remove each one to show the next, they're not always usable to make a whole statement. Photographs are two-dimensional and cannot show necessary volume or space relationships.

Helpful Hints

• Justify the kinds of photographs you will show and whether that's the best or the only way to make your point.

• Aerial views are extremely helpful to orient place, topography and layout. Close-up images in conjunction with this orientation are extremely useful.

• Use only professional photographers to take, print and/or enlarge your pictures. Poor pictures look amateurish and don't make your points well. Remember—we're a sophisticated, visual society now and photography has graduated to a fine art. We know the difference.

• Make sure your pictures make their point clearly. Don't present too much information at a time. Pinpoint what you want the jury to see by composition and contrast.

Slides

Strengths

They're a quick, clear way to show pictures to many people at once. Color and image reproduce very well. They require only small, compact, portable equipment—an inexpensive reproduction device that can handle many pictures in a small space. Pictures bring variety, pleasure and another point of view.

Weaknesses

You must darken the room (creating the old sleep syndrome). You lose your audience and your eye contact with them. We associate slides with Aunt Harriet's trip to Europe or baby Jean's first steps—i.e., boring. They are static images with no ability to flow or blend into the next scene. Even built-in dissolves don't help since, as soon as the next slide is in place, it's static again. You cannot talk over a slide for more than ten to fifteen seconds at most before people become bored and restless since nothing visual or active is happening and they can register and understand a visual image in two seconds unless it's very complex or unfamiliar. Even then, ten to fifteen seconds seems long. Each change erases the previous picture—there is no chance for comparison or reinforcement. They're not eloquent in explaining concepts—only facts or details. They're not as useful in the jury room as charts are.

Helpful Hints

• Use a Daystar projection device. It is a self-contained screen, projector and slide-tray unit all in one that does not require darkening the room. Since it is self-contained, you can step in front of it without throwing a shadow, and the screen is large enough for the judge and jury to see. (These can be bought or rented.)

• Do not show diagrams as slides. You cannot sustain the interest for long. You cannot change or write on them, and they disappear when you show the next picture. Charts are far better for lists, graphs, etc.

• The best reason for slides is to show pictures. Practice how to make verbal connections to cover changes between slides, and also practice how long to keep each one on. Get a little advice from advertising people who give slide presentations.

• You can repeat certain slides at the end for emphasis or for a lingering last look. Choreograph what goes first, what explains the story and what goes last, like a final chord, for impact.

• Put slides in logical visual order—long shot (overview to orient us), medium shot (isolating the area to analyze) and closeup (a hard, tight look at details). Also make them chronological unless you wish to use a flashback technique. (What happened; let's go back and see why and how.) Be sure the jury is always clear about the subject and oriented to what they're looking at and where it fits.

Videotape

Strengths

It's the visual coin of the realm—familiar to everyone. We all associate the television set with entertainment and pleasure. We also believe television more than film since we're accustomed to getting our news from it and have seen hard, brutal truths in documentaries, breaking news stories and global events there. Videotape plays noiselessly, through a simple television set as opposed to film, which plays through a noisy projector. You don't have to turn out the lights to see it (or even turn them down). It's much cheaper to make than film since videotape requires no developing and is reusable. You can instantly check on whether you got the desired pictures when you go out shooting on location. The editing process is much simpler than film, since sound and picture are edited as one. It flows and can sustain interest much better than static pictures or slides, as it re-creates reality. It can tell stories or zoom in for closeups easily. Like film, it's multidimensional, using sound as well as sight.

Weaknesses

It's still an expensive and time-consuming process. It's hard to go back to repeat an image or pluck out one scene in order to make a point. Stop action freeze-frames don't hold very well. It forces the eye to concentrate on a narrow field of vision, which is tiring. Although you can do it in sections, a videotape statement is generally all of a piece, shown from start to finish, making its impact, and then ending. You, as a lawyer, cannot be involved in its truthtelling; it speaks for itself. Since we expect to be entertained by television, and entertained at a fast pace, dull people speaking on tape and factual data or static images (like depositions) become irritating and boring more quickly than in a live presentation. Therefore, it's not an all-purpose visual aid.

Helpful Hints

• Pick your subjects and be clear about your reasons for using videotape.

• If you need to do a television deposition, try to get it done in a television studio, or at least with two cameras to vary long shots, closeups and medium shots as well as angles, to sustain visual interest. Be sure your witness is lightly made up for the television lights or they'll look ill, tired, tough-guy blue-bearded or perspiring and nervous. Pay attention to the visible background behind the speaker and to the seating arrangement. The tape is on for quite a while.

• Shop for a professional production company. See samples of their work. If you're doing a documentary, after you explain what you want, ask for a story board to be developed that outlines the sequence of the "plot" to be shot as well as showing the images that will show what you want to say. Discuss and revise script and images then. Don't wait till the tape is shot to make changes. Anticipate and get everything agreed upon *before* the shooting and editing or you'll be out a lot more money.

• Don't try to show intellectual concepts on video. That's better in an interaction between you and the jury. Show facts and details, action pictures, evocative scenes and places, clarification of complex processes that only video on location can get.

• The tape should be short—no longer than nine to twelve minutes—because that's the usual length of time between commercials and people are accustomed to that rhythm.

• You can show videotape in sections, stopping the tape to recap and explain further and then starting it again for the next section. This makes for more participation and clarity. Don't count on the freeze-frames; do it in sections with a natural beginning and ending to each one.

• Be sure your playback television monitor is big enough to be seen by all. Also, notice if any light hits the screen and adjust it.

If there is a glare, place a piece of cardboard on top of the set and extend it forward. It will cast a shadow and darken the screen.

In all the above choices, be sure you justify the use of the medium you choose. Is this the best device to tell your story? How about the weaknesses—can you overcome them? Knowing them, is that particular format still worth using? Be knowledgeable about your choices, and then, think about the jury and about what you, before you understood the case, wanted to know and how you wanted to learn it. What should they see? Would this visual explain it best? What else did you want? What else would they need?

* * *

And now, to conclude: Exhibits can be simple. Don't get trapped into thinking that bigger is better and expensive is more. Remember, the reason for making and using visual exhibits is to show rather than to just tell and to clarify by using that most powerful learning sense—sight. Don't forget the basic ingredients of involving the jury, letting *them* see in order to believe, giving them power and independence to learn on their own, and making complex information organized and memorable. Too opulent, glamorous exhibits speak about your client's money, and overload makes juries glassy-eyed. But no do-it-yourself home movies! Make your visuals look professional and interesting.

Stay active with your exhibits. Participate with them. Use them to help you explain. Make them attractive and appealing by being aware of the principles of effective design. Get professional help. Ask questions, and be sure your visuals do what you want them to do. Trust your instincts and your knowledge of juries to help you choose. Be very clear about what you want your exhibit to say and do. Form follows function. And enjoy exploring new modes of communication. They'll expand your horizons as an advocate.

To complete the concepts I raised in this chapter, here is a quote from Judge Rudolph Pierce of the Massachusetts Superior Court on using visual aids:

> I view the challenge of translating technical data into information easily understood by the lay juror as the crucial challenge facing the

trial bar in today's world. Indeed, the viability of our jury system itself (and, with it, the moral authority of the judiciary as a co-equal branch of government) depends in no small measure on the skill of the advocate in translating the complexities of today's ever more convoluted and involved society into terms that can be readily and fairly dealt with. With this premise, then, I favor all sorts of multi-media presentations of evidence—film strips, video tapes, "day in the life of " presentations, diagrams, chalk-talks, the viewer, the use of transparencies and anything else that will enable the jury to actually *understand* what is being presented. It's up to the judges to ensure that the techniques used are fair and do not unduly highlight just one aspect of the evidence. Thus, without detracting in any way from vigorous advocacy, these presentations must be seen as something of a joint venture. The slanted, inaccurate, or unduly prejudicial presentation does more harm than good and ought to be firmly excluded. Any technique that accurately and adequately conveys information, however, ought to be welcomed, explored and utilized to the full. In this regard, reference ought to be made to Federal Rule of Evidence 1006 and its state court counterparts involving the summaries of evidence. It seems to me that computer simulations, graphs, and even video depictions may be admissible if accurately done.

9

NON-VERBAL
COMMUNICATION

Think about the number of ways in which you instantly know the
mood of your husband, wife, children, or colleagues. Or, remember your childhood: how well you knew exactly when your father
was mad or your mother was going to yell at you for something.
This is true not only with familiar people you've shared many experiences with; you also know when you're a hit or when someone's
disinterested.

How do you know? What are the signals? Sit down right now
and write a whole list of clues of how you know your husband or
wife is anxious or upset, how you know when your children have
done something wrong and are feeling guilty, what you remember
of the signals that said, "Father is angry, I'd better not talk to him
now," or when you know you've made a score.

Now look at your list. See how many items describe how that
person looks, the way they sit, tap their foot, clasp their hands,
drum on the table, make eye contact or even snap the evening
paper.

We become automatically more attuned to non-verbal communications whenever we try to evaluate people's feelings. How
people look and act matters more than what they say. The most
important point is that we all do this instinctively and are capable
of making pretty accurate judgments, because unconscious, spontaneous non-verbal communication is actually a much more elo-

quent, dependable truth-teller than words, which are edited and chosen before they are delivered.

Experts agree that between 65 and 93 percent of the impact or meaning of a communicated message is carried by the non-verbal behavior that surrounds an oral message. While verbal language is conscious, rational and *describes* emotion, non-verbal language is unconscious, subjective and *expresses* emotion. The amount of inadvertent communicating you do non-verbally can markedly alter what the jury hears and thinks. This chapter, therefore, will be devoted to an index, a glossary of the forms of non-verbal communication and their perception by people—jurors, lawyers, judges, all of us.

WHY WE OBSERVE EACH OTHER

Our interest in each other comes from a basic need to identify friend or foe. There are endless nuances after that, such as, "Do you really love me?" or, "Can I trust you again?" However, the atavistic instinct for self-preservation is at the core of how we evaluate everyone. We all want to feel prepared, to feel safe and able to handle anything that comes along. Therefore, we have a great need to scrutinize each other, to be able to predict what's happening and what's coming next, to evaluate the mood and quality of any interchange or relationship.

Given such vital motivation, it is little wonder that we have become so good at it and that our instincts are so sharply tuned. Our instincts don't even break the conscious surface when they operate, but speak to us at the subconscious level, where we process and act on them, never really needing to know why or how.

Words vs. Body Language

Non-verbal signals are much more powerful than words because your native language requires only 15 percent of your brain to understand it. But a non-verbal signal is unique and original, not a classifiable symbol, like a word which always means the same thing. Non-verbal language is much more physical and compelling.

It has much more energy than words. It is bigger, involving muscles and tangible parts of the body, as opposed to words, which are more ephemeral and abstract, icons only your brain processes.

Why Non-verbal Language Compels Attention

The brain requires organization. The brain requires that each thing in our experience make some sense, that it have sequence and logic, that it have a beginning, middle and end, that it fits the circumstance, and looks like something we have seen before, especially when dealing with emotion and human experiences, about which we are all instinctive experts. Otherwise it upsets us.

Non-verbal language assails you and demands attention. You automatically want to understand what happened and why it happened. It captures your attention totally as you try to decipher and understand what you see people do so you can assimilate its meaning. Since it is often not directly applicable to what else is going on, i.e., what is being said, non-verbal behavior is almost like an obligato, another sound that is taking place while your mind is absorbing what is considered normal human interchange. It is challenging, often enigmatic, or so blatantly at odds with the situation that it sets up an instant internal dialogue as you fight with yourself to create some logic out of what you hear versus what you see. "He said that, but he doesn't look like he means it," or "He says it's sad but he doesn't sound or act sad."

What Makes Us Notice

People notice non-verbal communication most of all when it differs from the norm. We are quite accustomed to seeing people walk at a normal rate of speed on a street. Think for a moment about how quickly you notice and how you feel when you see someone running. When you see someone suddenly stop or look up. You need to check it out or automatically follow his line of sight to understand what happened to make him do that. This is true in every phase of non-verbal communication. Anything that looks different from what we normally and naturally do, which is not instantly absorbed visually, is something that is worthy of note and predictably will get people's attention. Try standing still and looking up in a crowd. Watch what happens. Since the symbols of common danger or curiosity are easy to recognize, people respond to them automatically. Just about everyone will look up, some persistently, others casually, to see what you're seeing, but they will glance up just the same.

When we see aberrant or unusual behavior, we know that it is in response to something. Normally, the response is to an outside force, but our system is so clear that we will respond or pay attention just as quickly when the stimulus or non-verbal behavior has to do with inner forces. What you are thinking or feeling is reflected in your non-verbal behavior. We automatically measure that against what we think is warranted in a given situation and what behavior normally fits that mood or activity. Deviations from the norm make us automatically register what mood that behavior signifies and even why it is there.

How We Gather Non-Verbal Information

We use our eyes in a certain sequence in pursuing this process. First we look at the face, most particularly the eyes. These windows to our inner selves are the most expressive physical attributes we have. We then look at the whole face to see if the eye expression fits its frame. "Are you consistent with what you're saying?" We check not only the facial expression but also the features to help us judge whether that person is pleasant, attractive, dour, old, young, tough, strong, docile and so on.

Next we go to the posture or the hands. This sequence is a matter of individual habit based on the individual's past experience of what part of the body matters most and what has been a source of information and/or fixation in the past.

The hands are a great source of expression. Because they are free from gravity, with infinite variety of movement possible, and the hidden implication of their ability to do harm, we are quite sensitive to hand gestures.

Posture is the frame on which the body hangs. It tells of physicality and strength, as well as one's attitude toward self.

Stance and spatial closeness register danger very quickly as well as giving many other signals as well.

How We Understand It

Non-verbal signals require that we first go back into our own index, our own reference library, of when we have seen that movement before. What does it remind us of? What does it look like? Is it familiar? What stereotypical gesture is it like and what does it mean? How does it make us feel? This is the first step toward trying to quickly absorb it and make it fit, to understand and put that non-verbal signal in the proper perspective. If that doesn't work, then it requires even more of our attention to understand. It requires more thought, more processing and more commitment from the viewer. Then the non-verbal language becomes another message being delivered at the same time that the voice is speaking, and is much more compelling, as we try to understand and combine it with what is being heard.

The final product of this internal dialogue, setting one set of signals up against another, is what we do, all the time, without ever thinking about it. When it comes to the conscious surface, if it ever does, it sounds like "I don't know why, but I just didn't trust him." "My gut feeling about that is. . . . " "Well, he or she talked a good game but there was just something about him or her that bothered me."

*   *   *

If you agree that the other system of communication, the un-conscious, non-verbal system, is alive in all of us, both as senders and as receivers, then the following guide will be helpful to check out what you see and what it means. It will focus particularly on what the jury sees in you that you might want to be aware of and perhaps work on. In your need to be eloquent, clear and persuasive, habits that get in the way of the jury's hearing you without distraction are important to note. Also, there are many positive communicative uses you can make of non-verbal language that can be very useful for you to know about and incorporate in your repertoire.

FORMS OF NON-VERBAL BEHAVIOR
AND THEIR EFFECT

Eye Contact

Eyes are where we look to uncover the real and private person. We all look into them, deeply, for meaning and for answers. They are the one thing in the face that is most uniquely different, from person to person. There is color in them, a sense of life, a shine and reflection in them. Eyes change shape. You can voluntarily change the shape as you squint, stare, glare or close them. They have lids which can hide them and shut the world away. They cry, involuntarily, and express emotion when the rest of you is trying very hard to deny it. They show anger and hostility before almost any other part. In general, they show the unique inner qualities that all of us have and many of us try to hide. That's why we look to eyes most of all when we want to get to know someone.

Eye Contact is Commitment

The jury looks at your eyes because your eyes will give them your commitment. Further, when you make eye contact with them, your eyes give them great power. You not only say, "I see you," you also say, "Look at me, I will let you see me." As you make eye contact, the juror is looking at your soul, your sincerity, your intention, as much as you are at his or hers. Jurors use contact with your eyes most often to find the truth, while your mouth is trying to say something that you may have decided is a better idea.

Eye Contact Makes Juries Feel
Important

Eye contact makes them feel recognized. It makes them know that you really understand who the consumers of your information are, that they are the center, the focus, the people you're trying to tell this to. When you look at them, you acknowledge their existence and their uniqueness. You're not speaking to the multitudes, "to whom it may concern," nor are you speaking to hear yourself talk. There is a link to the jury when you make eye contact and that is very important.

Eye Contact is Riveting

Eye contact makes people pay attention. You can grab a juror and cause him to listen by the force with which you look at him and the implied demand that he look back at you. It also focuses the jury's attention. If you keep looking at something or someone, soon everyone else will look there, too, just like looking up on a crowded street as I mentioned earlier.

Eye Contact Makes You Vulnerable

Eye contact is often hard to do. Just for fun, wherever you're reading this, try to make eye contact with someone and hold it for a while. What happens? It's startling, isn't it? It makes both of you feel uncomfortabale after just a little while and you find yourselves looking away. Now try to do it on purpose with someone else and tell them to do it back to you. What happened? You laughed, didn't you? Both of you giggled, right? That always happens because you're shocked at being so instantly vulnerable and at confronting another person so blatantly and overtly.

We all walk around all day with our armor on, saying, "I can control what anybody knows about me. I would never show this. I don't want them to know about that. I will handle it." And suddenly there you are—bald, bare, naked—when you look each other directly in the eye. In that sudden moment, you find vulnerability—theirs and yours. You slice through the facade. This is hard to do given our need for privacy and secrecy. It becomes embarrassing, and most people flinch and turn away. But it's a very good exercise for you to experience. You need to learn how to make eye contact, to dare to be out front, committed *and* vulnerable. Not only is it a vital tool to keep an audience's attention, but if it embarrasses you and you look away, you'll look evasive, like you are avoiding them, you have something to hide or you're not really forthright and honest. Wavering in your eye contact or avoiding eye contact with the jury makes you look suspicious or uncommitted to them and your case.

Eye Contact Gives Reassurance

Holding your witness in contact with you through your eyes gives him a sense of stability, and connection to his friend in court. It becomes a lifeline or an anchor to hold onto. It also tells the jury you won't let them go, when you are addressing them.

Eye Contact Gives Information

Watching reactions tells you who's nervous, who's getting angry, who's bored and not listening, who's confused, who disagrees. Whether it's a witness or the jury, you gather vital information when you look.

Eye Contact Energizes You

You get feedback from looking. The jury will give you energy and approval or skepticism and negative responses. Either of these can galvanize you into action. Approval sets you up and makes you feel like "you're doing just fine, keep it up." Seeing disapproval or, at the least, confusion, pushes you to try harder and think quickly of another way to explain. Watching your witness or the opposing witness gives you a clear sense of what he's doing and what you should do next.

Eye Contact Says Accusation

When someone looks in your eyes, accuses you of something and holds eye contact, it is twice as intimidating as only hearing the words. You feel called to attention and forced to answer back in some fashion because you are being watched. So, in cross-examination, eye contact is invaluable as a technique for intimidating opposing witnesses.

Eye Contact Says Sincerity

The jury notices how much eye contact you make with your witnesses when you talk to them and, most of all, when you listen. They notice when you look away and when you look back; they check it against the standard of what's being said to see if you're sincere and attentive enough.

Generally, then, eye contact is the first non-verbal signal. Master how to achieve and maintain it and when and why to use it.

Hands

After the face and eyes, the hands are the most telling aspect of the human body. They are free to move. They do not fight gravity. They are eloquent because they are parted at the end into five fingers that can make for an endless variety of shapes, movements, strength and grace.

Hands are really extraordinary. They are used for violence, for gentleness, for accusation, for affection, for writing, for strength and for our amazing ability to use tools and rise above our four-legged neighbors. They are extremely important in explanation, as an adjunct to who we are and what we mean.

Since hands have a potential for doing harm, wanting to show that you mean no harm means showing what you are doing with your hands. Extending the right hand in a handshake, for example, means a benign approach to someone, actually an outreach and a reassurance against harm.

Looking back on history and seeing the symbolic vestiges that remain in our society today we see how hands were always used to show intention. The salute, for example. The Romans originally developed a salute in which you clenched your right fist and raised your right hand to shoulder level, to show unity and that there was no weapon in the hand since most of us are right-handed.

During the Middle Ages was when we developed the traditional salute that we see now, where the right hand comes up over the right eye. In those times, knights wearing armor used to ride around with their visors down. In order to show friendship, they identified themselves by pushing up the visor with their right hand, which then came to rest above the right eyebrow. It not only showed the face of a friend, not foe, but also exhibited the weapon-less right hand. That gesture remained as only a symbolic greeting but, to this day, the atavistic concept of an open visible hand is still important as reassurance.

Open Hands Are Eloquent

Pick up your hands and look at them. Turn them over on both sides. Now relax them, palms up. When they are relaxed, the fingers are slightly curved. In order to open them fully, you have to make a conscious effort to straighten the fingers and extend the hand. That means that if you intend to be giving or outreaching, you must invest some effort in it. Look at the shape and the gesture of an extended, palm-up hand. What adjectives describe it? Open? Generous? Giving? Combine it with extending the arm. Asking? Now turn your hand over, still fully extended. What does that look like? Calming? Benign? Move it up and down. What does that call to mind? Reassurance? Patting someone? Each movement speaks and evokes ideas, doesn't it?

Closed Hands Mean Tension

Now clench your hands and see how that feels. It requires even more effort. You not only bend the fingers down, but you also clasp the thumb over them to hold them in a fist. Do it hard. Feel your arm muscles tighten. Notice your neck, back and shoulders respond. Look at your face as you do it. Your expression changes, doesn't it. Does your jaw clench? Your lips pinch? Your eyes grow narrow and cold? It creates not only the symbol of a fist as a weapon but the symbol of tightness, of withholding, of anger and potential threat. There is tension within the speaker. Holding your hands closed says that you're holding back some energy which would normally express itself through the free use of the hands and relaxed fingers, as well as the rest of the body.

So, open hands equal sincerity, generosity, entreaty and lack of concealment, and closed hands are tense and secretive, some-times even threatening.

Hidden Hands Look Furtive

Hands behind the back or in the pockets have particular meaning. If we talk about wanting to see your hands because they are such an extension of you and your intentions, then we also want to be sure that you are consistent and sincere at all times, that you're not giving us a double message. While you may be speaking softly and in a friendly manner, if the jury sees tight, clenched hands, nervous, flicking gestures or hands held behind the back in a military posture, this automatically tells them you're not being totally honest. If you're holding on to your wrists, rather than letting go, perhaps it's because you don't trust what else you would do. (Remember that famous gesture of Peter Sellers in "Dr. Strangelove," when he kept holding onto his hand because every time he let go of it the arm would fly up in a Nazi salute?) When we see people with their hands closed, clasped or clasped and hidden behind their backs there is the feeling of tension or withdrawal from an open and outreaching communication process.

Hands in the Pockets for Men

These have quite a different image. Stand up and look at yourself in the mirror right now and put your hands in your pockets. It automatically calls to mind a whole series of male movie star stereotypes: Jimmy Stewart, Gary Cooper, John Wayne, shuffling one foot behind the other, kind of relaxed and informal. As a man, it says to the jury that you are in a more relaxed and informal mode than when you are at your Sunday best formally making a speech. People don't normally make a speech with their hands in their pockets.

Some judges don't like it. I hear lawyers criticizing other lawyers for doing it. I do not mean to suggest it to you one way or another; I only mean to tell you what the implications are and when you might therefore want to use it. It is an informal gesture, implying ease, effortlessness and a generally comfortable state of being. For those people who do fidget a great deal, it gives them something to do with their hands until they get themselves in order. One hand in the pocket also gives you a chance to gesture with the other. This creates a sort of interesting midpoint between being relaxed and informal and also being active and involved.

I know a 6'4" ex-football player, solidly built, of an altogether imposing size, who is a superb and powerful trial lawyer. He could be a rather intimidating figure in the courtroom, except for the fact that he tries every case with both hands in his pockets for the entire trial. This instantly gives such a disarming, relaxed kind of an image that the jury relates to him quite differently than if he stood up, squared those football shoulders, looked down from his lofty height and proceeded to boom out his message.

This is a unique, personal approach and works for him, but as a rule of thumb, I'd suggest one hand in a pocket, not two. It leaves one free to gesture, and looks less blatant and confrontive than two hands tend to be, although my friend carries it off to feel like, "Aw shucks, just curious. Just gonna ask you a few questions." Or "Y'know, I was just thinking. . . . "

Hands in the Pockets for Women

Curiously, this gesture creates unique issues for women lawyers. Since the initial stereotypical image it brings to mind is the male cowboy, it can be misunderstood. It looks tougher and more aggressive on a woman and not as casual. It sometimes doesn't look serious enough. In either case, I suggest you use it sparingly. If you are a free-moving, restless, physical woman, it (just one hand) might be in your repertoire but since it is a gesture that can be misunderstood, I'd be careful of it. Look at yourself in the mirror. What image does it portray? If you like it, go ahead, but notice your jury's age level to predict if they'd see you as a competent, executive, professional woman or Annie Oakley.

Using Two Hands

Usually people gesture with one hand, but some people use both. Richard Nixon was quite well known and caricatured for using that famous chopping motion with both hands. If using both is your natural tendency, leave it alone. But do understand that it can be a rather harsh gesture.

Two hands have a finite quality to them—"It's as big as this," or, "This is definite," rather than a one-handed gesture, which is lighter and more vague. One hand leaves the ending of the gesture to the viewer's own imagination, while two hands speaks of the exactness of your version and your view. It's a strong gesture and can be used if what you mean is to be very definite. One hand, palm up, moving laterally, is the ultimate gesture of sincerity and a desire to explain. Palm down is negative and final.

Finger Pointing is a Problem

Pointing your finger looks like a remonstrance or an accusation, reminiscent of all the times you got in trouble as a kid. Although you only mean to use it for emphasis in addressing the jury, it often looks like you're pointing at them accusingly. It makes them feel defensive.

It's also a gesture that is too attacking to use on a witness. If you find yourself doing it, just open your hand. Five fingers are benign; one is not.

Holding an Object in Your Hand

Be careful what you hold in your hand. Don't point with a pen or pencil. It has a point. It's a slightly hostile weapon. You are not writing or marking something down in your book; at that moment, you are talking. The jury expects you to be free. Also, a point implies that if you touch someone with it, it will make a mark on his or her clothing. So it's accusing and slightly lethal looking. It's also removed and impersonal. You're sending your energy and intention through an inanimate object, not your natural self. It shows a power differential between you and them.

What else could you hold in your hand besides a pen or pencil? Some people want to know what to use to gesture with because they have such difficulty with their hands. You might think in terms of holding your notes, which are paper. It is a little harder to hold the legal pad since it has a hard edge to it and it's not very graceful or eloquent. It doesn't bend easily. It's clumsy. It becomes a symbolic tablet before you and gets in the way. I would suggest that you get rid of it, because then your hand is free to make many more gestures than only waving the pad up and down or back and forth.

Taking off your glasses or gesturing with them is very effective. It spells intimacy. It says, "Let's get closer to the truth," or "Look, let me level with you." This gesture is probably reserved for people who wear the little half-glasses for reading. For the others there's a major drawback. If you wear glasses all the time, taking them off will suddenly strike you blind and you will be addressing a sea of split-pea soup. Just be sure, if you do it, that you know where the jury is before you take them off. . . .

Gestures

Gesture is actually a physical extension and manifestation of what you're saying. In an effort to make yourself clear, you are moved to reach beyond mere words to emphasize, underline, call attention or make clearer. It adds a physical dimension to oral presentation.

What gestures you use come from the parts of your body that you feel are most eloquent or where you express stress. Mainly, however, your gestures are defined by your background. If your family was very animated and physically expressive, that lasts. You adopt the gestures you've seen, even some you didn't like. It's fun to watch a videotape of yourself talking and recognize, with a start, that you sound and act just like one of your parents, a sibling or an admired relative. We also adopt gestures we like from the heroes or heroines of some point in our early lives. But since gestures are so unconscious, we're hard put to consciously add new ones as adults.

Gestures are quite recognizable, but we also indulge in some that have no apparent meaning. They are usually the spill-over from stress and nervousness. These are the most noticeable to the jury since they take the longest to understand and categorize and do not automatically relate to anything you're saying.

The most important single truth about gestures is that they must be consistent with what is being said and with your own basic style and persona. If not, they register as bizarre and untrue, and render the communication given untrustworthy.

Gesture is Energy

Gesture is not only eloquent and narrative, it is also a visible extension of the physical energy you expend in your work. It shows eagerness and excitement and demonstrates your level of commitment. Not only does it raise the energy level of the lawyer, but it adds to the interest and energy of a passive jury.

Gesture is Punctuation

Gesture is very valuable as abstract movement when used for punctuation to show a new idea or another topic. Speaking in outline form, gestures can help underline, emphasize, connect or isolate key points. Describing a list of points by saying "1-2-3" as you chop the air or show each finger reinforces the order of your thinking and the points you make. Gesture helps the jury delineate and organize. It can be a visual reinforcement or embodiment of your text or outline on the printed page. Gesture in your verbal presentation helps you to clarify things.

Gesture is Description

In using description and word pictures, gesture can embellish words like "big" or "very small." It can help visualize the shape of "a winding road" or "an overhanging light," extending the jury's vision and helping the jury to see and imagine more. It can eliminate many words and make a statement more succinct and memorable. It's also irresistible. How else could you describe a spiral staircase?

Gesture Can Never be Arbitrary

Gesture must grow from content. Asking "Should I use my hands?" "Should I move here?" or hearing the oft-repeated complaint, "I never know what to do with my hands," worries me. Hands are useful only if they grow out of something else. A gesture is only meaningful if it's needed; if it actually punctuates, clarifies or enlarges what you're talking about. It doesn't have any meaning at all if it's something you do because you think it's time to make a gesture.

Gesture has to be consistent with what you're saying and what you're doing. Its main impetus is intention. What are you trying to say and what can you do that will help people understand?

Gesturing Towards a Witness

Sometimes a lawyer has a tendency, with unconscious gestures, to emphasize his own irate approach to his subject or what is being said, especially in cross-examination. Be careful that your gestures don't betray you. If you point a finger, the jury will get involved in a duel with you. Instead, find ways to use gestures similar to those you used with *your* witness. Try using your voice, language, and spatial relationships instead. They may be a little safer.

The same concepts apply with the opposing lawyer. Since the jury is waiting for a fight, see if you can find ways that don't symbolically look too pugnacious. Jurors often feel that somebody with a short fuse may be losing, and gestures betray your level of anger and impatience.

Repeated Gestures

Many lawyers will repeat a gesture from force of habit. For example, one holds the thumb and forefinger together while he's explaining. Another holds the fingers of both hands pressed together, almost as if in prayer. Very often, these are gestures that you saw your father or an admired older person make. These gestures looked authoritative to you so you tucked them away in the back of your mind. Now, quite unconsciously, they come out. These gestures matter because, although they unconsciously remind *you* of other authorities in your life, they may be a confrontational or enigmatic image for jurors.

If you hold your hands together, think of separating them. Notice and just open them. Pick up something or put a hand in your pocket. The prayerful gesture is too parochial and reminiscent of a preacher, just as the pointed finger reminds us of a teacher or an irate parent. They both imply a certain kind of pressured correctness which doesn't give you the freedom to be the multifaceted person you'd really like to present. These gestures are quite rigid and they linger in the mind. By the way, rubbing the nose looks nervous and not neat. Avoid it.

In general, any gestural habit that you have and continue to repeat looks false and becomes useless or attracts such attention that it becomes more important than your message. When you use one gesture for many kinds of description or emphasis, it becomes a little troublesome to the jury because then it looks unreal. If you are talking about different things, you should be able to free yourself to do different gestures that match what you are talking about.

The best way to discover if you use repeated gestures is to do an argument or opening statement before a videotape camera and then play back and study it. You see your habitual gestures most clearly when you fast forward the tape as you watch it. Regular speed tells the story, too. It's just slower and a little more agonizing to watch. Fast forward not only shows you your gestures, it'll give you a laugh at the same time and is therefore a kinder way to do self-criticism.

Misunderstood Gestures

There is one classic pattern I see men doing with some regularity. I call it the "Fig Leaf." It's a kind of self-protective posture where both hands are clutched or clasped directly in front of you, at the level of the crotch. That's the essence of a self-protective statement and looks just like "Help! Don't hurt me!" to the jury. That's hardly the image you want to portray, I'm sure. If you do this, stop before it's misunderstood.

Put one hand on a table or podium. Put one hand in your pocket. Hold your notes until you get over it. Since that particular image is so noticeable, it becomes fascinating to the jury and eventually injurious to you.

Aggressive Gestures

Putting your hands on your hips is a confrontational, aggressive gesture and rather pugnacious (go look at it). For women, it looks petulant and impatient. One hand on a hip is less so but still gives the impression of some irritation or accusation. Leaning the top of the body forward can look pugnacious, especially if connected to threatening words or facial expressions. Be aware of these.

Gesture is useful and eloquent, but many lawyers find using hands and gestures difficult or feel self-conscious using them. To discover more about creating natural gestures and hand movements, look at the exercises in Chapter 10 to help you develop your own natural style.

POSTURE AND STANCE

How you stand, how you take your piece of the turf and what shape your body creates in space is another important silent statement.

There is effort in fighting gravity. How aggressively you fight it, how upright you are, how secure and comfortably your body overcomes the downward pressure and still looks relaxed and free—that's what your posture comes from. It tells others how you feel about yourself and how positively or negatively you react to outside forces, natural or man-made.

Shoulders

Round Shoulders

The shoulders are the biggest give-away. Shoulders rounded forward have a slightly apologetic look and give a withdrawn, internally focused, unsure impression. A sunken chest, rounded back and sloped shoulders look physically weaker and insecure. There is an air of incompetence and self-doubt.

Thrust-back

Shoulders thrust back sometimes look belligerent, pugnacious or aggressive, especially if the chest pushes out at the same time. Since they are hyperextended past the natural center line of the body, they look tense.

Squared Shoulders

Easy, natural, relaxed, squared shoulders with arms and hands hanging effortlessly make people look more self-assured, stronger, more competent and positive, more physically healthy and more eager to be involved. Your arms move more naturally and the chest and back are relaxed and in alignment.

Head

Squared shoulders and straight spine give the head a proper base to sit on so it can look out clearly and directly. Round shoulders cause the head to thrust forward and the eyes look up from under the brows rather than straight out. The major cure is the classic one of practicing walking with a book balanced on your head. Working out at a gym helps strengthen and realign your musculature. It's worth doing. (See Chapter 10 for exercises to improve posture.)

Stance

Another aspect of how you stand on the ground is stance—where you put your feet and how you distribute your weight. Here again, people make assumptions about you by the way you stand. In different regions of the country there are different responses to and stereotypes about stance. What works in Texas won't necessarily work in Boston, but the basic generalities are true everywhere.

To understand this better, stand in front of a mirror and try these experiments. Do what all the following italicized headings say and look at the result. Then read the effect they can have.

Standing Balanced Equally on Both Feet, with Feet Slightly Apart

You are grounded, in balance. It is hard to push you over. Your weight is distributed equally on both feet and you are much less vulnerable. This stance makes you look solid and secure, in charge and in control of what you're doing. You're able to push off and go at anything, in either direction.

Standing with Most of Your Weight on One Foot

In this easy posture, able to pick the other foot up off the ground, you are now actually quite vulnerable. I could knock you over because all your weight is on one side and I need only tip you a little to push you off. This stance is softer, easier, shows trust that no one will knock you over. It's much more relaxed than the first one, more casual.

Putting Your Feet Very Close Together

If you stand with your feet together, actually touching, your weight equally distributed between both of them, you are still quite vulnerable and could be pushed over because you have a very narrow base. But you're giving another message. You're not at ease, you're uptight. Look at it. What words come to mind? Prim, proper, correct, exact. It looks tense because one must make a great effort to stand that way. It is neither comfortable nor physically efficient. Your weight is not well distributed because your shoulders and hips are much wider than the small balance point made by your feet, and the balance is all wrong. People don't naturally stand that way; it takes effort to "come to attention" and hold it. It says you are aiming to please, to be above reproach. Such a stance would make the jury wonder about your rigidity, your tension and insecurity.

Standing with Feet Wide Apart

This is unnatural and confrontational. It exaggerates your solid base, implying that you need to be ready to move, ready for anything. The implication is that you expect trouble or hostility. It looks aggressive, macho and unduly physical if you only mean to talk.

Shifting Your Weight from One Foot to the Other

This looks like you're anxious or uncomfortable, not only with your stance, but with the job at hand. Of course, standing for a long time can make you restless, but such constant shifting makes the jury feel like you're still in temporary quarters and that you haven't yet finally settled down to your space and the business at hand. You seem distracted, trying to find your own comfortable place before you can get to telling them what it is they're supposed to be hearing.

Leaning (On a Table, or a Lectern)

If you lean on something, that, strangely enough, doesn't look as though you're leaning for support, but rather that you are in a more relaxed mode. You look easy and not so charged up. It shows confidence and trust to lean against a table or a lectern without fear. The implication is that someone *could* pull it away from you and make you lose your balance, but you feel so competent that this wouldn't faze you. Actually, you have trust and expect good things, not bad, to happen to you. It looks unstressed and easy and speaks of your feeling so relaxed that you needn't stand erect but can just "ooze" over the furniture a little.

When to Lean

At the beginning of your opening, or of your direct, cross or final argument, when you need to get the adrenals going fast, leaning against something, though remaining upright, is useful. You have just been sitting and now need to stand up and charge through the gate, running, all at once. It is helpful to ground yourself, to lightly lean against or just touch a piece of furniture for stability so that you don't wander aimlessly or shift your weight. Trying to get grounded and find a position or a posture that finally makes you feel comfortable, rather than just standing in the middle of the air, is hard. When you start talking, adrenalin surges into all parts of your body and causes a great deal of extraneous movement. But if you lean against or touch something that is solid and "there," it seems to lean back giving you some support and strength. It also grounds you solidly so that you don't wander while you're getting yourself going. Then, when you're feeling comfortable enough, you can move, all of a piece; purposefully, not aimlessly.

Establishing a Comfortable Stance

In the courtroom, establish your posture and your stance this way: Get up and go to your chosen spot. Find your turf. Take time to find your space. Take a deep breath. Think for a moment about what you're going to say and what you want the jury to know. Then, standing still, start to talk. That is a calm image for the jury, which allows them to focus on what is being said and what is being answered, rather than being concerned about whether you'll ever get yourself in order. And it's a calm place for you to get up to speed.

Looking Self-Contained

If you are involved in a very bitter exchange, a trial where there is much hostility and heat between the lawyers, where the issues at stake are very emotional and there is a great deal of battling to be done, it is a good thing to discover ways to ease up during the trial by being conscious of where and how you stand. Start off in a comfortable position before you leap out. It will soothe you. Stand up slowly. Recognize how some of these stances you've just experimented with feel to you and how they look as well. What effect do they have on the jury? What effect do they have on you? This will help you to choose one over another.

Showing Another Side

Experiment in front of a mirror when you prepare your trial, to get a clear image of how you want to look. It is important for you to show some vulnerability sometimes. Therefore, as you see these images of possible stances, choose the times when you would like to use the more vulnerable and human ones that let you look thoughtful, internally reaching for something, and when you might want the two-fisted "don't mess with me" stance. This is true for men but especially true for women. Women should select their posture and stance after they experiment with how it looks and how it feels. What looks tough for a man may be all wrong for a woman. A woman just standing quietly, easily, is most compelling.

Movement

Here's a curious fact. Movement in the courtroom is controversial. Many judges require lawyers to stand still and use a lectern. In some jurisdictions, lawyers must examine witnesses while sitting at counsel table. What are the judges actually restricting?

In my conversations with judges, the reasons I hear are that it is "more dignified," "more serious," "not so distracting," "not too intimidating to witnesses."

Let's look at this issue more closely, at its most basic.

Movement is life. From birth, we respond to moving stimuli and we respond to stimuli by moving. The body energizes itself through movement; we stretch, we get up and walk around when we're tired of being in one spot or one focus. We express ourselves best, most naturally, directly and unselfconsciously, through movement—hugging, hitting, running away or toward, pointing, gasping, jumping up with glee, surprise or pain. As an audience, watching any aspect of human behavior or communication, we are automatically drawn to something that makes movement.

If one of the reasons for making restrictions on movement in the courtroom is what's best for the jury, the above-mentioned insights should give pause. Such restrictions breed artificiality and fly in the face of the most natural behavior for lawyer and jury.

Jurors need the surrogate movement of lawyers in the courtroom to re-charge them in their passive state. Their eyes become unfocused from concentrating on a stationary target. They're less likely to pay attention and will lose concentration more quickly if all they hear is a voice and they see nothing move. These are some universal truths. But there are additional components.

The lectern is a most intimidating structure, calling forth pejorative images of people who tell us what to do or think, who criticize us, who pontificate; people who are different, singled out, perhaps better, more important or more powerful than we are. Is this the best kind of image an advocate can use to reach out, to clarify and explain to the jury? Is the lectern and all it connotes a more fertile, reassuring setting for the jury to focus on than a human being who is fully involved and committed, drawing closer, moving, trying to help them understand in a natural, energized way?

Not only is the lectern a visual barrier to making contact with the jury, and thus the issues of the case, but sitting at the counsel table is even more so.

Sitting hinders the ability to produce clear, audible speech for many people. It sharply dampens the energy flow of the lawyer and that between lawyers and witnesses. Thus the content of an examination is impinged upon, and the jury cannot relate as well to it. Sitting lowers the level of concentration of the lawyer as he or she fights his or her charged-up body to be calm and sit quietly, artificially, while every pore and gland is in its most highly sensitized state.

Can this help the trial to be more fairly and forcefully presented? Does this give the client the best chance for his or her lawyers to be at the top of their form?

So much for my advocacy of movement in the courtroom. I hope to develop a dialogue around this issue with the powers that be.

Now, for those who are permitted to move.

When to Move or Change Positions

When you are tired, one of the best things to energize you is walking. Do so. Force yourself to start walking. Standing still drains you even further, and that is the time for you to break and move. This makes your muscles discharge more electrical energy to your head, revitalizing you. Try not to fall into a rigid posture or stillness during each of the aspects of the trial.

Another idea is to use movement as demarcations and visual punctuation for various sections within your opening statement, your argument or examinations. Going to another spot makes the jury turn over the page they've been mentally writing on.

When to Leave the Lectern

I have already discussed the lectern throughout the book. Remember what that image means, how often you should leave it, and the reasons that you would like to move yourself to the side, to give that sense of warmth and greater informality.

If you are only using the lectern to rest your notes upon, by all means, leave it whenever you wish to signal the jury that you're starting a new subject.

Leave it whenever you want to move into something that is tender, emotional or sensitive.

Another time to leave the lectern is for transition, when you wish to go from a series of facts to a series of impressions and descriptions by the witness.

Of course, in your address to the jury, it is always a good idea to leave the lectern as much as possible because that's the time when you want to be with them, on their side, hardly distanced from them.

Walk and Talk

Walking and talking is another issue. Some people are pacers. Some people's energy level causes them, at all times, to need more physical expression as an outlet for the amount of adrenal energy they are putting out. It's not just the energy to ask questions that you must handle. It's also the resultant surge of energy that comes from your tension and anxiety as well as your concentration. If that's your situation, then it's a good idea to walk and talk because it would be more destructive for you to withhold your natural behavior. You would put out other signals that would let the jury know there was an enormous amount of physical tension building up. The jury would see and hear it in your voice, your body language, your rhythm and pace. So, give yourself permission to move more, knowing that that's who you are. However, be sure it's tempered with quiet times, with times of stillness, so the jurors can concentrate better and feel some nuance and contrast in what you are saying.

Walking and talking indicates a more casual delivery than just standing still. Therefore, walk and talk during less important matters or as lead-ins and transitions. Walk and talk as you fill in or amplify. Knowing the variety of issues in your case, you know that not everything can or should be introduced with the same steady outpouring of energy and emphasis. Pick your times, for contrast and interest.

Movement Creates Interest

Another aspect of walking and talking is that you are filling the jury with more of a sense of involvement, purpose and activity than they normally would have if they only sat and watched you standing still. It takes more concentration to follow a moving target which generates interest as the eye continues to change focus against a changing background. It's a challenge to listen and follow movement, making the jury stay with you.

Cover Your Thinking

Walking is an excellent way to cover your thinking time. It's always a problem in a trial to find a way to think without too long a pause so the jury doesn't sense that you're at a loss for words or ideas. Walking covers the gaps and, like a pause or silence, it gets the jury interested in what will happen next. But remember, when you are ready to deliver the zinger, the key question or the focusing point, stand still. When you stop, it is almost like an exclamation point. This causes the jury to notice, to pay attention and to listen hard to what comes next.

Go to Your Notes

Walking is not only a good way to cover thinking time, it can cover going to your notes so you can formulate what you'll say next. The jury understands about your notes; they give you credit for your preparation and permission to look at them from time to time. Walking to them is both purposeful and self-explanatory. This is especially effective if you walk slowly and deliberately, exhibiting no panic. You look very much in control. It makes a break in the steady stream of talk and it does give you a graceful way to collect your thoughts, check on what else you wanted to say or rephrase something.

Some lawyers cover this particular moment by asking the judge's permission, saying, "Your Honor, if I may have just a moment . . ." That also gives the jury a feeling that you are in control, that you don't feel desperate. The fact of your stopping, at any time, gives them a greater sense of your control than non-stop talking just so long as you handle it with seeming ease and purpose.

Walking During Cross-Examination

If you are doing a cross-examination, you might walk and begin a question at the same time. Then, when you stop, turn to the witness and say, "Isn't that a fact?" "Isn't it true?" or "Didn't you?" it makes all eyes turn from you directly to the witness, almost as if they were following a dotted line. Stopping is almost like a signal to look at what is about to happen next. The jurors, as well as you, wait expectantly for the answer, which wouldn't have quite the anticipatory build-up if you stood still, asked the whole question and then simply stopped at the end with, "Isn't that a fact?"

Walk with a Purpose

Be careful not to walk in a random fashion or to stop in the middle of a sentence. That looks strange. The jury will wonder, "Why did he stop and yet keep right on talking? Why in the middle of a sentence? There was nothing within the sentence that caused him to do that." Stopping "out of synch," only brings a feeling of vague discomfort or a lack of coordination and disjointedness. It becomes harder for the jury to follow. You need to give a smooth progression and logical transitions to the times you walk and stop.

Don't Pace

A word of caution: Don't be a pacer. The feverish nature of pacing and the repetitive rhythm you set up makes the judge and jury irritated and sea-sick. Make every movement count.

Coordinate your movements with what you're saying. Save movement for drama, emphasis or release; don't squander it.

*   *   *

Movement, then, is valuable for both lawyers and jurors. For lawyers, it relieves tension and keeps you functioning with every part of yourself working to do the best job you can. For jurors, it piques interest, changes focus, helps to clarify and energizes the proceedings for maximum attention.

Spatial Relationships

Whether to move is one issue. Where to move is another.

Everyone has a sense of territory or turf. We have become quite familiar with this through books and documentaries which describe this phenomenon in the animal kingdom, but we are not as keenly or consciously aware that this is true for humans as well. We are only aware of it when we feel errors of commission towards ourselves or when we watch others do it. When we sense that someone is too close or that they are invading what should be neutral territory, danger signals go off. Our deep-seated instincts about this are so finely tuned that we pay very little conscious attention to when we need to protect ourselves or to each other's sense of space and privacy. We just automatically do it.

Notice people walking on a busy street. The subliminal dance, the basketball feints we do to keep from bumping, confronting or otherwise touching each other are marvelous to see. Ride on a bus, or subway. See how we startle and instantly adjust when we accidentally touch someone or sit too close. Such a highly developed sense is of great value to jurors in the courtroom and they call on it to help them judge behavior throughout the trial.

How We Develop Spatial Criteria

Early conditioning. Instinctive spatial responses are developed based on personal and cultural needs and our interaction with our environment. The need for body space and personal distancing are much affected by growing up in an apartment, a city or on a ranch; by being accustomed to riding in a car, on a horse or on public transportation; by being small or tall, strong or non-physical, young or old, a man or a woman. Our early conditioning tells us what's comfortable and permissible, what's ordinary or strange, how our bodies have learned to respond to physical closeness or the need for room. It also gives us a clear vision of what is culturally acceptable behavior for our sexual roles; fathers shake hands with sons and hug daughters; boys scuffle in the schoolyard and play tackle football; girls don't fist fight but do put their arms around friends. All of these early experiences leave strong impressions about our comfort with personal space and closeness as well as what is seemly, acceptable social space-behavior in groups or with strangers.

Personal vision and confidence. For each of us, spatial needs change with how we feel about ourselves and where we are in our lives. They are affected by how we judge each situation and where we perceive danger or harm, whether to ourselves or to others.

We vary the amount of territorial privacy we need based on how we feel about other people, how much basic trust we have and what our past experiences have taught us as well as our own sense of self-confidence. Only consent and invitation allows us to transcend normal spatial barriers for intimacy. Feeling anger or threat increases the natural need for physical distancing.

Cultural factors. There are external factors that affect spatial closeness as well. Culturally, we vary tremendously in what is allowed between men and between men and women. Mediterranean men stand much closer to each other than we do, touching and embracing as a matter of course. This gets the Anglo-Saxon American male very nervous! Frenchmen kiss women's hands; we shake. Frenchmen kiss men on both cheeks; we think that's silly. In the good old USA, Western and Southern men, who live closer to the soil and to physical involvement, slap each other on the back, while Easterners stay cool in their white-collar format and consider a handshake quite enough, thank you.

Men vs. Women

For women, getting close has connotations other than it does for men. In many ways, it connotes sexuality rather than a combative threat. Women do not see physical response as their answer to conflict or threat. That isn't built into their culture and it's not what they learned to do. Women respond to threat or violence by trying to talk their way out of it. Unlike men, whose fists clench when confronted, who tested themselves by scuffles in the schoolyard, women expect to find verbal ways to handle such a problem. They handle conflict and emotions in alternative ways because they weren't trained to resort to physical blows. Therefore, women feel extremely threatened by someone who is big and tall mainly if he moves in a threatening way and looks menacing. They see no equality of options there. They can only hope they are *clever* enough, because they are not *strong* enough to handle it. On the other hand, big, gentle men give the feeling of comfort and security. Women are ever on the alert for the invasion of their territory by physical intimacy. That's where the cultural bans lie. Yet women are also allowed to show physical affection and warmth through contact from an early age. In general, women allow people to get much closer to them than men do, especially in relationships with the same set.

Techniques in the Courtroom

Now let us tie this information directly to the courtroom. Here are some general principles of human territorial behavior and how they also operate in a trial:

• A territorial imperative or invisible spatial shield exists for us all, yet it is different in degree for each of us and different as the situation demands.

• You must be an astute observer to understand enough about a situation to know whether you are permitted to get close and whether observers, in this case jurors, will feel that you have trespassed, according to their innate sense of correct and acceptable behavior for that situation.

• Variations in our culture tell us about men and women, women and women, men and men. Since men have traditionally thought in terms of solving things physically, jurors see a man as a threat when he gets too close to a witness sooner than they would a woman, because they think of the inequality of relative power and, subliminally, potential harm. Knowing women don't normally resort to physical violence, the jury gives more trust and permission to them to get closer. Therefore, how close you get also pertains to gender and relative power in any courtroom situation.

• Physical size has much to do with the jury's response, as does youth and vigor, even eye contact. All of these feed our stereotypes and our anticipation of other people's intentions and what will or could happen.

• Subject matter determines how close the jury thinks is seemly: more intimate subjects, such as wanting to support an upset witness or wanting to get more personal with the jury, permit drawing closer and give a subconscious logical explanation for your doing so. Conversely, hostile exchanges imply some danger and require distance and safe space.

• Cool, abstract, conceptual dialogue does not imply physical closeness; it actually asks for room to turn inward privately and consider. Your ideas can get close; you shouldn't.

That's what happens in the courtroom. Someone starts to do something, and it's almost as like the beginning of a sentence. The jurors, as observers, fill in the rest based on conditioning. "He is walking towards him and he will . . ." "She feels afraid because . . ." or "So now he should . . ." It is filling in the last half of that sentence that makes jurors want to stop you sooner or later.

People's assumptions when they watch any interaction, are based on what is going on. What any relationship means affects us all automatically. This evaluation process goes on all the time during the trial. What is your relationship to that witness, the jury, the judge, the opposing counsel? Given these assumptions, how close or far away should you be from that other person? What's right? What's comfortable for both? What do the jurors, as observers, think you should do?

How Close Can You Get to the Jury?

In your opening statement, think about how little they know you. How welcome are you in their territory? How much will be permitted? How close would *you* let another unfamiliar man or woman come to you? What would feel right? Consider how big you are. Consider the sound of your voice. Is it a large, deep, booming voice? Are you a slow, formal speaker? These would further reduce the reasons for you to come any closer, because you are just getting acquainted and you might look and sound formidable. They also know you're trying to sell them your point of view. Remember, American sales resistance and suspicion is at an all-time high. Snake oil is now sold through mass media and we all go for a beer during commercials.

So, do not draw too close to the jury until they have had a chance to get to know you, like you, and respect you well enough to give you permission or invite you to enter their space.

The other reason you are given permission to draw closer is the material that you are talking about. If it's intimate, personal, small, emotional, if it deals with one person and his feelings or a tragedy that took place, then it is more logical for you to want to come closer because your voice will naturally drop. You will not be booming, formal or cerebral then. But if you're in the midst of a factual explanation of the issues or your theory of the case, there doesn't seem to be any reason to draw nearer.

How Close is too Close?

Research has shown that there are four general spatial settings to use as a general rule of thumb when evaluating distance.

- public setting—12 feet to infinity
- formal social setting—4 to 7 feet
- informal setting—1-½ to 3 feet
- intimate setting—0 to 1-½ feet

My suggestion is that you should almost never touch the jury rail. Women are given permission to do this more often than men, but generally speaking, that is still a jury's territory. It is the outermost boundary of their space, and invading it is presumptuous. You're exhorting them, at the behest of the court. They're recipients. They haven't said, "Pull up a chair and tell us." So you must ingratiate yourself enough to be allowed to come so close to their space. Save it, perhaps for the final argument and then only if you're such a "good ole boy" type with an outreaching, warm and informal style that in real life you'd find it natural to sit on the arms of their chairs.

Be Careful Not to Overpower

You should always be aware of the fact that a standing lawyer addressing the sitting jury makes them feel powerless. The closer you get, the more it forces them to look up at you. Not only is it difficult to do if you're tall, but it is also resented, particularly by men who feel challenged and subconsciously threatened by having to look up at another man. This is especially true if you're young and they're not, or strong while they're not. It makes them feel inept and competitive. They get a sense of being overwhelmed if you tower over them, looking down upon them. Recognize that some jurors may feel this way, trapped as they are in their wooden box, when you make choices about where to be in court.

Also recognize the ethnic mix of your jury. What do they think is the norm in their basic culture. How close is comfortable for them? Factor this in as well.

How Close to Get to the Witness and Why

The jury evaluates your behavior toward a witness as a paradigm of how you feel about people and how you would treat them, the jurors. *How* you get the information colors what the jury accepts from the witness. Let's discuss direct examination first.

In a direct examination, your first purpose—nurturing, supporting, getting the witness to feel good, comfortable and safe enough to talk easily—indicates that you should start a little closer to him. In this way, he doesn't feel quite so isolated in the "electric chair" where he has just sworn his life away on the Bible. Then, as you get to the point in the story where you want him or her to emerge, to be seen and heard alone, and to be more credible, you can move back and let him or her take center stage. Independent testimony then carries even greater weight.

In cross examination, the jury looks for hostility. They antici- pate that you are bound in one way or another to enter a duel, hoping to sink the blade to the hilt. Therefore, it is important for you to keep rather far away from that witness, particularly at the beginning, so that the jury does not automatically start responding to conflict. If you're cool and easy, they can become interested in the material that you are pursuing, in the facts that you are looking for, in those Agathie Christie clues I suggested you use, instead of becoming involved in who's tougher, who's fighting whom, or how imposing you are. The jury sees the territory around the witness as being almost a protection, a moat, and you must be careful not to tread too close to it because they will feel that you are being intimidating. There has to be a logical reason for you to get close.

Even when you impeach a witness and bring him the deposi- tion that you wish him to corroborate, be careful. It is valuable for you to step back and let the deposition speak for itself, to let the power stem not from you, but from the paper, the incontrovertible truth, the facts. Show it, but in your movements be aware that you have now trespassed territory that is quite sensitive in the minds of the jury. They see the witness as sitting boxed-up in the witness chair, isolated and vulnerable, as *they* would feel. Don't overstep these bounds and lose your edge in the fight.

Using Space to Intimidate

There are some subtle ways to use space to intimidate a witness. The lectern is an excellent barrier. Formal and ponder- ous, it distances you from a witness you're cross-examining and sends a "no more Mr. Nice Guy" signal without blatant aggressive- ness on your part. It makes you look authorative, powerful and righteous and invokes images of a preacher, professor or person in authority.

Slowly moving in on a witness during the examination is an- other effective device. The "impending doom" syndrome raises the witness' anxiety level. It dilutes their concentration, and as they falter in their answers, the jury gets pre-occupied with that, rather than your proximity. Be very careful using this, though. If you're not subtle and don't make the forward movement imperceptible and slow, the jury will see you as a bully. Be sure not to end up too close.

Relative Size and Gender Between Lawyer and Witness.

Many lawyers who are large should really think carefully about how close they will get to a witness, because it may be misunderstood. Also, lawyers who are small or highly charged and move very quickly are sometimes not at their best advantage when they move closer to a rather large, formidable figure. There is some strength in a sizeable, stolid, seated figure, and you don't want to look like a ferret running around looking for an opening. Think through the specific case to recognize who are the players, what are their roles and what would be a comfortable distance for you in relation to that. If you try to imagine yourself walking along the street with this other person, understanding his or her personality and yours, and that person's relationship to you, what would be comfortable? Where would you sit with him or her in your office? How close would you stand if the two of you were talking at a cocktail party? If you begin to develop such images, you begin to imagine how the jury will see all of this, because they are evaluating you in terms of natural human exchange.

How to Earn Permission to Get Closer

If you are going to change your spatial relationship, it does require almost a little introduction. You could cover your move by introducing a subject that obviously requires that you get closer. "Let's take a closer look at this," or "Now let's really focus on . . ." This means that the next material is something that requires proximity; it gives a reason for you to draw closer to witness or jury.

Another way is to show your sensitivity to your witness' position. "I recognize that what we're about to discuss is going to be difficult for you, and I just wanted to assure you that, if at any time you wanted to stop, or you need a drink of water, just let me know." That is another time when, obviously, you are moving to a closer, warmer, friendlier mode, and therefore it is "legal" for you to get closer to the witness. It is also understandable for the jury. And that eliminates any undue response to your moving in on someone's territory.

*   *   *

The key thing to remember about non-verbal communication in the courtroom is that the jury sits still. They watch you and evaluate every part of your non-verbal behavior without realizing that they are doing it. But they notice everything. Just as at the beginning, in the opening statement, they were trying to figure out a lot about your personality type and the kind of human being you are, so, too, they continue judging those human aspects of you, since they are the jury's major measuring stick.

After a trial I have asked jurors to tell me what the lawyers said or imitate what they did. The non-verbal communication wins, hands down. They can take your stance and imitate your gestures. When I ask about what else they responded to, they talk of the visuals and catch words, but they also mention the physical relationship to witnesses and to them. How close or far away you stand gets connected to how threatening or understanding you seemed or how formal or warm or friendly you probably are in real life. Your non-verbal communication is a vital part of your work as an advocate.

10

DEVELOPING NEW COMMUNICATION SKILLS

Well, we've almost come to the end. What's left? Assuming you agree with many of the concepts you've read about and want to include these new ideas in your courtroom repertoire or learn how to eliminate some destructive habits, how do you do that?

Change.

Easy to say, hard to do.

Consciously trying to change unconscious behavior is threatening to us for several reasons:

• There's often a gap between who we are and who we'd like to be. This goes back to our early days of being criticized and told how to behave, which implied that who we were already was not acceptable or good enough. We started way back then to develop role models of who we would like to become and how we would like to improve, secretly knowing we would probably never be able to.

• We behave unconsciously and therefore are not aware of what we really do and how we act, especially non-verbally. So we don't know *what* to change.

• We don't know how we come across. We assume our intentions are clear to everyone and are shocked to discover the difference between how we feel and how others see us.

• Our forms of communication are deep habits by now, so it makes us very self-conscious and very uncomfortable to purposefully monitor our unconscious behavior and try to change it.

• Since these habits are so old and so deeply ingrained, we think it's probably impossible to change them now. We can't imagine the "new you," and are therefore reluctant to give up the familiar for the unknown, the possibly worse "you."

Therefore, faced with change, we create resistance:

• "That's impossible. I've been talking like this all my life. It's too late."

• "Listen, I'm doing just fine now, winning cases. Why should I change?"

• "How can I do that? Everyone will watch me experiment."

• "It'll make me uncomfortable and interfere with my thinking in the courtroom."

• "How do I know I'll like the changes I make?"

• "What if I can't change it? Then I'll be stuck knowing my natural behavior is unacceptable and I can't replace it. I'll be in worse shape than before."

The answers are:

• Don't start change in the courtroom. Practice beforehand.

• Your changes should always be true to yourself and your own basic nature. You'll stay within the basic parameters of your most natural style anyway, no matter what you do.

• What you will change are your concepts. The new information you've gotten about the jury will automatically trigger new behavior in you as you try to satisfy needs you didn't know the jury had.

• Accept this new information in light of the new knowledge we're gaining about better communication between people anywhere, anytime. Let go of bad habits as the best of what we knew yesterday.

• Don't recriminate, just look at today and tomorrow. Don't dwell on yesterday's mistakes. Move on and grow.

• There's not "one way" or "the best way" to conduct any trial. Good communication is based on your needs and the jury's needs, what techniques get messages across more effectively and your best judgment of how to include them all in trying your case. It's an amalgam of all of these. Your "best way" for this particular trial will change with the next case and the next jury.

*   *   *

Having said all that, let's proceed.

I'm sure you already recognize some individual areas you might like to work on. Let me describe some of the most common habits that recur most frequently in my work and suggest some exercises to do to make some changes. See if any of these are familiar.

Just remember, it feels funny to become deliberate about unconscious behavior. Be prepared to laugh and feel funny in the process. Use that laughter to relax you, not discourage you. Use it to spur you on with some new energy. Your friends, colleagues and family will be willing guinea pigs to give you feedback. If you stick with it and really devote yourself to doing the work of change, growth is not only possible, but inevitable.

Eye Contact

Remember what eye contact can do for the jury and how it improves your image as a committed, sincere communicator. It's a valuable tool and well worth developing. Practice eye contact as often as possible. But let me warn you—it's such an intimate and committing thing that, if you're not accustomed to it, it will make you feel funny and self-conscious at the beginning. But stick with it. It gets to be a habit.

Start with Yourself

Stand still in front of a mirror and just look at yourself. (No flinching, now.) See how it makes you feel. Notice how your eyes change expression, become more open, expressive, vulnerable-looking. Look carefully at your face and notice your features; see yourself as a stranger might see you. Teach yourself to keep your eyes from moving away. Practice just holding your gaze, settling down into it and getting comfortable. Meet an expression of the inner self. That's at the heart of eye contact.

Really Look at Others

Look at service people, salespeople and, most of all, members of your family. Learn to keep eye contact while you're talking or explaining. Discover how you feel and understand that making eye contact makes you vulnerable. Not only are you empowering the other person by saying, "I see you," but you're also letting them, actually asking them, to see *you*. Although you may be a rather private person, there is no room for privacy or hidden selves in the world of performance and advocacy. Your audience sees you, all of you, and judges the composite. They'll know if you're not with them or not all there. Therefore, it is very important not to let the private self interfere with the public performer.

As you practice, think of eye contact in several ways:

- really seeing someone and making him or her important;
- your commitment to communicating with someone;
- your desire to reach out and to let him or her see you; and
- as fact finding and discovery. Notice the clues you pick up as you look—other people's gestures, their nervousness, their inability to look at you.

See how much more energized and focused you get when you make and keep eye contact. This will carry over into the courtroom, helping you discover your jurors and letting them discover more of you.

Reading from Notes and Keeping Eye Contact

Sometimes you must read from a document and lose eye contact or you may still prefer to write out your statement. Even if you've mastered outlines, you should still learn how to only pop a look down at them without losing eye contact with your audience. Here are some practice tips to improve your ability to use notes and still stay free to be eye-connected to the jury.

• Use a mirror. Drop your eyes down, grab a few words, then look up and connect with your eyes in the mirror again before you talk. Keep talking while practicing, dropping your eyes down and looking right up again to find your eyes.

• Use the words as a springboard. Let your eyes drop, hit the words and bounce right back up to keep looking at yourself. The focus of concentration should be finding yourself (the listener) in the mirror, not only looking for the words on the page.

• Be especially careful not to drop your whole head. Just your eyes are enough. You can catch four or five words at a time.

• Practice writing your notes with only the barest of clue words. Action words or major fact words are most effective.

• Number your points and list them vertically down the page. This gives you their order at a glance.

• Learn what kinds of underlining are most useful to you and stand out for emphasis (capitals, underlining, colored pencil, spaces on the page, notes in the margin).

Another way to practice getting your eyes off the page and continuing to stay visually connected to your audience is to actually read a text aloud. This is especially useful when you must read from a document. Do this before a mirror, too.

• Read from a newspaper or a book. See how often you can look up and find your eyes again.

• See how many words you can actually grasp and say before you pop down for another group.

• Work on always looking at yourself (your audience) at the beginning and end of a sentence, a phrase or an idea.

• Train yourself to find the right time to break and look down and to know when you must hang on to the viewer to finish or make a point.

• Try reading aloud to a member of your family and find their eyes. Feel how the thrust of your energy connects you to your audience and is linked to what you get back from them.

Remember that the reason for eye contact is that the best form of communication is dialogue, rather than internal monologue from you to a vague whom-it-may-concern. Your eyes on your words is a monologue; maintaining eye contact is dialogue. You must not only include your recipient; you must sustain and keep them with you.

Voice

Your voice is a primary tool in being heard and understood and in commanding attention. There are several kinds of voice problems: loudness, pitch and monotony.

Projection

The way to project your voice is with air. Vocal chords vibrate on air but many people are in the habit of speaking after the air is gone from their lungs. That makes for a thin, flat and powerless delivery.

A major problem is the ability to speak loudly enough. It's too theoretical to say "louder" or "softer." How much is loud enough? Therefore, you need a tangible image:

• Use a wall to project against. Stand opposite a wall and try to hit the wall with your voice. (Close the door of your room to eliminate unwanted gigglers).

• Take a deep breath first. Then speak. Hit the wall. Say, "Hit the wall." "Hello, I'm glad to see you." Using "H" sounds makes you expel air and gives strength to the voice.

• Keep lengthening your distance from the wall, but be careful not to let all the air go at once.

• Practice lengthening the numbers of words you can say before you have to take another breath. Feel when your power wanes and breathe in again *before* that happens.

• Put your hands on your diaphragm. Breathe in. Now challenge yourself to see how slowly you can let the air out.

• Make a sound like "Aaaah" and push with your diaphragm and abdominal muscles as you slowly expel the air. Practice this until you're comfortable. Feel how your diaphragm and abdomen actually control the air, pushing it up and out of your lungs.

• Now practice this with a candle. Stand before the flame, at mouth level, and try say long, slow vowel sounds preceded by "H"; "Ha," "Hee," "Hoo," "Ho," and "Hi." See how long you can keep the flame fluttering. Increase the distance each time.

• Try to blow it out with the force of a single sound. Increase your distance each time.

• Now see how many sentences you can say with equal power before the air is gone. Start with just two sentences and work up to as many as eight. It may help to read these sentences from the book and measure yourself by the number of "bullets" you can cover.

Breath Control and Phrasing

Breath control is very important, since you can't stand before the jury gasping and panting. It also gives you the freedom to stop when you want to, for phrasing and emphasis, not just for air.

You can save this for the shower, but it's excellent practice to sing.

• Hit loud, high notes and come down the scale, letting the air out slowly.

• Start low and go up the scale.

• Sing a song and breathe in at the end of each phrase. Don't start the next phrase until you fill your lungs by breathing in deeply.

• Try taking smaller, shallow breaths if the rhythm and music don't have a natural stopping place.

• Make your breathing rhythmic. Be aware of music and words and don't interrupt a phrase. Feel your diaphragm doing the work.

• Try to hold the end note of each phrase. See how you can control the air as you let it out slowly, making the note last longer.

Another issue is phrasing, stopping when the content tells you to. Practice the following phrases.* Pause wherever you see

---

*From Lyle V. Mayer, *Fundamentals of Voice and Diction*, 6th ed., copyright 1974, 1978, 1982. Wm. C. Brown Publishers, Dubuque, Iowa. All rights reserved. Reprinted by permission.

the two vertical lines. Breathe only at the vertical lines, not in between.

• It is not the quantity of the meat// but the cheerfulness of the guests which makes the feast.

• Old friends are best// King James used to call for his old shoes; they were easiest on his feet.

• Give and take makes good friends. //To find a friend one must close one eye, //to keep a friend—two.

• "That which is good to be done, cannot be done too soon// and if it is neglected to be done early, //it will frequently happen that it will not be done at all."

Now try this exercise again, breathing indiscriminately. Do you see how it interrupts the sense of the phrase and the sentence?

Try marking a transcript of yours with these pause and phrasing lines. Read it aloud and hear how they organize your thoughts and how much more sense it can make to the listener.

Developing breath control is vital for anyone who relies on oral presentation. Your words must be controlled, with you breathing only when the content requires a pause, for you to make maximum use of them. Remember as you practice to always breathe in and push air out toward your imaginary audience.

Pitch

Lowering the pitch of your voice is necessary simply because lower tones are easier to listen to for a longer period of time. They also sound more serious, credible and grown-up.

Here, too, you need a tangible goal, a comparison, so you know what "lower" is and how it feels. Lowering your pitch is physical and muscular. Therefore, feeling it in your throat and discovering what muscles you need to use will teach you how to recreate it, as well as conditioning your voice muscles to automatically respond that way.

The secret of low notes is lengthening the vocal chords. Look at a harp. The little high notes come from the short strings and the big, deep notes come from the long strings at the other end. If you have a high-pitched voice, either your vocal chords are short or you've been in the habit of tightening and pinching them, which creates a higher sound. The goal, then, is to open the throat and think of lengthening and stretching the vocal chords.

Singing is the best exercise. We all know what scales sound and look like.

• Start singing at your normal tone. Put your fingers on your throat (gently) and feel your "Adam's apple" move as you go down the scale. Just do four or five notes for a while. Now repeat the last note three times. Now sing each note five times.

• Try the word "Ah"; then "Ha"; then combine them on each note. Move smoothly down the scale. Notice the vibration in your throat and what your Adam's apple does each time as it moves down. Be aware of and capture that feeling in your throat.

• Use "Mi, mi," "Do, do," "La, la," any combination of a consonant and a vowel ending, as you descend the scale.

• Start with doing the exercise five times and work up to ten times each time you sing a note.

• Add notes until you can sing a whole descending scale (eight notes).

• Practice until it's comfortable and doesn't feel or sound like gargling. Depending on the actual makeup of your vocal chords, you may only be able to do four or five notes. That's fine. Don't push or strain. The goal is a comfortable, natural sound.

After about a week, start practicing this, too. Sing the scale down three notes, then, start "talking" by singing on that one note.

• Recite a poem, the pledge of allegiance or anything you'd like to say on that note. Just get in the habit of making words in the lowered sound.

• You can progress to lowering the note further, but not until you're totally comfortable at the new, lower range.

• Keep your fingers on your throat to become more aware and conscious of the feelings in your throat.

Next, start *talking*, not singing, at your normal tone. Consciously duplicate the scale and lower your voice two notes. Keep talking. Practice this for awhile.

• When it's comfortable, talk your way down three notes and on the new note. Actually, your goal should be to lower your voice only two or three notes. That's probably enough in most cases.

Finally, start using this new sound in conversation. Make yourself aware and train your ears to hear your pitch and tone. Reproduce those "lowering" feelings in your throat as you talk normally.

• When you hear your voice going up, visualize lengthening your vocal chords. Think "relax," "stretch," "lengthen," or see the high-to-low, short-to-long strings on a harp in your mind.

The essence of teaching yourself a new pitch is sharpening your awareness of tonal levels and how your throat creates the lower notes. Remember to breathe with all of these. Your sound is made by riding on air. Use it.

Nasality

Another problem people have is producing sound in their head and expelling the air through the nose, creating a nasal sound. This is a difficult sound to listen to. It sounds whiny, ineffective and, since it blurs the consonants, is unclear.

What actually happens when you produce a nasal tone is that you close the throat and mouth as the major conduits for forming the words that you float on air. Instead, you push air and words up toward the hard palate and out through the nose.

Try saying these few phrases and exaggerate the nasal quality, forcibly pushing air through the nose each time you say "n" or "ng."*

• "Nan and Dan pranced and danced along."
• "The nine dancers planned to do the can-can on the sand."
• "Randy asked the man if he panted in the snow."
• "Singing is nice for Nancy."
• "Max and Manny hung the laundry on a frame."

---

*From Lyle V. Mayer, *Fundamentals of Voice and Diction*, 6th ed., copyright 1974, 1978, 1982. Wm. C. Brown Publishers, Dubuque, Iowa. All rights reserved. Reprinted by permission.

See how when you say "n" nasally you can't open up again to let the other vowels out through your mouth?

To change this habit, think of sending the air through the mouth from the throat. Visualize the open passage and see how the air travels through it. Form "n" or "ng" by touching only the tip of the tongue to the palate, not the broad, flat middle section of the tongue. Don't block the air from continuing to come from your throat out through your mouth. Just interrupt it by lightly touching the tip of your tongue to the front of the roof of your mouth, behind the teeth.

- Practice just saying "n" or "ng" that way.
- Re-read and practice the phrases shown above that way.
- Become aware of producing sound in a much lower part of your head than you presently do.
- See the mouth, jaw and throat in your mind whenever you speak. Focus on imaginary arrows sending words out through your mouth, not your nose.
- Be aware of all this in daily conversation, and work on it.

Monotony

Dull, uninteresting or monotone deliveries are sure tickets to slumberland for the jury. Not only do they get lulled by an unvarying voice but they can't tell the wheat from the chaff. What's important? What's exciting or shocking? What's touching? I find this to be one of the single biggest problems trial lawyers have—the inability to create interest and nuance in their voice and speech.

The difficulty is that you're so used to your voice and so involved in the content of your words that you often don't know if you are monotonous. So, take a test. You need something tangible to work against. The key ingredient here is a tape recorder.

The big effort will be to make your voice-line much more varied and interesting. Pauses, phrases, highs and lows are measurable. Test yourself daily.

- Tell or read a story, with action, characters and descriptions, into a tape recorder. Now play it back and with pencil and lined paper, follow the pitch and tone levels of your voice. Draw a horizontal line representing your voice and let it go up and down, crossing the printed line as you follow the inflections.

• Follow the phrasing, too. Pick up your pencil every time you hear a pause. Now look at your "chart." Test it. How interesting is it? Are there many interruptions? Too many? Are the phrases short and choppy? Are your lines long and unending, with no waves in them?

• Keep this chart and your cassette of the original story you read. Practice with them every day. Date each new entry. Comparison is encouraging and educational.

• Find the best parts of the story. Where is the excitement? What do you want the listeners to remember? Now build up to these key points using your voice to create accent and anticipation.

• Build suspense as you work toward the climax. Pause. Make us hunger for the next word.

• Listen again to the cassette. Is it happening? Are you interesting? Keep working.

• Now read a factual news account into a tape recorder and replay it. Is it interesting? Is it clear? Do you care if you hear any more? Of course it doesn't have pictorial scenes or exciting action in it. There's more challenge here, but it's also more like what you do in court.

• Challenge yourself. Can you make the factual news story as interesting and varied as the fiction piece? How do you use your voice to clarify and underline?

• Take the story apart. Underline it, based on what is important. Use the phrasing marks learned on page 466.

• Read it with an attitude. Decide what your point of view is and demonstrate it to your imaginary listeners.

• Try this on your family. Can you keep their interest?

• Test your audience. Read pieces to your family or a friend and ask what they learned. What were the key points? What do they remember? Decide in advance what you want them to know. Then see if they got it. All you have is your voice, nuance and phrasing to help you. Don't stand or gesture. Just talk.

• Now do this with an editorial, to practice persuasion. Read aloud, trying to persuade people of your point of view.

• Read this to an audience. Get feedback on how convincing you are. Does your voice become shrill, harsh, overbearing, too passionate?

The essence here is to experiment. Find out what you really sound like. Explore what it feels like to pause, to make your voice go up and down, to add more notes to your normal speaking style. Try lowering your voice to a whisper or raising the level to a major statement, even exploring angry or loud sounds.

Use your family. They're much more like a jury than you or your colleagues. I'm sure they'll welcome the chance to participate in your career—even to getting a little extra time with you. Kids love this. You make them instant experts and they're *very* truthful and quite perceptive. Try your opening and closing on them. They're great critics.

Exercises for Inflection*

To develop more skill, here are a series of exercises to help you focus on producing interesting delivery of individual words or phrases:

Say "Oh," suggesting the following meanings. Do not say the words, just say "Oh" and make it sound like what the word implies.

- elation
- fear
- pity
- amazement
- mild surprise
- horror
- sarcasm
- doubt
- anger

---

*Ibid.

- hesitancy
- disgust
- evasion
- indifference
- finality
- curiosity
- great surprise
- bashfulness
- gratitude

Read each of the following first words aloud, using an appropriate inflection based on the sentences or phrases in parentheses. They will help you determine a specific meaning for each word, but do not read the sentences or phrases aloud, just the first word:

- So (we've caught you at last, you rascal!)
- So (what's it to you?)
- John (is that you tiptoeing upstairs?)
- John (what do you mean by coming in at this hour?)
- Stop (here?)
- Stop (at once!)
- Please (don't hurt the puppy.)
- Please (this is the last straw!)
- Why (I've never heard of such a thing.)
- Why (I'll tell you why.)
- Yes (I'm not so sure.)
- Yes (I'm positive.)
- Well (this is just what I expected.)
- Well (have you made up your mind yet?)
- Ah (the poor thing.)
- Ah (I'm tired.)
- Mary (who?)
- Mary (that's who.)
- Gosh (I dropped a button.)
- Gosh (I flunked three courses.)

- Boy (isn't she a beauty?)
- Boy (I've had it!)
- Really (did it actually happen?)
- Really (don't ever speak to me again.)
- Help! (I'm drowning!)
- Help! (why should I?)

Read the following, placing a slight pause between the two words. Use a higher pitch on the second word than on the first. Then try pitching the first word higher than the second. Try accenting the first word. Then accent the second word. Think through what you mean to imply each time, and what the action around that phrase might be.

She did?	Of course.
Don't stay.	So what?
I'll go.	Try that?
Oh, no.	All right.
I should.	I'll bite.
How much?	Which one?
But why?	Why not?
What time?	Not now.
Who's there?	I have.
Oh, gosh.	Try again.
Right now.	That's it.

Repeat the above exercise, using a pitch which is lower on the second word than on the first.

In the following sentences, the position of the word indicates the location of the word on a musical scale and the relative size of the jump or skip up and down the scale. Read them straight, then in an exaggerated manner. Experiment and vary the ways you can read them for new meanings. Be very aware of whether or not your voice actually follows the placement of the words on the scale.

```
       be
To
         or
            not        that
                  to        is the
                  be              question.
```

```
I                                              tomorrow.
won't                    won't
     answer                    answer
                   now,    I
                   and
```

```
                              here?
                home        sitting
          you          were
Were               or
```

```
       now
              forever
Speak              hold
                        your
          or                   peace.
```

```
         do
   I      it
      say    do
If          it
              fast.
```

```
                              mean?
                         you
                     what
                to understand
         supposed
   I
Am
```

Smile,   that,

     when you say

               my friend!

Now you're ready for the part you never got in the school play!

Speech Habits

We all have speech habits that are simply ways to stall for time while we think, or represent the way our mind manufactures words and sentences before we say them.

"Um—uh"

This is a common habit and comes from looking for the next word. People who say "uh" between every few words think horizontally, in sentences. Therefore, the next *word*, not the next *thought*, is what they're thinking about. Since they can't see the whole picture, they get stuck.

Suggestion: Think of focusing only on action words or a major noun as you develop a thought. Go for the idea. Trim out all the prepositions, pronouns, adjectives and connectors. Think of leaping to the major point in each sentence. Then leap to the next idea. The little words will take care of themselves. Write notes that way—a key word, not sentence—to avoid looking for the next consecutive word and letting the little ones get in the way of making a point.

Choppy, Unconnected Phrases

If your speech doesn't follow the natural rhythm and meaning of your words, but stops arbitrarily in the middle of a thought, it's very hard for a listener to follow. Listen to a tape recording of yourself speaking extemporaneously to discover if this is what you do.

To develop flow, you need to feel phrasing as one does in music or poetry. Mark up a piece of writing paper with phrase lines to connect ideas and smaller thoughts within sentences like this:

To be   or not to be

that is the question.

Then practice reading into a tape recorder to get the feeling of flow and longer, connected ideas. Taping yourself and playing it back is the only way to get a feeling for this.

You should try practicing and recording short, extemporaneous speeches after you get the feeling for reading. Think through to the end of your sentence. See the period. Don't stop till then.

"And . . . , and . . . and . . . "

It is a very common habit to connect all your questions in examination by beginning each one with "And." It is disconcerting to listen to, not only because it becomes predictable and monotonous, but because you are going from one subject to another unconnected subject yet linking them with "and".

Change this by imagining a large capital letter on the first word of each question you ask. As you keep seeing the "A" come up, your mind will make you aware of your first word—"And." You'll hear it and can then make a conscious effort to find a variety of real words to begin with.

Gesture

"I don't know what to do with my hands" is one of the most common complaints I hear.

As I've told you, gesture is punctuation. It's very useful for emphasis and underlining, as well as being a stimulant to the audience and an outlet for your physical energy. But it only works if it's natural to you.

Don't Be Compulsive About Gesturing

"I'm standing in front of a group, performing. I have to do something dramatic. I can't just talk . . . ."

Not true. Consider the fact that you are talking to individuals; they happen to be sitting next to each other, but each one perceives you by himself. They don't get a collective sound; they only hear you talking to each of them, personally. Therefore, all you have to do is focus on improving the way to talk to a single person.

To do this, rely on your instincts. Enhance what's native in you. You don't have to try too hard or to emulate some manufactured ideal. It's best to be natural. If gesturing is natural to you, it will come. If not, don't push. You're at your best when you're relaxed, not orating.

Discover Your Natural Gestures

Here's an exercise. What we're going to do is discover yourself and let your natural form and style come out. Let's find out what your most common gestures are when you want to make a point.

Read an editorial or a "letter to the editor." Now take a point of view about the issue. Oppose or agree with what you read.

• Stand in front of a mirror and argue your point. After you stop laughing, get on with it and find out what gestures you normally use.

• Don't do anything on purpose. Let it happen and see what's natural to you. You will be quite surprised. You're not as stiff as you think you are.

• Discover what your natural gestures are. What do you automatically do for emphasis? What happens? Try to be relaxed and natural. Just argue.

• Notice hands, arm gestures, how your feet are planted. Get comfortable with what you do. (Doesn't look so bad, does it?)

• Discover if you tend to stand rigid and still. Do you point your finger? Is there one gesture you repeat? How do you hold your hands?

It's important for you to know what you look like. It will help you, when you get up, to trust yourself. When you do, you can let go of your concern about gesture and focus on what you're saying.

Videotape is a great way to see many things. Just don't get too critical and paralyze yourself. If you decide on doing this on videotape, get the camera set up and then just stand in front of it and do it alone. A camera-person can inhibit you and make you feel self-conscious.

What if You Don't Gesture?

Don't arbitrarily "add-a-gesture." Your metabolism and/or previous cultural experience may not incite you to move around much or be physically expressive. That's all right, but it would help for you to get a little more uninhibited.

To discover ways to use gesture as punctuation, try this:

• Think about what you're saying. How would you write it? Visualize the punctuation marks you'd use. Where would you put commas, paragraphs, exclamation points?

• How can you act out these marks? Find physical, visual equivalents with hands, movement and stance.

• Gestures are especially useful when listing several points under one heading. Try using one hand for emphasis, to make them clear (even if it's counting out the numbers by showing your fingers).

People who don't gesture need to experience it. Sometimes it's easier to focus on something other than your own speech to discover your basic physical movements, to get the feeling of what gesturing feels like and what kinds you like or lean toward.

• Put on an orchestral record or tape. Choose a piece of music you know. Now let yourself conduct. Don't use a mirror, just feel the movement. Let it happen.

• Notice your arms. How do you indicate one section or another? How do you emphasize? How do you indicate quiet moments?

• Try disco or aerobic dancing. You may need to loosen up and get in touch with your body. Take a class. Anonymity helps, or you may feel safer doing it at home, if you're not used to it.

• Your kids or your wife can help free you. Let them show you movements. Try to imitate.

• Watch video music shows and dance along.

• Experiment with movement using your arms. Swing them, flex them. Use your hands. Notice if you're more comfortable with large-muscle movement or smaller hand and feet movement. Do you like to move or stand still?

The fact is that as a trial advocate, you are a performer. Gestures are extremely eloquent and useful tools not only for explaining but for keeping everyone's energy and interest level up—yours and the jury's. It's worth experimenting with and loosening up. Get in touch with your body. It will release you. However, if it's too alien to you, don't force it. Just add what's comfortable, even if it's only a change in your stance or walking a few steps.

Posture and Stance

Posture affects how you look to others and the assumptions they make about your being uneasy, ineffectual, secure or belligerant (as described in Chapter 9 pp.440–444). To improve your posture you first need to discover what you normally do.

• Stand in front of a mirror. Close your eyes and relax your posture until you feel natural and comfortable. Now open your eyes and study yourself. Notice your shoulders, hands and head. Where is the tension? How far off an ideal center plumb-line, dropped from the top of your head to the floor, are you?

• Try walking a few steps up to the mirror and then stop. Capture your normal posture and freeze it. Don't edit, adjust or choreograph. Get as close to natural as you can. Look at your head, your shoulders, your hips.

• Turn sideways to the mirror. Keep your natural posture. Remembering that your spine is in the back of your body and your head sits on your spine, where is your head? Is the chin out beyond the front of your body? Is the head thrust forward? Is it pulled too far back with the chin pulled in and the neck rigid?

• Look at your back. Is the natural spinal curve distorted with the upper back too curved or the pelvis tipped too far forward with a consequent arch in the small of the back?

Now that you've gotten a good, hard look and are thoroughly upset with how badly you stand (since we all have developed distorting and compensating habits through the years) let's get to work to recapture the natural body alignment.

Shoulders and Head

• Stand up against a wall with your feet about four to six inches away from the wall. Lean against it. Get the feeling of your upper back flattening itself against the wall. See what it does to your

shoulders and chest—how it opens them up. If you're round shoul-
dered, you'll really feel this. If you normally hyperextend and
throw your shoulders too far back, you'll find yourself rounding the
shoulders a little to get the broad upper back flat against the wall.

• Notice your head, neck and chin. As you push the head back
to sit on top of the spine, beware of the muscles you use. Close
your eyes and concentrate. Feel the muscles in your upper back,
shoulders, chest, neck—which ones are making the effort? Isolate
them in your mind. What are they doing? How does it feel?

• Step forward away from the wall. Try to recreate the feeling.
Check your alignment, in your mind; head on top of spine; shoulders easy; upper back flat; chest lifted; arms hanging at your sides.

• Now look in the mirror. Notice how your facial expression and
body image have changed as you assume this new, easier-looked,
more truly natural posture.

Another way to relax and realign the shoulders:

• Lift and hold two buckets of water in your hands. Stand still
first and feel where your shoulders have changed and how they are
placed. Look in the mirror. Relax your head. Roll it around and see
how it adjusts to the new shoulder placement when you bring it to
rest. Gently swing the arms, still holding the buckets (watch the
sloshing). Begin to absorb this new posture into your
muscle-memory.

• Now walk around with the buckets. See how your upper back
and chest feel and how your walking changes with this new
alignment.

• Now put the buckets down and check your shoulders again.
Do you hold them differently than you did? Walk around a little.
Stop and check the mirror. Can you recreate the easy shoulder-
posture you achieved with the buckets?

• Pick the buckets up again and see how much you still need to
do to compensate when you have the actual weight in your hands.

• Keep the image and the feeling of this correct shoulder placement and use it as a check point many times a day, especially in
times of stress, to create a new body habit.

To practice good head, neck and upper body posture:

• Place a book on your head. Notice how far back you need to place your head and how much you have to lift or lower your chin to create a level platform for the book.

• Look in the mirror, both front and side view, to see how your posture changes.

• Now walk with the book on your head. Aside from your awareness of balancing it, become keenly aware of where your muscles are working to keep it level. Notice how your chest and upper back muscles work to lift and change your alignment, how your neck pulls back, how your chin lifts or lowers. Absorb these feelings into your unconscious muscle-memory.

• Create an image for yourself that you can conjure in your mind without the book, to recreate this posture. Remove the book, walk around and think it. See if you can hit that posture again. Put the book back and see how close you come, how little further adjustment you have to make.

Another exercise for upper body and chest:

• Imagine a hook in the middle of your upper chest, about five inches above the bottom of your breast bone. Picture it attached to a line from the ceiling. Let if lift your chest up. Notice the muscles in the upper back—how they push and lift to support the lifted chest.

• Sit your head on top of that elogated spine. Feel the lifting in the upper spine and the neck. Lift the chin and feel the head and shoulders being light, all suspended and held by the hook in your chest. This creates an open-looking chest, flat upper back and good, easy head alignment.

Lower Back and Pelvis

Now let's work on the lower back, hips and pelvis.

• Stand against a wall, feet four to six inches away from the wall. Lean against the wall. Notice how much of your lower back touches the wall. Does your sacrum, that big, solid-feeling bone above your tail bone, touch? What has your pelvis alignment done to the small of your back? Put your hands behind your waistline. Is there a large space there? Does it feel tense and arched?

• Think of dropping the pelvis down in the back and lifting the pelvis up in front—like a fulcrum. Notice how you flatten the back against the wall as you drop the seat down and lift in front.

• Feel how the abdominal muscles tighten as you pull up in front. The weakness of these muscles is the reason most of us spill out in front and shorten the muscles in back.

• Hyperextend (arch) the back on purpose. Notice how the seat lifts up and how the abdomen pushes out. Remember this as the feeling you wish to counter-act.

• Don't tuck *under*. It's not a forward-back movement. It's an up-down movement, lengthening the spine *down* in back, lifting the pubic bone up in front, and shortening the abdominal muscles.

• Try to keep your knees easy but straight. You can't walk around with bent knees (unless you're Groucho Marx).

• Remembering the image of "*down* in back, *up* in front" walk away from the wall and, standing sideways to a mirror, look at your profile. Work on the pelvis area, tipping up and down, and see how it affects your posture.

• Create an image to make you find this posture again and start walking around with it. It does make you creep around for a while, as you concentrate, but it will become more familiar and easier every time you do it.

Posture is a habit. Changing any old habit is difficult and feels distorted and odd. It takes time to incorporate it and to feel natural with new behavior. But you *can* break old habit patterns and create new ones. It only takes motivation, some time and focused thought to develop new muscle memory. Working out at a gym helps strengthen and realign your musculature. But your conscious awareness of how you stand and move and working to change it on a daily basis by your awareness and realignment is the most important factor and the most rewarding.

Stage Presence

Just getting up to talk in court doesn't guarantee attention. Something needs to happen within you to make the jury sit up and take notice. Some people just naturally have "charisma" or seem to easily move into center stage and attract attention. Others need to work on developing this skill.

The goal of this exercise is to teach you how much energy and commitment you must put out to get someone to really notice you, pay attention and respond.

• Go up to a stranger and ask for information. The goal is to see if you can get him to *look* at you and answer you.

• Questions like, "What time is it? Where is such and such a street? Does the bus go by here?" are the sorts of things you can try, since they all have to do with a fact and require an answer. But the big goal is to get them to look at you when they answer you.

• Discover how much energy you have to put out to make people stop and notice you.

• How sure are you in advance that they will answer? How willing are you to look at them and make them look at you?

This exercise will help you find out what it's like to make real eye contact, and it's excellent practice for taking the stage in the courtroom. Find out what it takes to make somebody hear you. Its great to try this with strangers, because if you can really make *them* stop and respond to your needs, you've done it.

Clues: Begin with your commitment: You *want* this person to pay attention. You *will* it. Visualize his doing it. See yourself as successful. As you commit yourself, your energy will send the message across.

Think of the stranger's needs: Why should he bother listening? How can you get his attention? What can you do to make him focus on you and give you an answer?

Some possible openings: Make yourself vulnerable and needy. Try asking for help. "Excuse me, I see you're in a hurry but I need some help," "Sorry to trouble you, but can you help me?" "May I ask you something? I have a problem" or, "I'm a stranger here and a little confused." Try anything that gives the other person a sense of importance or value and shows that you recognize *his* needs before you tell him what *you* want. See if you can "command attention." What you'll soon discover is that, unless you make yourself visible, most people will ignore you. Find their sight lines and put yourself in them. And remember, it doesn't count until you get them to actually look at you, to see you. And—no touching!

You can try this with sales help in shops, with bus drivers or with people just walking or waiting for the light to change. Remember, everyone is in their own world. Find out what it takes for you to make them forget theirs and attend to you and your needs.

By the way—this exercise should be done with caution, to prevent ego damage or bodily injury.

Listening

To help sharpen your listening skills—so important in direct and cross examination and voir dire as well as client interviews—try these: (Use your friends or family: it's interesting at parties, too.)

• Sit in a circle or do this exercise one-on-one. Let each person prepare three sentences. After the first person speaks, the next person must repeat the sentence exactly before he can say his. Go around until all have tried it, if you're in a group.

• Then start again. The first person says a sentence, the next person repeats it and adds another phrase. The next person does the same and so on. You may not add a phrase until you have repeated the accumulated sentences exactly.

• Ask one person to read a paragraph. Ask him to drop clues of emphasis or emotional slant. How much can you repeat back? See if you can get the overall intention or the basic idea. How many details can you repeat? Let the reader question you for specifics. Do this exercise watching the reader, then with your eyes closed.

• This may be the hardest of all: For a few days see if you can repeat everything said to you at home before you answer. Not only will you sharpen your listening habits, but you'll be really listening to the people we all take for granted and tune out most often. (I can feel a warmer glow coming from the hearths of American lawyers even as I write this.)

Do all of these exercises, as simple as they seem. You'll learn a lot about what you miss and how much effort it takes to listen.

Observing

I've written enough throughout this book for you to now be a firm believer in the power of non-verbal communication. Focused and conscious discovery of how you use your instincts to make judgments about people will help sharpen your voir dire skills and your assessment of jurors and opposing witnesses, as well as clients.

• Begin to watch what you notice first as you see strangers on the street, in a restaurant or coming into your office. Keep a notebook. Start writing your priority list—eyes, clothes, shoes, weight, hair, hands, nails, voice. Then see if you can add a word to each of these. See what it is that interests you—color, texture, perfume, sounds, guessing the cost or size. Discover what you use as signals in making judgments.

• Notice people at parties. Guess their professions as you run down your personal checklist, then go find out if you're right. Question yourself to see what clues helped you make your decision. You'll begin to find out what stereotypes you rely on.

• Notice people you meet and give them names as you talk to them before you discover their real names. Sensitize yourself to many clues and how you characterize them by the name you decide on. See if your stereotypes work for you. See how often you're right. Giving someone a name or profession uses all your people-judging instincts. Find out how good yours are and keep practicing.

• Compare notes with a spouse or colleague. See what they saw and what judgments they come up with.

• Practice studying body language by turning off the sound on the television and watching only the gestures, spatial relationships, facial expressions and so on to see if you can figure out what's happening. Record how you feel, what you think they're saying. See how many details you can absorb—even from the surrounding environment. Then turn the sound on and check yourself out.

The best observation exercise is to notice your family and their non-verbal clues. Since these are the most familiar people to us, we are often much more instinctively aware of what else they are saying to us. Raise it to a conscious level.

• Make a list of what gestures and mannerisms spell out the following emotions with each of your near and dear ones: anger, fear, insecurity, happiness, trying to please, not telling the truth or wanting to tell everything. See how much you notice. Discover if it's accurate.

• Do this as a family exercise. Ask if your observations are correct. You might also ask how *they* observe you; what are *your* telltale gestures, characteristics, etc. (What interesting feedback you get about yourself and also about how well they know you!) These lists should be enormously useful as checklists for observing and learning more about all the players in a trial.

Asking Questions

Of course you know why this skill is important. It is valuable for you to find more human-scale, natural ways to ask questions, in informal settings, in order to develop an easier, more relaxed style in court. Sophisticated, subtle techniques for getting information from people often elude you as lawyers, since you work in a milieu where answering is required, not voluntary. Therefore, it is a technique that often needs polishing and honing, especially the listening and the subtlety. Remember—eventually you'll have an audience watching how you question so this should become a highly developed art that always looks perfectly natural.

• Set yourself a goal of a piece of information you'd like to get from someone. Then interview friends or strangers in a social setting. Try to discover something personal, like their most embarrassing moment, the turning point in their life or who was their hero at age 13 and why. Watch yourself. See how you go about setting the stage to get it.

• What is your opening question? How do you create a safe and warm environment? Is your friend willing or reluctant? What do you do to elicit more information? If you've already been doing your listening and observing exercises, you'll hear many clues and openings that allow you to move into areas that are normally closed. (See Chapter 2 on Voir Dire and Chapters 4 and 5 on Direct and Cross Examination for questioning techniques. Experiment with them.)

• Try it alone. Then let your spouse or friend in on what you're doing. Let them act as observer and get his or her input on how your experiment went, what you missed, how you picked up on a good point and so on. This is safer than just trying new ideas out in the courtroom.

• Notice what you do when you hit a stone wall. How do you get around it? Do you cajole, stay with it or drop it and change the subject? Force yourself to stay on the subject and find another opening to get in.

• Remember the basic principles of good communication: Tap into other people's self-interest. Give them reasons to tell you. Notice their agendas before your own. Look for clues as springboards for the next question. Notice how you close, how gracefully you finish the episode, leaving them comfortable and not feeling manipulated. These are valuable lessons for the courtroom.

*　　　*　　　*

In essence, this chapter should give you some ways to polish your skills, to explore new ways to communicate and to alter some habits. They should, at the least, raise your awareness of what you usually do. Have some fun experimenting.

11

ON JUDGES
AND BENCH TRIALS

I have been told by a number of lawyer friends that my next statement is open to question, but I shall make it anyhow and believe in it thoroughly.

Judges are human, too.

It may come as a distinct shock to some of you to think about that. Seeing them in the formal setting of the courtroom, you can forget that judges are human beings. Even before they were lawyers, which was before they were judges, they were human beings. They were conditioned by the same set of experiences all of us had: Boring teachers, lecturing parents, bad speakers, great expectations as curtains went up, getting lost during complex explanations—all of it. Therefore, the basic truths that apply to all human beings about our responses to the ways we communicate apply just as well to judges:

• Judges anticipate boredom in the courtroom as much as, or more than, jurors do.

• Judges, like jurors, have resistance to the spoken word.

• They're tired of having people talk at them, talk to them, talk down to or up to them and explain.

• They will also respond to all visual stimuli in much the same way that the jurors do, if not more so, because it simplifies and is more interesting and memorable than just talk.

489

• They also relate to the teller's personality.

• They, like all of us, like clarity and something that is interesting and makes a point.

Just as in each chapter I asked you to consider your audienc—
their expectations, needs and assumptions—before you begin any
part of the trial, I must now ask you to do exactly the same with
judges.

The next section will look at the many factors that act upon a
judge and his work in order to help you develop some perspective
about them and their role, their problems and pressures, their
needs which you may not have thought about before, and about
how and why they listen.

PERSPECTIVES ON THE JUDGE'S ROLE

Time

You have to remember that time is one of the greatest problems judges have. The dockets are incredibly full. Everything that
takes more time in a trial crowds up everything that comes behind
it. Judges have an inordinate number of things to do and are often
poorly staffed. They feel hurried and pressured. They need to get
right to their job as the finder of fact. Therefore, their irritation
rises in direct proportion to how much time you waste. Very often
you will hear judges say, "Get on with it, Counsel." This is not only
their impatience at the way you're trying the case, but also their
general sense of urgency about what else needs to be done and
what else is piling up. This deeply affects how they listen.

Concentration and Intensity

Let us consider the levels of concentration and intensity necessary in a judge's role as listener. Think about how sharply he
must listen, not only to the information that is being given, but also
to the way in which it is being given. He is judging two things at
one time; the process and the content. And the process is multi-

faceted; he must judge what happens between the two lawyers as well as what happens between each lawyer and himself. He must listen with a high level of intensity and concentration to the information that is given him. This creates extraordinary pressure.

A Single Focus for Your Energy

Think about it. The judge has to sit there, alone, with all your energy and eye contact directed solely at him. When you deal with an entire jury, you know to go from one juror (he's sleeping over there, so you don't look at him any more) to the one who smiles at you. There are choices and the jurors themselves don't feel as pressured because there is a sense of your advocacy being divided up among 12 people. In a bench trial it's not diluted at all. The judge is the recipient of a day full of advocacy from the two of you. "Listen to me!" "Listen to me!" "No, no, judge, not him—me!" "Listen to my side!" "Now hear my side!" Can you feel it? How intense and exhausting. It's easy to see how that can make him irascible and short-tempered or cause him to deal curtly or arbitrarily with an issue, just to be done with the assault.

Sole Responsibility to Decide

He or she must be not only the audience and absorber of the information, but at the same time must be able to keep the proceedings on track with instantaneous rulings, to make up his or her mind and to rule—alone. It is a solo process of a rare kind, not often required of most people in any of their endeavors.

It's just human nature, when we think about making a decision, to stop and talk to other people, to try out some ideas and gather some opinions about it before we decide. But in a bench trial, the judge's inner knowledge that the total outcome of the trial depends on him alone, not on the decision of 12 people, raises the pressure enormously. He cannot rule by consensus or majority opinion. The responsibility is his, totally.

It's common knowledge that we all basically hate making decisions because we could make the wrong ones. Here, too, the judge's basic human components are at work. Although he's prepared and feels confident in his knowledge (most of the time) and has chosen the role of decision-maker voluntarily, there is still the deeply guarded instinct of self-doubt at work. "What if I'm wrong?" This is especially true of jury-waived criminal trials where there is so much responsibility given the judge for being both right and sure.

Instant Decisions Based on Memory

Have you ever considered, as both of you stand facing the judge intently waiting for a ruling, what that feels like to him and what the judge is actually doing?

Consider.

Practically all the decisions judges need to make in trial are on-the-spot, instant ones based on memory and what they carry with them from past knowledge and experience. "I object." "Over-ruled." Each conflict requires an instantaneous judgement, which makes the judge riffle through his mental index cards, find the right precedent or application of the law, and rule. At once. Unequivocally. With utter conviction. No wavering. Not too much thinking (looks weak or unsure). Just pull up the right cite and judgement and rule.

It's not easy. The anxiety level in many judges is very high. Although some judges get used to it and thrive on the quick and impromptu, many find it very difficult. What's the effect? An overall internal unease during the trial, coloring the way they hear you and the trial, and how they act.

Physical Passivity

Sitting and listening—two terribly passive and powerless activities. In a certain way, it is even more difficult for judges than for jurors. Since both lawyers face the judge directly, they assault him with tremendous energy. It's hard to receive that much force sitting still. The physical animal in us needs to either recoil and get away from such an assault or to move out and counter-punch. However, judges are allowed to do neither. As the center of attention, visible to everyone, their behavior must be exemplary: a paragon of decorum, a symbol of rapt attention. Therefore, they are faced with the need to develop an unnatural, stoic posture of acceptance and attention. Their need to counter-punch gets buried in stolidity and silence. (Now do you begin to understand their squirming, twisting, tilting, pen twirling and looking off into the void?)

Although the judge, unlike the jury, has the opportunity to stop you and ask questions, and to be much more involved, the judge is still required, for long periods of time, to restrain the natural urge we all have to move, to get up and walk around as a break from working and concentrating really hard or just getting bored. Changing positions and moving energizes. Physiologically, thinking, listening and focusing are processes that use up great quantities of electrical energy inside the body. We release waste products from such activity into the blood and we need renewal. We need to move to increase circulation, thus allowing the body to recover and to rid itself of the chemically-induced lethargy that follows hard work. Yet the form of a trial denies this process. Recesses often arbitrarily follow the subject matter, not human need. Therefore, judges work counter to nature and this, too, takes its toll and affects how judges listen, think and behave.

They Are Demanding

As the finder of fact, they want to get at the heart of the matter as soon as possible. Since they know the process and what should be done, they expect excellence and they have little patience with equivocating, unpreparedness, vague concepts or sloppy meandering towards a point. They have a clear picture of how they want their court to run and anything less than that compromises their sense of efficiency and excellence in their running of a trial. So there is a high level of expectation, a keen sense of how things should be done and no forgiveness for not performing according to their lights, by their standards, in their court.

Judges are also Judged

Being the subject of a judge's unequivocal power in the courtroom as you see him or her rule impassively, abruptly, by fiat, sometimes makes you forget that there's another powerful presence in the courtroom.

Judges are keenly aware that *they* are being judged as well, while they do their task. They have great concern about protecting the record. Who wants to be reversed—found wanting or wrong? Although they mean to do their immediate job in the trial forthrightly and well, the fact of this possibility affects how they listen and how they rule, and hearing that inner voice remind them raises the anxiety level of their work. Don't forget they also face two other "higher courts" whose presence they feel looking over their shoulder as well—the press and the public.

Aloneness

It's hard to work alone and to be the only one who knows what you're thinking and doing. It's not only more pleasant, but also reinforcing and clarifying as well as stimulating to discuss and share information and ideas with others, to get feedback, argue and get input from peers. Yet judging is a solo effort, in every sense of the word.

A judge's life has to change from his days as lawyer or professor. He loses much of the pleasure and the cameraderie of just relaxing with his lawyer-colleagues and cronies, being able to drop into the old haunts to unwind, kid around, recap and chew over a recent case or discuss anything of mutual interest. As a judge, he must keep a distance between himself and the places where *you* bond, the informal "clubs" you create as trial lawyers. Judges must keep their own counsel. They must act more removed and judge-like. So, along with the levels of pressure and reponsibility, there is a loss of the gregarious life that he or she formerly enjoyed.

Judges are forced to be loners not only in relation to their work, but in much of their free time as well, as they read and deliberate alone, training themselves to be soloists, independent thinkers and the final, lone word. This affects their personalities and consequently their performance in court and how you see them.

Objectivity Hardens

In a great struggle to remain always fair and factual, judges try to lean over backward, away from feelings, instinct and prejudice. In their zeal to do this, they try to tune out their old systems and, in the process, atrophy their earlier, natural human tendencies.

That doesn't leave much room for yours in court. The end product often looks cold, enigmatic, unapproachable and unfeeling.

"The Court" Rules

Sometimes judges become alienated from themselves. They forget they're mere mortals and laymen in other areas. I know of a particular case in which a judge always referred to himself as "The Court" even saying, " 'The Court' is going to lunch"—seriously!

They live within formality and ritual, where lawyers (even old friends) treat judges with great deference; they're addressed as "Your Honor"; they have "chambers," not an office; their arrival in court is heralded and citizens rise when they appear. This sometimes causes them to lose their sense of balance.

They're Trying the Case, Too

There is another major issue. It's delicate and subtle, but one that I think would cause lawyers to understand something else about the psychology of a judge as listener. There is competition between you and the judge.

Judges (almost all) were once trial lawyers. Therefore, there is an irresistible urge to critique you. They see every case as a possible case of theirs, and this automatically sets up a challenge to imagine how they would do it. They see and hear the points you raise in the case and become twice as critical when they see inefficiency, points badly made, issues missed, no visuals, and disorganized examinations. While they're watching and listening, they're also critiscizing and comparing.

To understand the implications of this, let's find the source. Let's take a look at who becomes trial lawyers and what key personality traits you all have in common.

Trial lawyers have:

- a remarkable will and need to win;
- a strong ego that thrives on performance and being the center of attention;
- self-confidence enough to make you believe you can win;
- a desire to compete, to get in there and fight, to show who's best, toughest, smartest, most analytical;

• an enjoyment of moving people around, affecting them, even bending them to your will;

• a creative instinct for problem solving and unique solutions;

• a real excitement about analyzing; unravelling the knot of a problem to see its parts, its cause and its cure;

• a love of brinksmanship, of testing yourself against the dangers of trying a case and losing;

• a kind of daring which enables you to improvise and draw on your own resources spontaneously, under fire.

Now read these personality traits over again, not as a checklist for yourself (which I'm sure you've already done), but with the image of such a person being relegated to merely sitting and watching the action as a judge.

They are like retired race horses. Once they're in the gate, with that familiar environment and tension, the adrenals surge at the opening gun and part of them is running around the track with you and competing, while the other part, the newly trained, controlled part, sits back, considers and listens.

Judges can't help still being a little competitive, critical of you and of your process and presentation. They still play the game vicariously. As they oversee two other people doing it, if they were good trial lawyers, they really want to say, "would you please . . . just a minute . . . let me take this robe off, climb down there and show you how to do it, dummies!" If they were not very good, they may feel threatened and intimidated by any highpowered talent they see.

The personality traits I mentioned above don't just wither and die. They're forcibly buried by an intellectual decision and intention to become a judge, but they never really leave. Therefore, they keep playing inside and can color how judges feel about who and what they have been listening to.

The Subconscious Enjoyment of Power

I started this chapter by reminding you that judges are human beings. As human beings, it's irresistible not to enjoy absolute power.

The processes of life deny absolute power to most mortals. We don't have power over life and death, illness, whom we love or who loves us. Most of us don't have the power to shape our financial destinies or determine how our children will turn out. Therefore, to come to a place in life where you can design your environment and cause everyone inside it to do your bidding and abide by your will is a remarkable state of affairs. It's great! Why shouldn't judges enjoy it? And use it! Of course, they're committed to dealing fairly and upholding and interpreting the law. If that wasn't extremely appealing and important to them they wouldn't have chosen the bench. But that little human "me" demon is alive in all of us and we wouldn't be normal if, sometimes, it didn't get the better of us. Don't be surprised. Power is universally pleasurable. Why did kings, why do presidential candidates fight so hard to get it and keep it? We all like it; it feels good.

A Kind of Exchange

To become judges, they have had to make some big changes and compromises in their lives. They go from being entrepreneurs to living on a fixed income. They usually take a large cut in salary which means learning to live on less while they watch you continue to make more and more money. Even though they planned it, it is a shock to see their standard of living and their easy attitude toward money change. What takes the place of all that? The relief from the pressure of an advocate's life? Some judges may need to justify their decision, since it *is* a mixed blessing—and costly.

Disillusionment

For some of them, becoming a judge turns out to be frustrating and a disappointment. Listening and deciding rather than doing, overcrowded dockets and plea bargaining, outrageous verdicts and unnecessary litigation sometimes wears out the pleasure, the glamour and the substance. Many lawyers enter the judiciary idealistically, imbued with excitement about what they can add and how they will interpret and use the law to deliver justice well and fairly. Many join for the creative and intellectual challenge. But reality intervenes. A goodly number are disappointed and live with regret. Imagine how this affects their functioning in the courtroom.

*   *   *

So, the sum is—human. To communicate with your audience of judges you need to see, feel for and understand them as well and as three-dimensionally as you do jurors. They too have human frailties they work hard to overcome. They are beset by many invisible stresses that are not usually acknowledged or accounted for by lawers. They react as people do—sometimes bored, impatient, defensive, concerned, unsure. To reach them you need to understand them better.

HOW JUDGES SEE TRIAL LAWYERS

Talking of understanding leads us naturally to look at what judges know or feel about you. In order for you to understand more about how judges see trial lawyers in trial (be it bench or jury) and to establish a basis for the next section on more effective techniques in bench trials, I gathered some unusual data.

Having informally questioned judges for years on their views of effective and ineffective trial advocacy and their particular needs in the courtroom, I decided to do a mini-survey with a number of them for this book. The areas I asked about included:

• Pet peeves about trial lawyers.

• What trial lawyers do wrong or badly most often (in jury and/or bench trials).

• What trial lawyers do not understand about the jury from their point of view.

• Judges' needs in the courtroom.

• How they wish trial lawyers to relate to them during a bench trial (formal, informal, more or less peronally, with humor, etc.).

• How trial lawyers should present complex, technical cases at a bench trial.

• Are visual aids and charts useful? Permissable

- What they do and do not want from lawyers.
- Additional comments.

Pet Peeves

Almost uniformly, judges complained about lawyers being long-winded, ill-prepared and downright boring. This may come as a great shock to you, but knowing and understanding this can help make you more effective. It can also explain some of a judge's impatience and irritation in the courtroom.

Errors

According to Judge William J. Bauer, Circuit Judge, U.S. Circuit Court of Appeals, 7th Circuit, Chicago, Illinois:

> It suddenly dawns on me that my pet peeves involve the lawyers' errors or omissions; they seem inseparable. Let me rise now to say that as an old trial lawyer, I was really disturbed only by a bad job of lawyering before me. Since I was never sure of what problems the lawyer was facing in preparation or scheduling, I was forebearing and patient. When the trial was over, however, and it became obvious that the only problems were mistakes on the part of the lawyer I ground my teeth. But bad lawyering is usually obvious from the opening gun and then *I* suffered. Matter of fact, justice, the client, the jury and I *all* suffered, and I wanted frequently to tell the lawyer to take up some less demanding occupation such as sky-diving.

Organization and Communication Skills

The organization of your presentation and examination is important to judges. Just as with juries, how well you communicate and whether you can keep their interest so they can really hear the case is of great importance to judges, too. One judge writes;

> Lawyers who fail to organize their arguments (to the court) or who fail to come to the point with some speed (judges are *supposed* to be able to follow an argument with some intelligence) drive me nuts. The writing skills of some attorneys are equally as defective, but a judge can skim the bad parts; poor oral communication just must be

suffered. Incidentally, repetitious arguments are really a problem. In a jury argument, some repetition invites learning; in an argument to the court it invites both boredom and irritation. Again, lawyers seem to think that the longer they talk, the better their chances for success. And you and I know that's not so—no souls are saved after the first ten minutes of the sermon.

A federal court judge said:

> There is an art in organizing material and trial lawyers must learn it. They need to develop a system to be able to lay their hands on each exhibit, or the cites of legal authority. They must learn to anticipate what the judge will need.

Boring

As far as boring is concerned, the judges agreed that lawyers often feel that because they are trying the case purely in front of the bench, and need not be concerned about the perception of lay people (the jury), they feel that it is possible to lapse into as much legalese and technical verbiage as they can possibly muster in an effort to impress the judge. What it really does is to turn the judges off, because to some degree, it sounds almost like you're being competitive with him, showing off all the knowledge you have. They can beat you at that, and what's more, they have the power. Don't assume that just because it's a trial all judges will automatically love it.

From Judge Robert J. Hallisey, Justice of the Massachusetts Superior Court:

> My pet peeve is lawyers who bore me to death with their cases. As I told you, I would rather be torn apart by lions than die of ennui! I have told the lawyers that we are really in an aspect of show business, and you cannot convince anyone unless you first get their attention.

Long-winded

There is impatience on the issue of how quickly a judge can grasp a point and that you can't shift gears when they do. The judges speak of how rigidly committed lawyers are to their design, that they over-plan and insist on continuing even when asked not to because the judge already understands. You also greatly overestimate how much you must explain.

From Judge Rya Zobel, Federal District Court, Boston, Massachusetts:

> Lawyers are too long-winded, both orally and in writing. They are often unable to get to the point or make their point. They go on and on, unable to shift gears and curtail their planned speech. Even when I say 'I've read the brief; do you have anything else to add,' they go right back and repeat the brief before me.

Another judge says:

> In criminal trials there are prosecutors that overtry a case. Having amply proved the defendant's guilt, they try to prove him, *very, very guilty*. It may be difficult to know without *vast* experience when to quit on a jury issue, but it shouldn't be hard in a bench trial.

Unprepared

A great lack of preparation was commented on by everyone. They say lawyers do not pay enough attention to basics, to being ready or clear or to putting forth your case efficiently.

> My pet peeve is lack of preparation in getting to the point—i.e., the inability to articulate a brief statement of the claim, the expert testimony of important liability and damages witnesses and to realistically evaluate their claims.

Yet another judge writes, with some forebearance, analyzing why so many lawyers are unprepared:

> The most common lawyer flaw in the trial of cases is coming to court *unprepared*. Most lawyers have the requisite skills to try a case. The economics of practice, however, force attorneys to accept more cases than they can reasonably handle. In jurisdictions where there is a significant backlog of cases waiting to be tried, it is only in this fashion that attorneys can assure a reasonable cash flow to support

themselves and their office. The trouble is that attorneys will, not infrequently, get caught short and be called to court on cases upon which they are utterly unprepared. I offer no remedy for this affliction other than stating that the combined efforts of the bench and bar to reduce the backlog will help us both . . . Until the Nirvana is achieved, the most common grievance of the bench seems to be the unprepared attorney.

The complaints also listed being unprepared with evidence or not producing witnesses on time, disorganized demonstrative materials or a general rambling presentation of the case that did not handle the key points sharply and make them logical and clear.

Personal Respect

Other pet peeves dealt with respect for the judge's privacy and attention to his or her responses.

Once I have indicated that I am taking a recess, arguments and questions ought to cease. Nothing is worse than being interrupted by some comment half-way down the dais on your way out of the courtroom. For at least 100 years, judges in this country did not wear robes. Now we do. I am accustomed after five years to wearing mine on the bench but feel like a perfect idiot when standing around anywhere else with a robe on. When a lawyer interrupts me on my way to my chambers with some question, I find it most offensive. I'm not going anywhere. I usually work full days every day. I will be back. The matter will keep. It is a misplaced sense of urgency indeed to importune the judge on his way off the bench. I don't like it.

Or this:

Do not interrupt the judge, even when the judge interrupts you. Wait till he or she finishes the comment or question.

What Lawyers Do Wrong Most Often

Judges often feel that the lawyer has no sense of time, a crucial commodity to judges. They say a lawyer feels that, because he has the floor, he is allowed to speak as long as he wishes, without recognizing when he has come to his point, made his point and is ready to move on. They feel that a lawyer often reiterates a point because he hasn't thought it through, or tries to discover his point as he presents his case. The judge, as an experienced spectator, cannot only get the point very quickly, he feels patronized when you puree it. Here are some major grievances:

Time Management

From a Circuit Court judge:

> Since the discovery tools are better in civil cases, the lawyers should be better able to avoid "waiting for something to turn up." Still, the abuse of discovery and the dragging out of both the plaintiff's and defendant's cases are a problem. Jurors have a limited attention span and judges have limited time. The waste of jurors' attention or judges' time is truly detrimental to the case. Reducing what should be presented to only that which is necessary, without scrimping, should be relatively easy. Unfortunately, it comes with many years of experience.

Another judge writes:

> My needs in the courtroom are simple—I need some real help in scheduling my time. Litigation is so pervasive and time so limited that every hour I lose hurts. I think that most lawyers are aware of this and with rare exceptions, try to stick to a schedule that is realistic. But to show up late, or ask for a delay at the last moment, or delay a settlement until the morning of the trial so that it is impossible to schedule some other matter, is nerve wracking and thoughtless.
> Incidentally, bench trials are much faster than jury cases and the judge can absorb more information more quickly than a jury. Ergo, the plan of the trial should be worked out with this in mind.

A Federal District judge said:

> It should be clear that the contemporary trial judge not only must possess all the traditional judging skills, but must also be an effective time manager. The effective trial lawyer should be aware of this added facet of the judicial role.

Lack of a Theory or Clear Objectives

From Judge William J. Bauer:

> Next to unpreparedness as an evil is that attorney who thinks that by trying the case he will come to discover the theory upon which he can prevail. Such an attorney may ostensibly be well prepared, i.e. he has done extensive discovery and has a great mass of evidence to offer. Unfortunately, it is all mush. He has no idea of the legal requirements of his claim and even less as to how to go about fitting his evidence in a persuasive fashion to supporting them. Instead, this lawyer believes that coming in and telling his story in exhaustive detail is the route to success. Nothing could be further from the truth. It is not the function of the court to try the case for the attorney and to discover and explicate theories unknown to the attorney.

From another federal judge:

> Next on my list are lawyers who have no clear idea of where they're going and try the cases as though they are hoping something will turn up. Sometimes an obviously guilty defendant insists on a trial and all the poor lawyer *can* do is hope that something turns up; however when the same lawyer does it trial after trial I know that he can't evaluate a case and therefore can't even advise a client when it is time to pack it in and ask for mercy. (No one—not even me— wants real justice; we all want mercy.)

The Scheduling of Witnesses

This was a touchy subject, since a number of judges commented on it. The errors they complain about deal with not thinking and planning ahead and the attendant poor scheduling wasting the court's time:

Several judges wrote:

> Lawyers who either schedule all witnesses to appear at once or cause long waits between witnesses are an irritation. This is a hard one and some pauses are inevitable. Reasonable pretrial preparation, however, can reduce the problem to an acceptable level—or the attorney should have "routine" witnesses available to fill in the gaps.

*   *   *

Cumulative evidence should be avoided at all costs. If one or two witnesses can testify to an occurrence, there is no need to bring in three or four. Simply advising the judge that there are other witnesses who would testify to the same effect may be enough.

*   *   *

The trial lawyer should attempt not to run out of witnesses during the day so that the trial has to be recessed prematurely. This occurrence does not permit the judge to use his or her court time fully. If this should happen because of a reason beyond control of the lawyer, he or she should agree to let the other side present part of its case out of turn—rather than waste valuable courtroom hours."

Complaints About Objections

. . . Excessive pointless objections. This problem frequently results from poor preparation and/or a misunderstanding of the Rules of Evidence.

*   *   *

Inappropriate arguments on objections, i.e., anything but a crisp statement of the claims, e.g. hearsay, leading beyond the scope of the witness's competence, etc.

*   *   *

Then there are the lawyers who object to questions or evidence when the matter referred to can't possibly hurt their cause. This also irritates the hell out of jurors; I've watched their reaction.

Arguing with Opposing Counsel

Superior Court Judge William Young of Massachusetts;

A trait which, perhaps more rapidly than anything else, makes me livid, is the attorney who starts arguing directly with his opposite number in the middle of a trial. Nothing more quickly causes the judge to lose control and be relegated to the sidelines of the action than two attorneys who commence shouting at each other. Counsel ought always remember that they must, during the trial, either be questioning witnesses, addressing the jury at the appropriate times, or addressing the judge. Of course counsel can quietly go over to the other counsel's table to seek a stipulation, discuss the admission of evidence, or whatever. What is not permissible is to start interrogating the opposing counsel in the hearing of the jury or dur-

ing arguments before the judge. *All* arguments, no matter how personal, must be addressed to the judge and, through him, to the position asserted by the opponent. Not only is this more seemly, it
prevents a shouting match and permits the judge to control the proceedings with the minimum of judicial intrusion.

What Lawyers Don't Understand About the Jury

Judges are in a unique position to watch the jury and see their reactions in a way you cannot. While you are busy presenting, arguing,
questioning and persuading, the judge sits not only as another consumer, another member of your audience, but also as a keen observer of the jury's reactions. Therefore, they can critique you not
only for themselves and what they want you to do, but also as they
observe you and the jury.

All the earlier comments about judges' pet peeves and what
you do wrong also apply to how juries react as well. Here are some
specific comments:

Explaining at Their Level

Passing some minor points (such as the irritating repetition of every
one of the witnesses' answers) I think that lawyers usually start their
presentation at too high a level of abstraction. That is to say, they do
not start off by explaining the case in terms that a layman would understand. They usually have lived with the case so long they think
everyone understands the general context, and they plunge right
into the disputed points, with inadequate sketching out of the
background.

*   *   *

Lawyers insist on using legal language, especially in a jury case.
What a mistake! They should ask judges to explain phrases like
'liquidating damages' before they try to use those words.

*   *   *

Failure to address the evidence to the fact finder (jury or judge) i.e.,
the failure to adequately explain technical language, questions and
answers asked and given on the assumption that the fact finder
knows more about the subject of the inquiry than he or they do.
Poor use of visual aids (demonstrative aids) to pictorially present the
evidence—the notion that a picture is 'worth a thousand words.'

Using Visual Aids

There is generally, a poor, if not disastrous, use of demonstrative evidence. Too many small photographs are still being used in the courtroom; overhead projectors, large blowups of pictures and large, clear understandable charts are seldom used. Lawyers seem unable to take advantage of the explosion of knowledge explaining how effective the visual aids are in educating people.

Lawyers forget to notice the sight lines of the jury and are not aware enough of whether the judge and/or the jury can see the exhibits well.

Jury Reactions

Lawyers don't really notice juries or judges' reactions. Juries are very uncomfortable with overbearing cross-examination. If lawyers noticed their reaction they might change their approach or cut short a cross after they've made their point.

*   *   *

These are only a few comments but the subject matter might look familiar to you since I have continually stressed these points throughout the book. (It's nice to have corroboration.) The essence of the comments dealt with not recognizing the jury's level of understanding, their need for explicit information without overload and their sensitivity to the human interplay in the courtroom scene.

What Judges Need

Judges feel that much more efficiency and clarity in the trial would result from careful pre-trial preparation. They have very real goals and compelling reasons:

Pre-trial Preparation

I need some time in every case to hold a pre-trial conference with counsel. This applies to both civil and criminal litigation. The pre-trial conference enables me to learn the issues, spot the expected rough or complex points in the trial, assess the nature of the evidence, and plan—that's the key—how to conduct the trial in a fair and seemly manner. Without a pre-trial conference, the unexpected can, and too often will, crop up in the middle of a trial, skewing the thing in front of the jury and making it far more difficult to get everyone back on track. I much prefer a pre-trial conference where these matters can be raised. I conduct such a conference in every case.

*   *   *

While I'm not often favored with one, I really do need, and much appreciate, a trial memorandum from the parties. Such a memorandum sets forth the party's theory, outlines the expected proof, and supplies a rationale for the points in contention and the major matters of disputed evidence law. Such a memorandum, if comprehensive, lends its own structure to the trial and cannot help but aid the attorney who has fairly and carefully presented the issues.

*   *   *

One absolute rule: Judges *do not like* surprises, and if a lawyer is about to embark down an unusual road, he should signal the court ahead of time (not an ex parte communication but a motion that clearly signals the unusual path about to be taken).

*   *   *

Most well-prepared lawyers can anticipate evidentiary problems and potential conflicts long before trial. These, if at all possible, should be brought to the court's attention before trial, so that they may be resolved without interrupting the flow of the trial.

A number of judges had very definite rules about what they expect in pre-trial.

Technical data should be prepared in advance and marked for admission. Any questions of admissibility should be resolved in advance and stipulations or rulings gotten *before* trial.

There was also much written about the need for the sheer support of secretarial help, especially at the state court level. It sheds some light on aspects of the judge's life you never see or know about.

I think most of us feel that what we need most is a secretary to help us get our things typed up. To the extent that you deal with memory, you know how fast it fades. Sometimes we have to dictate something into a machine, and we do not see it in rough draft for a week or so, by which time our recollection of the details of the trial has faded badly, and sometimes even our own contemporaneous notes have become incomprehensible.

This is an interesting point since it can challenge you to make succinct written materials available to the judge.

Bench Trials

Lawyers often say after a seminar on communication techniques that will reach the jury, "Yes, that's fine, but what about a bench trial?" With very few alterations the same basic truths apply to judges *and* juries. Think of what the judges complained about— boring, long-winded, vague, disorganized and unclear material. Those are the same complaints jurors have, and for the same basic reasons. You, the presentor, are not living up to their needs. You must recognize that you don't have carte blanche with anyone's attention span and interest level, be it judge or layman. You need to understand your bench trial audience and go through the same process you do for juries.

Design your presentation for the judge and his or her unique set of circumstances. Understand his needs, give him only what he wants, and can use, no more, in an interesting, incisive, economical manner. But remember, as one judge put it: "A judge-only trial is not merely a streamlined jury trial. It is an entirely different species of the genera." Here are some specific preferences and critiques from judges:

Efficiency

From Judge Marvin Aspen, U. S. District Court, Chicago, Illinois:

Generally speaking, it is amazing how many lawyers are unable to shift gears from their jury trial modus operandi to effective advocacy in a bench trial. With staggering court calendars, most judges these days are keenly time-management oriented. This means that the trial lawyer should try not to burden the trial judge with unnecessary data or procedure, but rather should get to the core of his or her case as quickly as possible consistent with full representation of the client's position. To do otherwise, in my view, would be psychologically counterproductive to sound advocacy at a bench trial.

Judge Hiller Zobel of the Massachusetts Superior Court writes:

Lawyers arguing a simple motion before a trial judge expect (nay, demand) as much time—or more—than the Supreme Court allows for a full-scale constitutional case.

Another comment from Judge Aspen:

I would suggest that whenever possible, counsel should stipulate as to the accuracy and presentation of uncontested facts. Even when the other side will not so stipulate, it makes sense for the attorney to indicate to the Court his or her willingness to agree to the uncontested facts in order to shorten the trial time.

Methods of Witness Examination

There was also comment on the ways in which lawyers examine witnesses, especially in bench trials:

From Chief Judge Manuel Real, Central District Court of California:

Give me a modicum of credit for intelligence. I can read and I can see. Lawyers have witnesses read from a document and I've read it before the trial. In any case, I have it before me.

Another District Court judge writes:

In a bench trial, lawyers should not insist on a rigid order for the presentation of witnesses. Although this may be desirable in a jury trial, most judges are able to put the evidence in proper perspective at the close of trial even though it may not have been presented in chronological or other systematic order.

Still another says:

Lengthy "all-over-the-lot" cross examination is bad enough during a jury trial, but is especially deadly at a bench trial. Most witnesses are not destroyed in the Perry Mason mode of cross examination. The effective advocate should not burden the judge with a rambling cross examination, which will have little effect on a sophisticated trier of facts assessing the credibility of the witness.

How to Present Technical Complex Cases

Judges feel lawyers are too often unaware that the judge does not wish to become an ultimate expert on how to build a nuclear energy plant. He only needs to know enough about the technical aspects so that he can judge the norm and see whether or not this or that aspect was in order and why not. Being given too much technical informatioin is as tiresome to him as it is to a lay audience, because it's not all that necessary. He wants clear presentations, more efficient presentations, and anything that will keep his interest, since he has as much difficulty listening to technical data in oral argument as the lay public does.

Again from Chief Judge Manuel Real:

> Teach me. Don't gloss over data making me think you know it all so I must rely on you. Judges are generalists. It's a layman you're talking to when you get to the technical aspects of the case.

District Court Judge Robert Mehridge of Richmond, Virginia:

> You've got to treat the judge as any simple untalented person. Engineering is just not my cup of tea so I want the lawyer to take it step by step and explain. Don't assume I know anything. I want you to assume only that I know the law. Outside the law I confess to a numbness of the brain.

Use of Visual and Demonstrative Materials

They uniformly recommend the extensive use of visual aids. They complain that lawyers do not use enough visuals, not only to clarify technical data but to make any concept clearer. They say that lawyers feel that because every word would be something that the judge would understand, they need not use the kinds of aids which are by themselves not only efficient, but much more interesting and clarifying:

The best way to handle technical material is to have some simplified diagrams or exhibits, and to figuratively walk the jurors and/or the judge through the process step by step, explaining to them the inter-relationship of various aspects of the technical material. For example, showing a diagram; then tracing over the process in color which makes it simple and understandable. A simple model is also very useful.

Judge Rya Zobel of Boston:

The teaching function is more difficult in a jury case. There are not only more people to teach but one must arrive at a lower common denominator. Also, the judge is reluctant to interrupt the flow of the presentation with questions. In a bench trial the judge can and does question but is *extremely* responsive to very well prepared graphics that clarify and simplify the case. Lawyers should be aware of what the judge knows and wants to know and should gear graphics and explanations only to those areas necessary. One must use teaching aids in a technical case designed to assist in understandng the concepts.

Ways to Argue

I'm sorry to report that there is not a clear consensus here. It seems to depend on individual tastes and preferences.

Here are some specific preferences and critiques, as vaired as they are, from the judges:

One Federal District Court judge said:

Opening statements, if not waived, should be short and directly to the point. Arguments at the close of the case should avoid dramatics which might be effective for the jury, but would appear as contrived to a trial judge. In other words, the intensity of advocacy should be toned down. The appeal should be to the intellect, not to the emotions.

Another said he liked a bench trial done as a jury trial, "with full opening statements, emotional final arguments, detailed qualification of the witnesses" and so on. He said, "I really don't make up my mind till after the trial and want all the evidence and advocacy I can hear."

Judge Robert Mehridge, of Virginia, said:

> Opening and closing argument need not take so long nor be too simplistic since the judge knows the law. Fight the law but don't explain. Don't make friends with me, I'm different from juries. I am more impressed solely with facts and the law rather than personalities. Although personalities can affect a judge, save it for the jury.

Judge Hiller Zobel:

> Given that counsel always wants to file not only post-trial briefs but also lengthy proposed findings of fact, oral argument (entertaining at best, boring at worst and in any event, evanescent) is a waste of the lawyer's efforts, the court's good will and the client's chances.

Other judges commented:

> Not just a factual presentation. Get into the law in order to get rid of some basic issues. Mix questions of law and the facts. Do not just give a factual approach.
>
> *　　　*　　　*
>
> Emotional argument has no place. I'm a professional. They are professionals. We know what we're doing. A lawyer who attempts to get emotional tells me "my case is not that good and I want you to feel it, not think about it."
>
> *　　　*　　　*
>
> Influenced by emotional argument? I'm a human being and it would be untrue if I said No. I do take extra precautions in an emotional case to deliberate in order to be objective.

Incidentally, here is a hint:

> I don't like lawyers to continually wander or pace. It makes me seasick!

How to Relate to the Judge in a Bench Trial

All were in accord, preferring a more impersonal, professional attitude, not one that was "fawning" or "obsequious."

> Frankly, I don't care about how lawyers relate to me in a courtroom as long as it is *impersonal, not fawning* [his emphasis], and always to

the best interest of the client. That permits arguing a point but not fighting with the judge. Looking hurt or snarling after an adverse ruling gains no points with either the judge or the jury (even though the client might think the lawyer is a real scrapper—the client's wrong and so is the lawyer.)

Judge William Young, Superior Court, Massachusetts, said:

Attorneys ought to treat judges before whom they appear as a fellow professional and ought to seek to understand his problems and perspectives during the trial. At the same time, the attorney ought to have respect for himself as a professional and for the role he plays in the trial process. During the trial of a case, it is the two trial attorneys who are the hardest working professionals in the courtroom. They are entitled to respect and understanding as they practice their profession. When I teach lawyers, I like to emphasize that attorneys ought to think of a courtroom as a brain surgeon thinks of his surgery. That is, it is in the courtroom where the lawyering profession attains its highest standards. Courtroom advocacy actually defines the profession. Since that is so, attorneys ought to act at home in the courtrom and ought to exude an air of professional competence and serious dedication to the tasks at hand . . . Since the judge is necessary for the proper trial of the case, attorneys ought to act with appropriate respect for his professional competence. Obsequiousness is out. Not only is it disingenuous, it is actually demeaning to the judiciary and the bar alike. Judges in a democracy are not Lords in Chancery. It is quite proper to vigorously argue one's case before them as one would before a fellow professional, understanding that in this case the fellow professional may have the final power of decision. What is silly, however, is to keep arguing once the decision has been made. The proper role is to press every reasonable point thoroughly and vigorously and to preserve one's rights to appeal if the ruling goes against you.

A Federal District Court judge said:

I run a very formal court but not in a stiff manner where one cannot smile. However, I want strict adherence to the rules. Friendliness is fine, but don't let the bars down. The courtroom manner should be the same as with a jury.

Another Federal Court judge added:

I prefer to maintain dignity and rules about courtroom behavior. That implies formality and I like lawyers to observe these for either jury or bench trials. I do not like lawyers to talk to each other, only to address the court. One accords respect to the court—not the person of the judge. I don't appreciate bowing and scraping—rather, maintain distance, and respect for the institution.

*   *   *

Now—how do you respond to what the judges complain about or want? As with all critiscism, the best way to get over the smarting is to attack the cause constructively and begin building.

EFFECTIVE TECHNIQUES IN BENCH TRIALS

The communication techniques described throughout this book aimed at making your material more interesting and more effective, at clarifying through organization, reinforcing or explaining through the use of visuals, seem to be as true for judges and bench trials as for juries.

The language needed may not need to be as simplistic or appeal to the emotions as much as it must for a jury, but a variety of communication techniques is as welcome to one person as to many and actually, even more so. The judge's total job is getting talked at, and anyone who can rise from the crowd of lawyers and be more interesting and more concise, who can use more effective techniques to be understood or who can find a new way to present information commands favorable attention.

Therefore, to focus your thinking further about bench trials and to give you a few more techniques, consider the following:

Know Your Audience

You need to know and understand your judge just as much as you need to know your jury. Research your judge and argue to that particular individual. Fashion each bench trial to the unique consumer and how he or she will listen best.

Discover how he or she usually runs his or her trial. Are they quick? Impatient? Thoughtful?

Read some things he or she has written to get a better sense of his or her innate style. That's the form of communication the judge finds most comfortable and he will probably have a preference for it. Don't change *your* style like a chameleon, but be aware of his preference for a more cerebral and legalistic style, a crisp, clear, efficient one or a more colorful way of writing and speaking, and tailor your rhythm and organization to it.

Find out what makes him or her listen--what are his or her basic interests, hobbies, family, lifestyle? This will help you choose your analogies or references. We all identify and feel comfortable with the recognizable and the familiar, whether they are people or things.

Re-read the first part of this chapter about the judges's role and problems. Understand the general needs of all judges, and then focus on them in relation to your particular judge's circumstances. The old adage about knowing your audience is never more important than in this intense relationship.

Be Prepared

Do you know how cross you get when you're ready to eat and there's no waiter, and then the food takes forever? The judge is geared up for the trial. He's "ready to eat." He expects efficiency and professionalism; motions made, documents in order, witnesses ready, basic procedures well executed. That's minimal. When he sees that any part of the trial, which he expects to go as a matter of course, is fumbled and not efficiently done, then, before your talent as an arguer or a persuader fully comes into play, he is already irritated and suspicious of you and your prowess as a lawyer. If he is critical of your performance at the start, that can color how your case is heard. Be terribly careful to have all details in order, but most of all, be clear about the issues of your case. Judges are trained, experienced listeners. You can't fool them if you're unprepared.

Jury surveys show that jurors really admire and respond to tidiness of counsel's papers and exhibits, readiness of witnesses and no delays in the trial. Judges feel the same way, even more strongly.

Organization Is the Key

Organize your thoughts and the issues logically. If you separate your points and then, as one of the judges suggested, analyze what evidence, documents, special needs and considerations belong to each point, you will be ready to summon them at will and your presentation will be much smoother and less interrupted.

Draw up a checklist. Review the order of your evidence. What issues follow logically and what pertains to each?

Presenting your argument with great clarity and order allows the judge to concentrate and move along with you, instead of flailing about in a sea of disjointed, unconnected arguments and thoughts.

Edit for the Bench

Although you try cases before juries, you must learn to shift gears for a bench trial:

• Short-cut long explanations with crisp cites and efficient explanations.

• Remember how much judges understand about the law—speak shorthand about that.

• Remember how little they know about your case and its technical aspects—speak longhand about that.

• Remember they can ask questions and they will.

• Give them your theme, the basic outline of the case, the topic headings, followed by the facts and good explanations so they are well informed and can focus on where they want more information.

I get many opinions on whether or not they want full, emotional openings and closings. Know your judge. Think through how much introduction you need and why, but to be safe, always err a little on the side of brevity. Exercise some discipline, before the trial, in your preparation. Don't leave it to the judge to sift and sort his way through all your materials.

Build Your Points

Making an orderly and logical progression of your material as it unfolds before the judge is very important. But also think of the drama involved. Where should you begin? What are the highlights? What clinches your points? How do you build to a climax? What do you tell last, as the crescendo or wrap-up?

Finding the most interesting way to tell your tale is as important to the judge as it is to the jury. Timing does make a difference and affects the way you hear what comes before and after.

Scheduling Witnesses

As the judges suggested, schedule your witnesses so that there are no gaps that waste the court's time. Another important issue is arranging the order of witnesses to maintain interest, as well as to tell the story coherently.

A dull case can be made interesting by manipulating the order of your witnesses. Think through the different qualities of your witnesses and see how they can provide variety and contrast in terms of personal style and energy, as well as content.

Clear, Concise Technical Information

I cannot tell you how many times judges say, "Anything that is of a complex technical nature, don't send me the tomes. Get down to the basics and show me the heart of it in the same way that you would a jury. If I need to know more, I'll ask for more."

Don't start out asking them to understand how a whole railroad car is made. Figure out what they need to know in order to understand why a wheel fell off. If there is material you want them to read in advance, screen it. Don't send a library. Choose what's necessary, and be sure they get it in plenty of time. It's easier to absorb your explanation if they're already oriented, but choose wisely. If you're not an engineer, that stuff can be deadly!

sharp word for it, by all means, but only if it's your strength. If it isn't, don't bother. Go for efficiency instead; they'll love you more.

You can also give a judge respect without being obsequious at the same time. Being a grownup, a competent professional who is doing his or her work, is really as much as a judge wants. He or she likes to look at another adult. He or she is not really impressed with someone who tries to curry favor. He or she sees through that rather quickly.

After preparing the case as professionally as you do, allow yourself to stand as an individual before the judge, arguing with verve and commitment, to the best of your ability. Special tricks or ploys won't do it. Good advocacy is what the judge most expects and requires.

Also, don't let him push you around. Some judges are bullies, but most of the time when they are acting unfairly they are acting out of impatience or a misunderstanding of your position. When you are being brow-beaten, insist with dignity and strength that your side be fairly considered. Most judges will respect your duty to your client to stand your ground.

Respect

Always look at the judge when you address "Your Honor." Many of them comment on this. That form of address becomes a habit for many of you and is often just a throwaway line.

Don't Grovel

Judges tell me they resent when you say, "Thank you, Your Honor," after a judge has ruled against you. They say things like, "Do they think I'm such a fool? They're saying they're delighted that I have just overruled them? I know as well as they do that I've just hurt them. And I mind terribly if they either toady to me, and say, 'Thank you, Your Honor,' which doesn't impress me at all, or if they think by saying 'Thank you, Your Honor,' they're trying to tell me that it didn't bother them. I know exactly what I did, and it is condescending and patronizing, as I see it, for them to say, 'Thank you, Your Honor.' They have nothing to thank me for. I am doing my job as a justice. I am ruling for the court and there is no per-

sonal involvement here, and I resent when they make it personal."
Don't say thank you when they rule *for* you, either. That makes it
sound like a favor.

Don't Show Off

You touch a competitive nerve when you start vying for legal
knowledge laurels with judges. It's their job to know more rules
and, even more important, to know how to interpret them. And
even *more* important, it's their court and you can't tell them how to
rule. Remember their competitive trial lawyer spirit is already at
play, as is their subliminal enjoyment of power. If you try using
bigger words or more obscure cites in an effort to show off, it will
backfire.

That doesn't mean not to legitimately argue your points, but
do it objectively and with respect. Keep it short, simple and
straightforward and eschew the florid and pedantic. (See what I
mean?)

Another point—don't show off your newfound technical vocabulary (which you just learned from this case) or play "who can
be more obscure" with an expert. This has the same effect on a
judge as it does on a jury. No one likes being left out or watching
someone else be smart.

You and the Other Lawyer

It becomes tedious to watch you compete with your opposite
colleague before the bench. This, judges often feel, wastes time.
They are not interested in that kind of wrangling. It feels like two
kids fighting for their parent's attention and approval. Don't set up
the judge as a referee. Choose carefully when, how and why you
argue with the opposing lawyer. It can cost you good will and develop the suspicion that your case is not too strong.

What if the Judge Hurts You

In the midst of your big performance, with all your adrenals
running, filled to the brim with advocacy, what if the judge rules
against you or reprimands you in some way? Doesn't it make you

feel chastised or humiliated before opposing counsel or your client? It can surely make you angry.

My advice is to separate yourself and go on to the next point. Like professional athletes, try to drop the double fault behind you and re-energize to play on. Get up for the next issue. What's done is done. Use it as a catalyst to sharpen you as to what to do now and what to do next. The big thing to understand is that recrimination or focusing on the injustice (if that is the case) can only hurt *your* further performance, not the judge. Too much arguing will kill you.

Want to get back at him? Get brilliant! Show him how you recover. He'll admire you for it and listen harder. We learned to shun a sore-loser or cry-baby on the playground, the street or the little league team. It helps to understand *why* they rule arbitrarily or harshly sometimes, as I explained at the beginning of this chapter. But, most of all, remember what you're there for. Set your counter-punching ego aside and look at the work before you. Do *that* well and you'll get your strokes later—when you win.

Jury-waived Trials

An interesting footnote: When you waive a jury, especially in a criminal case, you should be aware of the special psychological stresses on judges and the implications it has for them.

First, the stresses. One person is, literally, judge and jury. In close factual cases, most judges feel much happier if an anonymous slice of the community determines "whodunit," especially when the verdict's consequences are so personal and can be so dire.

Witness credibility is always very troubling, but in a criminal trial they are often complex and hard to read fairly and impartially. This, too, creates great stress for judges.

But there is another issue as well. Judges sometimes feel that a jury waiver conveys an explicit message that the defense lawyer thinks he or she has a better chance of acquittal if the judge alone tries the case. That produces an instinctive reaction (not always acknowledged): "I'll show him or her." Judges hate to be thought of as soft touches.

Therefore, be especially sensitive to these issues in such a situation. Be super-prepared and above reproach, and be sure your case has good foundation and cites to fall back on in order to give the judge ample support for your position. Plead such a case being fully aware of his or her needs and also of the assumptions about why you waived a jury.

*   *   *

To sum up: Stop and analyze your view of the bench. The insights into the judge's role, its pressures and problems, and his or her responses to them should give you a better understanding in preparing bench trials. What the judges wrote about how they see you and what they want and need should give you pause and stimulus to look objectively and critically at your performance in court.

Find a more human approach to judges. Treat them with the respect that the office and their fund of knowledge deserves, and that the system of law in this country requires. Figure out what a discreet distance is, notice how they respond and what they like. Use the same instincts you would in judging your presentation to jurors. Be interesting. Be clear. Be aware of your audience. Feel the judge's reaction and imagine his response as a person, not just as a judge. Don't take liberties with his being required to listen—make him or her want to.

12

A FINAL WORD

In a sense, the value of all we've shared together in this book is directly related to the effect it will have. My goals, as I began writing it, were to make some changes. I wanted to re-introduce you to your familiar territory—the trial—with a new point of view. I wanted to help you see what's really going on on the other side of that jury-rail or bench and engage you in a quest to understand more and to see why. I wanted to give you new tools based on that bed-rock of understanding, to make you more effective, more comfortable and more helpful in the courtroom. I wanted to inspire you to try new ways, to breathe new life into your old modes of doing your work. And I wanted to make you feel safe enough to absorb these challenges and to use them.

It's been a hard labor but filled with excitement as I imagined you reading my book, raising your eyebrows, looking off and thinking, arguing with me and, hopefully, laughing often. I feel that I know you and that now you know me, too. You see, we all share that incredible gift the jurors bring to the courtroom—the human instinct to understand, to perceive and to know each other. Yours is alive and well, inside your navy blue lawyer suit or dress. Trust it. Use it. Pull it out of those legal mothballs and rely on your basic gut people-instincts to give you the final word on everything you do in the trial. That's where the jury is. *That's* what makes juries listen.

INDEX